# VEHICULAR
# ACCIDENT
# INVESTIGATION
## and
# RECONSTRUCTION

# VEHICULAR ACCIDENT INVESTIGATION
# and
# RECONSTRUCTION

## Donald J. Van Kirk

**CRC Press**

Boca Raton   London   New York   Washington, D.C.

## Library of Congress Cataloging-in-Publication Data

Van Kirk, Donald J.
    Vehicular accident investigation and reconstruction / by Donald J. Van Kirk.
       p.  cm.
    Includes bibliographical references and index.
    ISBN 0-8493-2020-8 (alk. paper)
    1. Traffic accident investigation. 2. Traffic accidents. I. Title.

HV8079.55.V36 2000
364.1'47—dc21
                                               00-044487

© 2001 by CRC Press LLC

No claim to original U.S. Government works
International Standard Book Number 0-8493-2020-8
Library of Congress Card Number 00-044487
Printed in the United States of America  1  2  3  4  5  6  7  8  9  0
Printed on acid-free paper

# Abstract

This book was written with a mentor–student relationship in mind, including the use of commentaries from real-world accidents. The basic tools and equipment of the profession are discussed with reasons for using each. Detailed analysis of scene investigations with comprehensive diagrams showing the development of scale drawings and methods to locate witness marks and debris are provided. Extensive real-world photographs and diagrams are used to analyze vehicle damage and witness marks. Vehicular occupant kinematics, as well as pedestrian and motorcycle accidents are discussed in detail. A short history of the various safety equipment used in today's vehicles is included as basic information. Computer accident simulation and animations are discussed with recommendations for their use. Development and use of exhibits and sources of information are reviewed. Expert depositions and courtroom appearances are discussed along with unusual case histories and a new look at ethics for the investigator/reconstructionist. This book should be a constant source of information and reference.

# Acknowledgments

I am grateful for the invaluable assistance, friendship, and encouragement of Mitchell Marchi for proofreading the majority of the manuscript and drawings and for giving freely of his wealth of automotive knowledge; for the friendship of Paul N. Cross and his assistance in developing many of the drawings needed for a better understanding of the printed word; and finally for the encouragement of my many friends in the legal and medical profession and their friendship over the years of our association.

# Author Biography

Donald J. Van Kirk, B.S.E.E., M.S.E.M., M.B.A., P.E., has been a forensic engineering consultant for 15 years. He is retired from his consulting firm and devotes his time to a few major cases a year and to speaking engagements. For the previous 20 years he was employed as a senior engineer at Ford Motor Company in special vehicle engineering. He developed and taught a course titled Human Tolerance Design Data for Automotive Engineers for company personnel, and he worked with the Office of General Counsel involving corporate litigation on product liability cases.

Mr. Van Kirk received his B.S.E.E degree in 1964 and his M.S.E.M. in 1969, both from Wayne State University; and in 1975, an M.B.A. from the University of Michigan. During his graduate work at Wayne State he worked for the Biomechanics Research Center, where he acted as project engineer on a government and private industry research contract to determine human tolerance to impact from analysis and reconstruction of automotive accidents. He set up and trained five teams (two men each) of accident investigators to obtain pictures and measurements of deformations of the interior and exterior of a vehicle. He also worked with approximately 50 insurance companies and the local and state police groups in southeastern lower Michigan. The second phase was to simulate these accidents in the laboratory. He assisted in the design of a device to slow down the vehicle using a specific pulse shape similar to the vehicle crush characteristics. In addition, he participated in many other private and public contracts involving the determination of human tolerance design data. The results of this work were published in peer review journals.

Van Kirk's work has been published by the Society of Automotive Engineers (SAE), Stapp Car Crash Conference, and American Association for Automotive Medicine (AAAM), and in the *Journal of Forensic Sciences*. He has presented papers before scientists and engineers in Shanghai and Guangzhou, China; the Legal Assistants Association of Michigan; and the International Association of Forensic Scientists Triennial Conference, Vancouver, B.C., Canada, and Adelaide, Australia.

A member of the National Society of Professional Engineers, Van Kirk served the Michigan Society of Professional Engineers as President of the

Fairlane Chapter and as a State Director. He also belongs to the American Academy of Forensic Scientists, where he has been named a Fellow; the National Safety Council; the American Society of Testing Materials E-30 and F-8 Committees; the Michigan Association of Traffic Accident Investigators (MATAI); the American Board of Forensic Examiners, where he was named a Diplomate; the SAE's Biomechanics Subcommittee of the Human Factors Committee of the Head Restraint Subcommittee — Body Seating, and the SAE's Accident Investigation Practices Standards Committee. He holds a patent for a cold weather diesel starting aid.

Van Kirk's recognitions include a Community Service Citation, from Ford Motor Company; Outstanding Service Award, Dearborn Exchange Club; and Man of the Year Award, Dearborn Exchange Club. He is listed in *Marquis Who's Who in the Midwest*, *Who's Who in Masonry*, *Personalities of America*, 3rd ed., *Community Leaders of the World*, *Men of Achievement*, 11th ed., *Directory of Distinguished Americans*, and *Who's Who in the World*. In addition, he has received the Outstanding Service Award from the Dearborn Exchange Club, and the Editors Award from the *International Shrine Clown Association Magazine*.

# Personal Comments

Accident investigation/reconstruction is more than just a job or even a profession; it is more art than science and requires a dedication greater than a commitment of time. It takes constant reading, study, and analysis of accident information and case reconstructions to keep improving your performance, both in the field and in the courtroom.

The one fact that must be uppermost in your mind is that you are dealing in one way or another with a human life. In the case of criminal work, there is a direct connection, and the detailed analysis of your investigation and reconstruction could be the difference between freedom and incarceration. In the case of civil actions, your analysis can help the injured party recover his/her health and financial losses. You may be instrumental in discovering a major defect in a product, possibly saving lives, but surely eliminating injuries from these products. In the end, you find out your expertise helped people who were in great need of assistance at a specific time in their lives, especially when you receive those thank-you letters.

Let it always be said that you did your best for your clients and the people they represent. You will always be able to sleep at night with a clear conscience.

Donald J. Van Kirk, P.E.

# Introduction

During the last 25 years I have read dozens of books, magazine articles, and technical papers on accident investigation and reconstruction. Many were written with the assumption that the investigator/reconstructionist already had a specific level of work experience or educational background in his/her newly chosen profession. This is usually not true. This text begins with the assumption that the reader has little or no experience in accident investigation and reconstruction. Many experienced investigators have published informational material through various professional societies; unfortunately, it is difficult to provide sufficient, detailed information for the novice in 10 to 20 journal pages. Several years ago I decided to write a book that would not only tell but also show the novice and the experienced investigator what system or method has worked best for me, and why it should be used even with its limitations.

Many field investigators today use techniques they have been taught, but they cannot describe why the method is used or what its possible limitations are. A goal of this publication is to show these limitations.

Investigators must continually update their skills by studying the latest improvements in equipment and techniques. Attending conferences can help. The investigator must realize that an equipment sales person is trying to sell a product. It is advisable to investigate any product by questioning people who purchased it and used it under conditions similar to yours. This book introduces old and new equipment and techniques and their good and bad points.

Textbook theory is acceptable to illustrate a specific class of situations but does not tell you that the particular example does not fit all the problems you may encounter in the field.

The investigator must be taught to analyze each accident situation and then to make a judgment based on the evidence discovered at the scene. It is no longer necessary to memorize specific classes of examples when the investigator can determine for himself or herself what the situation is and the best way to handle it.

Most methods used to solve particular problems work if the analysis is done within the limitations of particular techniques. As an example, the investigator *cannot apply* the four-wheel skid equation to every situation unless all four tires were actually locked up and skidding. Each situation must be analyzed to determine what method must be used to solve the problem, while staying within the boundaries of that particular situation based on the available evidence.

Details, details, details provide the information that accident investigators and reconstructionists need to complete the analysis and to provide an opinion. This text spends a great deal of time showing the investigator why and how the details of an accident are the most important parts of any investigation and reconstruction. Many investigators agree that only the details matter. The rest of the information is easy to obtain; the hard work is digging out the details.

Sir Arthur Conan Doyle and his alter ego Sherlock Holmes were probably the best investigators/reconstructionists who ever existed. Doyle was asked many times by Scotland Yard to assist them in many high-profile investigations. Doyle was trained as a medical doctor and learned that in medicine, as in other facets of life, the details are the most important part of any project or program. He showed the world how important details are and how to use them through the exploits of master detective Sherlock Holmes.

In the story, *A Case Of Identity*, Holmes states, "It has long been an axiom of mine that the little things are infinitely the most important." I would suggest that every investigator read or reread the exploits of Sherlock Holmes and study his methods and the deductive process he uses to solve cases. Pay special attention to his knowledge of many subjects and the analysis of details he uses in his deductive reasoning. The details he sought solved all his cases. Look for the details and then follow them to a logical solution.

# Table of Contents

**1  Why Investigate Accidents?**     **1**

Economic Costs     1
Human Costs     3
Causes of Accidents     4
Methods Used to Estimate Costs     5
     Economic     5
     Comprehensive     5
How to Reduce Vehicular Injuries     6
Reasons for Investigating Vehicular Accidents     7
Investigative Organizations     8
Databases for Road Conditions and Use of Restraint Systems     8
Prevention and Elimination of On-the-Job Injuries     9
Criminal and Civil Litigation     9
References     10

**2  Where Do I Start?**     **11**

Requirements for Accident Investigators/Reconstructionists     11
Sources of Additional Training     11
Basic Knowledge for the Investigator     15
Fresh Scenes     19
Stale or Aged Scenes     21
References     23

**3  Tools and Special Equipment for the Investigator**     **25**

Preparation     25
Basic Tool Kit     25
Special Equipment     27
Photographic Equipment     32
Video Equipment     35

Special Safety Equipment or Gear 36
Office Equipment 37
Computer Needs 38
   Printer Needs 39
   Computer Programs 40
Ownership of Documentation 41
Ownership of Evidence 42
Technical Library 42
Internet 43

**4**    **Scene Investigation**    **45**

Collisions — Vehicular 45
Accident Scene 47
   Urban Setting 47
   Rural Setting 47
On-Scene Sketches 67
   Methods for Plotting a Curve 68
Visualization 72
Traffic Light Timing 73
Tire Marks 74
Real-World Scene Photographs 77
Water on or over the Roadway 87

**5**    **The Vehicle Exterior**    **89**

Memorializing Accident Vehicles 89
   Videotaping at Accident Scene 91
   Using Still or 35-mm Camera at Accident Scene 93
Exterior Details to Be Noted and Recorded 109
   Metal Folds 109
   Paint Transfers 120
   Weld or Base Metal Separation and Rust 122
   Scrapes, Gouges, and Scratches 125
   Aluminum vs. Steel Wheels 129
   Tires 131
   Missing or Misplaced Components 132
   Underside of Vehicle and Use of Tow Trucks 133
   Fluid Leaks 133
   Headlights, Taillights, and Side Marker Lights 135
   Unexplained Damage 138
   Vehicle Deterioration and Rusting 138

**6  Vehicle Interiors**                                      **141**

Collisions — Occupant                                          141
Obvious Interior Deformation                                   142
   Windshields                                  142
   Rear Windows                                 147
   Instrument Panels                            148
   Steering Columns                             155
   Steering Wheel Rims                          157
   Sun Visors                                   159
   T-Tops, Moon Roofs, and Sunroofs            160
   Rearview Mirrors                             162
   Seat Cushions and Seatbacks                  163
   Headrests                                    165
Less Obvious Interior Deformation                             166
   Moldings                                     166
   Checklists                                   166
Types of Impacts as Related to Interior Deformation           167
   Side Impacts                                 167
   Rear Impacts                                 173
   Rollovers                                    176
Smears and Blood Pooling                                      180
Comment on Restraint Systems                                  180
References                                                    180

**7  Restraining Systems**                                   **181**

Standard Restraint Devices                                    181
   Shoulder/Lap Belts                           182
   Air Bags or Supplemental Systems             202
   New Developments                             207
Restraint Devices for Special Occupants                       209
   Pregnant Women                               209
   Children                                     210
   Converted Vehicles for the Handicapped       212

**8  Vehicle and Occupant Accident
Investigation Forms**                                        **215**

Vehicle Data                                                  215
Tire Data                                                     217
Exterior Damage Sketches                                      219

Damage Measurements                                              219
Occupant Area Intrusions                                         221
Internal Damage Sketches                                         223
Internal Contacts                                                223
Interior Seats, Headrests, and Steering Wheel and Column         226
Seat Belts and Air Bags                                          227
Occupant Information and Injury Data                             229
Soft Tissue Injuries                                             229
Internal Injuries                                                229
Skeletal Injuries                                                230
Injury Mechanisms                                                231
Notes and Injury Countermeasures                                 233

**9    Occupant Kinematics                                       237**

Terminology Definitions                                          238
Basic Systems of the Human Body                                  239
   Skeletal System                                239
   Muscular System                                242
   Nervous System                                 242
   Cardiovascular System                          244
   Visceral System                                245
Anthropomorphic Dummies                                          245
Impact Acceleration                                              246
Linear Acceleration                                              247
   Positive Direction Coordinates                 247
   Rotational Directional Coordinates             247
   Caudocephalad Acceleration $(+G_x)$            248
   Actual Incidences of Vertebral Injury          248
   Experimental Studies                           248
   Impact Acceleration to the Lower Limbs         249
   Impact Acceleration to the Head and Face       250
   Facial Impact Acceleration                     252
   Impact Acceleration to the Neck                252
   Impact Acceleration to the Chest               253
Longitudinal Acceleration $(+g_x$ and $-g_x)$                    254
   Forward Acceleration $(+g_x)$                  254
   Backward Acceleration $(-g_x)$                 254
General Physiological Effects                                    255
Lap Belt Injuries in Aircraft and Automotive Accidents           255
Occupant Injuries                                                255

Cadaver Experiments 256
Anthropomorphic Dummies 256
Large Animal Experiments 257
Actual Injury Reports 257
Lateral Acceleration ($+g_y$ and $-g_y$) 258
Lateral Impacts — Animal Experiments, Lap Belt Only 258
Anthropomorphic Dummy Experiments 258
Volunteer Experiments — Full Restraint 258
Combination Lap and Shoulder Belt 258
Summary 259

**10   Accident Reconstruction   261**

How to Become an Accident Reconstructionist 261
How is a Reconstructionist Defined? 263
How to go about Starting the Reconstruction 263
Sample Case 265
What Was Learned? 271
What Was Required to Solve the Case? 272
What Happens When Details are Insufficient to Prove
the Hypothesis? 272

**11   Severity Indices   273**

Traffic Accident Data Index 274
Scale Validation 275
Vehicle Deformation Index 275
Requirements for a Deformation Index 276
Description of the Vehicle Deformation Index 277
Conclusion 283
Development of a Medically Acceptable Injury Scale 285
A Review of the Present Scales 285
American Medical Association Abbreviated Injury Scale 287
Injury Scale Uses 291
A Detailed Injury Scale for Accident Investigation 293
Definition of Detailed Injury Criteria 293
Accident Data 296
Conclusions 298
Discussion 298
References 299

## 12 Motorcycle Accidents 301

Factors Involved 301
  Size of Vehicles 302
  Headlights and Taillights 302
Details to Be Investigated 302
  Braking System of Motorcycle 303
  Witness Marks on Accident Site 303
  Witness Marks on Motorcycle 303
  Measurement of Angle of Impact 304
  Oil Trail 304
  Determination of the Motorcyclist's Point of Impact 305
  Motorcyclist's Helmet 305
  Inspection of Inoperative or Deformed Motorcycle
    Components 305
Determination of Velocity of Motorcycle at Impact
  by Alternative Method 306
References 312

## 13 Pedestrian Accidents 313

Details to be Determined 313
  Direct Impacts from Front of Vehicle 313
  Pattern of Injury to Pedestrian 314
  Determining Pedestrian Rotation 314
  Impacts to Vehicle Windshield 315
  Dents in Vehicle Exterior 316
  Sideswipe Type of Impact 316
  Comparison of Vehicle Exterior Surfaces 316
  Rearview Mirrors 317
Determination of Pedestrian's Walking or Running Speed 318
Determination of Distance Pedestrian Is Thrown 318
Determination of Impact Velocity 319
Witness Statements 320

## 14 Scale Drawings, Surrogates, Animations, and Computer Simulations in Preparing Exhibits 323

Developing Exhibits 323
  Photographs 323
  Scale Drawings 324
  Measurements 324
Surrogates 327

Animations 331
Computer Simulations 335
Conclusions 338

## 15 Mathematical Analysis 339

Linear Motion with Constant Acceleration 341
Definition of Terms 342
   Perception and Reaction Time 342
   Coefficient of Friction 344
   Drag Factor 345
A Detailed Description of Figure 15.1 347
   Problem One 347
A Detailed Description of Figure 15.2 353
   Problem Two 353
Appendix 15.1 Equation Workbook 363
A Detailed Look at Appendix 15.1 371
   Section A — Distance Equations 371
   Section B — Velocity Equations 374
   Section C — Momentum Equations 379

## 16 Sources of Information 383

Weather Sources 383
Meteorology Experts 384
Vision and Lighting Experts 385
Vehicle Statistics 385
Accident Intersection Data 387
State Highway Department Photographs 387
Construction Zone 388
Power and Telephone Poles 390
State Maintenance Records, Roads, and Trucks 392
Aerial Photographs 392
Vehicle Information 393
   Full Size Body in White Drawings 393
   Preproduction Defect Reports 394
   Warranty Reports 394
   Customer Service Bulletins 394
   Recall Campaigns 395
   Endurance Testing 396
   Laboratory Testing 396
   Federal Motor Vehicle Safety Standards Test Results 396
   Barrier Crash Tests 397

Independent Agencies 397
Database Analysis 398
Medical and Scientific Journals 398
Data Research Companies 399
Human Factor Data 399
Trade Associations 400
Professional Associations 401

## 17 Deposition and Courtroom Appearance 403

Expert Witness and Use of Videotape Recordings 403
Major Studies 404
Expert Witness's Use of Videotape 405
Pros and Cons of Videotape 406
Nonverbal Communication in Expert Testimony 407
Pretrial Preparation 409
Physical Appearance 409
Establishing Qualifications 410
How to Describe the Research 411
Video — Visual Aids 411
Briefly State Overall Conclusion — Then Explain 411
Transcending Your Ego 412
Hypothetical Questions 413
Cross-Examination 414
Handling Attack 414
Summary 415
Nature of Jury Response to the Expert Witness 416
Source Credibility 420
Conclusion 425
References 429

## 18 Educating the Client 431

Technology and Basic Language 431
Terminology 431
Preparation for Deposition 432
Mutual Building of Trust and Understanding 433
Interrogatories 433
Discovery 433
Questions about the Scene and Vehicle 435
Unusual Case Histories 439
Case One — Injury to Cervical Airway 439
Case Two — Dragging Death 440

Case Three — Suicide by Self-Decapitation     441
Summary     442
References     443

## 19   Ethics     445

Derivations and Definitions     445
Recommended Text on Ethics     446
    The First Commandment — *Your Ear Shall Hear; Your Eyes Shall See*     447
    The Second Commandment — *Do Not Utter a False Report*     448
    The Third Commandment — *Do No Unrighteousness in Weights and Measures*     449
    The Fourth Commandment — *Love Your Neighbor as Yourself*     450
    The Fifth Commandment — *Do Justly, Love Mercy, and Walk Humbly*     450
    The Sixth Commandment — *Bring Healing and Cure*     451
    The Seventh Commandment — *You Shall Surely Tithe*     452
    The Eighth Commandment — *Remember the Sabbath*     452
    The Ninth Commandment — *Acquire Wisdom*     453
    The Tenth Commandment — *Know Before Whom You Stand*     454
Suggested Conduct for Professional Investigators/ Reconstructionists     456
References     457

## Glossary     459
## Index     467

# Dedication

This book is dedicated to my dear wife Wyva for her constant faith and encouragement over the many years of my work in forensic engineering and for allowing me to commit to the printed page my education, experience, training, and passion for the art and science of accident investigation and reconstruction, and to my daughter, Cheryl, her husband David, and my granddaughter Samantha for putting up with my unending discussions of the various portions of this book and for allowing me to complete this work and miss the many good times families may only experience once in their lives.

# Why Investigate Accidents? 1

"It is a capital mistake to theorize before you have
all the evidence. It biases the judgment."
**Sherlock Holmes**
*A Study in Scarlet*

## Economic Costs

Each year in the U.S., 93,400 people die from unintentional deaths and
20,700,000 incur disabling injuries. That means that 35.2 people die per
100,000 people in the U.S. The term "unintentional" covers most deaths from
injury and poisoning. Excluded are homicides (including legal intervention),
suicides, deaths for which none of these categories can be determined, and
war deaths. Unintentional deaths include motor vehicle, public, nonwork,
work, and home accidents. The total cost of unintentional injuries in 1996,
$444.1 billion, includes estimates of economic costs of fatal and nonfatal
unintentional injuries: employer costs, vehicle damage costs, and fire losses.
Wage and productivity losses, medical expenses, administrative expenses, and
employer costs are included in all classes of injuries.

Motor vehicle costs include property damage from motor vehicle accidents. Where costs of on-the-job damages, motor vehicle accidents, and fires
include the value of property damage, the costs of home and public accidents
include estimated fire losses, but do not include other property damage costs.

Besides the estimated $444.1 billion and economic losses from uninten-
tional injuries, lost quality of life from those injuries is valued at an additional
$1027.9 billion, making the comprehensive cost $1472.0 billion.

It is sometimes difficult to comprehend numbers this large and it is
helpful to reduce them to quantities we might encounter in everyday life. As
an example, the cost for all injuries would mean that $0.68 out of every dollar

paid in 1996 federal personal income taxes or $0.58 of every dollar spent on food in the U.S. in 1996 would cover those costs. Look at motor vehicle accidents with an economic cost of $176.1 billion dollars; this cost was equivalent to purchasing 680 gal of gasoline per registered vehicle in the U.S. or a $20,700.00 rebate on every new car sold in 1996. The total death rate for unintentional injuries has changed less than 0.05% from year to year. It is interesting to note that the age group in which the highest number of unintentional injuries and deaths occur is from 25 to 44 with 27,400 people.

Motor vehicle deaths are the second largest category under intentional deaths with 43,300 people. The death rate is 16.3 deaths per 100,000 persons. These deaths include the chemical or electrically powered highway transport vehicles in motion (except those on rails), both on and off the highway or street.

In 1996, the National Safety Council reported that 43,300 people died in automobile accidents. That is still the sixth leading cause of death in the U.S. The first five causes are heart disease, cancer, stroke and pulmonary disease, and unintentional deaths. In 1995, the second leading cause of death in automobile accidents involved people in the age group from 15 to 24 years old. In 1996, this group shifted to the 24- to 44-year-old groups with 14,600 deaths.

Is this change in the age groups an indication of things to come? Will this group of people continue to move up the ladder, causing the largest number of deaths each year? In 1994, motor vehicle accidents were the leading cause of unintentional injury deaths overall from birth to age 78. The distribution of 1994 motor vehicle fatalities shows a sharp increase for persons aged 9 to 19, rising from 160 9 year olds to 1238 19 year olds.

Approximately 43,300 people are killed each year. That is a little less than a third of the number of people who fill the University of Michigan football stadium on a Saturday afternoon. It is almost incomprehensible to believe that those men, women, and children will never be able to touch the lives of another human being, perhaps find a cure for a major disease, set new world records in sports or, yes, even become the President of the United States. Putting these numbers into everyday parlance for a better understanding of how many people were killed or injured unintentionally translates to a death every 12 min, 5 people per hour, 119 people per day, or 30 people per week.

There is one injury accident every 12 sec, which means there are 300 injuries per hour, 7200 injuries per day, or 50,400 per week for a total of 2.62 million in 1996. More precisely, while you are listening to a 10-min safety speech, 2 persons are killed and about 390 will suffer a disabling injury. The costs will amount to $8.4 million. On the average there are 11 unintentional injury deaths and about 2360 disabling injuries every hour during the year.

Each year many people for one reason or another must go to an emergency room for some type of medical treatment. Usually these rooms are overcrowded. Why is this? In 1994, there were approximately 93.4 million visits to emergency departments of which 39.6 million were injury related. That means 15.3 visits per 100 persons on an injury-related basis. Motor vehicle accidents, traffic and nontraffic, make up 3.973 million visits or 10% of this total, thus making them the cause of the highest number of emergency visits.

People who visit the emergency departments most often are in the 15- to 24-year-old age group. One good piece of news in all of these statistics is that the highest number of motor vehicle deaths occurred between 1969 and 1973. Since that time, the number of deaths has decreased with the exception of 1978 to 1981.

In 1996, there were 38,200 fatal accidents, 1.6 million disabling injuries, and 9.6 million property damage accidents for a total of 11.2 million accidents involving motor vehicles.

Although the number of deaths per vehicle mile has decreased each year, the American driving public has increased the number of miles driven each year, and the number of vehicles registered, along with an increasing population.[1]

To understand what types of accidents these vehicles were involved in, consider the following: in 1996, vehicles collided with pedestrians, causing deaths only 6000 times and 64,000 injury accidents, while collisions with other motor vehicles occurred 19,300 times and produced 1.14 million injury accidents. Of those 19,300, the highest number resulted from an angled collision with another vehicle. The highest overall number occurred in a single vehicle accident into a fixed object, which accounted for 12,000 deaths and 262,000 injury accidents.

## Human Costs

People never seem to think about the number of those killed each year in automobile accidents but seem to remember the number or men and women killed in the nation's terrible wars. The following statistics shed some light on these facts. More people have been killed in an automobile accident in this country than all the U.S. military personnel in all the wars in which the U.S. has ever participated. Between 1900 and 1970, motor vehicle deaths in the U.S. totaled more than 1.8 million. From 1775 to 1970, 1.152 million U.S. military personnel were killed in the principal wars this country fought to preserve peace.[2] This is a terrible and frightening thought.

Why has the public not tried to stop the needless slaughter caused by vehicular accidents, as it tries to stop the nation's wars? Remember the junior and senior high school students wearing armbands or identification (ID) bracelets for the men who were missing in action or were prisoners of war (POWs)? What about the teenage drivers in U.S. hospitals who will never walk again — who cannot continue their education because of a serious brain injury? Nobody wears bracelets for them, and their friends in high school knew them. Why are there no marches to Washington, rallies, or whipping the American people into a frenzy as we did for our friends who were presumed dead or missing in action? During the various wars, the populace knew who the enemy was; now it is not so sure who or what the enemy is in the war against vehicular deaths. Maybe Pogo, the comic strip character, said it best, "We have met the enemy and he is us."

*Commentary: Between 1970 and 1980, I gave vehicle safety speeches to driver education classes. My first words to the class were, "Look at the student on either side of you because in less than one year one of you will be involved in a motor vehicle accident and one of you will be involved in a fatal accident." This did not seem to impress the young drivers. I showed them films of controled crashes at the Automobile Manufacturers' proving grounds; I showed them still photographs of actual on-scene accidents with all the blood and horror; yet they still were unfazed. Many young people in those days wore elephant hair bracelets or dog tag bracelets or just ID bands with the name of a servicemen believed to be missing in action.*

*The idea of someone close to them such as their mother, father, sister, brother, or best friend being seriously injured or killed in an automobile accident did not seem to be as important as people they did not know in a country they knew very little about who were involved in a war they could not understand. No amount of preaching, cajoling, or even begging or pleading, as well as showing young drivers statistics that proved their age group had the highest death rate and injury, would impress them. I think it was because they did not want to believe that their own generation could be at fault. That is one reason I gave up lecturing — because nothing I said made a difference.*

## Causes of Accidents

Accident investigators have identified bits and pieces of the problem; they have won a battle or two here and there with solutions to problems such as an improperly constructed road, poor overhead lighting, or even a vehicle defect, but still continue to lose the war. For example, it is known that 10,900 people between the ages of 15 and 24 and 4300 people over the age of 75 died in vehicular accidents in 1995, and that alcohol is a major contributor to these fatalities. However, real answers to these problems have not been found.

Also identified is the fact that in all motor vehicle accidents the 15- to 25-year-old age group leads the grisly death list with the exception of pedestrians and pedal cycles. *These statistics have been known for over 50 years.* That is why families who have a driver in that young age group all pay more for insurance.

About half of all motor vehicle deaths occur during the day and half occur at night. Death rates based on mileage, however, are about four times higher at night than during the day. Believe it or not, the highest death rates do not occur in the winter with icy roads and poor visibility, but between June and October when the weather conditions are usually the best.

The time of day is an important factor in accidents. Of all motor vehicle accidents, 21.8% occur between 4:00 and 8:00 p.m., with the highest number (3.8%) occurring on Friday afternoons at the same time. Drivers are all in a hurry to go somewhere and forget that their first job is to drive the car safely to get there. On the weekends 4.3 to 4.6% of the accidents occur between midnight and 4:00 a.m. That would appear to be the time in which the bars close and alcohol becomes the prime moving force in fatal accidents.

These statistics may not impress you because an accident has not happened in your family. Therefore, put aside the numbers for a moment and look at the cost of these accidents to you as part of the American public.

## Methods Used to Estimate Costs

There are two methods used to estimate the cost of an accident: one is economic and the other is comprehensive.

### Economic

Economic costs are a measure of the productivity lost and expenses incurred because of accidents. In 1996, it was estimated to be $790,000.00 per death or a total of $34.2 billion, with $32,200.00 per disabling injury for a grand total of $83.72 billion.

### Comprehensive

The comprehensive costs are even greater. They include not only the economic costs but also a measure of the value of lost quality of life associated with the deaths and injuries, that is, what society will pay to prevent them.

Estimating each death as being worth $120,807 and each incapacitating injury, worth $138,000.00, yields a total dollar value of $358 billion or slightly more than one third of a trillion dollars lost. These dollars could have been used in the fight against cancer, diabetes, hunger, poverty, poor education, or any other number of problems this country is facing today.

What about the pain and suffering those families have undergone because of the loss of a family member? Perhaps a great artist, a composer, a scientist, an engineer, a lawyer, a minister, a historian, or even another President of the United States has been lost. The list is endless, but the lost potential will never be known.

## How to Reduce Vehicular Injuries

Many people recommend the way to reduce the risk of moderate-to-critical and fatal injuries is to use the lap and shoulder belts provided in the vehicle. It is estimated that when people do use these restraint systems, the risk of fatal injury to front-seat passengers is reduced by 45% and the risk of moderate-to-critical injuries is reduced by 50%. As of December 19, 1996, 49 states and the District of Columbia have mandatory seat belt laws, the only exception being the state of New Hampshire. Safety belts provide the greatest protection against occupant ejection.

Among crashes in which a fatality occurred in 1995, only 2% of the restrained passenger car occupants were ejected compared with 25% of the unrestrained occupants. According to observation surveys conducted by the various states, 68% of passenger vehicle occupants used their seat belts in 1995. Between 1982 and 1995, the highest number of lives saved by the use of seat belts reached 10,000 in 1995. This is an appalling figure when considering the fact that the country of Australia during the first year of mandatory seat belt usage had a usage rate of approximately 92%. The difference is that the Australians have strict enforcement with strict penalties attached to violators. As a result, their injury rates are much lower than those in most countries.

Air bags, combined with lap/shoulder belts, offer increased protection for most passenger vehicle occupants. The overall fatality-reducing effectiveness for air bags is estimated at 11% over and above the benefits from using only safety belts. The benefits of air bags outweigh the risks. An estimated 475 lives were saved by air bags in 1995.

At the same time, 40 children and 30 adults (through July 1, 1997) were killed by air bags that deployed in otherwise survivable crashes. Of the children, 10 were in rear-facing infant seats placed in the front passenger seat and another 26 were not restrained in any way. Of the adults, 16 were not properly restrained.

There is only one way to stop this epidemic on the nation's highways, and that is to investigate each accident and to find out how and why it happened. When this is determined, action can be taken, just as any scientist or doctor does when he/she knows what is causing an epidemic: He/she fights back, destroys the cause of the disease, or finds a way to keep it in check. This is what the investigators and reconstructionists must do. This is their quest. This is the reason I am writing this book.

## Reasons for Investigating Vehicular Accidents

Vehicular accidents are investigated for a number of reasons. All states and the federal government require that an investigation be done to record the data and hopefully the facts surrounding that particular accident. In many states, especially in larger cities, accidents are not always investigated at the scene unless there is an injury. The parties can singularly or together go to the police station and have a report made concerning the accident. This is usually done for insurance purposes. Many times the officer/clerk recording the information may get the scene drawing or the names of the participants wrong, or the street names in the wrong place on the form. Usually both parties do not go to the police station and as a result only one side of the story is recorded. When and if the other party shows up the clerk many times may say that the accident has already been filed and does not take any further information.

In fatal cases, the law in most states requires that a comprehensive and thorough investigation be conducted. In many police departments there is a special team that handles only fatal accidents. This team is generally called the fatal squad. These specialists on such a squad have more training, are better equipped, and usually have more experience than the average road patrol officer.

A major problem is the amount of detail that these reports contain. The investigator at the scene controls the situation. It is his/her duty to include as much detail as possible in all the reports. Rain, mud, snow, heavily traveled highways, and low ambient temperatures all contribute to "getting the job done as quickly as possible syndrome." It is understandable how these types of conditions can influence any investigator to cut corners. Unfortunately, this can happen too many times, especially as the investigator becomes callused to the grisly scene he/she is exposed to day after day and year after year.

Think about the investigator who has done a less than adequate inspection of *your* accident. *Your* future may be in the balance based on that investigation when the prosecuting attorney decides to bring charges against *you* for vehicular homicide. For instance, assume a single piece of evidence was not noted by the investigating officer, such as a skid mark from the other vehicle showing that the driver tried to stop but was driving too fast for conditions.

## Investigative Organizations

The federal government, the insurance companies, and the automobile companies have been investigating accidents since the late 1950s to determine the effectiveness of the safety devices that they have placed on their vehicles as well as the problems of highway design and the drivers' interaction with both of these items. Many health-related organizations have tried to use these same data along with emergency room data to determine the cost of accidents, in real dollars and other costs to society such as lost time on the job, lost production, etc. These databases have grown over the years and are constantly being updated. There have been many studies conducted by independent organizations using these databases to compare all the contributors to the accidents such as small vs. large cars, older vs. newer cars, and cars vs. trucks. Many studies also have been conducted to determine the most vulnerable seat in a car. Each of these studies has helped vehicle designers, health professionals, and insurance companies to determine methods to increase the protection of vehicle occupants, better ways to bring medical aid to the scene of the accident, and changes in insurance rates for safer drivers and cars. For example, investigation of accidents led to the confirmation of the effectiveness of the air bag as a supplemental restraint system for today's cars and small trucks.

## Databases for Road Conditions and Use of Restraint Systems

Many states and local governments have started special databases to improve the dangerous roads and intersections, and to increase the use of restraint systems. Much use is made of these databases for information about drivers (i.e., old vs. young, and experienced vs. learners). Even the effects of seat belts being used in one accident vehicle vs. no restraint systems being used by the second vehicle occupants have been compared. The most recent studies have been into areas such as child seats and deployment rates for air bags. Research and accident investigations have shown that many child seats were unsafe and not effective based on federal government testing. This finding led the Department of Transportation to initiate a recall campaign against the manufacturers. Air bag systems have fast deployment rates to ensure the bag is inflated before the occupant slides forward into the instrument panel or steering wheel.

Preliminary studies have shown that adults small in stature, such as women, in vehicles with the fast-deploying air bags have suffered moderately severe injuries such as fractures of the forearm and severe eye injuries. There have also been cases of facial burns due to the heat generated by the gas used to fill the bags.

Changes are being made in the design of the inflator system of air bags. Some manufacturers have adopted a special key system to allow the occupants too small in size to turn off the air bag. There is also work being done on a "smart" bag system that will not fire when a small person is in the seat. Accident investigations will prove how effective these changes will be in tomorrow's vehicles.

## Prevention and Elimination of On-the-Job Injuries

Accident investigation is a necessary part of all manufacturing industries today. It answers the question, "What happened and how can we prevent it from happening again?" The National Safety Council has been a leader in this field to minimize if not eliminate on-the-job injuries. Work by the council has spread to all phases of the commercial and industrial workplace. This advisory body has a database of accident investigations, both in the workplace as well as in the home. The council also has been a proponent of carrying good safety habits from the workplace to the home. Many products have been investigated and information is available through the National Safety Council.

The advent of the Occupational Safety and Health Administration (OSHA) and the state OSHA groups have, through the information gleaned from accident investigations, expanded safety training for workers in all industries as a result of studying these types of accidents. It is evident that accident investigation has and will continue to save people's lives and mitigate their injuries through the data that are collected properly and very carefully. The data collected and evaluated by safety professionals may one day very well save our lives or those of our loved ones.

## Criminal and Civil Litigation

Accident investigation has also been used in both criminal and civil litigation. A team of trained investigators examines each fatal case; many times, more information is needed, so the reconstructionists perform a detailed in-depth probe. The findings are then sent via report to the prosecuting attorney for the county or district where decisions are made concerning the criminal action to be taken against the driver of the vehicle. Many times, however, there is no further action taken and the charges may be reduced from vehicular homicide to gross or even ordinary negligence. A civil suit may be an outgrowth of a fatal or nonfatal criminal case.

This action may be brought against a driver for personal injury or death, and a product liability case may be brought against the vehicle manufacturer if the attorney has sufficient information about a defect in the vehicle design. Without the most complete details gathered at the scene, an innocent driver may spend the rest of his/her life in prison or a plea bargain may be entered for the guilty driver and he/she may go free, which is worse.

It is up to every investigator to bear these thoughts in mind when investigating the first or the 500th accident of his/her career. Investigators should do the very best they can each and every time they are called on to do so.

*Commentary: Several years ago I was reconstructing a case where a police officer was called to the scene of an accident in which his daughter had been involved. He was not aware she was one of the injured parties and it was not until she was taken away in the ambulance that he realized it. He completed his work at the scene and then took himself off the case for obvious reasons. He, of course, followed the case with increased interest. You never know what circumstances you may find yourself in at the scene of an accident. He did his best.*

# References

1. *Accident Facts — 1997 Edition*, National Safety Council, Itasca, IL, 1997, 10, 78.
2. *Accident Facts — 1996 Edition*, National Safety Council, Itasca, IL, 1996, 63.

# Where Do I Start?

2

"To a great mind, nothing is little."

**Sherlock Holmes**
*A Study in Scarlet*

## Requirements for Accident Investigators/Reconstructionists

At the present time the author knows of no formal requirements at the state or local level for accident investigators or reconstructionists. Police officers, sheriffs, county deputies, and other peace officers who work the road patrol and investigate accidents are not always designated as accident investigators, even though they have attended the police academy. These academies do have within their curricula several hours of training in investigative techniques such as the use of measuring tapes, scene drawings, and information gathering from the principals and witnesses.

These law enforcement personnel usually assist another officer from their own departments who has been designated or is considered a qualified accident investigator/reconstructionist. The on-scene officer may instead call in a state trooper who has been qualified by the state police as an accident reconstructionist. This is usually the case in small towns, villages, and even small cities, and basically is how the road patrol officer gets on-the-job investigation training.

## Sources of Additional Training

Many local law enforcement departments may not have sufficient funds to send personnel to one of the special one-day or weekly schools that are held each year in the state or in other parts of the country. There are several schools across the country where a formal education is available in criminal justice. These usually require 1 to 2 years of commitment and can lead to a bachelor's degree. Many of these schools allow private individuals to attend and others only allow police officers in attendance due to funding limitations.

Many regional or community colleges offer courses in public safety, scientific investigations, or even crime and evidence analysis. (For further information, check with your local community college about its curricula). These courses are usually taken over several weeks and contain such specialty subjects as lamp filament analysis, truck tire data, and semitractor driving and handling.

Many states or counties have associations of investigators that hold seminars on a semiannual basis. These inform the members of the latest developments in investigation and reconstruction techniques or in the latest changes in the law such as the graduated licensing procedure for young drivers.

The Institute of Police Technology and Management (IPTM)[1] from the University of North Florida at Jacksonville has courses on accident investigation and reconstruction. The institute was created and designed to provide management and training to municipal, county, state, and federal law enforcement officers. They train both civilian and military law enforcement personnel throughout the U.S. and overseas. The faculty consists of professionals with practical law enforcement skills, many years of police experience, and necessary academic backgrounds to effectively train in-service law enforcement officers. When necessary, the faculty is supplemented by highly qualified experts from government, private industry, and the academic community. The IPTM programs are specifically directed toward the operation and supervision of command law enforcement personnel.[1] The traffic accident reconstruction course is an 80-hour course and requires that the student must have attended the advanced accident investigation course.

The University of California at Riverside also has traffic accident investigation and reconstruction programs.[2] The Riverside extension program has the Traffic Accident Investigation Training Institute, which consists of 180 hours of course work. This program covers the principles and procedures of collision investigation, immediate collision investigation, skid mark analysis, and advanced collision investigation. In addition, it offers electives such as basic computer-aided collision diagramming, low-speed impact, accident photography, and human factors. (See Chapter 10 for more details about reconstruction courses.) Special electives are selected according to the needs of the student and can include accidents involving pedestrians or bicycles, detection and investigation of staged accidents, speed determination from crush analysis, and commercial vehicle reconstruction.[2]

The oldest school to establish a formal accident investigation training school is the one located in Chicago, Illinois, called the Northwestern

University Traffic Institute (NUTI).[3] It was established in 1936 for the purpose of expanding the scope of university level education and training in traffic safety. Since that time, the institute has broadened its original objective to include training in police operations and management. Representatives from federal, state, and local law enforcement agencies, as well as members of foreign agencies, attend the institute's many and varied programs.

NUTI also publishes many research programs and provides on-site technical assistance. The courses available include accident investigation I and II, and vehicle dynamics. The institute also includes courses in microcomputers using commercial software for reconstruction of the accident. (See Chapter 10 for additional details.)

For those students interested in independent study programs and the freedom of self-paced study, the school offers courses in tire examination, drawing after-accident situation maps, photogrammetry for traffic investigation, measuring the road at the accident scene, and other police-related matters. Textbooks and other course-related materials for individual study and refresher programs are sold there for those seeking to increase their skills with the latest techniques.

The Civil and Environmental Engineering Department of Michigan State University,[4] through its highway traffic safety programs, has an extensive schedule of police traffic accident investigation courses. These are offered each year through the university's facilities as well as at several local community colleges and selected police or sheriff's departments. The sequence of courses being offered covers the basics and several advanced courses in accident investigation and reconstruction. The program includes initial investigations, follow-up investigations, accident photography, perspective grid mapping of evidence, tire dynamics and examination, lamp examination, commercial vehicles, motorcycle accident investigation, vehicle motion and injury causation during collisions, vision, night visibility and lighting requirements, vehicle/pedestrian collisions, advanced traffic accident reconstruction, vehicle damage measuring for computer-aided reconstruction, computer-assisted traffic accident investigation, basic REC-TEC computer program, advanced accident reconstruction using the basic REC-TEC program, reconstruction formulas, computer-aided drawings, EDCRASH computer simulation programs, and heavy vehicle accident reconstruction.

In addition, several new specialized courses are being developed at Michigan State University including railroad grade crossing crashes, report writing/case preparation, testifying as an accident reconstructionist, accident reconstruction physics, and investigation/reconstruction of emergency vehicle accidents. From time to time the school offers refresher and update courses to upgrade the skills of older graduates.

The Michigan Association of Traffic Investigation and Reconstruction (MATIA)[5] has a spring and fall seminar that covers many different subjects as well as demonstrations of investigation/reconstruction techniques and staged accidents with new safety devices such as the antilock braking system (ABS). Several organizations such as the National Association of Professional Accident Reconstructionists (NAPARS)[6] and the American Council of Traffic Accident Reconstructionists (ACTAR)[7] have an examination that the individual can take to become certified as an accident reconstructionist by that specific organization. Each of these organizations may have retired peace officers on their staff as well as graduate engineers to assist each other in developing techniques useful in accident investigation/reconstruction.

The Society of Automotive Engineers (SAE)[8] has a subcommittee called the Accident Investigation and Reconstruction Procedures Committee. This committee is made up of SAE members who are involved in some manner or forum in the field of accident investigation or reconstruction. Many of these men are graduate engineers working in industry who use this information or are full-time investigators/reconstructionists. There are part-time committee members who are on the staff of a college or university on a full-time basis and will act as investigators/reconstructionists when called on by a law firm, an insurance company, or a company looking for product information. The SAE *does not certify investigators or accident reconstructionists.*

Experts in the various fields of engineering can send a course syllabus to the SAE to develop and teach many one-day or partial week courses throughout the year at the various conferences held throughout the U.S. These courses have been useful to the investigator/reconstructionist working in the field; unfortunately, many times they are too advanced for the novice. Other special groups or organizations such as the bar association, expert witness listing companies, and legal assistant associations have put on seminars throughout the U.S. to increase the knowledge of their members through the use of experts in the field of accident investigation/reconstruction.

Some specialized professional associations such as the American Academy of Forensic Examiners[9] have developed seminars for their annual meetings. They encourage their members to develop correspondence courses in their specific specialties, which can then be offered through the association to all its members.

The most qualified investigators the author has had contact with are private investigators, commonly known as private eyes (PIs). Many if not most of these men/women have been peace officers in different organizations and have gained their knowledge the hard way, through the school of experience and dedicated work in the field of investigation/reconstruction. That is not to say that these men/women have not taken any formalized training. They are hard-working, dedicated people trying to determine the truth concerning any accident they may be called on to investigate and/or reconstruct. There is a formal course available at the Henry Ford Community College in Dearborn, Michigan, that helps an individual to become a PI. This is the only one in existence that the author is currently aware of.

## Basic Knowledge for the Investigator

The accident scene contains the majority if not all the evidence as to what occurred before, during, and after a collision. It is up to the on-scene investigator to determine, locate, photograph, measure, and preserve this evidence. All the formal or informal courses that an individual may take do not always prepare him/her to be an accident investigator.

The first requirement of an accident investigator is an inquisitive mind. This means that he/she is always asking questions such as why, what, when, and how. The investigator must be interested in learning the answers to these questions at each and every accident that he/she investigates. Many times when faced with adverse environmental conditions, such as rain, snow, or cold temperatures, it is easy to forget the reason the investigation is being conducted. The answer to these questions can only be determined when the investigator has an eye for details. It is easy to see the larger pieces of evidence scattered about the accident scene. The investigator should photograph, measure, and construct a rough sketch of the scene with the location of the evidence.

In addition, the entire scene from several different directions and locations should be videotaped. This means the videotape operator must walk the length and width of the accident scene and tape the scene from the direction the vehicle was coming, from the direction it was going, and from both sides of the accident scene so that a panoramic view of the scene is developed. This can aid both the reconstructionist in developing his/her opinion at a later date and also in providing background information for the tryer of fact. Once this is done, it is then necessary for the investigator to begin to dig for details of the accident. As an example, if the engine has been thrown clear of the vehicle itself, it is mandatory for the investigator to determine how and why the engine was thrown from the vehicle and to establish why it ended up in a particular location. This would include looking at the exterior damage of the engine and also at components such as previously damaged or broken engine mounts, weak or rusted frame and/or support members, and transmission and drive shaft. Every piece of evidence that has been displaced from the vehicle has to be documented as to how and why it ended up where it did. This is the effort that the investigator must put forth in every investigation he/she conducts. Another necessary element for investigators at the scene is to be able to use their imaginations and place the vehicles involved in their minds' eye so that they literally develop a possible scenario of the movement of the vehicles prior to impact, through the collision to their final resting point. They are better able to do this when they are viewing fresh witness marks left by the vehicles before, during, and after the collision. By performing this imagery in their minds' eye, it is possible to develop multiple potential scenarios until one is found that matches the majority if not all the physical evidence such as the witness marks, missing vehicle components, and damage to the vehicles available to the on-scene investigators. The investigators make notes of each of these and later develop the best scenario for their review and comparison with other data such as witness statements and depositions. They then check out their scenarios against the statements of the principals involved, obtained at the scene of the accidents or those taken at a later date.

Finally, investigators must also have the ability to place themselves in the various positions inside the vehicle, once again through their minds' eye. This can be of great assistance in trying to determine what actions or reactions the drivers of both vehicles may or may not have undergone during the three phases of the accident: precollision, collision or impact, and postcollision. It can also assist investigators in determining the trajectory of the various occupants in each vehicle during the collision phase of the accident. When the medical information becomes available, they can match up the injuries to each of the occupants with the damage found inside the vehicle. Then these can be compared with the investigators' scenario developed at the scene when they placed themselves in the various occupants' positions inside the vehicles.

These last procedures are not easy to accomplish. It takes constant practice and adherence to a strict methodology that must be done at every accident scene. Each accident is different; *the method of investigating an accident is not.* Whether the vehicle is a total disaster or only has minor damage, *the method by which the investigation must be done has to be exactly the same each and every time.*

*Commentary: Many investigators have asked me over the years why it is necessary to conduct the accident investigation in exactly the same way. I have always answered that question in this manner.*

*If I continually adhere to the same pattern of investigation I will never forget to do any single portion of the procedure necessary to complete the detailed analysis of the accident scene.*

*Shortcuts such as only taking pictures of the damaged side of a vehicle or only taking two or three pictures of the damage without any detailed photographs of the damaged and undamaged portions of the vehicle may lead you to forget to take other steps that are necessary for your analysis. Shortcuts also open the investigator up to criticism during the deposition or trial by the opposition. As an example, consider the following hypothetical question from the opposing counsel: "Sir, why did you take pictures of only one side of the vehicle? How do we know that is the only portion of the vehicle that was damaged or that there may have been existing damage that cannot be seen?" What answer would you give at your deposition? It would appear that you are trying to shortcut the job or that you are inefficient and sloppy in your work ethic and the remainder of your opinions may not be worthwhile. This, of course, could lead to a poor reputation and eventually to very little or no work whatsoever in your chosen profession.*

Professional accident investigators/reconstructionists have a duty each and every time they undertake an accident investigation and/or reconstruction to do the very best job that they can for their clients. This does not mean that they should slant their work in favor of their clients. It means they should walk the tightrope of independence and that, if necessary, their work could be used by either side of the litigation.

*Commentary: I had one case in which I was hired by both the plaintiff and defense counsels to determine what occurred in a multiple car accident. A vehicle traveling at high speed went down an expressway off ramp and onto a city street. The vehicle went through a stop sign and struck the front of a vehicle, causing it to spin violently in a counterclockwise direction and to slam up against a telephone pole. The high-speed vehicle was redirected off the second vehicle and literally ran up and across the wall of building, rolling over onto its passenger side, ejecting two occupants, and losing two wheel assemblies. When I explained all the details to both parties, they agreed that the study and analysis was free of bias for either side.*

The first fact every investigator must remember is that he/she must start each investigation with an "open mind." That means not starting the investigation with a preconceived notion of already knowing the answer. Even if he/she has done 50, 100, or even 1000 investigations of the very same type, there are always differences in each accident investigation. The investigator cannot know everything about the vehicles, the road, the weather, or countless other factors that make up an accident prior to starting the investigation. For example, there may be some unusual pieces of equipment added to the vehicle by the owner or the company that provides the vehicle, which is unknown to the investigator.

*Commentary: An article recently appeared in a major newspaper concerning an accident investigation by a very prestigious organization that brings home this very point. The accident involved what is commonly referred to as "sudden acceleration."*

*The investigator had done a considerable number of very similar cases in the past and did not want to look at another case, claiming he already knew the answer. The driver put his foot on the accelerator instead of the brake, and the car shot forward, impacting another object and causing severe injuries and death. The investigator eventually looked at the vehicle involved and could not find any rational explanation or defect in the vehicle so he concluded that he was correct in his original assumption that the accident was completely due to driver error.*

*A few months later the investigator was giving a seminar to a group of investigators on this simple case, as he described it, and was explaining it to his audience when one of the investigators stood up and told him he had the very same thing happening in his vehicle, but without an accident. With that, the speaker went outside and looked at the vehicle in question and found that another switch had been added to the electrical system in the same electrical path as the brake pedal switch that had been installed by the manufacturer. The brake pedal switch was installed to prevent the vehicle from developing a sudden acceleration when shifting from park or neutral to drive by requiring that the driver depress the brake pedal activating the switch. In some manner that was not explained in the article, the second switch somehow diverted energy from the brake pedal switch, making it inoperative; and when the vehicle was shifted into drive, there was indeed a sudden acceleration. This is a classic example of an investigator starting his primary investigation with a closed mind — he thought he already knew the answer to the reconstruction.*

*It is possible that the investigator may have had indications by the information given him by the client that the case was very similar to one or even several cases that he had before. Never fail to do a complete and exhaustive, detailed investigation of the entire accident, including the vehicle, before rendering an opinion that you may one day regret and that under certain circumstances could cost you your career.*

When starting a case, many investigators, especially the less experienced ones, are overwhelmed by either the lack of or the stacks of information. All investigations and reconstructions start at the resting point of the vehicles at the scene. The scene of the accident holds the richest and most abundant amount of evidence and information, including:

- Location of the resting points of the vehicles
- Location of the occupants outside the vehicle, if they were ejected from the vehicle
- Location of accident vehicle debris
- Location of the skid or yaw marks from either or both vehicles
- Construction of the roadway — asphalt, concrete, or gravel
- Condition of the shoulders of the road — paved, gravel, sand, soft or hard, edge ruts, or no shoulders at all

- Condition of the roadbed — potholes, washboard, edge nibbling, narrow lane widths, and improper or no lane markings
- Damage to the vehicle
- Components missing from the vehicles
- Location of the missing components
- Damage to the roadbed from the vehicle interaction
- Damage to the off-road environment such as fields, lawns, orchards, culverts, and trees

These data are easily seen and documented. The hard part is looking for details at the scene. This is where the investigators/reconstructionists must show their expertise.

Vehicles involved in a collision follow Newton's second law of motion, "Bodies in motion will tend to stay in motion until acted upon by an outside force." This basically means that vehicles do not make radical changes in direction or speed unless they strike an object or they are being struck. The only exception known is when vehicles become airborne. When they touch the ground again, they perform weird gyrations and movements due to the location of the center of gravity of the vehicle as well as the uneven ground area where the vehicle is impacted.

## Fresh Scenes

Unfortunately, very few investigators have the privilege of a "fresh" scene, (i.e., one that is investigated within a few hours after the accident). Most get their first look when the scene is a few weeks to a year old. This time lag creates many problems in terms of the data available for analysis and reconstruction.

Those investigators who have the luxury of a fresh scene may be overwhelmed by the quantity of information. It appears that there is so much available that it begs the question, "Where do I start?" The following is a checklist on how to get started:

- If at all possible, secure the scene from both pedestrian and vehicular traffic or have someone else do it, preferably the police.
- Souvenir hunters, gawkers, and thrill seekers may remove and trample evidence such as footprints and tire marks in the snow or dirt, or may even take parts of the vehicle that they think they can sell. They have been known to remove clothing and purchases made by the occupants of the vehicle prior to the accident, or even to move the bodies at the scene to hunt for money and jewelry from the accident victims themselves.

- Photograph and videotape the entire scene as soon as possible, even while rescue personnel are doing their job.
- Many times a rescue squad cuts the posts that support the roof of a vehicle and bend them out of the way for easier extrication. The deformed metal of the vehicle is under stress from the collision. The removal of the roof relieves the stresses and the shape of the vehicle changes. These changes may affect the depth of the deformation that many times is used by the investigator to determine speed at impact. When the amount of deformation is incorrect, then the speed at impact is incorrect. Many on-scene photographs fail to get close-up views showing that the support posts of the roof were either cut or sawn off. When this happens it is difficult to determine the condition of the roof, especially if the vehicles have been junked before the investigation starts.
- Start by making a rough sketch of the scene. Always include the northerly direction with an arrow. Locate the positions of the vehicle as accurately as possible with respect to pavement lines, pavement edges, grass vs. gravel, etc. This sketch can help if there are no photographs due to a camera failure or if the photographs become lost or misplaced for some reason. Detailed dimensions can be taken later in the inspection for a finished sketch.
- Measurements, photographs, and videotaping of the witness marks such as skid or yaw marks are mandatory. Especially, record the start and end points. Remember to consider the shadow marks, which make up the start of the skid marks. Location and measurements of marks in the snow are very significant, especially if the vehicles were sliding sideways.
- Locate the major components of debris patterns. Then measure the distances to the extreme portions of debris that form some type of geometric shape. These shapes are usually conical unless the vehicle splits apart, in which case there will be a trail of debris that must be marked, measured, and photographed.
- All the details are added as soon as the injured parties have been removed for treatment. These include the measurements of damage inside the vehicle as well as the exterior damage. Blood spatter, shoe prints, and locations of broken glass should make up a portion of the list of details needed to complete the investigation.
- Photographs, videotapes, and measurements of everything else seen at the site, whether they appear important or not at the time, round out the inspection.

From this point on, the investigator should continue as previously described with the full and detailed inspection. The investigators should be continually asking themselves questions as to why or how certain marks were made or why certain marks are not present at the scene or on the vehicle.

If these questions cannot be answered at the inspection, then the investigator must start asking questions of the client and the witnesses to the accident itself. Many times it is necessary to obtain a previous accident and/or maintenance history of the vehicle to determine if any of the problems seen at the inspection were preexisting. This would include paint transfers, and damage to certain areas of the vehicle or vehicle glass, such as the windshield.

## Stale or Aged Scenes

Most investigators are thrilled to observe the scene within a month of the actual accident. Aged or stale scenes require a different approach to the question, "Where do I start?"

- At this point in time, a police department, sheriff's unit, or the state troopers should have completed the scene investigation and made their reports.
- Hopefully, there should be photographs of the scene with the vehicles still at their resting points.
- Many times these are taken at night, which usually means the quality of the pictures is poor, especially in close-up views of the witness marks on the road.
- There may be some pictures of the vehicles but usually taken too far away for any analysis.
- Many police department or state troopers go to the scene the next day and photograph the area, but unfortunately not from the same places the original photographs were taken.
- If the road is heavily traveled, then the skid, or yaw marks, and even gouges and scratches may not be as visible as they were on the night of the accident.
- Law enforcement officers may also take photographs of the vehicle at the police impound lot or the salvage pool. They usually do not get the views that an investigator/reconstructionist would require for an analysis.

What should the investigator do first? He/she should obtain a copy of the photographs and review them at his/her office. Become familiar with both the vehicle and the accident scene. Make a written list of the information that is missing or needing more detail. Review the UD-10 report and all other attachments such as the fatal report and witness statements. Then check the statements for positioning of the witnesses with respect to their location and what they may have been able to see at the time of the collision. At this time the investigator should be forming some idea of how the accident happened.

Next the details need to be determined. Take the photographs, police report, and sketches to the scene and determine the positions and directions from which they were taken. Look for specific landmarks such as cracks in the roadbed, or other unusual markings on the road surface near the locations of the resting points of the vehicles. These help in locating any residual gouges in the roadbed. Check to see if the police have recorded the gouges or other marks on their sketches. Depending on the length of time between the accident and the inspection, there may still be some portions of the skid marks visible on the roadbed. What is seen should be measured and recorded and checked against the police report.

If the police created a sketch with any dimensions, it is necessary that several if not all the dimensions be checked to determine their accuracy as well as their location. Try to locate the police determination of the point of impact (POI), if they made one. Starting at that point walk the roadbed, shoulders and areas beyond the shoulders on both sides of the highway, looking for debris. When accident debris is swept off the road, it is usually swept to the edge nearest its location. In other words, debris is not swept across the entire width of the highway. The location of the debris should be very close to the POI. This is one method of verifying the police POI with the actual POI.

If there is a difference of more than a few feet, then continue looking for pieces of the vehicle that can be identified as those coming from the accident vehicle or vehicles. Once these pieces are found, then look on the roadbed for additional scarring such as gouges and scratches to determine the new POI. If the accident happened in an urban setting then check the trees by the side of the road for damage. Then check the impact vehicle for embedded wood in any cracks or crevices.

*Commentary: I had a case where there was more than one type of wood embedded in the vehicle damage. Examination showed that one wood had been treated with a preservative. A second trip to the scene showed a piece of a wooden telephone pole was missing about 10 feet up from the ground. This was missed on the first inspection due to the height of the impact and the fact that the vehicle rotated about its longitudinal axis and came back down on its wheels without touching the ground with any other part of the vehicle. There was a large rock in the path that did not show any witness marks due to weathering.*

Never cease to question the evidence until it leads to a conclusion or there are no other data available.

# References

1. Assistant Director Institute of Police Technology and Management (IPTM), at the University of North Florida, Jacksonville, FL.
2. University of California Riverside extension program, 1200 University Avenue, Riverside, CA.
3. Northwestern University Traffic Institute, (NUTI), Chicago, IL.
4. Department of Civil and Environmental Engineering, Michigan State University, Lansing, MI.
5. Michigan Association of Traffic Investigation and Reconstruction (MATPA).
6. National Association of Professional Accident Reconstructonists (NAPARS).
7. American Council of Traffic Accident Reconstructionists (ACTAR).
8. Society of Automotive Engineers (SAE).
9. American Academy of Forensic Examiners (AAFE).

# Tools and Special Equipment for the Investigator

*3*

"It is my business to know things."

**Sherlock Holmes**
*A Case of Identity*

## Preparation

Before starting any investigation there is a certain amount of preparation necessary to do it properly and accurately. One of the main points to bear in mind is the distance the investigator may have to carry the equipment once the site is reached. Sometimes it can be to the farthest reaches of a junkyard; to a salvage company holding yard; to a private garage; or even to the back end of a barn where chickens, dogs, mice, and squirrels have made nests for themselves within the vehicle for several weeks if not months. Therefore the prepared investigator organizes his/her equipment so that he/she carries only the minimum necessary to accomplish the job if cartage for a long distance is required.

## Basic Tool Kit

The investigator's basic tool kit, as shown in Table 3.1, is mandatory. First remember that the initial inspection is not a major disassembly. If a more detailed inspection is necessary after completion of the initial work, then the investigator should ask the client to hold the vehicle and should get

**Table 3.1    Investigator's Basic Tool Kit**

Set of various size screwdrivers
Set of open and closed end metric and English wrenches
Set of 1/4- and 3/8-in. drive sockets, metric and English
Set of Allen wrenches
Jackknife with 4-in. blade
Special drive bits for screws used to hold tail- and headlight covers and lenses in place
Homemade 3-4-5 triangle

permission to disassemble it further in the proper manner such as in a heated garage or with a lift.

Many times it is necessary for the attorney to purchase the vehicle and make the necessary arrangements to hold the vehicle in a secured storage area until the opposing side has performed its inspection. The vehicle is then held until after the trial, depending on the possibility of an appeal being filed by any of the parties.

There are several types of disassembly. The first is a minor type where the investigator looks at easily removable components. The second is a moderate or medium heavy-duty inspection. This includes removal of large components or assemblies. The last and most comprehensive inspection is the disassembly of major components.

The minor type of disassembly includes taking off the front headlights, rear taillight lenses, and side marker lenses to analyze and photograph the condition of the filaments of the light bulbs. This can require several different types and sizes of screwdrivers: not only the common flat blade but also the Phillips, Torx and other special screwdrivers for the special screws that are used in today's vehicles. Wrenches, both closed and open, as well as metric and English, are also necessary. All manufacturers have not converted to metric, and because the average car on today's highways is at least 7- to 10-years old, you will get a mix of both types of hardware for some time to come.

A set of sockets is valuable but not always necessary. Both metric and English socket sets containing deep as well as short sockets are helpful. These might be left in the trunk, and if necessary, require an extra trip to retrieve them. Wide selections of Allen wrenches are a must. They are small and come packaged in several sizes for different uses. A 4-in. blade jackknife is always handy for many different uses. A homemade 3-4-5 triangle is a necessity when trying to determine and develop a curved road surface for mapping at a later date. By using a 12- × 12-in. piece of cardboard, mark off 6 in. on the horizontal surface and 8 in. on the vertical surface. By use of the Pythagorean theorem, the hypotenuse must be 10 in. in a basic 3-4-5 right triangle. Its uses are described later when mapping a curved section of highway. Depending on the investigator's specialty, such as trucks, motorcycles, or bicycles, he/she may want to include other special tools used on those machines but Table 3.1 includes the basic necessities.

Both the moderate and heavy-duty inspections should be conducted in an environmentally controlled garage with a lift. This is for the equipment and lighting as well as the safety and health of the investigator.

The moderate or medium heavy-duty inspection should include the removal of larger components or assemblies that are fairly easy to reach, such as front and rear seats, the entire instrument panel, spare tire, mounted tires, and some engine components including the alternator, air-conditioning units, etc. Further disassembly of these components may be necessary depending on what is found when they are first removed.

The heavy-duty inspection usually requires a mechanic with all the specialized tools that are required to disassemble the engine and/or transmission.

*Commentary: Unless you are an excellent mechanic or have Master Mechanic certification, do not undertake a heavy-duty inspection by yourself. It requires specialized tools and the work requires a lot of space, especially a hoist, oil and other fluid disposal, and chain lifts or equivalents to hold the engine or transmission. Spend your time more fruitfully overseeing the inspection and videotaping and analyzing the fractured parts to determine their role in the accident.*

## Special Equipment

A second carrying case is for the special equipment. This equipment case has been developed over a 25-year period. I have used each and every piece of the equipment on more than one occasion and have been glad I had it in the kit. Table 3.2 lists the special equipment. An explanation of the need for each of the items on the list follows.

**Chalk** — This is used to mark the beginning or the end of the tire mark or circle and outline the gouge marks in the roadbed. The gouge marks are readily seen with the naked eye but because they many times lose their depth of field when photographed, the chalk brings the viewers' focus back to the mark. During the photographic or video recording, it is necessary to outline the gouge and place an appropriate sized ruler next to it to indicate the size of the mark. An arrow drawn on the street or a 3 × 5 card placed next to the mark shows the direction of travel at the time the gouge was made. Both videos and still photographs must be taken as a series of wide angle and good "fill the frame" close-ups. These close-ups must be taken at different angles of the sun to ensure that the depth and direction of the gouge are easily discernible in the photograph. Tire marks present the same problem during photographic recording. They must be photographed at different angles to

**Table 3.2    Special Equipment**

Chalk
Red, black, white, and yellow colored grease pencils
Contour gauge
Blank cards (3 × 5)
Red, black, and blue felt tip pens
Tape measures — 12, 25, and 100 ft
Cardboard placard (12 × 12)
Children's play clay
Stick-on tape measures
Graph and plain paper
Menu board
Handheld compass
Surveyor's pins
Vehicle motion rods
Handheld magnifying glass
Small and large envelopes or plastic evidence bags to hold scene evidence fragments
Small and large tags to label evidence at scene
Handheld minitape recorder with extra tapes
Accident investigation forms
Lightweight vest with many pockets
Duct tape

ensure a specific refection of the sun off the surface of the roadway that best shows the length and width of the mark. In addition, it is necessary to photograph and videotape each mark from several different angles and locations to show the beginning, end, and middle of each one, especially any change in the tire mark directions and widths. Do not concentrate on close-ups. The investigator and reconstructionist must see the entire mark from several different angles to be able to understand how it was made. Chalk circles, with direction arrows or 3 × 5 cards to show the direction of travel, made at the beginning and end of each mark, give the photographer a starting and ending point of each mark, especially if they start and stop or rapidly change direction. Marking the roadway in chalk alongside the tire marks with dashed lines helps not only the photographer but also the investigator many months later.

**Colored grease pencils** — These pencils in several different colors are a must. The best colors are red, yellow, white, and black. These are used to mark out various details both inside and outside the vehicle. Inside the vehicle, circle skin transfer marks, and draw arrows to where a portion of hair or tissue may be lodged in the crack of the windshield or on the screw head in a molding. The different colored interiors require different colored pencils. Use them to mark the center location of the driver's and passengers' seats to determine seat locations and seating positions. Putting a white grease pencil circle around a blowout or cut mark on a tire when photographing them makes them much easier to see. Grease pencils are used on the outside of the vehicle to show the direction of scratches, dents, metal folds, and paint transfers. Use these pencils to show any details that need to be brought to the attention of the photographer and the reconstructionist.

**Depth or counter gauge** — This is used primarily on the inside of the vehicle to measure the depth of an impact from a knee or head. Remember that all metal has a hysteresis curve and the dent loses some of its depth over the first few hours or days. This gauge can be used on the outside of a vehicle when trying to show that a specific impact was due to a signpost or a small tree.

**Index Cards (3 × 5)** — These are necessary and can be used over and over again. When a close-up of a damaged tire or rim is needed, it is impossible to tell if it is the right or left, front or rear tire when all that is seen is the tire. Marking a set of cards as LF, RF, LR, or RR helps immensely at a later date during the reconstruction. A marked up set for the seat belt locations, LF-D, LF-O/B, RFP, RRP/OB, MP/R, and MP/F are also useful. These are the only ways to keep seat belt webbing photographs from getting mixed up. The cards also come in handy when locating debris along the side of the road. You can mark the location by the number of feet from the RP or give it a coordinate point $(x, y)$ from the RP for use in preparing the final scale drawing. Of course, all must be photographed using a general photograph of the area and then progressive close-ups.

**Red, black, and blue ink felt tip pens** — These felt tip pens can be used to make a rough sketch, which every scene investigation with very few exceptions requires. Using different colored pens for each vehicle's skid marks, plow marks in the field, and debris location makes the investigation a lot easier during the reconstruction. Marking telephone and powerlines, and fire hydrants in different colors is also useful.

**Tape measures** — These are necessary, even if a total station computer program is used to map the scene. At least three different lengths, 6, 12, and 25 ft, are desirable. Sometimes it is nice to carry a 100-ft tape for added assistance in locating the middle ordinate in certain yaw marks when later plotting them on the scale drawing. These materials are all used to locate and measure various damage to the outside and inside of the vehicle. An example would be the location of the impact star on a windshield from the head impact. The location near the top of the windshield means that the occupant was not belted, whereas lower stars mean the occupant was belted.

**Placards (12 × 12 or 24 × 24)** — These are made of heavy-duty cardboard and are made to fold into one 12- × 12- or 24- × 24-in. piece. When unfolded the placard can be twice as wide and even twice as long depending on what is needed. It is usually made from white cardboard and has an "X" taped or drawn on the inside surfaces. When these are placed in the photograph, then any measurements that are needed can be done with the placard as a reference of known distance. When photographing down or across a road, the camera shows a perspective or narrowing of the road. The use of the cardboard placard at the point of impact or even at several other places helps with determining distances from the photographs at a later date. It seems that no matter how much detail investigators strive for they usually miss an item that may be important and they cannot get back to the scene for any number of reasons. Thus, the width of the road at or near the point of impact (POI) can be found with the use of a placard, and one less "missing" item is found.

**Children's play clay** — This works great not only in the field but also at the office to simulate small objects of such shapes that appear in particular photographs the investigator is looking at but cannot retake. A lump of children's clay, the type that does not harden, can be pressed into any small object and positioned for the camera at any angle. It is very handy when parts cannot be taken away from the vehicle to be photographed later. The investigator can photograph them there with the clay in the position being sought.

**Stick-on pieces of tape** — These pieces that have been imprinted with marks (as a tape measure) are very good. These usually come in yellow and have black marks. They can be set alongside a dent or even through it to add depth to the photograph. A piece of foam board that is 4-in. wide and 2 ft long, alternately painted with black stripes 2 in. wide, can be used to show the center of the vehicle when taking photographs from any particular angle. It is also handy to show both the interior and the exterior of the vehicle, and the centerline of the seated positions of various occupants. The board also adds depth, and it is an excellent reference point for analysis at a later date when it is difficult to determine the length or width of a particular part of the vehicle.

**Graph and plain paper** — When doing a rough sketch scene or even a particular exemplar vehicle, it is much easier to use graph paper and keep shape and scale to the drawing. The sketch can be refined on a computer-aided design (CAD) program later with the dimensions and photographs taken at the inspection. The plain paper is for taking notes and making a sign for the photographer at the beginning of a roll of film. This ensures that the right photos get into the right case.

**Menu board** — A small inexpensive menu board works even better than plain paper, especially for multiple rolls of film and for setting up the videotape.

**Handheld compass** — This makes it possible to sketch a scene if there is no access to a mapping station especially when doing a curved road. Later in Chapter 4, how to map a curved road using a compass and a tape measure is described. A sighting compass purchased at an Army surplus store works well and is very helpful when picking out a specific spot for taking the next reading.

**Surveyor's pins** — These pins can be used when measuring long distances and when working with a two-man team. They can be moved from position to position to obtain great accuracy over long distances. They keep the tape taut at all times; if measurements are needed at right angles to the original ones, then an accurate position for those cross measurements are known by the location of the pins.

**Vehicle trajectory rods** — These custom-made hollow aluminum rods are 3 ft in length and have a 2-in. diameter disk welded to the outside of the tube at the top. The bottom ends are welded shut and tapered with a point to fit inside of another tube. Two dozen or so of these are necessary when showing the sliding, tumbling, or yawing motion of a vehicle in a field or alongside a road; and especially across a ditch or culvert when witness marks are not available. When the vehicle goes down into the culvert, one tube is pushed inside the top of another to reach a sufficient height so that the camera can see its trajectory. The rods are painted orange with alternating white stripes 2 to 4 in. wide. They are especially welcome when only a few areas are visible in a field. The location of these tubes can also be measured to determine the curve and the length of the motion.

*Commentary: A case was being investigated in which two high school students were racing from the new school outside of town back into town to the local pizza palace. At a curve one of the vehicles lost control and tumbled over a deep ravine onto private property without any marks between the impact point on the guardrail and the point of rest (POR).*

*Photographs taken at the scene by the police were made into 35-mm negatives and placed inside the viewing lens of the camera. The camera was then placed at a location where the photograph was taken by viewing through the lens and the negative at the same time. The exact place was found where the photographs were taken and the trajectory rods were placed in a path from the guardrail to the POR showing the path through the air.*

**Hand-held magnifying glasses** — These are used for many purposes but they come in handy at an inspection when looking at stickers on a truck for load validation or at the FMVSS stickers on a vehicle that may have been smeared or partially destroyed in the crash.

**Evidence tags** — All evidence collected at a scene must be either tagged, if it is too large for an envelope, or put into a plastic evidence bag with the proper identification on the tag or the envelope.

It is very easy to mix up the evidence once it is taken back to the office and it does not fit in the proper case file. Remember, it is the duty of the investigator to keep a chain of custody of the evidence once it is removed from the vehicle or the scene. If it is lost or misplaced, it could mean the loss of the case as well.

**Microcassette tape recorder** — This is the salvation of many investigators, not only for those who have bad penmanship but also for those who collect data in all types of foul weather. Rain or snow on paper can wash away an entire day of work in a few minutes, especially if ink is used. Documenting the site damage as well as the vehicle damage by tape recorder is essential. The investigator can ramble on trying to find the right word, can make notes about a particular aspect of the scene or the vehicle that he/she thinks may need follow up at a later date, and then edit the tape with just the material pertinent to the inspection. However, it is necessary to carry two very important items when working with electronic equipment, spare batteries and tapes. It is very embarrassing to have to leave the scene to find some place to buy batteries or tapes. The microcassette tapes are not that readily available in all areas of a state or even a city.

**Accident vehicle investigation forms** — These are a series of forms that should be used in the investigation of almost any type of vehicle. (See Figure 8.1 later for a sample form.) These differ slightly for the various vehicles being investigated. Many of the sheets are the same but others are changed as necessary. There are forms for the four-door sedan, two-door sedan, pickup truck, sport utility vehicle (SUV), straight truck, semitruck, step van, and station wagon. Ones for larger vans and minivans have been added. (These are discussed in detail later in Chapter 8.)

## Photographic Equipment

Table 3.3 is a list of the photographic equipment needed to perform an accurate and detailed investigation. This equipment is probably the most important set of tools needed. It memorializes all of the vehicles and scenes during the inspections. Without the proper equipment you will be unable to show opposing counsel or the jury the evidence you have discovered and the importance of such evidence.

**Single lens reflex 35-mm camera** — This is the best type of camera to purchase. The format is standardized and there are a variety of notebooks to show off the photographs that have been made specifically for the film size. They are easily enlarged and fit a standard foam board for exhibit display. They are lightweight, easy to carry, and easy to use.

*Commentary: I have found that cameras that allow the user to change the f-stop and shutter speed are the best. This gives the investigator many options for the variety of situations he/she may be involved in, such as a dark garage or*

**Table 3.3   Photographic Equipment**

SLR camera (35 mm) with 50- or 70- to 115-mm lens/UV filters
Wide-angle lens (25 mm, 1-in.)/UV filters
Motorized unit and data back for dates
Standard adjustable angle flash with detachable hot shoe with diffuser
Ring flash
Color film, 100 and 400 DIN, 24 and 36 exposures
Panoramic lens camera
Monopod or small tripod
Backup camera with all the above equipment
Waterproof carrying case

*warehouse, the underside of the vehicle, or even brilliant sunlight on one side and relative darkness on the other side. I have found over the years that I needed to carry only two lenses for all the different camera angles photographed during an inspection:*

1.   *A 50- or 70- to 115-mm zoom lens with a macro setting and a 25-mm or 1-in. fixed lens allow the investigator to take wide-angle shots of both the inside and the outside of the vehicle, especially in close quarters such as in a junkyard or at a salvage pool (where cars are placed very close together). The zoom lens gives the investigator wide latitude in medium as well as in closeup views.*

2.   *I have recently added a 2X tele-extender because it is useful for getting shots of small parts or close-ups under an instrument panel or of the underside of a vehicle. It is not necessary but there are times when the investigator wishes he/she had it in the field. Both of these lenses should have UV filters to clear up the haze in the background of all outside shots.*

**Motorized winder unit with a data back** — This is as close to a necessity as possible. The motor-driven winder unit allows shot after shot to be taken without dropping the camera from the eye to advance the film and then having to refocus it. In very cramped quarters such as the underside of the vehicle or the instrument panel, there may be just enough room to get the investigator's head and the camera in the same place. Once there, it is difficult, if not impossible to move his/her hands and face to wind the camera and try and refocus for another shot.

**Data back** — This has been a lifesaver in many depositions. There are many types that can be purchased but the one with at least a date option is recommended. The data back verifies when the investigator was at the vehicle or scene inspection and also helps to verify the ownership of the photographs. Most police departments do not have the funds for such special equipment.

**Large flash unit** — This is a must, especially one with a head that can be angled in several directions and with a diffuser to prevent bright spots. The unit must also be detachable so that a cable extender can be attached from the hot shoe to the camera. This helps in holding the camera to set up the shot. Then the flash unit can be easily detached and placed for maximum light on the object without disturbing the camera placement at a critical angle for light from the flash unit that may be blocked by a shock tube or tailpipe assembly. It cannot be stressed enough that a flash unit must be used in taking all photographs, both inside and outside of the vehicle. If sufficient light is available, then the flash will not fire; if there is not enough light, then the flash fills in the shadows and the photograph quality is vastly improved.

**Ring flash** — is something nice to have but not a necessity. It attaches directly to the camera lens and gives you a total ring of light around the subject without the problem of shadows or loss of light at the critical areas. It does not have a great deal of use in the field, but in the laboratory it comes in handy.

**Choice of film** — This depends on what is being photographed. Black and white film allows more contrast. If the investigator wants to show up the damage inside or outside of a vehicle or a crash site, then color is best. The new faster color films like the ASA 400 film allow the color laboratories to blow up photos for use as courtroom exhibits without the annoying graininess that was seen several years ago. Remember that film is cheap when compared with the initial travel time, other expenses, and traveling to a site a second time to take photographs because details were missed at first inspection. The vehicle may have disappeared by the time of the second inspection. Do it once and do it right.

**Panoramic lens cameras** — These are very inexpensive and can save a lot of time when trying to take photographs of an accident site from the four compass points. The print quality is good and the photos make a better presentation than several 35-mm prints taped together, which can never be aligned properly.

**Tripods or monopods** — Both serve a useful purpose but there is no need to take them in the field unless the investigator is inspecting components from the opposing side and is not able to take them back to his/her laboratory for analysis. Generally, leave them back at the storeroom.

*Commentary: You may believe you already have more than you need. I learned the hard way to always carry a backup camera, especially on long trips of more than an hour away from the office. It is rare but it can happen that you drop your camera and damage it to the point of not rewinding; the electronics may go bad at just the crucial shot, etc. Another camera case or a space in your original case for a second camera works well. It saves a lot of embarrassment and makes you look more like a professional.*

**Camera cases** — Although a well-known brand name case seems appropriate, the type of case carried is an advertisement for the cost of the equipment. The brand name case may not be waterproof. There is another brand that has a watertight seal, can take pressure changes in an airplane, and is nondescript enough not to turn heads. It also does not get banged up or scratched easily. In addition, the off brand comes with foam inserts that can be modified to fit and protect the shape of any camera and its associated equipment.

## Video Equipment

Today, it is imperative that every effort is made to make the vehicle investigation as easily understood as possible. This means in many instances that the use of a video camera would assist the tryer of fact to more easily understand what, where, and how the accident has occurred. The video camera has been especially useful at the accident site. Still photographs give a moment in time of the accident setting, but a video camera gives the viewer a much more accurate view of what happens at the site. It shows the traffic patterns of the vehicles, pedestrians, store and street lighting, traffic lights, and the effect of the vehicle headlights. The action at the scene is what is important. It is necessary that the scene be videotaped at least once at the same approximate time and date as the original accident if at all possible. A second taping during daylight or at other times of the year helps explain details such as the tree foliage growth, changes in road design, or even new or expanded housing in the area. Table 3.4 gives a list of video equipment that has been found to be useful.

**Table 3.4    Video Camera Equipment**

8- or Super-8-mm camera with carrying case
UV lens
Spare charged batteries
Spare cassettes of videotape
Menu board for case information
Battery checker
In-car battery charger
Monopod

**Video camera (8 mm or super-8-mm)** — A good quality video camera is the best. Remember it may have to be carried some distance to the actual site. It is also easier and lighter to use than a 1/2 or 3/4 in. VHS recorder. An 8-power zoom lens works well. Many cameras come with an attachment allowing the addition of other lenses for getting better close-ups of a particular object. The use of the additional lens is the choice of the user and depends on what the camera is to be used for. Good quality tapes are also essential. Record all the data on the 8-mm film and then transfer it to a standard VHS tape for the client, deposition, or courtroom use. Never release the master tape. Once it is out of your control you do not have power over what might happen to it. It can be changed, altered in some manner, erased, or even lost. You must have custody of the tape at all times just as it is necessary to have custody of the chain of evidence.

**Small heavy-duty camera bag** — This is also a must, and should have room for several tapes, spare batteries, and a battery checker. Many times the investigator may find that someone (not him/her, of course) forgot to recharge the batteries. A charging device can be purchased to plug into a vehicle cigarette lighter for charging the camera batteries on the way to the site or vehicle inspection. The device is also handy when taping a drive through on the roadway of the accident scene. It saves the life of the batteries and recharges them at the same time.

In this one instance a monopod can come in handy. When the investigator's partner is driving the car over the accident route, it is difficult to keep the camera steady when holding it. A monopod works well when placed between the person's legs on the floor of the car while taping the accident vehicle route. Once again, do not forget the menu board. It makes the tape look good, keeps the taped sections straight, and makes a great presentation.

## Special Safety Equipment or Gear

It is time to think of the safety of the investigator. Always remember that he/she is working on or alongside very dangerous roadways. The drivers "whizzing by" do not always see him/her and many drivers today like to see how close they can get with a "brush by." Table 3.5 lists special equipment for the safety of the investigator.

**Table 3.5   Special Gear Equipment**

| |
|---|
| (18 in.) Orange road cones |
| Orange vests |
| Flasher for car |
| Cellular telephones |
| Business cards and authorization from client |
| Appropriate dress for the weather: heavy layered clothes for winter, and sunscreen and hats for summer |

**Orange cones (18 in. high)** — These cones placed along the route the investigator is working may be a good deterrent, especially if placed about a foot or two into the roadway. Do not assume because the orange cones are on the road that they provide total protection. Always consider that the driver does not see the investigator or a member of his/her team during an inspection.

**Orange vests** — These should be worn by each member of the investigative team during the scene inspection. They make each person very visible, which is needed to catch the eye of the other driver.

**Yellow flasher** — When working alongside freeways or limited access highways, having a yellow flasher on top of the vehicle and keeping the vehicle between the oncoming traffic and the team help warn the traffic that something is occurring ahead (any warning to a driver is better than no warning at all). The flashing light indicates to the driving public that something is going on, in or on the roadway. Thus, they usually slow down and become *somewhat cautious*. At this time it can be dangerous to the investigator and his/her team as they undertake the inspection. They should never assume that the driver sees them even when all the safety devices are in place; it is better to be safe than sorry.

**Business cards** — Remember always to take business cards and some type of authorization from the client, verifying permission to inspect the vehicle or the site. This can save many trips and telephone calls to the client's office and lost time for the investigator.

**Cellular telephones** — These are essential. Being out of touch with the office can cost future business. A cellular telephone also has the advantage of locating a business that the investigator is having trouble finding, can help him/her in a foreign city when looking for a courthouse or a client's office, and lets the staff at the office know when he/she is available to answer messages. It makes good business sense.

*Commentary: Finally, somehow I feel that I should not have to say this but dress for the weather in which you are going to do your inspection. You would be surprised at the number of times I have seen other experts come out in the wintertime without layers of clothing, gloves, and even a hat. The same advice is true for the summertime. I always carried sunscreen in my case, especially when I did not know how long I would be gone that day. It saved a lot of sunburn pain and embarrassment.*

## Office Equipment

Today's investigator/reconstructionist must act and work as a professional. This means having the proper office equipment so that the reports, scale drawings, videotapes, simulations, and animations all have a professional appearance. What does this mean in terms of the equipment that must be purchased or leased to prepare these kinds of documentation?

## Computer Needs

No business office today can get along without having at least one computer. If the investigator/reconstructionist is working as a single individual or sole proprietor, then a single computer may suffice. If the investigator/reconstructionist is going to perform simulations and/or animations, then a computer dedicated to that work is needed because a significant amount of random access memory (RAM) as well as hard disk space is required. The rendering of an animation requires a significant amount of computer time when making the initial setup or any changes.

The need for the investigators/reconstructionists to keep track of the time expended on each of their cases goes without saying. There are several good programs available today to track time and expenses on a single-individual as well as a multiindividual firm. These programs allow the individual to prepare a detailed account of the time spent on each particular case. This is extremely important, because the client explains time and expenses to *his/her client* and the more details that the investigator/reconstructionist can impart on his/her time sheet the better it is for the client. Expenses are also tracked. Mileage, meals, parking fees, air or vehicle transportation, motels, and other necessities required during an out-of-state inspection should be detailed as much as possible, because these are out-of-pocket expenses. Billing to clients should be on a monthly basis. This informs them of the balance of their account with respect to the residual of their retainers as well as any balance due. This program can be used on a single computer for a period of time. Nevertheless, as the number of cases increases, the necessary amount of computer disk space is increased. Therefore, another computer may be required to continue this specialized function for the office.

Even a single-individual firm should consider networking the computers to keep all the data on the file server and programs on the individual computers. This makes backing up of the data on a daily basis much easier and can be done several times a day if necessary. A separate backup tape should be done for security and in the event of a fire, and that tape should be kept off the premises and changed daily. One of the worst things that can happen to a single proprietor is the loss of his/her financial data. It would literally ruin him/her.

Preparing scale drawings is a necessary function of an investigator/reconstructionist. They must be well done and appear professional for presentation at depositions and trials.

For at least 10 years, engineers have not been taught the use of drafting tools unless they worked as draftsmen prior to finishing their education as an engineer. There are now several good computer drafting programs available. Some of these are rather simple and others are quite complex, depending on the complexity of the case or work being done by the office. The choice of programs is strictly up to the individual. The learning curves of these programs are quite rapid and any individual with some computer experience can follow without much difficulty the tutorials that are usually included. If more detailed tutoring is necessary, many individuals or small companies in larger cities can provide this type of instruction to the investigator/ reconstructionist.

## Printer Needs

The next important piece of equipment is the printer. Laser printers are mandatory. For letters, they provide crisp, clean reports and look very well when placed in a presentation folder. For small-scale drawings they work extremely well. If color is desired, such as blue or red vehicles, green trees and shrubs, and yellow center lines, then a good high-quality ink jet color printer can serve very nicely. If at all possible, both types of printers should be used. For depositions or trial testimony, larger scale drawings are essential.

Good high-speed, colored pencil or colored ink drafting printers are available at reasonable prices. Many can be purchased after being used as demonstrator models. Call the local vendor and ask if they have any available. These printers can produce outstanding color scale drawings that can impress the opposing side as well as the jury at a trial presentation. It looks more professional and makes a better presentation if during his/her testimony the investigator/reconstructionist can point to the *red vehicle* and the *blue vehicle* as the principal ones involved in the accident, and then point *to green, yellow, or black vehicles* as the witness vehicles or vehicles that are just used to fill in the scene as it would have appeared at the time of the accident.

Remember that the presentation of visual data is a major part of the total reconstruction opinion. When the opposing counsel, jurors, or witnesses see color scale drawings that are neat, crisp, and clean, it is much easier for the opposing counsel, their expert, and the jury to understand the investigator's/reconstructionist's verbal comments when viewing the visual presentation. The opinion becomes easier to understand because the colors are present and easy to distinguish.

Consider for a moment the opposing expert. The investigator's/reconstructionist's data and reports as well as any scale drawings should be developed and written as precisely and as fully detailed as possible. When the opposing expert looks over these data, he/she must be able to follow them to their logical conclusion as outlined in the report. Nothing looks worse than going into court and having the opposing expert tear the investigator's/reconstructionist's reports apart because there are insufficient data to back up his/her calculations and conclusions.

That is why it is necessary for the investigator/reconstructionist to provide as much detailed information in his/her reports to his/her client and at his/her depositions so there can be no question raised by the opposing counsel and/or the opposing expert as to the validity of the conclusions or opinions. Some experts like to use only a minimum of data in their reports so that it is difficult for anyone else to follow their work. This is ludicrous. If the report, data, and calculations are complete and easy to follow, then the opposing side may decide not to continue with the case, saving the client money and time. The investigator/reconstructionist as the expert can gain an outstanding reputation as doing a full and complete reconstruction and report, which can enhance his/her credibility and case load.

## Computer Programs

Presentation of calculations is another important characteristic of any investigator/reconstructionist report. Once again, there are commercially available mathematical computer programs. These programs vary all the way from very simple to extremely complex statistical programs. Depending on the type of practice the investigator/reconstructionist is involved in, he/she may require one or both of these types of programs when developing a final report. Unfortunately, many of these professionals do not have good penmanship (this involves presentation as opposed to content).

Multiple pages of calculations that are not orderly do not flow from one step to another, or those not neatly done can easily lose the individual trying to understand what is being presented. These mathematical computer programs permit the investigator/reconstructionist to develop good quality presentations of mathematical computations that show the assumptions for each step and include all individual steps that then result in a final conclusion.

In addition, the use of these computer programs permits the investigator/reconstructionist to insert as much detail as possible when completing each particular step of the calculation. As an example, the basic equation sets forth the initial data, what is being assumed, and then the particular data for that step should be inserted. If the equation has several basic steps, then each of those steps should be done individually so that the opposing expert and/or attorneys can determine exactly what that particular calculation is trying to prove. Finally, the conclusion should be listed and it can be boxed in or underlined, as desired.

Programs such as these become more valuable when it is necessary to use a range of values such as several different coefficient of friction values or to assume a range of initial vehicle speeds. Then a table can be constructed with the given data and the calculated data can be set up next to it to show exactly the range of answers available. This makes it easy during the presentation to show the opposing counsel that the investigator/reconstructionist investigated a particular range of values for a specific equation and chose a median value based on information available at the time of the calculations. Again, the laser printer can make a very good copy of the calculations developed from a computer program.

## Ownership of Documentation

Attention should be given to what is referred to as the ownership of documentation. Any photographs (including all negatives), videotapes, calculations, reports, scale drawings, sketches, notes, audio tapes, and correspondence belong to the accident investigator/reconstructionist. Many times clients may request the negatives of photographs so they can have copies made. *Never, never* give up possession of negatives. The same advice is true for original videotapes, calculations, reports, scale drawings, sketches, notes, audio tapes, and correspondence.

*Commentary: In the early stages of my career I would allow negatives to be used by the opposing counsel to make prints for use by their experts. These negatives were lost. I hesitate to say that they were lost intentionally, but I will never know. In a particular trial, I was asked to testify and I had given my set of photographs to my attorney client. He then promptly turned them over to an associate, then to another associate, and then to another until the chain of custody was completely obliterated. In addition, the same thing happened with the negatives I gave to the opposing counsel and I had to testify in court without any photographs whatsoever. The opposing counsel refused to allow me to use copies of my photographs for my testimony. Suffice it to say that the testimony was not as accurate and as convincing as I would have liked it to be at the time.*

The investigator/reconstructionist should retain ownership of any material that is generated in the course of the investigation/reconstruction. He/she should make as many copies of any of the materials that have been requested by the opposing counsel but never, ever let the material out of his/her immediate control because he/she has the chain of custody of this evidence and it rests squarely on his/her shoulders to make sure the materials stay in his/her hands. With respect to videotape, the investigator/reconstructionist should always keep the original in his/her file, making copies from the original and not from a second generation print because the quality degrades too rapidly unless the original is used.

## Ownership of Evidence

The evidence that the accident investigator/reconstructionist collects at the scene or at the inspection of the vehicles becomes a part of his/her file. This means that he/she has the chain of custody of evidence and as a result is responsible for its whereabouts at all times. From time to time it may be necessary to allow the opposing expert to review the evidence in privacy. This author does not agree with that policy. Evidence has a way of vanishing or turning into a good part when it was originally defective. Remove the temptation. The same is true for the opposing sides wanting to run tests on the evidence. The investigator/reconstructionist should never let these tests be conducted without someone from his/her office being present and making a videotape of the entire procedure. The person viewing the test must have a technical background to understand what is happening during the test procedure.

Depending on the material being reviewed, the investigator/reconstructionist may be convinced by his/her client to let it out of his/her immediate control. Having the individual sign a release form, which stipulates the exact evidence that is being turned over to him/her, the date, time, and his/her signature, can accomplish this. In some cases, an expected return date of the evidence may be added.

*Commentary: If the evidence that you have obtained through your investigation is something that may be easily replaced, then never let it out of your control. For example, an air bag sensor, a seat belt assembly, or any other piece of equipment can be misplaced and another piece of equipment that does not have a defect that you found at the time of your inspection can be inserted in its place.*

The investigator/reconstructionist should only allow the opposing counsel/expert to inspect the particular part while he/she or someone from his/her office is present. In addition, to ensure that no errors are committed on either side, he/she should conduct a videotaping of the opposing expert's entire inspection. Copies of the videotapes can then be made available to all parties who wish to pay for them.

## Technical Library

A major part of the office of an investigator/reconstructionist should be the technical library. This library should consist of printed material from organizations that hold annual meetings where scientific and technical papers are presented for the information of its members. It is necessary that the investigator/reconstructionist should try to attend these meetings as often as possible. During cross-examination the opposing counsel in many instances may ask when the investigator/reconstructionist last attended one of those technical meetings in his/her field of expertise. It looks good to the jury when he/she can answer, "Last year." There is an interaction on a one-to-one basis with other experts that is helpful and develops a kinship between people who are always willing to assist one another in the same or complementary fields.

The library should also include information gleaned from investigations of previous cases such as technical manuals and bulletins that may be helpful on future cases. The calculations prepared for cases should also be saved and cataloged, because they can be an additional source for similar type cases.

Magazines are also useful for providing information and/or statistics on vehicles or other types of transportation that may be part of the investigator's/reconstructionist's field of expertise. Monthly or quarterly magazines are always helpful because they contain information that can be useful on a current case or in some future case. A database file can be compiled that contains the articles found in each issue so that the office staff can look at the file and determine if there is an article that can assist them in a particular reconstruction.

Repair manuals are often an invaluable aid during a reconstruction because they have diagrams of the assemblies and subassemblies of a particular product that is being investigated. These pages can be photocopied and marked up as necessary to be inserted in the final report to the client. Remember, a picture is worth more than a thousand words when trying to complete a report on the required date for the client.

Textbooks from professional and technical societies should also be obtained and used as reference material. There are occasions when the investigator/reconstructionist takes on a case in which a different perspective on the reconstruction is needed. Textbooks many times can provide insight that can be used directly or indirectly. This advice is especially true for the novice or inexperienced investigator/reconstructionist. Basic information from textbooks is always helpful and gives the novice an insight through the eyes of the author that may increase the novice's ability and expertise without having to actually experience each of these different situations.

## Internet

Today's investigator/reconstructionist must be acquainted with the use of the Web sites available on the Internet. Information can be found on virtually every subject or product that has been made in the last several years at least. There are Web sites for general information as well as specific information. For example, consider a commercial bus accident. Web sites are available that provide the investigator with information on general bus accidents as well as accidents to specific buses such as school buses, travel or motor coach buses, or city buses. There also are Web sites for giving statistics on number of accidents, number of injuries, and fatalities for each of the various types of buses. Standards for buses are also available; these include federal, state, or local standards.

The use of the Internet is an invaluable tool for any investigator's/reconstructionist's office. If it is not presently used, then certainly the investigator/reconstructionist should have a member of his/her staff take a formal course from a college or even a night school class at a local school system adult education program.

*Commentary: When my library became larger than one shelf and one file cabinet, I decided it was time to develop a database so I could find material much quicker than by using a file-by-file search through the cabinet or on the shelf. A simple database was designed so that I could find articles by a master subject, and then a simple keyword system was designed to find a particular area of interest. This database included not only the textbooks but also the monthly magazines by listing each specific article in that magazine. Single pages out of technical magazines were filed in a folder in the file cabinet and placed under general headings. These were then located in the database by that particular heading. Specific material such as calculations or drawings that were used on cases was also located on the database for future reference. I have found that the database has come in handy for use on appeals, which occur several years after my testimony is given. Unfortunately, your attorney client may not keep you abreast of the development of an appeal or in some cases may not even tell you that appeal is being made. It is much easier to review the material that you have developed and saved than to go back, read, and develop that same material again.*

A well-run, efficient, and professional office can enhance any investigator's/reconstructionist's ability to perform at a much higher level because all the tools that he/she uses on a daily basis are available. Without this equipment he/she may have to spend time searching for material at public libraries or special medical or technical libraries. As a professional working in today's environment, his/her use of the Internet can save time and make him/her look much better in the eyes of his/her attorney client.

# Scene Investigation

4

"They say that genius is an infinite capacity for taking pains."
**Sherlock Holmes**
*A Study in Scarlet*

## Collisions — Vehicular

Successful accident investigation requires a considerable amount of basic knowledge. To know what to look for, the investigator must have some fundamental knowledge of accidents, roads, and vehicles of all types, especially the dynamics of vehicular motion. All investigators must approach the scene with a plan for the investigation. Many times scenes are restricted due to traffic volume, time of day, changes in weather, or even new construction. They must be ready to revise their plan as the situation changes.

Many people assume that accident investigation and accident reconstruction are one and the same. The accident investigator "observes or studies by close examination"[1] and preserves and documents the evidence he/she finds. If the documentation is sketchy and the preservation photography is poor or disjointed, the reconstructionist cannot develop an accurate scenario of the accident.

*Commentary: In dealing with some investigators, paralegals, and a plethora of other pseudotechnical personnel, I have found that many appear to be in a hurry to get the job done. Some are not willing or able to follow even a rudimentary procedure to ensure that every piece of evidence has been collected, and misleading or confusing documentation has been eliminated. In investigating more than 5000 accident cases, I have developed a procedure that is outlined in Table 4.1.*

Vehicular accidents occur in an open environment, something unique to the forensic investigator. When investigating a murder case, for example,

**Table 4.1   Inspection Checklist**

### Accident Scene

Urban or rural
  Reference point (RP)
  Debris location and shape
  Point of impact (POI)
  Point of rest (POR) (if different than POI)
  Origin of initial actions
  Skid mark length, width, and starting and end points
  Roadbed and shoulder damage
  Road hazards, potholes, etc.
  Configuration details
    Stop signs, poles, and traffic lights
    Driveways, buildings, curbing, unique intersections
    Trees, culverts, mounds, fences, and posts
    Plowed fields, types of shoulders, gravel, blacktop

### Vehicle

Exterior
  14 Camera angles (minimum)
  Additional close-ups of damage
  Missing components
  Unusual or unexplained drainage
Interior (frontal, side, rear)
  Windshield bulge
  Instrument panel damage
  Sun visor and header damage
  Door trim panel abrasions and dents
  Seatback and cushion damage
  Observe all interior surfaces for abrasions, cuts, dents, or other unexplained damage

he/she often finds a very detailed, closed environment, which can be thoroughly examined and documented over any period of time necessary to complete the job. Vehicular accidents are exactly the opposite. By the time the investigator arrives on the scene, many pairs of feet have trampled over the area, including the impact and resting sites; and many pairs of hands have picked up, discarded, or moved around evidence that could have a bearing on the investigation.

The principal investigator is the individual who must control the scene. He/she literally has the life of possible criminal or civil litigation in his/her hands. The case can be won or lost through his/her foresight or thoughtlessness of investigatory techniques. The process is not any easy task. It requires thought, dedication, and a detailed plan. Thus, investigators must not only observe and document the obvious but also must be able to discover the not-so-obvious details that may have been moved, discarded, or even misplaced, thereby ensuring an accurate investigation.

The automobile accident consists of two, three, and sometimes four collisions. The initial or first (primary) collision is the vehicle colliding with another vehicle or another object on or off the road. The second (secondary) collision is the occupant colliding with the interior components of the vehicle (see Chapter 6). The third (tertiary) collision is the occupant engaging the vehicle restraint system, which usually produces some type of injury. The fourth possible collision is an injury due to the supplemental restraint or the air bag system (see Chapter 7). The air bag is the latest safety device; and the engineering, legal, and medical communities are just starting to see a different type of injuries.

# Accident Scene

The first part of the initial collision, the accident scene, is discussed and analyzed next. Accident scenes can be broken down into two locations: urban and rural.

## Urban Setting

In an urban accident, the investigator inadvertently deletes many details. A typical urban accident can be either a high- or low-speed accident and many times may involve a pedestrian.

The scene configuration shown in Figure 4.1 is a typical urban accident scene. It is drawn at a scale of 1 in. equals 50 ft. It contains left and right turn lanes, straight-through lanes, alleys, angled intersections, utility poles, fire hydrants, traffic signals, light poles, and buildings, basically everything that makes up a city street.

### Reference Points

The first step the investigator must take is to chose a reference point as the origin for all measurements. This point must be close to the center of the scene to eliminate long-distance measurements for the investigators. The reference point (RP) must not be the point where the accident occurred but a known point that will not change in 2 or 3 years, when another investigator or reconstructionist looks at the scene. A good example would be a telephone or utility pole. Every pole is numbered; if the investigator cannot find the number, he/she should check the engineering office of the utility or telephone company. From the office records, the number of the pole can be obtained by its location  Sewer grates or manhole covers are also good, but are sometimes difficult to use because they may be located inside the driving lanes. The intersection of two curbs has been used but the investigator needs to mark whether he/she is using the curb facing or the upper curb surface.

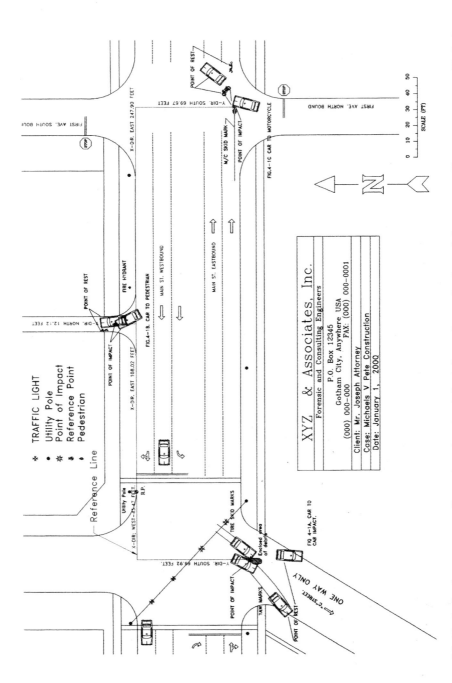

**Figure 4.1** Typical urban scene configuration showing left, right, and straight-through lanes, as well as stop signs, traffic lights, and angled intersection.

Under no circumstances should a tree that may die or be cut down be used, for any number of reasons.

Be as explicit as possible when describing the RP. Another investigator most likely will not be as familiar with it as the on-scene investigator is and may have trouble locating it at a later date. In Figure 4.1 a utility pole is chosen as the RP, but it is the intention to use the outside edge of the curb as what is commonly referred to as the reference line. When this is done, then explicitly state that fact. Make it as simple as possible for someone else to follow. Buildings, street signs, and traffic signs are all poor choices because they can also be changed or be moved for any number of reasons.

### Other Details

Note that the scale drawing also contains a significant amount of different types of information. The streets are named and have direction arrows, especially for left and right hand turn lanes. Stop signs, traffic signals, stop bars, pedestrian cross walks, utility poles, sidewalks, and lane markings are all included in the drawing to give as complete a picture as possible to the tryer of fact. Building outlines and names if possible can be included, especially if the resting point of the vehicles would be at or near a building.

Many investigators do not understand why all this detail is necessary. There have been numerous occasions when the on-scene investigators did not make a scale drawing or did not complete a rough drawing, but for some reason had incorrect dimensions on it. Most injury accident case investigations require that photographs be taken at the scene. By using the newly constructed detailed drawing and the photographs, the investigator/reconstructionist can place the vehicles in the same position as shown in the photographs. Without the detail it would be impossible and the testimony would be less creditable than it should be, especially if the opposing expert had done the detailed drawing and had shown the proper location of all parties involved.

*Commentary: It is not unusual for measurements taken at a scene to be incorrect by several feet. Assume that when placing the dimensions of the on-scene investigator on your drawing you may find one of the vehicles sitting on the curb but the photographs actually show the vehicle 3 ft away from the curb. By using the location of the vehicle with respect to the sidewalks, painted crosswalks, edges of buildings, or even cracks in the roadbed, your drawing will actually portray the scene and it will be complete and accurate.*

### Point of Impact

Three separate accidents are shown on Figure 4.1. The first is a car-to-car crash on a one-way street in an angled intersection (Figure 4.1A). A vehicle is struck in the right front fender on the passenger's side of the vehicle. Note the enclosed area of debris. A point just north of the most northern end of the debris is the point of impact (POI). In other words, the impact occurs before the debris strikes the ground because the debris must fall to the ground in a trajectory similar to a cannon being fired horizontally. Gravity is pulling the debris to the ground as it is moving forward. The distance from the first point of the debris to the actual POI is dependent on the speed of the vehicle at the time of the impact. The faster the vehicle is traveling, the greater the distance between these two points. The POI can never be the same as the start of the debris pattern; it is physically impossible.

The vehicle slows down because of the impact, but the debris, which was moving at the same velocity as the car prior to the impact, is now free to continue its forward motion because it has been released from its bond to the vehicle. Note the vertical line, which extends in the Y or northern direction on the drawing. This is the dimension that was taken by the on-scene investigator from the remaining debris pattern.

There is also a horizontal measurement taken from the intersection of the vertical line and the reference line to the extension of the RP. These two dimensions are shown only for the reader to see how the dimensions are taken from the RP, to the POI of the vehicles and all other information that appears on the drawing. These dimensions are not usually placed on the drawing; they are measured when drawing the rough sketch and/or listed on a separate sheet of paper. Table 4.2 shows a typical listing of measurements that are taken at an accident scene. Note that the locations of both sides of the vehicle are usually not measured, only those facing the RP. This can be a problem if the heavy damage of the vehicle may be toward the RP. The dimensions that were measured would show the distorted vehicle and would make it difficult to place the vehicle on the scale drawing with any accuracy.

**Table 4.2   Table of Measurements Taken by the On-Scene Investigator**

| Point | North | East | South | West | Comments |
|-------|-------|------|-------|------|----------|
| RP | pole north of sidewalk, reference line parallel to curb | | | | |
| A | 12.2 | 6.1 | | | LF tire |
| B | 22.6 | 8.4 | | | LR tire |
| C | 12.2 | 6.1 | | | End of skid |
| D | 35.1 | 15.21 | | | Start of skid |
| E | 8.6 | 9.5 | | | Start debris |
| F | 12.0 | 5.9 | | | Impact pole |
| Width of road 12 ft per lane, gravel shoulder 3 ft wide | | | | | |

*Note*:   Additional dimensions would be shown if other vehicles were involved or there were long and multiple skids on the road and in a field or lawn.

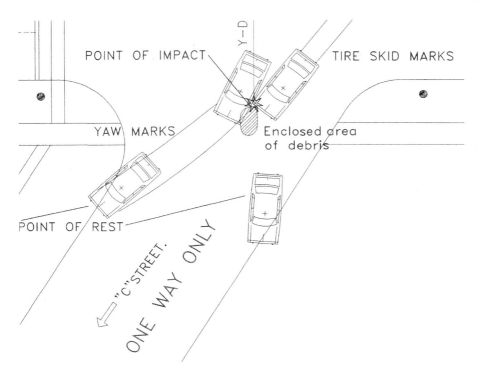

**Figure 4.1A** Car-to-car impact.

## Witness Marks

Another problem involves the skid and yaw tire marks. Some on-scene investigators take the measurements of all the tire skids or yaw marks and some only measure one tire. The question is, which measurements were taken, the left or right front tire? Another problem is, what part of the skidding tire was measured, the outside, inside, or center of the skid mark? These are usually never explained on the measurements report.

## Location of Debris

The location of the debris is another problem to look for. The on-scene investigator usually lists the large items such as a door; shattered glass particles, if in a single location; and the windshield or portions of the trim. Some investigators make a sketch of the pattern of the small debris and give the overall width and length of the pattern. This can be very helpful when trying to determine the POI.

Figure 4.1A is a larger scale drawing of the car-to-car accident. The scale is 1 in. equals 10 ft. The larger scale drawing is necessary to show the major portion of the scene including the original intersection, with the traffic lights

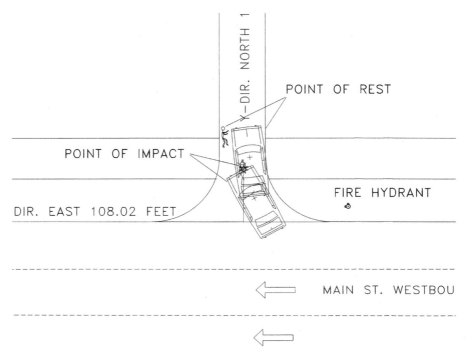

**Figure 4.1B** Car-to-pedestrian impact.

and the left turn lane. Note that the skid marks and the yaw marks are both shown and are easier to see. The POI and the point of rest (POR) of the vehicles are also shown. Both scale drawings shown in Figures 4.1 and 4.1A would be used at a deposition and trial to give a more complete understanding of the scene.

The on-scene investigator's measurements are usually drawn on an overlay sheet of clear Mylar to show the measurements taken at the scene, and if there was a discrepancy, then the overlay would be laid on top of the measurements taken by the investigator to show these differences and the results in the reconstruction if the on-scene measurements were used. The investigator should be ready to make adjustments in the on-scene investigator's scale drawing as the photographs of the scene dictate and should be sure to measure a sufficient number of details to make a drawing as complete as possible. When using a computer-aided design (CAD) program, the overlays are placed on different electronic layers and are switched on and off when needed. The base and overlay drawings can be enlarged on a high-speed plotter and used as deposition or court exhibits.

The second accident shown is a vehicle turning into an alley and striking a pedestrian (Figure 4.1B). Note that this accident is located to the east of

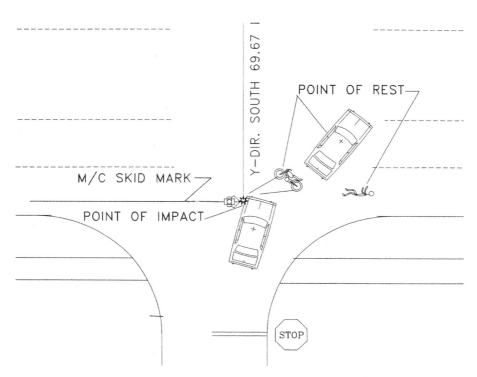

**Figure 4.1C** Car-to-motorcycle impact.

the RP but still uses the same reference line, which is south of the utility pole RP. Again, only the dimensions to the POI are shown for convenience. Figure 4.1B is a larger scale drawing at a scale of 1 in. equals 10 ft. Note in this particular drawing that the POI lies very close to the POR. The drawing shows one car setting on top of another. When presented at a deposition, an overlay would be made of the vehicle and the pedestrian at the POI and the base drawing would have just the vehicle and the pedestrian at their respective PORs. The overlay would be laid over the base drawing when needed to show the POI.

Note that a fire hydrant is shown in this drawing. It could have been used in this investigation as the RP, if necessary, because it will not be moved in the future. The location of the pedestrian's body can be a problem. Is the measurement taken to the head, center of the body, or the feet? Investigators/reconstructionists generally take the dimensions to the center of the body; however, if there is significant bleeding then measurements are taken to those points because they are easier seen in all the photographs.

The third accident shown is between a vehicle and a motorcycle. Figure 4.1C is a scale drawing at 1 in. equals 10 ft. In this accident there are no skid marks for the vehicle, but there are for the motorcycle. Note that they are straight and not curved at all. The cyclist went up and over the hood of the vehicle, rolled, and skidded to a stop.

In this case, the motorcycle is measured at its POR at the center of the front wheel, the center of the bike, usually the oil filter, and the center of the rear tire. These are fixed points and easily measured on the motorcycle itself.

## *Line of Sight*

One area not usually considered by the investigator in an urban setting is the line of sight obstruction from a building, house, telephone poles, hedges, and even fences that have more than a 50% open weave pattern. Unfortunately, not all of these items are listed in a typical investigator's report.

An on-scene investigator frequently overlooks many of these details because he/she does not consider them important. They are important and necessary for a complete investigation and a reconstruction. The sketch of the scene must include the location of these objects and the distance from them to the streets leading to the intersection.

Calculations can then be made using the estimated speed of the vehicles to determine when each vehicle would see each other as it approached the intersection. Figure 4.2 shows a typical urban setting at an uncontrolled

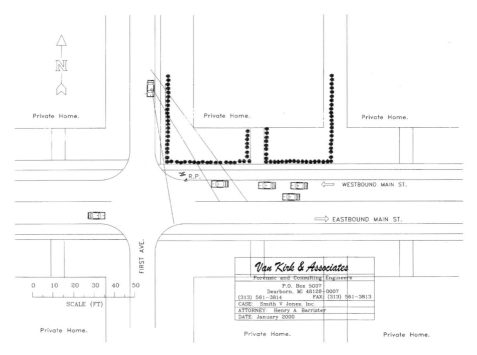

**Figure 4.2** Line of sight problems.

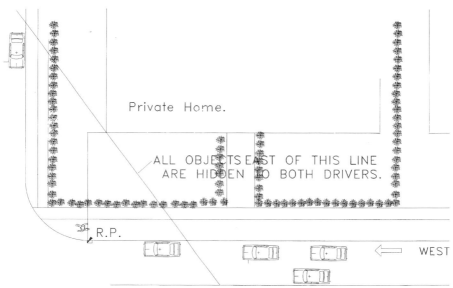

ALL OBJECTS EAST OF THIS LINE
ARE HIDDEN TO BOTH DRIVERS.

Private Home.

R.P.

WEST

**Figure 4.2A** Line of sight problem with house.

intersection. Note that both the southbound and the westbound vehicles and pedestrians are hidden due to several line of sight problems. Once again only the dimensions to the southbound vehicle and the various objects that caused the line of sight problems are shown. Figure 4.2A is a scale drawing of 1 in. equals 20 ft of the intersection. Note that the problem in this case is the corner of the private home. It blocks all views of both drivers and pedestrians as each approach the intersection. The positioning of the vehicles at specific points in time are critical to determine whether either or both vehicles had time to stop after seeing the other as it left the blind spot behind the house. It is necessary for the on-scene investigator to locate the corner of the house in his/her scale drawing so that a line of sight can be drawn and calculations pursued for speed and stopping distance.

Figure 4.2B is a 1 in. equals 20 ft scale drawing of the same intersection showing a parked car at the curb. This parked vehicle usually hides all westbound traffic to the extent that it cannot be seen clearly from the approaching intersection.

Once again, it is necessary to locate the parked car at the time of the accident as accurately as possible. Police photographs are very helpful if they were taken at the scene. If they are not available, then verbal testimony such as statements at the scene or deposition testimony have to be relied on to place the vehicle as accurately as possible. Figure 4.2C is again a 1 in. equals 20 ft scale drawing showing a very common problem in an urban setting, a

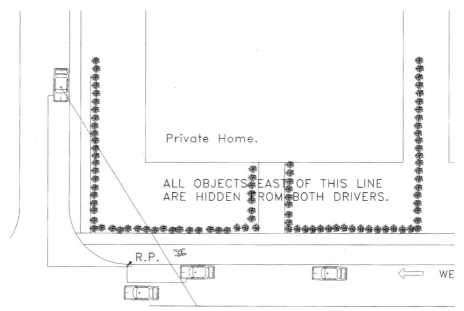

**Figure 4.2B** Line of sight problem with parked car.

large hedge located at the sidewalk in front of the home. This drawing does not show the height of the hedge, but it can be stated after the title or just added to the list of measurements taken at the scene.

Note in this drawing how the southwest corner of the sewer drain cover is used as a RP and the northern edge of the westbound lane is used as the reference line. Each of these is viable as RPs and reference lines, because they will not change radically in the near future. If they were changed, then a record of the construction would be available before and after the changes were made.

Drawings also contain a north arrow, a scale, a legend, a title block to show the name of the company or the individual doing the work, the client's name, the case name, and the date the drawing was completed. A typical title block is shown in Figure 4.3.

## Rural Setting

Many rural accidents occur at high speeds. Special attention must be given to the scene investigation due to the trees, culverts, fences, and line of sight problems that are different than those seen in the city. Many times a planted field is a problem at the time of the accident but months later the crop is gone and the field is lying fallow, and it is difficult to imagine that there was a line of sight problem.

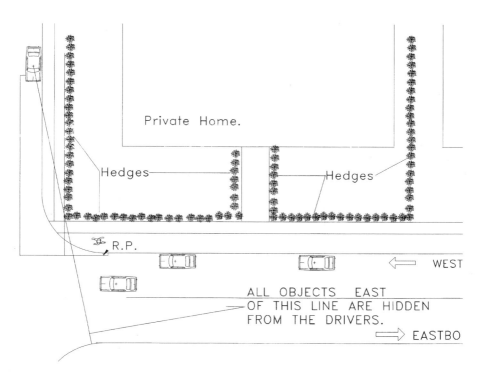

**Figure 4.2C** Line of sight problem with hedge.

Van Kirk & Associates, Inc.

Forensic and Consulting Engineers

P.O. Box 5007
Dearborn, MI 48128-0007
(313) 561-3814          FAX: (313) 561-3813

CASE: Anyone V Anybody

ATTORNEY:  John Smith

DATE: January 5, 2000

THIS IS A TYPICAL TITLE BLOCK SHOWING THE
NAME AND LOCATION OF THE FIRM, THE TELEPHONE
NUMBER, AND FAX NUMBER.
 A SEPARATE LISTING FOR THE CASE NAME,
NAME OF THE ATTORNEY, AND THE DATE
THE DRAWING WAS COMPLETED.

**Figure 4.3** Title block to be used on all drawings.

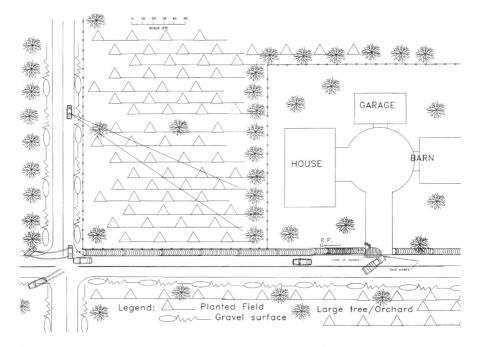

**Figure 4.4** Typical rural scene with all the elements shown.

Figure 4.4 is a typical example of a rural scene with all of the elements shown. Note the planted field at the uncontrolled intersection. At the time of the accident this would be a line of sight problem and must be listed as such by the on-scene investigator. In addition, there are the line of sight problems with the large trees acting as a windbreak for the house and barns, and with the orchards to the west of the southbound road.

Due to the change of seasons there are different appearing scenes in the spring, summer, and fall. Crops are harvested, trees have lost or just are regaining their leaves, and some trees may have been destroyed due to the weather. It is extremely important for the on-scene investigator to note and photograph these problems from the perspective of both drivers, especially at the eye height of the driver in the particular vehicle they were driving at the time of the accident. Trucks, semitrucks, and cars all have different driver eye heights, and what may have been invisible to one may not be true for the other driver. Figure 4.4A is a close-up view of the nearly blind uncontrolled intersection. Due to the planted field, trees, and fencing, the cars are almost invisible to one another until milliseconds before the impact. Neither driver had time to react until a few milliseconds before impact because there are no braking skid marks at their locations.

**Figure 4.4A** Close-up view of the nearly blind uncontrolled intersection.

The skid marks from the smaller vehicle are due to it being spun around by the larger vehicle at impact. Both will end up partially in a field and on the roadway. Note the use of a second RP marked RP2. Because the original RP was quite a distance away, it would require moving the tape measure several times, leading to errors. The second RP would eliminate such errors. Title blocks and measurements have been left off these drawings for clarity.

Figure 4.4B is a close-up view of another type of rural accident, especially if there is any dip in the road whatsoever to hide the smaller oncoming traffic. Note the direction of the skids of the motorcycle. They are straight and are angled toward the right side of the road. This generally would indicate that the motorcyclist saw the truck, and thought the truck saw him and tried to go in front of the truck (assuming the truck would not complete the turn). The RP is located at the Bell telephone box and all measurements are usually taken from the intersection of the line drawn from the Bell box to the fog line or the edge of the paved surface if it is in good condition. This makes it easier than having to crawl in and out of the culvert for each measurement. The motorcyclist landed in the culvert after impact. There will be signs of the impact in the soft ground of the culvert.

In this case, measurements need to be taken of the entire profile of the culvert so that it can be plotted and the exact location of the impact can be

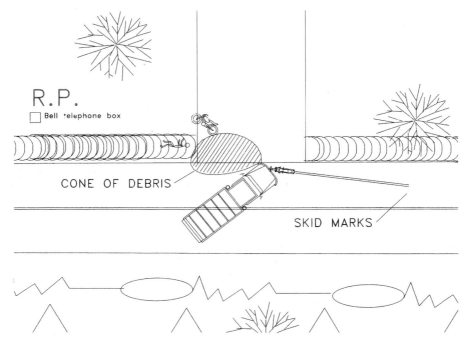

**Figure 4.4B** Close-up view of a motorcycle rural accident.

marked. The cone of debris and the motorcycle's final resting point must be measured and located from the RP. The location of the motorcycle must be measured using the axle of the front tire, the axle of the rear tire, and a center position of the cycle (which is usually the oil filter canister cover).

In a rural setting there may not be a pole of any kind. Look for a Bell telephone cable box, which has usually been placed about 30 ft from the side of the road. If all else fails, then use the middle of the closest driveway, but make sure it is designated as such on the sketch.

Do not use rural mailboxes. They may have been removed by snowplows and errant drivers, and are seldom placed in the same location. Take a photograph of the RP location. Use the menu board or a sheet of paper written with large block letters to describe the RP. Whatever location is chosen make sure it can be found in the future. Remember that all measurements for the entire scene are taken from this point. This includes all debris found at the scene as well as the final resting point of the vehicles. Many on-scene investigators mark the location of one or two tires of the vehicle closest to the RP. It is extremely important to measure the location of at least three tires, two of which are undamaged.

The width of the vehicle used on the scale drawing is determined by the track width of the vehicle, and the damage from the impact changes these measurements. Once all the measurements have been taken, check them against a visual location of the vehicles with respect to the edge of the road; the lane markings; or the point where any of the tires rest with respect to the curbs, lane markings, or driveways. Determine whether they are on top or just next to the curb or lane marking. Recheck all measurements before leaving the scene and especially before releasing any of the vehicles.

## Debris Pattern

An important area to be measured in detail is the debris pattern. This represents the pieces of the vehicle that were dislodged during the impact and kept moving with the same velocity of the vehicle until it lost its energy and came to rest, scattered along the highway and shoulders. Hopefully many of these components have not been moved by well-meaning citizens or just thrill seekers. The pattern is generally cone-shaped with the vertex of the cone being the *approximate point of impact*. As an example, consider a head-on crash between two vehicles. The dirt from the undersides of the vehicles and broken components, such as the grille and headlamp covers or trim rings, do not drop straight down to the ground. They have the same forward velocity the vehicle had prior to impact.

The vehicle stops but the dirt and the broken components continue to follow a trajectory like a horizontal cannon shot. The debris moves in the principal direction the vehicle was moving prior to impact but it is also being acted upon by the earth's gravity and is falling to the ground in a parabolic arc.

The pattern of the dirt and other components that fly off the car usually spread out in a conelike pattern with the lightest objects going the farthest from the POI. Measure the extreme edges of the conelike pattern and follow it back to its origin to locate a point very close to the POI. It is very important that all the debris be photographed and/or videotaped in the place where it came to rest. Scale drawings can never capture the true pattern of the debris. The same is true of gouges or scratches on the highway surface. There is never sufficient information recorded to do so.

## Roadbed Damage

Damage on the roadbed surface cannot be overlooked as an important piece of evidence. Gouges are usually made in the concrete or blacktop when an underbody component is forced downward during the collision and a portion of the suspension is broken or bent down far enough to come in contact with the surface of the highway.

The difference between a gouge and a scratch is the amount of pressure being applied at the time the component is being pushed or dragged along, depending on the direction of the vehicle at that time. Many times, but not always, the length and depth of a gouge mark indicate that the two vehicles are still in contact and moving along together in maximum engagement.

The investigator has to compare the gouge and scratch marks with the abrasions or asphalt on the undersides of both vehicles to be sure that they were moving together. In addition, other marks on or off the road must be examined and compared with the original gouge marks to determine how they lined up when the two vehicles separated.

*Commentary: In a case I was working on, I was told the impact occurred at the crest of a hill. Examination of the crest did not show any gouges or scratches on the asphalt surface although the underside photographs showed asphalt embedded into the oil pan nuts. By walking the site for another 30 ft, I saw that one of the vehicles had crossed the centerline and was impacted, leaving gouge marks. The angle of impact had caused the encroaching vehicle to be swept back onto its own side of the highway. Walking the scene always helps.*

While discussing gouges, it is important to view the underside of a vehicle at the scene. If the road surface is asphalt, then portions of the asphalt are forced into crevasses on the underside of the vehicle, and the direction in which the asphalt is embedded shows the direction of vehicle travel. Concrete road surfaces leave a white dust or powder on the underside components, causing the gouging or scratches. The concrete causes severe wear on the underside components and the direction of travel of the vehicle shows up as witness marks on that surface.

Tire marks such as *yaw*, *skid*, or *acceleration marks* tell another portion of the story of the movements of the vehicle, but at different points in time. Acceleration marks occur before a collision. Skid and yaw marks can occur before, during, and after an impact. There are three phases to a skid mark. First, the cleaning phase is when the tire is first skidding on the road surface after it has locked up. This cleans the road and the tire surface and is usually not detectable. In the second phase the tire heats up and the mark is slightly more than a shadow and begins to get darker. This mark is usually light and is not always detectable unless checked from several different directions. The third phase is the heavy black mark of the hot tire skidding on the road surface.

## Road Surface and Shoulders

The surface and shoulders of the road also hold evidence for the on-scene investigator. Large potholes, construction of the road or shoulder, or abrupt change in the surface of the shoulder or roadbed can indicate loss of control.

These marks are explained in more detail later. Humps, soft shoulders, and edge ruts can all lead to loss of control by a driver with the possibility of the vehicle being thrown into the direction of oncoming traffic. Edge ruts occur when a soft shoulder abuts the road surface and vehicles leaving the road surface continually drive over it, and depressing the surface.

When the edge rut gets to 3 or 4 in. in depth, it prevents the tire from rolling back up the edge of the roadbed and onto the road surface. As a result, the unsuspecting driver keeps increasing the left-hand steering input while maintaining the same speed. At some point in time, the rut becomes shallow or the tire climbs the wall of the roadbed. Due to the large left-hand steering input, the vehicle now makes a violent maneuver to the left resulting in a very quick and unexpected left turn. This action exposes the right or passenger's side of the vehicle to oncoming traffic, a potentially severe collision, and severe if not fatal injuries to the right front passenger.

*Commentary: Edge ruts are not as prevalent as they used to be with the advent of paved shoulders. The original shoulder paving was about 18 in. In later years it was changed to approximately 6 ft on some highways. Potholes unfortunately are still a major problem, especially in the northern climates with the warming and freezing of roadbeds.*

*Striking a pothole can cause minor to extensive damage to a vehicle, especially the front suspension. Damage can range from a blowout to a bent or fractured wheel rim to bent or fractured suspension components. Each and every one of these problems may cause a loss of control, sending a vehicle into almost any direction depending on the skill of the driver.*

*Always investigate the road surface for potholes, edge ruts, or anything unusual on the roadbed or shoulder surface when evaluating and investigating a scene. These types of problems are more common then most on-scene investigators have determined in the past.*

## Lighting

Loss of street lighting can be disastrous for the driver of a vehicle as well as pedestrians, motorcyclists, or bicyclists. Street lighting gives the vehicle driver a reference point for determining the distance and speed of approaching vehicles, the edge of the roadway, and the roadside obstacles. It directly lights or backlights pedestrians and cyclists helping the driver to see oncoming nonvehicular traffic. There have been several occasions where eyewitnesses have made poor evaluations of vehicle colors, speed, and location on a road due to a loss or partial loss of street lighting.

In rural areas where there is no street lighting the vehicular driver is totally dependent on the headlights of his/her vehicle. If these lights are not working or properly aimed, they can lead to severe if not fatal accidents.

## Poles

Telephone and utility poles when struck do not always fall over. This is due, of course, to the lines that are connected to the top of the pole. Sideswipes or even frontal impacts leave fresh marks on the wooden structure, usually by way of a chuck of wood being torn out of the pole itself. A portion of the removed wood may be embedded into a crack or crevice of the vehicle. At the very least, there may be scratches on the vehicle paint surface that are unusual because they have been made by the curved surface of the wooden or metal pole. Many times there may be a paint transfer, both on the pole and on the vehicle. This is more readily seen on a steel or aluminum pole.

The location of the impact on the pole, size, direction of paint transfer or missing wood, and impact height above the ground of these marks must be measured and recorded; and photographed with overall and close-up views from several different directions. It also is necessary for the on-scene investigator to check the area of impact of the vehicle and the pole to determine if all of the wood pieces are present. If all the wood pieces are not present, as stated previously, carefully examine the vehicle for pieces of wood lodged into any crevices of the vehicle. Still cameras as well as the video camera must also record the wood fragments. This is the investigator's *prima facie* evidence that the particular vehicle did strike the wooden pole.

*Commentary: I have seen poles with a section taken out of them so that the bottom of the pole does not quite reach the ground. The wires are stretched to their maximum in these cases.*

## Trees

On-scene investigators must continually look for the details of an accident. Trees that have been fully impacted, uprooted as they were driven over, or even sideswiped reveal another portion of the accident sequence. Impacts to trees can occur at any time during a collision depending on the velocity the vehicles possess at that point. The velocity, size of the vehicle, and size of the tree determine how the tree and the vehicle react to the collision. As with a telephone or utility pole, the exact location of the damage allows the on-scene investigator to determine the size of the vehicle, sometimes the color, and the direction of the impact.

Again, it is necessary to perform a detailed inspection of the vehicle exterior to determine the location of paint transfers, peculiar deformation, and any wood fragments that have been removed from the tree.

## Point of Impact

Determining the POI of any accident is never easy. It requires time, effort, and knowledge of physics (primarily the effects of gravity). Many times investigators report that the POI was the location of the debris. *This is absolutely incorrect.* It takes time for debris from the vehicle to reach the ground, especially when it is still moving.

Even if the investigator were to kick the snow or dirt from under the fender or quarter panel, which can be 8 in. from the ground, it would take 0.02 sec or 20 msec for it to reach the ground. Debris from a vehicle that was traveling at 30 mi/h and 44 ft/sec, and has come to rest due to an impact may travel 0.91 ft or 10.93 in. without any rolling or sliding after reaching the ground. It does not seem like much, but the error becomes cumulative, with respect to using it as the basis for the location of the vehicle at impact.

The end of a skid mark does not mean that it is the POI either. Remember that the impact may occur at anytime along the skid mark without leaving discontinuity, depending on the type of impact involved. A jog or discontinuity along the skid marks may mean that an impact occurred at that point, or that some piece of equipment failed. The on-scene investigator must confirm the POI by other evidence such as the start of the gouges near the continuity of the skid mark.

## *Point of Rest*

The location of the POR of the vehicles must be a smooth continuous movement from the POI. Vehicles do not move at right angles to their original paths unless undergoing a second impact or loss of control due to some type of mechanical failure. Sometimes there may not be enough evidence to establish a POI.

If this is true then by all means state the estimated POI explicitly in your report or that it was impossible to determine it. Do not pick any point just for the sake of naming one. Other evidence may come to light at a later date that may require a change in the assumed POI or may allow the investigator to accurately determine a POI. That is one more reason for detailing the evidence that may allow the location of the POI.

When the on-scene investigator finally establishes the POI, measure the distance from the RP to the established POI and record it.

In some cases, evasive action may have taken place prior to the impact. The on-scene investigator must determine if the abrasive action was precipitated by the driver or was due to some other problem. Look for a tire or suspension failure. Was there a child, tree limb, pothole, or possibly a small animal in the road that required evasive action? If an evasive action did take place, walking the scene back in the direction from where the vehicle came may reveal the origin of this evasive action.

Examine the curbs at the scene for tire or rim marks that may have caused damage. A driver falling asleep at the wheel or losing his/her focus on the driving task can hit a curb, causing a loss of control of the vehicle. A detailed inspection of the tires and rims of all the vehicles involved can later confirm this. Did the wheel rims scrape the curb or did the tires roll under so that the rim actually damaged the asphalt or cement? Look for fresh rim marks in concrete; also check the sidewalls of the tire for a fresh rubbing of the surface where it may have had impacted the curb facing. These marks may look whiter with no embedded grease or dirt. If rim and tire marks are present and do not appear fresh, record them anyway but note that they are not fresh. Is a portion of the curbing missing that an impact to the remaining curb edge may have caused the steering wheel to be pulled from the hands of the driver and thereby cause a loss of control? Measure and record each and every unusual mark, gouge, or vehicle component that is not natural to the scene.

The investigator must fill in as many of these details on his/her sketch as possible, as shown in Figures 4.1, 4.2, and 4.4. How close was the impact to the nearest driveway? How far is the POI from the nearest utility pole? Look both directions from the POI for damaged signposts, street signs, overhead street or traffic lights that may not be working, or anything unusual that would help to confirm an opinion.

There should be a lot of information on all the scene sketches, all of which can be useful to the investigator. It is important to show culverts or mounds that could possibly have been built up by road construction crews, different types of fences, open fields, plowed fields, gravel or blacktop shoulders, driveways, and other such details; any of these could act as a blind spot, a defect in the road, or a problem the driver of a vehicle would have as a potential loss of control.

Accident victims may be thrown from the vehicles and it is important to show on what type of environment they may land. Pedestrians who are thrown after impact from a vehicle may land on gravel shoulders, plowed fields, fences, or against trees. The medical report may tell you that gravel was found in the victim's head wound, while the investigator's report does not mention that the shoulder was gravel. Investigators must learn to fill in the drawing as completely as possible. There can never be too much information taken at a scene.

Remember the details when reviewing the checklist. In rural areas, debris is going to scatter over a long distance. Windshields can be displaced and thrown from a few feet to as many as 20 ft. Tire and wheel assemblies that come off vehicles can roll several feet before coming to rest. Look for these and other missing items from the vehicle during the inspection and locate them at the scene. The fractured or damaged parts that allowed a wheel assembly to leave the vehicle must be measured, photographed, and video-taped. Try to determine how these displaced and damaged parts reached their final positions, and take photographs before any object is moved.

Make sure that culverts are measured for width and depth, for the distance the start of the culvert is from the edge of the road, and at which point the culvert starts to turn downward. These measurements are extremely important if a witness reports seeing the vehicle jump or skid across the culvert. By using a simple ballistics problem approach, it is possible to determine what velocity the vehicle had when jumping the culvert. If the angle of departure from the road is known, or if it is a flat road and the distance to the landing point from the take-off point is known, then simple mechanics can solve the problem of determining the velocity.

Examine the roadbed shoulders for skid marks, torn up grass, and or scattered gravel; see if these marks continue across the culvert, or if there is a large deep gouge in the opposite bank indicating the vehicle had insufficient velocity to make it across the culvert and landed inside the culvert.

## On-Scene Sketches

Sketching a scene can be overwhelming to some investigators. As discussed in the previous chapter, if the investigator is prepared and has all his/her measuring and sketching equipment, sketching is not a problem. Electronic measuring devices such as a Sokkia Total Station should be used whenever possible. They, of course, would be the first choice because of being more accurate and easier to use. The associated software produces a scale drawing without all the fine details, but it is a very good beginning and can save a lot of time.

The following is a step-by-step procedure to prepare a scale drawing of a scene either by using a CAD program or by laying it out by hand with a "T-square," triangles, and a pencil. Assume that the on-scene investigator has made a rough sketch and he/she now wants to make an accurate scale drawing of the site. If the scene is a standard four-way intersection without an offset between the two roads, or other streets angling in or across it, then this step is easy. Just draw the four corners with the proper number of lanes in each of the four directions. Be careful to include partial right- and left-hand turn lanes.

Locate the RP as outlined previously. Having taken a sufficient number of measurements, locate the proper width dimensions of the traveled lane, curb widths, location and width of the sidewalks, locations of buildings, crosswalks, and stop bars on the road surface. Indicate utility poles by the number stamped or burned into each one. Mark the location of the stop or yield signs, especially their position with respect to the stop bars. Traffic light support towers, highway crossover traffic light support cables, and any freestanding traffic and the overhead lights must be located.

Remember to indicate if the traffic lights also contain pedestrian, walk–no walk, and crosswalk lights at the intersection. It is necessary to mark the existence of all driveways, bushes, or trees around buildings and homes, especially in the case of line of sight problems at the intersection. Measuring the height of the bushes or trees is especially important if they may be hiding a stop or yield sign or a parked vehicle. Fences along sidewalks can also create blind spots for drivers.

Note all fence locations and heights, even chain-link fences because under certain driving conditions the angle of the fence with the driver line of sight can cause a blind spot. Fire hydrants, mailboxes, and the location of stand-alone street lights are also important for vision problems, especially at night. Use the handheld compass to determine and show the direction north on the drawing. Remember to always make the top of the drawing the northerly direction, the same as it is on any commercially available street map.

If a building is not parallel to a street, use the compass to determine the angle of the building with respect to the street. This helps locate the building on the scale drawing. All final drawings must also include a title block as shown in Figure 4.3. It is important to show the opposing counsel and the tryer of fact when the original drawing was completed, and the case and the attorneys' name.

Curved sections of roads require more work when completing the scene sketch. When the investigator does not have any electronic means of determining the curve sections of road, he/she must use the less accurate but time-tested method of pencil, paper, compass, and tape measure.

## Methods for Plotting a Curve

There are three methods to plot a curve: the constant angle method, the constant distance method, and the median method.

### Constant Angle Method

In looking at Figure 4.5, start at the point where the curve begins to deviate from the straight road, and then sight the compass back along the straight section of road. Turn 180 degrees and sight along the curved section using the supplementary angle that was just determined. Measure 25, 50, or 100 ft along the straight-line extension from the straight section of road using the tape measure. In Figure 4.5, the first three measurements with the tape measure are 50 ft each.

Any distance is acceptable as long as it is recorded at each section being measured. It is best to use a consistent distance each time a measurement is taken for clarity, unless the curve is very small or tight and unusual dimensions are necessary to determine a sufficient number of points to draw the curve. Figure 4.5 shows the curve deviating away to the right from the straight line just laid out. Taking the homemade 3-4-5 triangle from the tool kit, place it so there is a 90-degree corner at the end of the measured length. Use a shorter tape measure, place it along the other leg of the 90-degree triangle, and measure the distance to the edge of the curved road. Record this

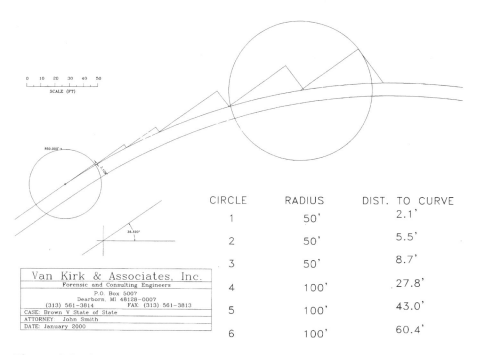

| CIRCLE | RADIUS | DIST. TO CURVE |
|--------|--------|----------------|
| 1 | 50' | 2.1' |
| 2 | 50' | 5.5' |
| 3 | 50' | 8.7' |
| 4 | 100' | 27.8' |
| 5 | 100' | 43.0' |
| 6 | 100' | 60.4' |

Van Kirk & Associates, Inc.
Forensic and Consulting Engineers
P.O. Box 5007
Dearborn, MI 48128-0007
(313) 561-3814          FAX: (313) 561-3813
CASE: Brown V State of State
ATTORNEY:   John Smith
DATE: January 2000

**Figure 4.5** Plotting a curve using constant angles.

measurement and procedure to the end of the first measurement. Note that in Figure 4.5 an angle of 36.320 degrees was measured.

Move the surveyor's pin up to the next 50-ft length and take another sighting at 36.320 degrees from due east. Follow the procedure in step one with the 3-4-5 triangle and the shorter tape to effect a 90 degree angle, and measure the distance back to the curved section of roadway. Note that this distance is increasing, as seen in Figure 4.5. The last three measurements were done using a 100-ft measurement to show the on-scene investigator how much faster the distance increases with a longer straight-line measurement. The sixth measurement plots only half of the curve. During the remaining plotting procedure, the distance continues to increase as the curve drops farther south. If there are drainage ditches or planted fields, then this method can be difficult to use.

### Constant Distance Method

Figure 4.5A shows the results of using this method. Use the same curved road, the same initial angle, and a distance of 100 ft in length for each measurement. Measure the distance from the initial angle that was parallel to the straight section of road, and at the 100-ft length measure the distance back to the curved road. This is 7.76 ft in Figure 4.5A. For step two measure

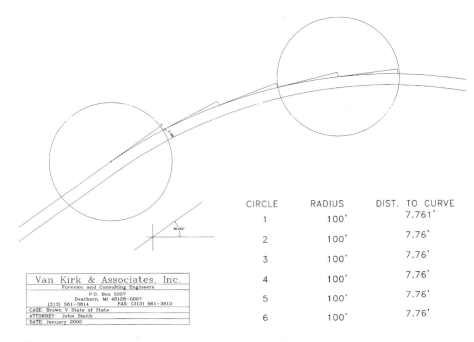

| CIRCLE | RADIUS | DIST. TO CURVE |
|--------|--------|----------------|
| 1 | 100' | 7.761' |
| 2 | 100' | 7.76' |
| 3 | 100' | 7.76' |
| 4 | 100' | 7.76' |
| 5 | 100' | 7.76' |
| 6 | 100' | 7.76' |

Van Kirk & Associates, Inc.
Forensic and Consulting Engineers
P.O. Box 5007
Dearborn, MI 48128-0007
(313) 561-3814        FAX: (313) 561-3813
CASE: Brown V State of State
ATTORNEY:  John Smith
DATE: January 2000

**Figure 4.5A** Plotting a curve using constant distance from a curve.

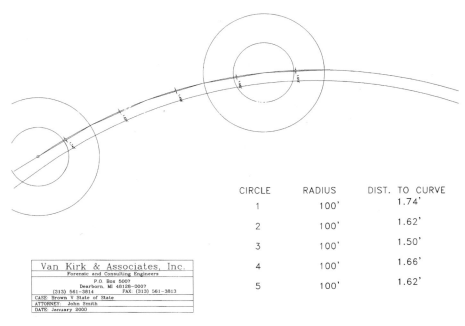

| CIRCLE | RADIUS | DIST. TO CURVE |
|--------|--------|----------------|
| 1 | 100' | 1.74' |
| 2 | 100' | 1.62' |
| 3 | 100' | 1.50' |
| 4 | 100' | 1.66' |
| 5 | 100' | 1.62' |

Van Kirk & Associates, Inc.
Forensic and Consulting Engineers
P.O. Box 5007
Dearborn, MI 48128-0007
(313) 561-3814        FAX: (313) 561-3813
CASE: Brown V State of State
ATTORNEY:  John Smith
DATE: January 2000

**Figure 4.5B** Plotting a curve using median distance from a curve.

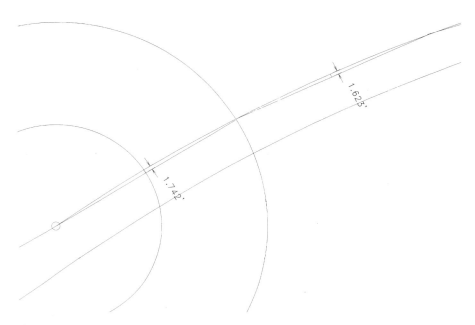

**Figure 4.5C** Close-up of median measurements.

another 100-ft length and with the shorter measurement tape and the 3-4-5 triangle, lay out the 7.76-ft length from the edge of the curved road.

Then from the starting point at the end of the first measurement, measure the angle from due east or due north. Note how close the straight sections follow the curved road. The distances are easier to measure, but it takes a little work to get the angles. Both of these systems work well in the urban or rural areas.

### Median System

One scene that presents a problem is a curved bridge over another highway. For these types of situations where there is little or no shoulder from which measurements can be taken, a third system was developed, *the median system.* This system is based on using a chord measurement from a circle (Figure 4.5B). Depending on the severity of the curve, any dimension can be used.

Many bridges have a small curve to them; then a 50- or 100-ft cord length can be used. Starting from the point where the straight section of road starts to deviate into the curve, measure the angle from either due north or due east. Then walk along the bridge measuring a 100-ft distance. Mark with a grease pencil the 100-ft mark on the bridge roadway at the outside extreme edge of the road.

Leave the tape in place, walk back to the 50-ft mark, and use the smaller 12-ft mark to measure the distance from the inside of the tape to the outside edge of the road on the bridge. Figure 4.5B shows how this procedure would be done on the same curve being used previously. Note that the halfway point is reached with only five 100-foot measurements in this case. Figure 4.5C is a close-up of Figure 4.5B showing the location of the measurements for the 100-foot cord length and for the median measurement, from the cord to the edge of the roadway surface. Note also that all dimensions on this curve were less than 2 ft and could easily be handled on a narrow two lane, curved bridge.

Once the on-scene investigator has completed the actual road surface dimensioning, the remaining details can be filled in on the sketch (as discussed earlier), with all the pertinent data needed to create a scale drawing for use at depositions and trials.

## Visualization

The accident scene is a major part of the investigation and reconstruction of any accident. It is both necessary and important that each investigator locates and records as much detail as possible when viewing the scene. Investigators must put themselves at the scene in their minds' eye, on the day of the accident. This scenario must play over and over in their minds, as a movie or a videotape.

The weather, the lighting, the direction, and the speed and maneuvers of the vehicles or pedestrians involved before, during, and after the accident must be visualized. Only when a mental image is firmly in place can the investigator look for the myriad of details that are crucial to the outcome of the case.

As an example, visualize the vehicle going off the road and rolling over several times. This prompts the mind to look for glass particles from the tempered glass side windows. If the front windshield is missing from the vehicle, it has broken its bond and has been thrown clear of the vehicle. If the occupants have been ejected from the vehicle, look for possible landing sites. These can include tall grass bent flat, gouges in the lawn or the gravel shoulder, or even blood spots. Remember occupants can be thrown forward or end up behind the vehicle's final resting place depending on when they were ejected from the vehicle and by what venue. Trampled or torn up grass are the witness marks of the path of the vehicle.

Work backward from the POR and look for damaged pieces from the vehicles. Photograph them in place before moving them. Broken vehicle components can be examined at a later date to determine when the parts were broken, and what effect they had on the accident itself or on just the movement of the vehicle.

Clothing or other objects ejected from the interior may allow determination of the point or place of ejection and possibly the speed of ejection from the distance they have landed from the vehicle. Once again, the cannon trajectory calculation is used.

Be aware that many fire departments wash down a highway or city street after an accident when gasoline or large amounts of fluids have been expelled onto the road surface. This practice definitely changes the debris pattern and destroys the fluid trails. To make sure that a wash down occurred after the accident, a check of the fire department's log of equipment and manpower use can indicate what occurred at the same site. In many states today due to environmental protection laws, it is necessary that soil from oil and gasoline spills be removed and taken to a plant for processing. This also changes the scene dramatically.

Finally, the investigator must always remember that accident scenes change every day. The more traffic that travels a road surface, the more changes he/she may find in the coefficient of friction for the road on the day of the inspection. Even a few hours after the accident the coefficient of friction is different than it was at the time of the accident. Also, trees and shrubbery not only change in size but also may be removed for disease or change in landscaping.

*Commentary: There have been instances in which an offending tree in an accident that resulted in the death of a teen driver was cut down by the father and hauled away. Roads are often widened as the area increases in population, thereby necessitating that the roadside trees be removed.*

Commercial businesses, houses, driveways, trees, telephone poles, curbing, and even the roadbed being resurfaced can all be impediments to the success of the investigation. The prepared and flexible investigator is not stopped by such problems. Many if not all these impediments can be overcome through various sources such as the newspaper reports of the accidents, on-scene television videos of the area, local people's memories, etc. (The investigator should seek all these details.)

## Traffic Light Timing

The timing of traffic lights has been and will continue to be a very important part of any investigation. Drivers today do not consider it a violation of the law to go through a "pink light" as they call it, one that is turning from yellow to red just before they enter the intersection.

*Commentary: Each motorist has had plenty of warning, usually about 4.0 sec that the yellow light is about to change to red. The motorists who are stopped at the crossing intersection and waiting for their signal to turn green are not looking at the driver about to run the red light. They are looking to speed away from the stop bar as quickly as possible. This "dumb" act on the part of both motorists has led to many fatal accidents.*

As intersections increase in size due to increases in the number of lanes, the number of vehicles that use such intersections increase. This requires a change in the light timing. Many traffic lights today have at least two and maybe four different timing sequences for the various traffic patterns encountered during the day — longer green lights for the morning traffic in one direction and longer green lights in the opposite direction in the afternoon. In between, the light may go to a relatively equal timing for normal traffic use. In some rural areas the light may go into a red–yellow blinking pattern after midnight and resume its normal timing pattern for the morning rush hour. The constantly blinking yellow light is used for the more frequently traveled road, and the blinking red light, for the less traveled road such as one coming from a subdivision. These pattern changes can be extremely important in any investigation. The county or city in which the accident occurred will have a record of the light timing sequence for any intersection.

Make sure that the light timing covers the same time of day that the accident occurred. The traffic light system has also become more complicated with time. Most if not all now contain some type of interference monitor for loss of power from natural or man-made circumstances. There is even a specific start-up procedure after a power loss. It starts up on a blinking mode for a set period of time and then switches to a regular sequence set for that time of day. Unfortunately this is not always true. Many times, as in all electronic equipment, both lights may flash red or yellow or both at the same time. Questioning of the city engineers, light designers, or installers can help the investigator understand the problem but may not resolve it. Because the lights have been installed and set up by humans, they are not infallible. Always remember to check the light timing with a stopwatch to see how close the settings are to the actual ones.

*Commentary: Yellow lights are generally set for 4 sec on a regular two-lane road; however, I have found them set as low as 3 sec.*

*When calculating the position of a vehicle in an intersection, this difference can change the location when determining distance and time relationships. Never assume any piece of data or evidence as being true and accurate.*

Check every piece of data, evidence, and fact for accuracy and truthfulness, if for nothing more than your own piece of mind.

## Tire Marks

As stated earlier, there are three basic types of tire marks left on a road surface by a vehicle: the yaw mark, the skid mark, and the acceleration mark.

A tire that is rotating and turning at the same time leaves what is called a yaw mark. This is a very distinctive mark. Instead of the tire leaving dark marks parallel to the direction of vehicle movement, there are striations in the marks at various angles to the direction of travel. The directions of the marks are dependent on the amount of "rolling under" the tread does during the maneuver. In addition, the entire mark is curved. The width of the yaw mark as well as the number and angle of the striations is highly dependent on the speed of the vehicle. Yaw marks can be made by both the front and rear tires and are dependent on the vehicle movement.

The investigator must be careful to check that the yaw marks have not turned into a sideways skid of the entire vehicle. This can be observed by measuring the width of the mark. Tire patch size almost doubles as the tire slides sideways. When the sideways skid does occur, then it must be documented by location from the RP and with photographs and videotape. There is a clear indication of the change when the investigator backtracks the tire marks from the POR of the vehicle to the end of the marks, which may be under the tires on the vehicle.

Acceleration marks are mentioned again at this point because some investigators have become confused when they see these marks at intersections where both acceleration and deceleration marks may be present. As discussed previously, deceleration or skid marks are made up of three phases. They start out light on the road surface, darken as the tires get hotter, and usually end abruptly. Acceleration marks are just the opposite. The tires are being rotated by the axle and when done fast enough, the outside of the tire — the tread — which is being held by the coefficient of friction between the tire tread and the road surface takes time to catch up to the rest of the tire. Therefore, the acceleration marks are heavy at the beginning and lighten up as the tire tread catches up to the rest of the tire.

The investigator must therefore walk the tire mark back from either end noting its change in darkness. If the end closest to the POR is darker than the other end, then it is a skid mark. If the mark is getting lighter at the POR, then it is an acceleration mark. If it completely disappears near the POI, it may be possible that the vehicle was accelerating prior to impact and lost control.

***Commentary:*** *Consider the example where a vehicle is accelerating from a green light and another vehicle is running a red light. The acceleration marks were just short of the POI and confused the on-scene investigator.*

Skid marks are left on the road surface when rotating tires lock up and no longer roll but skid along the surface of the highway. One, two, three, or all four tires on a car can lock up during a braking maneuver. The driver's foot applies significant pressure to the brake pedal causing the brake pads or shoes to hold the disks or drums from rotating.

Cars and nonarticulated trucks are designed so that approximately 60 % of the braking power is applied to the front brakes. This means the front tires will leave skid marks before the rear tires do. When only one set of skid marks is encountered at an accident scene, they should be the front tires. This means that usually the braking pressure is not set properly or there may be other problems with the brake system. The investigator must keep this in mind because when only two tires are braking, the braking capability is reduced by at least 40%, which increases the distance the vehicle requires to stop. Locking up the tires on a vehicle is not the most efficient and effective way to stop a vehicle. Once the skid begins the stopping of the vehicle is dependent on the coefficient of friction between the tires and the surface of the road.

The coefficient of friction ($\mu$) between a car tire and the road can be as low as 0.2 for ice or hard-packed snow or as high as 0.8 for new highways that have not been worn down by traffic yet. A dry concrete or asphalt highway has an average coefficient of friction of between 0.7 and 0.8. An experienced driver can brake the vehicle with a deceleration of 0.9 g, or sometimes higher, without locking up by pumping the brake pedal. He/she releases it just before the tires lock up and repeats the process over again until the vehicle stops.

Mud, snow, rain, or ice changes the road surface and reduces the coefficient of friction. The brake pads and shoes do not usually change the $\mu$ values significantly with the weather conditions. Antilock braking systems brake the wheels to the point of lock up, momentarily release them, and then pressure is reapplied to the impending skid level again. This process is repeated until the vehicle comes to rest. All the driver has to do with a vehicle equipped with an antilock braking system (ABS) is to apply steady pressure to the brake pedal and the system does the rest. *The driver must not pump the brake pedal* as in older vehicles without ABS; it prevents the ABS system from working properly.

One point every on-scene investigator must remember is that when a vehicle is skidding down a highway with the front wheels locked, it cannot be steered and the direction of travel of the vehicle cannot be changed. It is similar to driving on ice. The steering wheel can be turned from lock to lock but it has little or no effect on the direction the vehicle is traveling.

To steer a vehicle requires that a portion of the rolling tire act against the surface of the road, changing the direction of the vehicle. If the tire is locked up in a skid, then it is impossible to have a portion of it act against the road. Thus there is no steering during a skid. The vehicle continues to go in the path it started at the time the skid starts. That is why many cars run off a road or into a tree during a skid because the driver is still trying to steer the vehicle but is unsuccessful because he/she did not release the brake pedal.

The advent of the ABS eliminates the possibility of lockup because it releases the brakes just before lockup and then begins to brake again, giving the driver maximum effective braking when needed. Unfortunately, the ABS system is not available on all vehicles yet.

All cars and nonarticulated vehicles are designed to have the front tires brake first. This is to keep the front of the vehicle pointed in the same direction of travel during the braking maneuver. There have been instances where the rear brakes locked up first. In those cases the vehicle does a complete 180-degree turn and the rear of the vehicle is now heading down the road first. When an investigator sees only one set of skid marks at the scene, he/she must also backtrack to see if there has been a rotation of the vehicle at some prior time.

*Commentary: This may sound ridiculous because the on-scene investigator should be able to tell what type of impact the vehicle underwent by the damage it sustained. In multiple car impacts, it is more difficult to ascertain damage and more detailed analysis is required.*

Sometimes it is difficult to determine whether there were one or two sets of skid marks from the same vehicle at the scene. Careful analysis of the marks shows that one set of marks usually grows lighter as the pressure is released. This is the rear set of tires changing from skipping to rolling to prevent rotation of the vehicle. If the marks never change color and are dark right up to the POI then a very close look at the tire marks is necessary. The close-up look shows a difference between the distance separating the two tires on the front and rear axles. The rear tires are set wider apart than the front ones and a difference between the marks can be seen. This is called track width and the vehicle statistic sheet lists the track width.

*Commentary: When calculating speed from skid marks using the skid equation, be careful not to assume that there was a four-wheel skid. If the investigator cannot be sure of the number of sets of skid marks, then state at the beginning of the calculations that a four-wheel skid is assumed but give results for both a two- and a four-wheel skid. I have seen calculations where only one skid mark was visible in the photographs and the investigator calculated the speed loss using the four-wheel skid equation and never stated his/her assumptions. This, of course, means the vehicle velocity will be higher than it should have been because the drop in braking efficiency was not taken into account during the skid equation calculation.*

## Real-World Scene Photographs

The photographs in this section show the results of an accident in which a pickup truck exiting an expressway using the off ramp was impacted by a

**Photograph 4.1** View of the bridge over the expressway from the off ramp.

late model muscle car coming over the bridge at close to 100 mi/h. The bridge that goes over the expressway is high in the center and it is impossible to see any oncoming traffic on the bridge when on the off ramp.

Photograph 4.1 shows the bridge over the expressway from the off ramp as the pickup approached the intersection of the off ramp and the bridge lanes. Note that all views of vehicles are blocked. Photograph 4.2 shows the bridge lanes just before the pickup reached the intersection, and is taken behind the stop sign.

Photograph 4.3 shows the pickup bumper at the intersection and the driver can see only a few feet south of the center of the bridge. The pickup driver in Photograph 4.4 is half to three quarters of the distance into the right-turn lane. Notice the car in the opposing lane just passing the center of the bridge.

Photograph 4.5 shows a close-up view of the oncoming lane and the blind spot for the pickup driver that prevents him/her from seeing approaching traffic. Photographs 4.6 and 4.7 show the muscle car driver's line of sight as he/she clears the center of the bridge and approaches the intersection. Photographs 4.1 through 4.7 show the accident scene from the two principal directions the vehicles were traveling at the time of the accident. The complete photographic file is more extensive; only a small section was shown for clarity.

Many on-scene investigators take a photograph every 50 ft depending on the accident scene. The average car driver's eye height distance above the ground is 3.5 ft. Therefore, a profile view of the hill can be constructed and

**Photograph 4.2** View of the bridge lanes just before the pickup reached the intersection.

**Photograph 4.3** View of bridge lanes as the pickup bumper reached the intersection.

**Photograph 4.4** View of the bridge lanes when the pickup is near the center of the right-turn lane.

**Photograph 4.5** Close-up view of the oncoming lane and the blind spot prevents vision of approaching traffic.

**Photograph 4.6** View of oncoming driver's line of sight as he/she clears the blind spot, the center of the bridge, and approaches the intersection.

**Photograph 4.7** Closer view of oncoming driver's line of sight as he/she clears the blind spot, the center of the bridge, and approaches the intersection.

**Photograph 4.8** View of the skid marks from the 2 vehicles approximately 2 weeks after the accident.

a line drawn parallel to the hill to show where the muscle car driver would have seen the intersection. Conversely, the eye height of the pickup truck driver is approximately 6 ft. The overall height of the muscle car is approximately 5 ft. A line can be drawn on the same drawing showing the distance at which the pickup driver would have been able to see the highest point of the muscle car.

Once these distances are known, then a calculation can be made to determine the time it took the muscle car to reach the intersection at the speed he/she was traveling and to ascertain if he/she had sufficient distance and time to come to a stop.

The speed limit on the bridge was 55 mi/h. Photograph 4.8 shows the skid marks from the two vehicles that were taken approximately 2 weeks after the accident. Photographs 4.9 and 4.10 show the skid marks of the muscle car as it was leaving the highway and was heading off the road onto the grassy area next to the house. Photograph 4.11 is a closer view showing the impact to the right front tire of the pickup and the skids from the muscle car. Photographs 4.12 through 4.16 are different views of the grassy slope over which the muscle car traveled after the impact with the pickup truck. It should be noted that the muscle car was spinning, turning, rolling over, and sliding on almost all sides of the vehicle before it came to rest at the porch of the house in the background.

**Photograph 4.9** View of the skid marks of the car from the through lane as the vehicle leaves the highway.

**Photograph 4.10** Close-up view of the skid marks of the car from the right-turn lane as the vehicle leaves the highway.

**Photograph 4.11** View showing the skid marks from impact to the right front corner tire of the pickup and the car.

**Photograph 4.12** View of the grassy slope looking toward the house, showing the path traveled by the car after the impact with the pickup truck.

**Photograph 4.13** View of the grassy slope looking toward the road, showing the path traveled by the car after the impact with the pickup truck.

**Photograph 4.14** Close-up view of the grassy slope looking toward the house, showing the path traveled by the car after the impact with the pickup truck.

**Photograph 4.15** Long view of the grassy slope looking toward the house, showing the path traveled by the car after the impact with the pickup truck.

**Photograph 4.16** Long view of the grassy slope looking toward the road, showing the path traveled by the car after the impact with the pickup truck.

Once again, only a limited number of photographs are being shown for brevity. These photographs do show the directions of approach of the vehicles prior to impact, including all line of sight problems, road conditions, intersection controls, and general appearance of the scene. The second series shows the skid marks on the road from the POI to the point where they leave the paved surface.

The last series show the marks in the grassy slope, the direction of the plowing of the vehicle, and the number of times it struck the ground. Matching up the various portions of the vehicle that show the residue of grass and dirt embedded into cracks and other openings allows the investigator to determine the actual movement of the car as it moved across the field. There was a loss of skid marks due to the 2 weeks of traffic that traversed the scene. When matched up with the police photographs taken the night of the accident, the loss was not significant. There were a total of 250 photographs taken at the scene and almost 300 taken of the two vehicles to cover all the damage.

## Water on or over the Roadway

Standing water on a roadway must be designated on the scene drawing, especially the length along the road and the width, the distance the water extends across the usable lanes (i.e., one two or more lanes). Notations should also be made of the source of the water. These would include such details as backed up drain sewers, broken water mains, or just a heavy rain that did not drain off of the road. These problems may have been caused by poor design of the road or changes in the area along each side of the roadway such as a loss of drainage ditches due to residential building.

The reason it is necessary to include standing water is that three happenings can occur to a vehicle when it passes through standing water: (1) it can hydroplane, (2) it can yaw severely to the deepest part of the water, and (3) it can do both.

The following is quoted from*:[2]

Hydroplaning of tires occurs when the standing water can not escape the path of the rapidly approaching tire and thus the water forms a wedge ahead of and under the tire. [This raises the tire from the road surface.] As the tire is not touching the runway there is no conventional braking. However, if the length of standing water is long enough, even a free rolling wheel will slow down to a standstill although the aircraft or automobile is traveling fast. This is because the hydrodynamic forces on the tire from the wedge of

---

* Quotations from Reference 2, reprinted with permission from SAE Paper 900105. © 1990 Society of Automotive Engineers, Inc.

water produce a retarding torque. The essence of hydroplaning is the inability of the water to escape from the tire footprint area. Even shallow water, less than 1/2 inch deep, can sustain hydroplaning.

To overcome this problem water can be dissipated from the contact area by deep tread patterns on the tires. Hydroplaning causes control problems because the tire is not in contact with the road and therefore no friction is available for steering or braking.

The widely accepted concept that hydroplaning speed was simply proportional to the square root of the tire pressure turns out to be wrong. The formula just does not fit the experimental data. For normal highway speeds with water depths greater than 1/2 inch, water cannot get out of the way of tires with normal tread depth. This creates tire drag. Tire drag on flooded roads has hardly been considered a problem in research.

When a road is flooded all the way across, traffic normally moves very slowly. However, a single automobile may come upon it suddenly. Most drivers slow down before encountering the water so do not appreciate the high drag forces that can be generated at higher speeds of tires in water, slush and snow. This is because of the close proximity of entrapping structures such as fenders, engine, and underside of the automobile cause impingement drag. The inside spray from the tires impacts these structures. Also the water momentum is changed as the vehicle carries some of the redirected water forward. The retardation at 90 km/h (55 mph) in 5 cm (2 inches) of water is about 1 g, which is more than can be achieved by the brakes on a dry road! [A vehicle that encounters water over the road that is mostly in the curb lane can give the driver significant control problems.]

Asymmetrical tire drag at higher speeds shows that water drag is proportional to depth and to speed squared. The effect on the vehicle dynamics is now studied where the wheels on one side of the automobile is traveling through a significant depth of water thus creating an asymmetrical loading which causes a yaw torque.

# References

1. Van Kirk, D. J., A scientific approach to documenting evidence for accident reconstruction, *J. Forensic Sci.*, 29(3), 806, July 1984.
2. Hight, P. V., Wheeler, J. B., and Reust, T. J., The Effects of Right Side Water Drag on Vehicle Dynamics and Accident Causation, SAE paper no. 900105, 1990.

# The Vehicle Exterior

# 5

"You know my method. It is founded upon the observation of trifles."

**Sherlock Holmes**
*The Boscombe Valley Mystery*

## Memorializing Accident Vehicles

The best place to photograph an accident vehicle is at the scene. Unfortunately, most investigators do not have that luxury. Photographing vehicles at the scene is better because of the relationships of the scene data to the vehicles present. There is no guessing at this point — the story is in the evidence found at the scene. If this is not possible, then there are several options available to the investigator:

1. If the vehicles are still at an impound yard and the portions of them that contain the damaged areas still exist, then a proper investigation can be done. Because the vehicle is still in the impound yard, it has probably only been handled once and only by the wrecker crew. This may limit the amount of damage done to the vehicle when it was moved from the accident scene. However, be assured that there will be postaccident or handling damage, which the investigator must sort out from the accident damage.

2. If the vehicle has been released by the police and has been taken either to the home of the accident victim or to an insurance salvage pool, the vehicle has now been handled three or four times as it was moved from the impound yard: by the wrecker, by salvage pool people on their lot, and then by those who loaded and unloaded it at the final destination. Parts may have fallen off or been removed by parties unknown in the process.

3. If the vehicle has been taken out to a farm, yard, or garage, or if the case was settled by the insurance company, then this is where the greatest amount of noncollision damage can occur to the vehicle because it has been moved five or even six times before getting to its final destination.

During each transfer the vehicle is either hauled by a wrecker by its rear wheels (if they can still rotate), or pulled onto a tilting platform of a truck and then slid off when it reaches the destination. Many yards do not have tilt trucks so the forks of a "hi-lo" are slid, hopefully, under the vehicle; then it is picked up and usually dumped on the ground or on top of another vehicle. These material-handling trucks can cause an enormous amount of damage to the vehicle during the transfer process. If the vehicle has had severe damage to the frame or unibody making it unstable, it can be torn completely into two parts. This complicates the investigator's job.

The investigation can be relatively easy or difficult, depending on the location of the vehicle. Countless times the vehicle is squeezed in between two other vehicles at a salvage or junkyard. This makes it impossible to take overall pictures of either one or both sides of the vehicle and even many critical close-ups. Standing on top of the vehicle next to the subject vehicle allows a fairly decent photograph to be taken. If this does not work, ask the salvage pool operator to move the vehicle into the open. This may require some money to change hands but the photographs are necessary. Vehicles located on a farm or in true junkyards are the worst. In both cases, animals, both domestic and wild, may have taken up residence in them. This obliterates many of the fainter interior marks. The weather takes it toll also by cleansing the interior and exterior of dust marks, blood spatter, mud, shoe polish marks, strands of hair, skin transfers, and other witness marks. The animals, of course, leave their droppings, hair, and bits of food, bringing with them flies and fleas; these do not help the investigator when he/she is trying to get a close-up of the inside of the vehicle.

*Commentary: I always carry bug repellant in my equipment case as well as sunburn lotion. Many times I have used an aerosol spray room deodorant to improve breathing for a 1 to 2-hour inspection.*

This is a description of the potential loss of evidence that can and does occur when the investigator cannot perform a vehicle inspection within a short period of time. If the inspection is not carried out within a period of 6 months to a year, a great deal of evidence is lost and usually never recovered.

Just because the witness marks inside or outside the vehicle are no longer visible, does not mean they never existed. Therefore, it is necessary for the investigator to carry out a detailed examination of all the available remnants of the vehicle and to dig for any portion of the remaining evidence that may still be there. As an example, at this point the scratches from the impact may only be seen by looking at that part of the vehicle at an angle so the reflected light brings out the deeper part of the scratch, losing only the surface scratches.

The results of such a detailed inspection are then compared with any and all photographs that were taken at the scene by the police, firefighters, TV news people, or even relatives a day or so after the accident. These comparisons may reveal many details of the collision that were lost in moving the vehicle several times, in weathering, from animals and their droppings, and from the carelessness of the wrecker driver when he/she threw parts inside the vehicle while cleaning up the scene before moving the vehicle.

## Videotaping at Accident Scene

The next step that the investigator must take is to videotape and photograph the exterior of the vehicle. Videotaping the vehicle at the scene gives the tryer of fact a broad overview of the vehicle as first seen. The camera angles should mimic those used in the 35-mm still photographs as well as all other angles of the vehicle. The resolution of the video camera is not as good as print films so the camera must be moved to the left or right as well as up or down to get a better depth of field view of the vehicle deformation.

Both the video and still cameras should be mounted on a monopod when used at the scene. The videotaping should be done as a scene in a movie. Start by setting the camera so it is facing the front of the vehicle. Set up the camera with the menu board of date, time, place, case name, and number. Most video cameras are automatic and do not require any extra setup effort other than to ensure the switch is in the camera position and not on playback.

Make sure that there is sufficient videotape to do the complete inspection and that the batteries have a full charge. Most of the video cameras today only require a very low-light level, which means they can be used in darkened warehouses or garages without the need for artificial light. This does not mean that the camera operator does not have to provide extra light for shooting inside as well as on the underside of the vehicle. A camera-mounted, high-intensity light can be purchased with the camera or a portable light source can be used when setting up the shot to get the best focus (especially if the vehicle is in an unlighted barn or storage garage). If an outside power source is available, then by all means use it. The more light there is, the better the depth of field can be seen to show the total amount of deformation.

Each sequence must be set up before recording to ensure that all portions of the vehicle are in focus during the zoom in and out for recording a close-up, and all deformations are clearly visible. Once the portion of the vehicle has been checked out and the camera position is set, the operator then pushes the fade button and the record button. The scene slowly becomes brighter as it fades into view; then the operator can zoom in and out to fill the frame of the lens and to show the details of the evidence from the collision.

Once that portion of the vehicle has been completed the operator then touches the fade button again and the scene fades to black. Fading in and out is done for at least three reasons: (1) to insert other menu boards with special text if required at a later date; (2) to make a cleaner shot and to allow the investigator/reconstructionist time at the deposition or trial to explain what will be seen in the next shot for the tryer of fact; and (3) to keep the viewer from getting seasick watching the scene bounce up and down as the operator walks around the vehicle trying to avoid stepping on scattered components.

*Commentary: I once used videotape taken by a police officer, digitized it, made single frames from it, and placed them on a laptop computer to be used instead of still photographs that no one had taken before the vehicle was destroyed.*

**Never** walk around the vehicle with a handheld video camera; it results in bad videotape. Never under any circumstances try to describe the damage at the same time taping is being done.

The ground is usually uneven and littered with rocks or debris. Twisting an ankle is very possible because it is impossible to watch the ground and stay focused on the vehicle at the same time. The video ends up with a vertical bounce at the very least, as well as missing parts of the vehicle, and often has some footage of the ground and/or of the operator's feet.

*Commentary: I have reviewed footage taken by investigators that had so much vertical bounce that everyone who viewed the tape got nauseous after watching only 3 or 4 min of it. What was even more peculiar was that the investigator was walking down a straight and level paved road at the time the videotape was taken.*

Improperly set up, unfocused, or bouncy videotape destroys the credibility of the tape for documentation as well as for evidentiary purposes. Many investigators try to record voice on the tape at the same time. This is impossible to do. A shaky audio as well as a bouncy video is the result. The volume, pitch, and diction of the operator's voice can vary and sometimes become inaudible, resulting in a loss in credibility.

A secondary problem is the background noise. Even as close to the microphone as the operator may be, passing cars, trucks, or construction equipment can drown out his/her voice. The video camera operator is not aware of the noises from passing vehicles, a factory that is under full production, or even other people who may be talking at the scene, because he/she is focusing attention on getting the best possible video of the vehicle damage. The omnidirectional microphones pick up all the extraneous noises and conversations and record them along with whatever is being viewed at the time of the inspection. Many times voices can be heard that have nothing to do with the part of the vehicle being viewed, and it is annoying and in some cases may be embarrassing to the people who do not know they are being recorded. Your local video store sells dummy plugs that can be placed in external audio jacks to prevent the recording of any audio. The videotape is a much better exhibit if there is no voice on it and instead the tape is narrated at the deposition or trial. In this manner the investigator can present the investigation sequence without distracting ambient noises.

*Commentary: Another reason not to record the audio during the inspection is that many times when making the initial tape, which may become the final inspection, there may not be sufficient information about the accident. Thus, any scene narration may not point out the particular area of the vehicle you may want to highlight after the reconstruction is completed.*

Close-ups of deformed areas should follow the wide-angle shots on the tape. If the client wants a special sequence of the inspection, be sure to tell him/her there are extra expenses involved in editing the tape. It is always better to see a wide-angle view of the deformation and then see a close-up followed by an extreme close-up if necessary.

Always remember that tape, like photographic film, is cheap compared with another visit to inspect the vehicle again because a dent or another area has become important during the analysis of a witness transcript or a portion of a police report.

The investigator must keep taping the damaged vehicle until he/she has gone around the vehicle at least twice and is comfortable with the reviewed tape results. It should go without saying that the tape should be reviewed at the inspection site to ensure that the video camera was working properly and that the investigator obtained the necessary footage to show the damage of the entire vehicle, inside and out.

## Using Still or 35-mm Camera at Accident Scene

At least 18 different camera angles are required as a minimum to adequately cover the exterior of a vehicle. The first sequence of photographs must establish the type and make of vehicle by overall views. This confirms that it is the vehicle in question. It is necessary to verify that the vehicle is a two-door sports coupe, convertible, or family sedan. If this is not done at the outset of the inspection, it may be difficult to compare the photographs taken later with the ones taken at the scene.

Figure 5.1 shows the four wide-angle views that must be taken first: front, rear, and one from each side. These shots may require the use of the 25-mm or wide-angle lens. The use of the lens may be dependent on the distance the photographs can be taken from the vehicle.

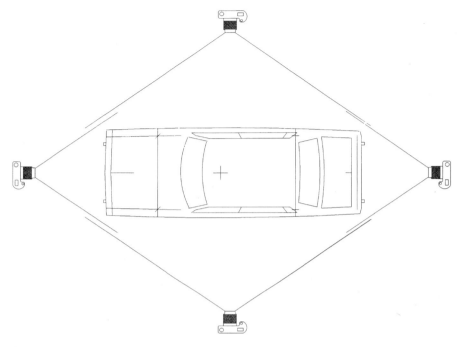

**Figure 5.1** Four wide-angle shots for overall view of the exterior.

Photographs 5.1 through 5.4 show actual pictures taken at a junkyard several months after the alleged accident. Notice that the vehicle is sitting atop a van. This is not unusual if the investigator is called into a case several months after the case has been filed. Notice that the photographs establish the make and model of the vehicle and also general damage areas.

This vehicle could have been removed from the stack and photographs taken a second time, but the damage seen and the case requirements did not warrant the cost and possible hi-lo damage from being moved again. Additionally, there were no suspension components and the vehicle was close to its proper attitude as though it were sitting on its own suspension.

Photographs 5.5 through 5.8 are of a more normal inspection. In this case, the damage is more severe and the vehicle still has the suspension in place and mostly undamaged. Figure 5.2 shows the next sequence of photographs to be taken. Those of sectional and medium close-up camera shots afford a closer look at each component and show a different view of the extent of the damage. Photograph 5.2 shows the required shots of the major sections of the vehicle (i.e., the front fenders, front and rear doors, and rear quarter panels). These views can generally be taken with the zoom lens without having to move the camera too many times. The same distance should be kept from the camera to the object when shooting from side to

**Photograph 5.1** Front view of a vehicle.

side. It is easier for comparison and the presentation looks better at the deposition or trial. Also if possible, take an overhead view of the hood, roof, and trunk lid without endangering the camera operator.

*Commentary: I have found it very handy to purchase a lightweight vest with many pockets. Once you get behind a vehicle, after maneuvering around two or three others, you find you do not have enough room to get the shot you need. Without the proper lens or light source you either take a bad picture or go back to the camera bag for another lens. The pockets are also handy for carrying marker strips, extra film, 3 × 5 blank cards, and bug repellent. Grease pencils and colored pens fit nicely in the upper pockets.*

Photographs 5.9 through 5.13 show the second sequence of photographs. Notice that all the views are not present. This was due to the way the vehicles were squeezed together in the yard. Photographs 5.14 through 5.19 show all the sectional views and they are approximately the same size and fill the majority of the frame. Figure 5.3 shows the three-quarter or angular views.

**Photograph 5.2** Left side view of a vehicle.

**Photograph 5.3** Rear view of a vehicle.

These are taken from the left and right front corners of the vehicle as well as from the left and right rear corners of the vehicle.

Photographs 5.20 through 5.23 exemplify the photographs that can be taken under extreme conditions. Why are these special views necessary? Damage to the top or side of the vehicle shows up the best at these angles.

**Photograph 5.4** Right side view of a vehicle.

**Photograph 5.5** Front view of a more severely damaged vehicle.

If the impact was from the side, the depth of penetration should be seen. A three-quarter view along with good close-ups shows this depth. These views also show the spread of the damage (i.e., how far along it extends from the front to the rear or from the roof to the rocker panel). Figure 5.4 shows four

**Photograph 5.6** Left side view of a more severely damaged vehicle.

**Photograph 5.7** Rear view of a more severely damaged vehicle.

additional views that should be taken from the front and the rear of the vehicle. The camera is sighted along the side of the vehicle with no more than one half of the vehicle showing in the frame.

**Photograph 5.8** Right side view of a more severely damaged vehicle.

Photographs 5.24 and 5.25 are good examples of why these shots should be taken. Note that in the right-hand view or the driver's side, the front of the vehicle is pushed toward the passenger's side. Note that the remainder of the vehicle from the door rearward is undamaged. In the opposite or passenger's view, the remaining rear of the vehicle is concealed by the damaged front end, which has been pushed to this side of the vehicle.

Figure 5.5 shows the complete camera angles of mandatory photographs that must be taken. These photographs must be considered as only a minimum number of views. Remember, shooting extra rolls of film is cheap when compared with the time in getting additional photographs after trying to relocate the vehicle. It may prove fruitless if the vehicle has already been destroyed.

Photographs 5.26 through 5.32 are detailed photographs that must be taken to complete the inspection. In this particular case, the alleged accident was a rear-end impact with whiplash-type injuries. These photographs show that there was no damage to the exterior sheet metal as well as the bumper and taillights. The photographs of the underside of the vehicle show the Poly Gel Mitigators (PGMs), which should have been stroked showing that there was at least a minor type of impact. The sticky tape attached to the PGMs shows they are almost equal in stroke length and did not undergo a stroke, because there were no witness marks left after the stroke (case closed).

The 18 required photographs are not sufficient to show the entire detailed close-up damage on the vehicle. The camera operator is required to use

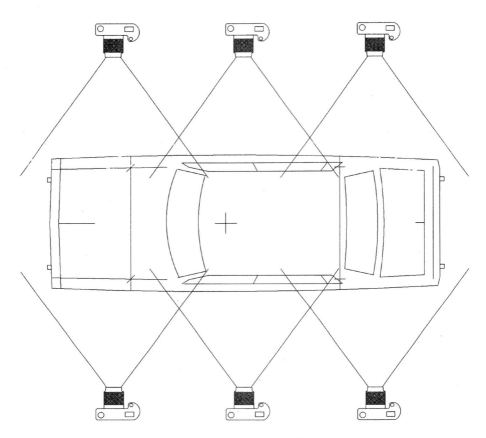

**Figure 5.2** Camera angles for sectional shots of front fenders, front and rear doors, and rear quarter.

his/her skills and to determine the best angles to show the damage. Many times several shots from slightly different directions are required to cover the deformation zone. Photographs 5.33 through 5.44 show medium and close-up views of the front fender damage. Notice that there are several shots that appear close in angular directions but each shows a different depth of the damage. Note also that photographs were taken of the area of the right front fender as it was pushed back into the door opening. This is induced damage, a result of moving the car and not due directly to the impact itself.

Measurement of the depth, in inches, should be taken using a set of tape measures that are perpendicular to each other at the deepest portion of the deformation. Sometimes a heavy-duty string tied at both ends of the vehicle can act as one tape measure or baseline; use only one tape measure. Place the tape at 90 degrees to the string and find the deepest portion of the damage and record it. Then, measure along the length of the string from the

**Photograph 5.9** Close-up views of the left front fender.

**Photograph 5.10** Close-up view of the left front door area.

beginning of the deformation to the end and have the location and length of
the deformation marked on the diagram.

**Photograph 5.11** Close-up view of the left rear quarter panel.

**Photograph 5.12** Close-up view of the right front fender.

If the investigator has a client who is interested in trying to reconstruct the accident using one of the various computer modeling programs, he/she needs to divide the component such as a door or quarter panel width into six equal parts and measure the depth of each part of the deformed area.

**Photograph 5.13** Close-up view of the right front door.

**Photograph 5.14** Close-up view of a right rear quarter panel.

The investigator must remember that one of the measurements being taken must include the depth of the deepest deformed area. Investigators inadvertently have forgotten this, and as a result the computer program does not generate the correct answers because it does not have the actual depth of the deepest part of the deformation.

**Photograph 5.15** Close-up view of an undamaged right front door.

**Photograph 5.16** Close-up view of a damaged right front fender.

Close-ups must be taken of all the damage; these views must show the depth and direction of impact as seen from each of four directions, top and bottom, left and right. There are many details to look for when determining

**Photograph 5.17** Close-up views of an undamaged left front fender.

**Photograph 5.18** Close-up view of an undamaged left front door area.

which close-up to take. These include metal folds, paint transfers, scrapes, gouges, and remains of blood and human tissue. Always remember that a close-up view without a moderately close view and a long view of that same area of the vehicle is useless.

**Photograph 5.19** Close-up view of an undamaged left rear quarter panel.

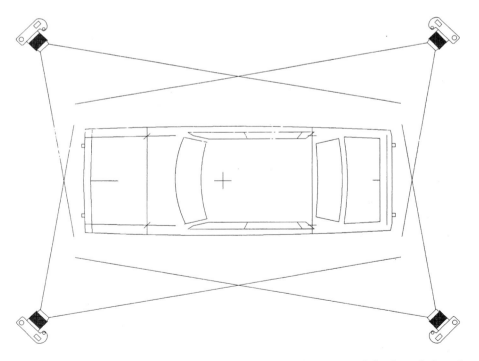

**Figure 5.3** Camera angles for three-quarter or angular views of the front left and right and rear left and right corners of the vehicle.

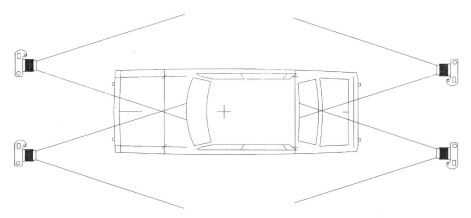

**Figure 5.4** Camera angles for sighting along the side of the vehicle, both from the front and from the rear.

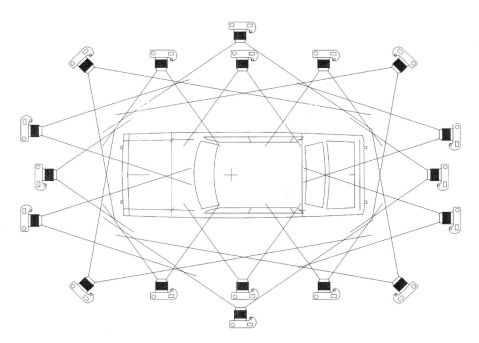

**Figure 5.5** Minimum required camera angles.

**Photograph 5.20** Three-quarter view from the front right side.

**Photograph 5.21** Three-quarter view from the rear right side.

**Photograph 5.22** Three-quarter view from the front right side.

**Photograph 5.23** Three-quarter view from the front left side.

## Exterior Details to be Noted and Recorded

### Metal Folds

The metal used in cars has been decreasing in thickness for many years. The thinner gauge metal folds over more easily and gives the investigator

**Photograph 5.24** Induced damaged front left side.

another tool to use in his/her investigation. Metal folds occur at impact when one portion of the metal is pushed over or under another portion. The direction of the folds, such as front to rear, indicates a frontal impact. There can be metal folds in many different directions on the same vehicle. This would usually indicate that the vehicle underwent more than one impact. It could also mean that the vehicle rotated or flipped over before the second impact.

It could, in addition, mean that the vehicle was struck by a second or even a third vehicle such as happens in a chain reaction collision during a fog or an icy condition on a bridge overpass.

Each of these metal folds must be analyzed to determine how they occurred and how many vehicles were involved. The on-scene investigator

**Photograph 5.25** Direct damage to the right front side.

**Photograph 5.26** Right rear three-quarter view.

**Photograph 5.27** View across the rear of the vehicle.

**Photograph 5.28** Three-quarter view from the rear left side.

looks for paint transfers from the other vehicles, embedded wood fibers from trees or from utility poles, dirt or grass stuck into wheel wells, bumpers, and metal folds. Rollover damage is easily seen by the collapse of the roofline or the fenders or the hood.

**Photograph 5.29** Unstroked left side PGM from under the rear bumper.

**Photograph 5.30** Unstroked right side PGM from under the rear bumper.

The scene must also be examined for witness marks off the road surface on a grassy slope of open or planted field to see if the vehicle has undergone the possibility of a rotation.

Photograph 5.45 is an example of metal folds in a trunk lid. Note that the sheet metal has been pushed forward towards the front of the vehicle as

**Photograph 5.31** Wide-angle view of an unstroked left side PGM from under the rear bumper.

**Photograph 5.32** Wide-angle view of an unstroked right side PGM from under the rear bumper.

**Photograph 5.33** Low-angle frontal view.

**Photograph 5.34** Close-up view of the left front headlight and grille.

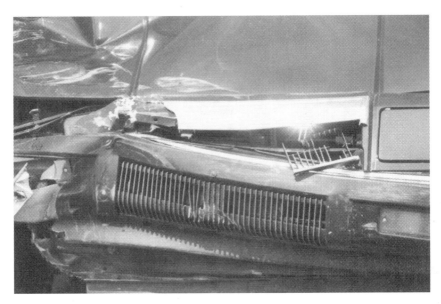

**Photograph 5.35** Close-up damage, center grille area.

**Photograph 5.36** Damaged left front headlamp and grille area.

well as from the outside toward the middle of the vehicle. There is a sharp indent approximately half way along the upper edge of the trunk lid. Photograph 5.46 is a rear three-quarter view showing where the corner of the box of a utility truck has penetrated the soft, right rear quarter panel and

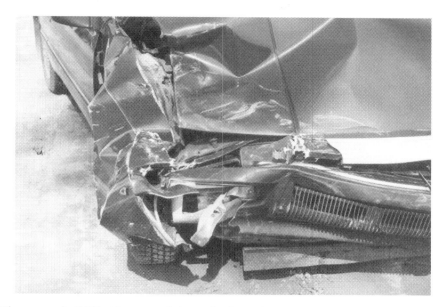

**Photograph 5.37** Close-up of the right front fender and hood.

**Photograph 5.38** Right side damaged hood.

in so doing has deformed the truck or deck lid inward. This action caused the rear edge of the deck lid to be pulled forward, resulting in the second metal fold. The first deformation is direct damage and the second is induced damage.

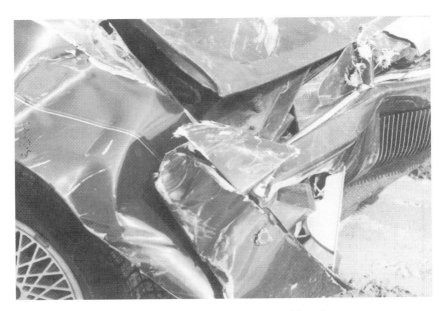

**Photograph 5.39** Damage to the fender, grille, and hood.

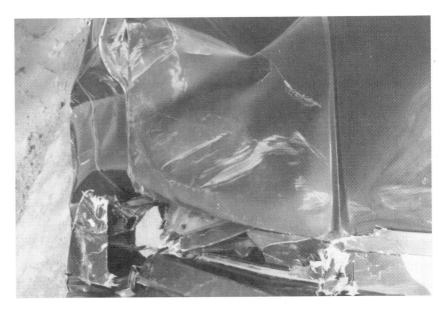

**Photograph 5.40** Right side hood, grille, and fender.

Photograph 5.47 shows a complete fold over of the metal on the right side of the hood. Note the larger impact area on the fender. This impact

**Photograph 5.41** Long three-quarter view of the right side of the vehicle.

**Photograph 5.42** Close-up view of the right side and grille and bumper.

extends up into the hood and pushes the metal over onto itself, showing clearly the direction of impact.

**Photograph 5.43** Close-up view of the right side fender and hood from the rear.

Metal folds are also useful in determining when a vehicle has rolled over and in what direction and possibly how long it stayed in that position. The number of road abrasions on the metal is an indicator of this. The deeper the abrasion is, the longer the slide time in that position. Sometimes there will be two or three different directions of road abrasions on a vehicle's surface. Each of these must be located and plotted for angle and direction of slide.

Many times the on-scene investigator sees a fold mark and an abrasion under the fold. This indicates that the abrasion occurred first followed by an impact that folded the metal over on itself. When the metal is folded over, the vehicle then slides over the depression of the fold and the scratches show on top of the folded metal. These are clear indicators that impact occurred first and then the vehicle slid over onto the deformed area at a later time.

## Paint Transfers

Paint is transferred from one surface to the other during the impact phase of the accident. In each collision where the metal is undergoing elastic deformation, it generates a small amount of heat. This heat is sufficient to cause the paint on both surfaces to soften to the point where they are deposited on both surfaces. As a generalization, a paint transfer starts as a small thin line and increases in width and thickness along the direction of the transfer. The end is usually abrupt with a full width and thickness. This is not always true in a sideswipe or glancing impact.

**Photograph 5.44** Close-up view of the damaged right front fender and right front door.

Photographs 5.48 and 5.49 show both paint transfers and metal folds. The metal fold is so severe that it ripped open the sheet metal of the door. Note the paint on the outside edge of the outside rearview mirror as well as the interior of the dent. Close examination of the paint transfer shows that it starts out small on the right side of the photograph and gets wider and thicker toward the left side of the photograph. Note how the paint ends abruptly at the left edge of the dent. This indicates that the impact started at the right side and went to the left. The metal was deformed and pulled back on itself so quickly that it tore itself apart trying to conform to the shape that was striking it. The tear also indicates that the metal was not drawn slowly into that shape so it would have time to stretch and conform; it was pulled and pushed rapidly causing the tear. Photographs 5.50 and 5.51 show a paint transfer from a sideswipe. Note that there is no denting of the metal on a paint transfer that ends at the trim ring around the taillight lens.

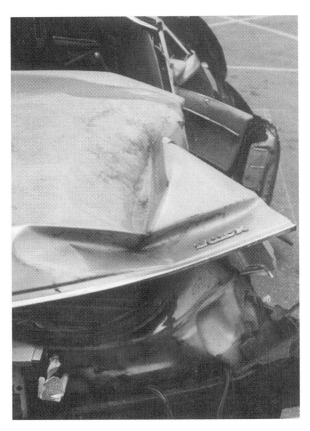

**Photograph 5.45** Metal folds in a trunk lid.

Photograph 5.52 shows a rub stripe transfer mark. The mark is straight and has no curve to it, as a tire would leave. Again there is no deformation. Note several smaller marks to the rear of the large thicker mark. These are due to the striking vehicle bouncing at the end of the motion between the two vehicles.

Paint transfers are important in multiple impact situations. In some cases the paint transfer may reveal multiple colors in the same transfer. This has been used to show that the vehicle had been in a previous accident or it was stolen and repainted. In either case, that is a clue to the investigator to look more closely at the vehicle. There could have been a bad repair job such as poor welds that broke free at the time of the initial or secondary impact. The parting of metal in such a quick manner does not absorb energy but exposes the occupants to more and possibly severe injuries.

## Weld or Base Metal Separation and Rust

There are some accidents where the struck vehicle has undergone an enormous amount of deformation, but the collision was low speed and the vehicle

**Photograph 5.46** Rear three-quarter view of the right rear quarter panel.

should not have sustained such damage. There are several reasons why such deformations occur: (1) the vehicle has been repaired from a previous accident and it was not done properly; (2) spot welds were improperly placed too close to the edge of the metal or are missing; (3) fillets or other supporting brackets were not installed at all; or (4) the good metal was welded to poor metal that did not hold in a low-speed impact. Also bad or poor welds can occur when spot welder tips are not properly cleaned and shaped.

Other problems include an insufficient number of welds at specific locations as specified by the manufacturer, or the metal not properly located before welding (i.e., one piece of metal did not sufficiently overlap the second piece as it should have when spot welded). Photograph 5.53 shows the inner hood separated from the outer hood. Note the poor condition and placement of the welds.

Another reason for deformation is the amount of rusting the vehicle has undergone previous to the accident. Surface rust is not a true indicator of the condition of the body of the vehicle. The on-scene investigator must look under the vehicle as well as under the hood and inside the trunk. This also means picking up the carpets or other material in the vehicle to see if rust has accumulated there. The same must be done inside the trunk. The carpeting must

**Photograph 5.47** Complete fold over of the metal on the right side of the hood.

be lifted to determine if or where the rusting has started, and the depth and the location of the rust pattern must be determined. It is not unusual in the northern climates to see a hole underneath a carpet near a wheel well.

The loss of sheet metal thickness due to rusting results in a loss of energy absorption of the vehicle at impact. Deforming sheet metal absorbs energy. The thinner the sheet metal, the less energy is absorbed.

*Commentary: Taking a paper clip and bending it back and forth until it breaks easily demonstrates this principle. It takes several bends before it happens. Now take a heavy-duty paper clip and try the same thing. It takes considerably longer and it may not fracture because the metal work hardens and takes more energy to bend it each time.*

The less energy absorbed, the more the vehicle will be deformed, until it literally compresses into a flat object at the point of impact. Vehicles are designed to deform at specific places and with specific rates of deformations. Too much deformation intrudes on the occupant's compartment, which

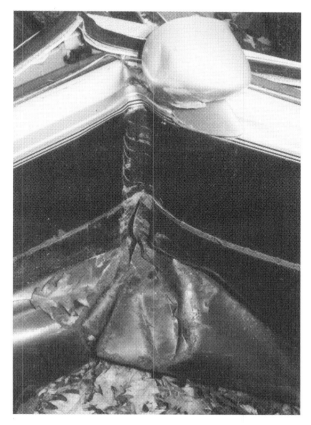

**Photograph 5.48** Both a metal fold and a paint transfer.

produces severe to fatal injuries. Insufficient metal deformation subjects the occupants to forces greater than the restraint system can protect the occupant against, and the occupants sustain injuries from the restraint system.

## Scrapes, Gouges, and Scratches

It is necessary to make a good photographic record of the scrapes, gouges, and scratches on the vehicle exterior. Scrapes can be due to an impact, or they can occur during a rollover and subsequent sliding of the vehicle along a hard surface such as a street or vertical concrete barrier. Many times a vehicle changes direction during a slide. The investigator knows this by the direction of the scratches. The depth of the scratches also shows the length of time that particular portion of the vehicle was in contact with the surface on which it was sliding.

Heavier objects such as larger stones or heavy pieces of metal left on the road can make scrapes on the vehicle as it slides along. Gouges are usually

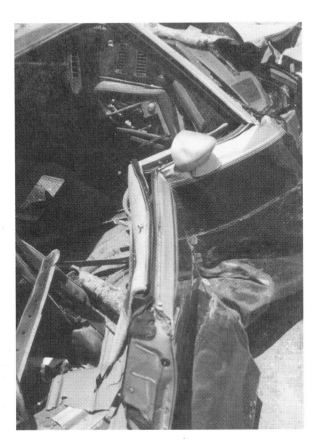

**Photograph 5.49** Metal folds in two directions.

of the puncture or ripping type. Suspension components or engine parts that have come loose from a vehicle have caused gouges and tears during a collision. Many times the rough edges of the "W"-shaped posts used for highway signs can cause a ripping or tearing of the sheet metal of the vehicle.

The shape of the tear can tell the investigator the direction of impact. A tear is usually a teardrop shape with the small end at the beginning of the tear. As the collision continues the tear gets wider and wider until the metal completely separates from itself or the collision stops.

Rips or gouges usually just penetrate the sheet metal pushing the edge of the hole inward. The gouge or rip may get larger than the original hole and takes the shape of the object causing the damage.

Large, heavy-duty trucks have lug nuts that extend beyond the surface of the tire rim. If that truck were in a skid, had its front wheels locked, and collided with a car, the lug nuts would penetrate the sheet metal of the car, causing a distinct puncture pattern.

**Photograph 5.50** Long view of a paint transfer without metal damage.

**Photograph 5.51** Paint transfer from a sideswipe.

*Commentary*: Consider the case where a large tow truck was towing a Thunderbird from a location in the country to a garage in the city. The tow truck driver approached a blind intersection and did not slow down, even though he was aware of the intersection. A vehicle crossing the path of the tow truck came from behind a small hill that had blocked the view of the tow truck

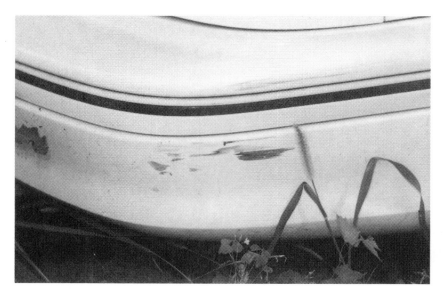

**Photograph 5.52** Rub stripe transfer mark.

**Photograph 5.53** Inner hood separated from the outer hood panel.

*operator. The truck driver locked up his front wheels and skidded sideways into the side of the car, leaving a large and very distinct lug nut hole puncture pattern in the door of the vehicle.*

## Aluminum vs. Steel Wheels

Many vehicles today have aluminum wheels. These types of wheels are more easily damaged but also retain the damage better than the older steel wheels. Two vehicles that are sliding past one another as a sideswipe show scratches or some gouges in the metal of both rims that the investigator is able to locate and determine the direction of the impact.

**Photograph 5.54** Wheel rim and tire damage.

During a head-on collision the rims of one or sometimes both vehicles will show deformation extending from the rim to the axle in a radial-type pattern. Due to the design of the rim it bends inward toward the center. Some investigators have not been able to determine whether the rim damage was from another vehicle or from the curb as the vehicle ran up over it and onto the sidewalk. Nonmountable curb damage always involves both the inside and the outside of the rim. Curb damage is quite different from other types of damage in that the deformation is broad and very rounded. Vehicle-to-vehicle impacts are not. They usually involve only the inside or the outside of a rim, depending on the direction of impact. Steel wheels, on the other hand, require a heavy impact to cause the same amount of damage. Photographs 5.54 and 5.55 show wheel rim and tire damage. Note that the rim shows a relatively small flat spot and the tire is blown out just above it. The severe impact caused the blowout and the rim damage. The other rim damage was due to a second impact.

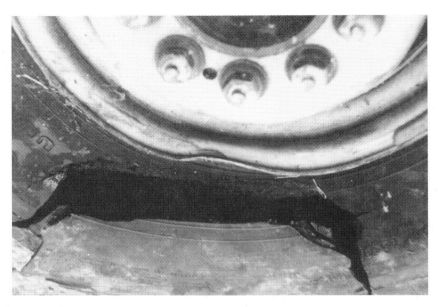

**Photograph 5.55** Close-up view of a wheel rim and tire damage.

When vehicles lock up their wheels and slide sideways, the tire rolls under and the wheels move over the top of the rubber tires so that the tread is no longer in contact with the road surface. This is evident by the rub marks on the sidewalls of the tires.

If the sliding vehicle has enough velocity, it moves completely over the top of the tire and the edge of the rim comes in contact with the road surface. The rims scrape and sometimes gouge the concrete or asphalt surface of the road. The rims are in turn damaged by the road surface. The keen-eyed, on-scene investigator can see traces of aluminum that are left on the road surface after the sliding action. These indicate the direction of travel of the wheel and tire during sliding. Unfortunately, they do not stay very long on the concrete surface because they are adhered to the upper most surface only and are easily rubbed away by traffic and weather conditions. A relatively small, single location of the grinding of the rim edge indicates that the tire was locked up when it was sliding, but only for a short period of time. The peripheral length of ground edge of the rim is an indicator of the velocity the vehicle had as it started its sideward maneuver. Grinding a third to a half of the tire rim indicates that the tire was at some time partially rotating because it would be impossible to grind that much of the rim during a single sliding maneuver. Of course, if the entire rim shows grinding marks, then it was rotating for the entire time it was sliding.

Steel wheels have a small hubcap to protect the lug nuts or a larger wheel cover. These wheel covers have been known to pop off during an impact or a sideway slide of the vehicle. The wheel covers are usually made of aluminum and damage easily. Unfortunately, they may roll for several feet along the highway and it takes a little effort to find them. Once the wheel covers are found, however, they can supply another part of the accident puzzle, such as impact damage from a sideswipe, puncture marks, or any witness marks that occurred during the collision. Never forget to check for all the details of the accident however small or seemingly immaterial.

*Commentary: One case showed the need to check the details of all the vehicle components. A wheel cover was missing when the left front tire came off a truck. When it was found the grease cup was embedded in the wheel cover itself, indicating the entire wheel left the spindle at once and then impacted the fence post later in the accident.*

When a vehicle slides sideward in an unmowed field, the tire separates slightly from the rim but not off the bead. During the separation time, the tall grasses and weeds get pushed into the opening and are pinched between the tire and the rim. As the tire moves across the field, it breaks the grasses free from the shaft and they stay embedded between the tire and the rim.

The weather often washes away any scuffing of the tire sidewall, but the tufts of grass reveal to the investigator that the tire was sliding on a grassy surface. The wheel assembly may or may not have been rotating at the time, depending on where and how much grass is located in the rim/tire interface. Grass embedded along a major portion of the rim may be considered a sign of a rotating tire for some period of time.

## Tires

Every part of the vehicle can help to solve the accident puzzle. The tires are no exception. The tread area shows a flat spot when a tire has been locked up during a skid or yaw. It also shows the direction of the yaw or skid by the witness marks on the tread when matched to the position on the vehicle.

When a vehicle is sliding sideways and the tire sidewall gets tucked under the rim, the tire shows abrasions or severe scrubbing of the sidewall. This is true whether it occurs on the roadway, on a gravel shoulder, through a field, or on a lawn.

The rubber surface is marred in some manner. The deeper marring occurs on the roadbed surface as opposed to the grassy surfaces. The accident investigation form shown in Figure 8.1 has a special place to note the condition of the tires. The observations should include the general condition and the damage such as cuts, blowouts, air leaks before and after the collision, tread depth, and tire sizes.

A condition overlooked by many investigators is the tire size and width. This is especially true with older vehicles. Many drivers do not pay attention or do not care about the size of a tire when purchasing a replacement. One tire on a car that is a size smaller or larger changes the way a vehicle handles. Tires that are too wide rub on an inner fender or even a portion of the suspension during a steering maneuver. A smaller tire rotates faster than the others and as a result wears faster and gives the driver problems handling the vehicle during an emergency.

If the investigator is lucky enough to have photographs taken at the scene by the police, it is a good idea to check for two items: (1) were any tires flat, or aired out at the scene, and (2) have the tires and/or wheels been changed by persons unknown between the accident and the inspection? This is important because of the possible information the tire may contain for the reconstructionist.

*Commentary: I have had a person or persons unknown change the tires and/or rims before or during the time the vehicle reached the holding areas. The reason I say unknown is because no one ever tells you what happened. "It came in that way," is a favorite answer.*

Blowouts and cuts must also be carefully examined. Scene photographs play an important part in this portion of the investigation. An examination of the rim can confirm the damage to the tire. If only the rim or the tire is damaged, then something is wrong. This possible error must be noted in the inspection report. It is necessary to follow up when finding such details as tire changes have occurred. These details could be very important to the accident investigation.

## Missing or Misplaced Components

When viewing the vehicle, either the exterior or the interior, be sure to note any missing parts. These are the details that must be dealt with at both the scene and the subsequent vehicle inspections. Is the windshield or rear window missing? Has it been broken out from the inside or outside of the vehicle? Are the pieces of broken glass on the highway or inside the vehicle? Did an emergency crew remove it during the occupants' extractions?

Make it a point to determine how the windshield was removed from the vehicle. Locate it and place it on a white surface if possible. The concrete roadbed can serve as a white background. Photograph the windshield and look for any head impact stars. Look for damage to the edges from being pried out by the emergency response people. Check the peripheral edge of the glass for any adhesive that holds the glass to the "A" posts. Under Federal Motor Vehicle Safety Standards (FMVSS) the windshields must have a certain percentage of retention of the peripheral rim. If the adhesive is spotty or missing in several places, it could easily have been pushed out when the occupant was ejected from the vehicle.

Photographs 5.56 and 5.57 show two views of a fractured windshield in place in a vehicle. The first one was taken without a cover to block out the sunlight. The camera was tilted to bring out the fracture lines. They are still not quite distinct enough to determine what caused them. Photograph 5.54 shows the same windshield photographed straight on with a cover to block out the light. It can easily be seen that the upper right fracture is a true head impact star with a tissue smear leading up to it. The lower left is a stress fracture.

## Underside of Vehicle and Use of Tow Trucks

Check for undercarriage damage by having a tow truck lift the vehicle and take pictures of the underside components. Remember the gouges that were made on the road surface? Now is the time to check the underside of the vehicle for confirming witness marks. The underside of the vehicle shows scratches, some deeper than others, and bits of concrete; however, more readily discernible are chunks of asphalt that remain embedded between components under the vehicle. The length, direction, and depth of the scratches and gouges coincide with the damage seen on the road. The stiffer and heavier portions of the underside of the vehicle cause the gouges.

Look for broken or fractured components that show witness marks such as asphalt on the fractured surface or concrete dust. This confirms that the fracture occurred prior to the gouging and other additional vehicular movements.

In some accidents the underside of a vehicle may be driven downward so hard that components are broken off. The detail-minded investigator first sees what is missing or broken and then locates the component if it is not connected to the vehicle, and determines what happened to it. Detailed evidence such as this allows the reconstruction of the accident at a later date. The more data available for analysis, the better the reconstruction is.

## Fluid Leaks

Today's automobiles contain many different types of fluids. The investigator must be familiar with all these from the standpoint of color, smell, viscosity, location in the vehicle, and what effect the loss of the fluid would mean on the operation of the vehicle. Brake fluid is usually clear and thin in viscosity, and smells somewhat sweet. Engine oil is dark yellow or black depending on how long since it was changed, and it feels and tastes greasy.

Transmission fluid is pink and not as thin as brake fluid. Antifreeze is usually green and is almost as thin as water. Under extremely cold temperatures, it becomes thicker. Gasoline is usually colorless, has a distinctive odor, and is thinner than water. Diesel fuel is quite dark, has a distinctive odor,

**Photograph 5.56** Fractured windshield in place, without a cover to block out the sunlight.

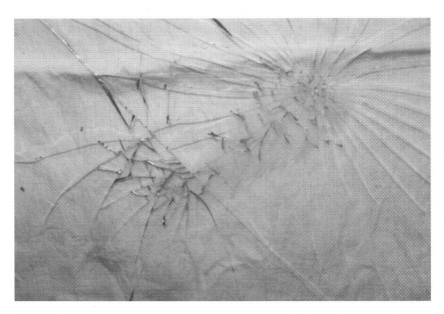

**Photograph 5.57** The same windshield photographed straight on with a cover to block the light.

and is heavier than gasoline. Oil, diesel fuel, and antifreeze do not dry up very quickly and leave a residue that is easy to spot at the scene or in photographs taken at the scene. The location of the fluids at the scene indicates the direction of vehicle movement after impact and gives an approximate location of the point of impact. Swirling motions of fluids on the road surface are indicators of the rotation of the vehicle after initial impact.

Remember that all roads are crowned from the center to the edges by approximately two degrees to allow the rain to run off the traveled surface. Unfortunately, the fluids from the vehicular accident will do the same thing. The investigator must be aware of this and take it into account during the inspection process.

Fuel tank damage is becoming rare these days unless there is a massive rear-end impact that destroys the vehicle. In these cases the tanks are ripped apart. Some vehicle manufacturers are including bladders inside the fuel tanks to control the fuel after impact and keep the fire hazard to a minimum. The inquisitive investigator is interested in any fuel tank damage, especially small cracks or punctures to determine if the condition existed prior to the accident sequence. This damage can be accident induced but not to the point of tank rupture.

**Commentary:** *An example of fuel tank puncture was seen in a case in the southern United States, which involved a fire as well as heavy damage from being rolled, pushed, or driven off a mountain road. A detailed examination of the fuel tank showed that there was a puncture in the tank that was the exact shape of the sharp end of a tire iron and had a patch over it.*

*Examination of the patching material revealed that in a fuel fire the material would melt. The hole in the tank was punched in after the vehicle was pushed off the road; and after the fire, the owners came back and patched the tank.*

## Headlights, Taillights, and Side Marker Lights

Modern motor vehicles use light bulbs in a 12-volt system that serves as the the main power source for the reflective headlight, taillight, and side marker lights. The filaments inside the bulbs glow a dull red when electricity is applied to them. This makes the filament wire much softer than it would be when no electricity was applied.

Photograph 5.58 shows a normal brake light bulb. During a collision the filament stretches in the direction that the accident occurred if the lights were on prior to the collision. Many investigators use the deformed filament to determine if the headlights and/or taillights were on at the time of a collision. The investigator must be very careful when using this method of determining if the lights were on at the time of the collision. The main reason is that the point of collision must be very close to the headlights or taillights for the stretching to occur to any degree. Photograph 5.59 shows a rear taillight bulb with the one filament stretched but not fractured.

Dual filament taillights have separate filaments for the brake lights and another for the normal running lights. These brake light filaments also show this distortion after the impact if the brakes have been applied before the collision. If the collision is severe enough, the heated filament fractures. Photograph 5.60 shows a fractured filament. In some instances a cold filament may also fracture during a collision.

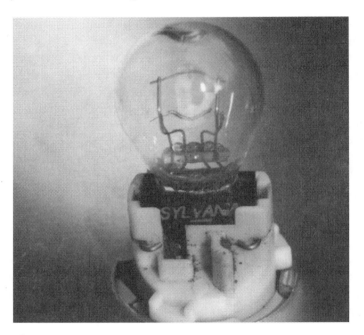

**Photograph 5.58** Normal brake light bulb.

There is a definite difference between a cold fracture and a heated filament fracture. A cold filament fracture has sharp edges at the ends. A heated filament fracture has a rounded globular like end. This is due to the fact that the metal is hot at the time of the fracture and the warm metal takes the most economical form, which is that of a sphere.

***Commentary:*** *It is difficult to determine if a light bulb had a cold fracture prior to an accident, especially if the direction of the collision is different from the direction of the stretch or fracture of the filament wire. All investigators must be very careful not to use this as the only method for determining if the lights were on prior to the collision.*

Whenever possible the investigator should use redundant methods to determine his/her opinion. In this example, the investigator should check the

**Photograph 5.59** Rear taillight bulb with the one filament stretched but not fractured.

**Photograph 5.60** Fractured filament.

position of the headlight switch. If the headlight switch is pulled away from the instrument panel, that would corroborate the fractured filament wire as meaning that the headlights were on at the time of the collision. Most wire filament experts agree that the point of the collision must be within 12 to 18 in. of the headlights. Anything greater than that leaves significant doubt as to whether the deformed or fractured wire filament was disabled during the collision.

When removing the light bulbs from the vehicle the investigator must take great care. It is necessary that each bulb position in the vehicle be marked and photographed in place before removal. The bulbs should be placed with the metal ends pushed into the bottoms of Styrofoam cups. This protects the bulb from external shock. Each cup can be marked with the position of the bulb as it is removed. A second cup can be placed over the first to protect the bulb.

Close-up photographs should be taken with the bulb in place and then later with the bulbs mounted on Styrofoam cups using a close-up lens and indirect lighting. Special tools might be required to remove the trim rings or reflective lenses on taillights to photograph the bulbs in place. Removal of the bulbs is usually accomplished from inside the vehicle, in the trunk area. Videotaping of the removal process is always helpful in showing the investigator's client and the opposing clients the procedure that was carried out when obtaining these bulbs and the condition of the light assembly prior to removal.

## Unexplained Damage

In every accident there is damage to the vehicles that is difficult if not impossible to explain. If the impact was to the right side of the car and the left front window is missing, look where the glass pieces have landed. If the damage is inside the vehicle, then it could have been caused by the emergency service (EMS) people trying to extricate the occupants, or even a rock thrown through the window after the collision (look for the rock too). If there are few or no glass pieces inside the vehicle, then it may be possible that during the accident sequence the driver's head struck the side window and fractured it and the pieces fell into the street. The investigator needs to check the medical data for the driver to see if he/she sustained an impact to the head. There are many types of unexplained damage. The investigator with the inquisitive mind and an eye for detail makes note of all particulars and follows up on all of them trying to find an answer.

## Vehicle Deterioration and Rusting

The physical condition of a vehicle structure is a major concern in an accident. Rust and deterioration have major bearing on the crashworthiness of the vehicle and the safety of the occupants.

Vehicle sheet metal, especially in the unitized body design, is the energy-absorbing structure of the vehicle. If welds are bad or missing, the vehicle does not act as a unit as it was designed to do. The failure of one component affects the entire structure.

The same is true if the sheet metal is rusted at the time of the accident. The more rust there is, the less energy-absorbing capabilities the vehicle has. This is because rusted metal does not absorb the energy of impact and the vehicle suffers more crush or deformation than it should; as a result there is more intrusion into the passenger compartment and a greater degree of injury to the occupants. Many investigators use vehicle deformation to determine, or approximate, the "delta V" or change in velocity the vehicle underwent during impact.

The investigator must remember that the rusty condition increases the deformation and gives a false impression as to the change in vehicle velocity. Make extensive notes on the rust condition of every vehicle inspected. These data can be helpful on future cases, because a pattern emerges from the information collected.

*Commentary: There is no rule of thumb as to how much rust reduces the energy-absorbing capabilities. The more the rust, the less energy is absorbed.*

*Time on the job looking at hundreds of accidents is the only way to learn what you can use to assist in your determinations of speed.*

# Vehicle Interiors

# 6

"I make a point of never having any prejudices, of following docilely where ever fact."

**Sherlock Holmes**
*The Reigate Squires*

## Collisions — Occupant

As mentioned in Chapter 4, a vehicular accident consists of two, three, and sometimes four collisions. The second collision takes place when the unbelted occupant strikes some component or components inside the vehicle, usually before the vehicle comes to rest. The rest of the accident scene and the exterior of the vehicle show the investigator what the vehicle did immediately preimpact, at the point of collision, and post-impact. The vehicle interior, on the other hand, yields information to the investigator concerning the components that the occupants struck during the second collision. This information allows a biomechanics expert to match the occupants' injuries with the interior component damage if possible. In general, the investigator must look for the usual dents, dings, and broken plastic parts of the interior components. The more subtle the witness marks are, the harder they are to decipher, especially after the vehicle has been allowed to stay out in the weather for any period of time.

Information is in the form of witness marks left on the various interior components and can include smudges from human skin (sometimes referred to as skin or tissue smears), dings, dents, blood spatter, strands of a human hair caught in various cracks or crevices, shoe polish smears, clothing transfers from the impact, cracked glass, or bent or broken knobs within the instrument panel. The job and duty of the vehicle investigator are to locate, classify, manage, and report each piece of evidence inside the vehicle.

## Obvious Interior Deformation

The first and most obvious source of witness marks is the windshield.

### Windshields

Every investigator should know the history of the development of the present-day windshield to perform an accurate investigation. Newton's second law of motion — "a body in motion will tend to stay in motion until acted on by an outside force" — acts on the occupants during the collision. Milliseconds before a collision occurs the occupants and the vehicle are traveling at the same speed. When the vehicle is subjected to a collision with another object, its forward motion ceases but the occupants continue with the same velocity, obeying Newton's second law of motion, and stay in motion until acted on by some external force.

This means that a belted or unbelted occupant continues to move in the same direction as he/she did prior to the collision. In a frontal collision, the occupants slide forward on the seat toward the windshield pivoting about their heels, which are on the toe board of the floor pan. Fully restrained (lap and shoulder belts, and air bag) occupants move forward until they contact and take up the slack in their restraint system and start dissipating their energy and stretching their restraint belts and impacting the now inflated air bags. This continues during a collision until the occupant's kinetic energy is totally dissipated, moving forward without impacting or only slightly impacting any interior components until the vehicle completely comes to rest.

Unbelted occupants continue to move forward on the seat, pivoting about the ankle, the same as a belted occupant, toward the windshield. Their knees strike the lower instrument panel, dissipating a portion of their kinetic energy. This initial contact causes their bodies to rotate upward toward the windshield in a curvilinear movement, lifting them up from the seat and continuing forward. (No reference to airbags is made here, due to location of the bag and size and location of occupant. Motion after impact with the bag can take on a variety of directions and velocities.)

Depending on the seated height of the occupant, his/her head may or may not strike the header, the steel portion of the roof that connects the roof to the rest of the vehicle. If the forehead misses the header, then it or the occupant's face itself may strike the inside glass surface of the windshield. This usually results in a smear on the inside glass surface before the glass fractures. The smear is the initial point of contact with the inner glass of the windshield.

In the early 1930s Ford Motor Company pioneered the use of laminated safety glass for windshields. The following is excerpted*:

---

* Excerpted from Reference 1. With permission from Wayne State University.

Cellulose nitrate was laminated between two sheets of annealed glass to produce a shatter-resistant windshield. Unfortunately the cellulose nitrate interlayer was unstable, and discolored and became brittle with prolonged use. In the late 1930s a new material was developed for use as an interlayer, polyvinyl butyral. It had higher impact strength and did not discolor or embrittle with age. In 1962 the Automotive Crash Injury group of Cornell University published listings of the major causes of occupant injuries during automotive collisions. Based on a number of occupants exposed to the hazard, 17.1% are injured by the windshield. During the late 1950s and early 1960s numerous tests were conducted to determine the mechanism of injury due to the windshield. Head form drop tests showed that at speeds above 13 mph, the head form would consistently bulge the windshield and then penetrate the glass sandwich as the interlayer was torn.

The penetration exposed the head form to shards of glass. As the head form tried to return, the bulge in the glass collapsed, reducing the diameter of the hole that the head form had made going through the windshield.

This prevented the head form from returning and produced what was called the "horse collar" effect.

Tests conducted at Wayne State University Biomechanics Research Laboratories, with instrumented human cadavers and anthropomorphic dummies, showed that once penetration occurred and the head was returning back into the hole, it tended to impact the lower edge of the hole causing severe lacerations and bone fractures. During this forward and return trip the head would many times oscillate in the plane of the glass causing several distinct lines of facial lacerations. Safety personnel generally agreed that windshield injuries could be decreased if the penetration could be reduced without increasing the deceleration levels beyond human tolerance levels. In 1962, Dr. G. Rodloff demonstrated that a dynamic improvement in penetration resistance resulted when the interlayer thickness was doubled; its moisture content increased from 0.5% to 1.1%. Previous windshield constructions had the bond between the glass and the interlayer as strong as possible.

This assured the maximum amount of glass retention when broken but only a few thousands of an inch of interlayer was available to stretch. Therefore the interlayer would fail in tension. When the interlayer moisture content was increased to an optimum value, the bond strength was weakened to the point where the glass would separate from the interlayer at the broken edge of the glass.

This allowed a longer length of plastic laminate to stretch allowing a deeper and larger bulge to absorb greater energy levels without the inner later being torn due to high tensile strengths.[1]

Figure 6.1 shows the difference between the 15-mm tight-bonded interlayer and the improved 30-mm high-moisture interlayer, which allowed more stretch of the interlayer plastic.

STANDARD LAMINATED GLASS

Tight bond between glass and plastic interlayer permits only a small amount of plastic to stretch, allowing easy penetration

IMPROVED LAMINATED GLASS

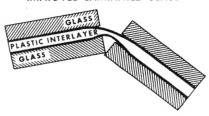

Loose bond between the glass and plastic interlayer permits considerable amount of plastic to stretch, thus reducing the liklihood of interlayer failure

**Figure 6.1** The difference between the 15 mm tight bonded interlayer and the improved 30 mm high moisture interlayer

This research by Ford Motor Company along with many other works caused the federal government to establish the new high penetration resistant (HPR) windshield as the standard for all vehicles. It is made up of two layers of glass with a 30-mm plastic interlayer between them. All three layers are bonded together to form a "sandwich" of protection for the human head. Both glass layers are made of thin glass. The inner glass is made of annealed or soft glass that has the stresses removed. The outer layer is heat tempered on the outside surface. This tempering toughens the surface to damage from stones and other debris, which minimizes fracture or breakage.

Due to the smaller pieces of glass and the deep pocketing effect during impact, the face and head are not subjected to the severe disfiguring or fatal lacerations as previously seen. The occupant walks away with just minor scratches to the skin that heal without any other medical action other than just cleaning and removal of the debris.

*Commentary: There were several other attempts at improving the HPR design for a few years after acceptance by the federal government. One glass manufacturer tried to chemically strengthen the outer layer to make it tougher. It worked, but not significantly better than heat tempering, and it was more expensive. A second improvement was to have a stress riser built into the glass surface. This allowed the glass to break at a predetermined level and location. It was hoped this would help to minimize the possible effects of concussion due to impact with the windshield. Again, it was not significantly different than the HPR system.*

There are three types of windshield damage. The first type of damage involves stress cracks that are caused during the collision when the glass is struck on one of the edges. The glass is pushed sideways and cracks emanate from the point contact.

The second type comes from impact to the outer layer by a rock or some other foreign object that is thrown or dropped from an overpass onto and sometimes through the windshield. This, in some cases, produces a "stellar pattern" that is on the outside surface only. The fractures do not go through to the interlayer unless there is a complete penetration by the foreign object.

The third and last type of damage is the impact of the human head. This impact causes a bull's-eye or stellar pattern to the windshield, which starts from the inside and as its energy level is increased it penetrates to the outside layer. Damage occurs to both layers of glass in the form of a circular (stellar) pattern, with cracks radiating from the center. If there is a low-speed impact, then there is little or no pocketing of the windshield sandwich. If the speed at impact is very low, there may only be a few cracks and no stellar pattern at all.

Photograph 6.1 shows a windshield with only stress cracks. Note that there is no pattern and the cracks emanate from the point where the stresses were imposed. In this case, they were imposed on the upper left or driver side of the vehicle due to a side impact collision. Many investigators mistake the point where the stresses are imposed as the head impact area. This is due to the severe cracking of the glass at the point where the glass is broken up into tiny pieces, and it is difficult to determine the point of origin of the impact. Stress cracks are due to an outside force being applied, usually at or near the edges. Therefore, an impact on an outside edge of the glass is almost always a stress-induced impact. The only exception would be a pedestrian impact.

There have been instances where the pedestrian has struck the upper, or outside edge, of the glass producing a stellar pattern impact, which has been mistaken for a stress crack. In those cases the investigator must look for other evidence such as the windshield being pushed inward from a shoulder or hip impact as the pedestrian is rolled over the windshield and onto the road surface. Hair, blood, or tissue being smeared or caught on the edges of the glass would also show that the impact was not a brick- or rock-type impact. With stellar-type impacts to windshields, the investigator should look for tissue smudges or hair transfer on the inner glass surface. This smudge may look like a smear that usually starts above the center of the stellar pattern, is somewhat rounded and greasy at the start, and tapers down until tissue adheres to the glass surface. Depending on the size of the bulge, hair and sometimes surrounding tissue are caught between the edges of the fractured glass.

The stellar fracture and also the pocket of glass that holds the head both grow in size and in depth as the vehicle speed at impact increases. The pocket

**Photograph 6.1** A windshield with only stress cracks.

caused by the head impact is made up of small pieces of glass. These pieces act as wedges and open up during the impact; as the head returns inside the vehicle, the pieces come together and pinch the tissue or hair off the head or face. A piece of tissue or strand of hair taken from the vehicle can later be matched up with the missing tissue or hair of the occupant. If a positive identification is required, then laboratory tests can be conducted matching the occupant's DNA with a DNA analysis of the samples taken from the vehicle.

Determining which occupant was driving at the time of a collision many times may be dependent on what the investigator finds at the scene. Matching procedures such as those just described can be very important, especially when one of the occupants dies at the scene. Photographs must be taken of the stellar pattern from both the inside and the outside of the vehicle. Measure the location from the side and the top of the glass surround molding. This measurement is important during the reconstruction to show the seated height of the occupant and also to show if the occupant was unbelted at the time of the accident.

*Commentary: There have been several research programs conducted in various parts of the world to reduce the severity of lacerations resulting from windshield impacts. The main thrust of this research has been through the use of thinner glass in the windshield sandwich, usually in the area of 2.5 to 3 mm thick. Those investigators interested in further information should consult the* Transactions of the Society of Automotive Engineers (SAE) *for 1969, 1970, and 1973; and also the 1973* Conference of the American Association of Automotive Medicine.

It must be remembered by the investigator that the windshield is a part of the total restraint system because it keeps the occupant from being ejected from the vehicle. The Federal Motor Vehicle Safety Standards (FMVSS) require that the windshield be fixed in the frame in such a manner that after a collision, 90% of the windshield is still fixed or bonded to the frame of the vehicle. A great deal of research has gone into the bonding system presently being used on cars and trucks today.

Windshields have caused concussions in some people. If the investigator has a case where there is a report of an occupant with a concussion, do not rule out the windshield as a source of the concussion, without a detailed and thorough investigation of the windshield itself.

Front windshield vehicle glass is different than side or a rear window glass. As previously described, the front windshield is made of two layers of glass that are bonded together. The inside layer is made from annealed glass. The outer layer is made from heat-treated tempered glass. Side windows and rear windows are made of a single layer of glass that has been heat tempered to give it a toughened inner and outer surface.

This glass is thinner than that used in the past and allows the automotive designer to curve the glass to fit the vehicle "tumblehome" (curving inward) design. The side and rear window glass requires a greater impact to fracture it unless it is struck very near the edge. It then shatters into many tiny pieces that produce only small lacerations when striking human tissue. There have been occasions where the occupant's head has struck the side windows and has resulted in a concussion. These are readily verified by tissue smears on the inside surface. Be careful not to confuse tissue smears with hair oil from a driver or passenger resting his/her head on the glass window during a trip. Smears are usually shaped like a teardrop and are smudgy. Hair oil smears are usually round and hairlines can be seen on close examination. Rear windows are made of the same glass as the side windows and have the same properties.

## Rear Windows

Rear windows play a part in rear impacts. If the front occupant seats collapse rearward then the occupants can move rearward toward the rear window. If the occupant's head strikes the rear window, the impact can cause the head to be pushed forward while the remainder of the body is moving rearward.

This dual action has fractured the cervical spine causing paraplegia or even quadriplegia due to the tempered glass not fracturing at a lower level of force. The greatest advantage of the tempered glass is the fact that it resists small impacts such as stones and other small foreign bodies, and when fractured it turns into tiny pieces of glass that do not produce major lacerations.

*Commentary: Many times the investigator must determine if the fractured side windows were up or down during a collision. Most side windows in today's vehicles are installed in a full frame. When the glass is in the upright position, there is a frame around the glass on all four sides.*

*If the glass was broken when it was in the up position, the frame still has very small pieces of glass stuck in it in several places. Generally, when these impacts occur, the majority of the pieces of glass are outside of the vehicle. Photographs of these fragments of glass help prove the case.*

*If the window was down, then it is necessary to spread the inner and outer door panels and look between them with a flashlight. The remainder of the glass is either in a frame or down in the bottom of the door. If the window was partially up at impact, then the pieces in the frame tell you the position of the glass at impact.*

*It is important to review any photographs taken at the scene of the accident as well as completely documented police reports, to determine the entire condition of the vehicle immediately after the accident when the investigator performs his/her inspection. The inspection may take place within a few days to upward of a year or more from the original date of the accident. The condition of the vehicle can change dramatically during even a short period of time. The vehicle glass can especially change due to children throwing stones or dropping large heavy objects on it.*

If the side and rear windows have been broken by foreign objects thrown from the outside of the vehicle, then the glass fragments are inside the vehicle. If the glass was broken from the inside, then the fragments are outside of the vehicle. There are, however, those rare occasions when a collision is at such an angle that the glass fragments are at least partially driven inside the vehicle. Those cases require an investigator to search the scene for tempered glass fragments to ensure the mode of glass fracture.

*Commentary: Consider the case where a young girl was the right front passenger in a vehicle that was struck on the right side. The right side window fractured and drove the glass particles into and through her cheek, lodging them in her throat. The paramedics were able to remove them at the scene.*

## Instrument Panels

### Upper Surfaces

Instrument panels were originally designed to hold the wiring and subassemblies of the gauges and other instruments for the driver's use in operating the vehicle and not to absorb the energy of impact. Not until scientists started to research and analyze accidents did they discover that unbelted occupants slammed into the panel with their chests or abdomen during a collision. Experimental testing with the use of the lap belt showed that the occupant's pelvic girdle was held in the seat and prevented him/her from sliding off the seat and into the panel. However, the upper torso and head were allowed to rotate forward about the hips. These actions allowed the head to come crashing down on whatever was in front of the occupant.

Instrument panels were made of metal with no padding. The relatively strong and unpadded panel caused severe head and facial injuries. One of the early design changes was to move the panel forward, giving the upper torso and head room to swing forward and miss the panel during a collision.

With all these design changes there were other problems brought to the forefront. It was found that some of the occupants' upper torsos rotated down toward the floor and their heads struck the floor pan with great force, causing severe injuries. This was demonstrated by research done at Holman Air Force Base by the 6571st Aeromedical Research Laboratory in 1969 and 1970.

*Commentary: Those interested in further information can review the* Fourteenth Stapp Car Crash Conference *transcript published in 1970 by the SAE.*

The next step was to pad the upper surface and forward edge of the panels. The forward edge or eyebrow of the panel was more heavily padded than the rest of the panel. This helped greatly but the padding was not always successful in reducing facial injuries due to the relatively nondeforming panels supporting it. Today, panels are still padded but not to the same degree. The panels have been designed to absorb the energy of impact from both the unbelted and belted occupant.

With the increased use of restraint systems, especially shoulder belts and air bags, the instrument panel facial injuries are bordering on being a rare incidence in a collision. The investigator must still inspect the panel for damage to the upper surface. The investigator may feel with his/her fingers a depression in the padding, but this is not always successful, because the material itself may not retain the deformation. The most reliable method is inspecting for the tissue smear. This requires a keen eye to observe such marks at various angles to the head impact.

*Commentary: I have found that Polaroid sunglasses can sometimes be of assistance in locating smears both inside and outside the vehicle. Using this smear as a starting point, place your fingers on the upper surface of the padded panel and probe along the surface of the panel. The metal or foam underneath the padding may have been deformed due to the collision.*

*The occupant's head or chest can cause this deformation. The occupant's injuries are reflected in the panel damage. A non-deformed surface many times results in a contusion on the forehead or a fracture to the facial area. The panel surface has been designed to deform at a level below that which causes a serious or life-threatening injury to the occupant at specific vehicle velocities.*

The eyebrow or extreme front edge of the instrument panel has more padding than the upper surface. This is for the protection of the unbelted occupant. Because there is not a steering wheel in front of the right front passenger, then he/she must depend on the energy-absorbing qualities of the instrument panel.

## Lower Surfaces

The lower surface of the instrument panel where the glove box is generally located is usually not padded. This is the area where the right front passenger's knees impact in an accident. On the driver's side of the vehicle, the driver may impact the lower instrument panel, which is located on either side of the steering column.

This is the first point of interaction between the unbelted occupant and the interior of the vehicle during a collision. The belted occupant may also strike the lower panel if he/she has long legs or moves the seat close to the steering wheel. The lower panel is also designed to absorb energy at a level below that which causes serious injuries to the upper leg or femur and knee–thigh–hip complex. By impacting the lower panel the occupant expends a portion of the total kinetic energy he/she had prior to the initial collision by deforming the lower panel, and has less energy to be absorbed by the restraint system and the other interior components.

The remainder of the energy must now be expended by other means. If the occupant is unbelted, he/she must rely on the energy-absorbing steering column or impacting the lower instrument panel to expend the remainder of his/her energy. If the occupant is belted, then the upper restraint system as well as the energy-absorbing steering column absorbs his/her energy, or if he/she is the right front passenger, impacting the upper instrument panel absorbs his/her energy.

Unfortunately, the more vulnerable portions of the body such as the abdomen or face and head are the areas that impact these other devices. If the occupant's energy level is greater than that which can be absorbed, he/she may suffer additional injuries that can be life threatening if not fatal.

In 1964, a series of experiments were carried out at Wayne State University to measure the forces that cause injury to the knee, thigh, and hip; and to evaluate, among other criteria, the effect padding would have on these injuries. A crash simulator was designed and built by the General Motors Research Laboratories and installed at the Wayne State University, Biomechanics Research Center. Both instrumented cadavers and anthropomorphic dummies were used in the study. The following are portions of the ground-breaking research that was done during that period*.[2]

---

* Excerpts from Reference 2. With permission from Wayne State University.

In a survey by ACIR of injury-producing rural accidents between 1953 and 1955, 55% were of the front end type (ACIR, 1961). Of these injury-producing accidents, 46% of the injuries were to the lower extremities. The instrument panel caused 22% of the "injuries of any degree" and was second only to the steering wheel in the number of injuries produced; 5% of the moderate to fatal injuries were attributed to impact to the instrument panel. In this category it ranked third, with steering wheel and ejection being first and second in that order. Kulowski's book *Accident Injuries of the Conjoined Femur* (Kulowski, 1964) points out the many injuries to the knee/thigh/hip complex are from impact to the instrument panel.

His findings — which represent a limited population — shows that out of 321 automobile injuries to the knee, thigh, and hip, 48% (155) involved the knee. He includes the supracondylar and condylar portions of the femur, patella, tibial plateau, and proximal end of the fibula in this group.

Twenty-nine per cent (91) of the 321 injuries were to the hip and buttocks, which include the acetabulum, proximal end of the femur down to the subtrochanteric level, and the adjacent pelvic area.

Twenty-three per cent (75) of the 321 involved the thigh and femoral shaft. Although the exact cause of the injuries in this series of cases is not known, it is presumed that many of them were the result of the knees striking the instrument panel.

The ACIR survey showed that occupants striking it in 23% of the cases permanently deformed the instrument panel pad. Since the incidence of instrument panel damage corresponds closely to the number of injuries, one might conclude that the force required to deform the panel is above the human tolerance level in all cases. There are, however, some accidents in which the instrument panel is deformed by knee impact without injury (noninjury accidents are not included in the ACIR survey).

It follows, then, that instrument panels are, in some instances at least, marginal from an injury-producing standpoint.

When considering whether or not a panel is safe, many variables must be remembered. Probably the most important is the part of the body striking the panel. Fractures of the facial bones occur at very low force levels (Patrick, Lange, and Hodgson, 1963; and Patrick, Lissner, and Gurdjian, 1963) while thoracic and knee impact forces in excess of 1000 pounds may not result in injury. The face usually hits the top of the panel with a large downward velocity component while chest and knee impacts are essentially in a horizontal direction.

Thus, the panel should have asymmetrical deformation characteristics — a lower force required to deform it in the vertical direction than in the horizontal direction. Energy must also be considered as it establishes the amount of deformation required.

Since kinetic energy is a function of velocity and mass, the velocity of impact and the size of the individual determine the amount of deformation required at the sub-injury force level. The shape of the force–deformation characteristic is important from the energy consideration. If minimum deformation is desired for a given maximum force level and impact conditions, a constant force–deformation characteristic is required. Any other characteristic will require greater deformations. In the foregoing qualitative analysis of instrument panel injury potential, human tolerance to impact forces has been mentioned several times.

Unfortunately, quantitative data on human tolerance to knee impacts are scarce. The basic research program to establish impact tolerance levels of the knee/thigh/hip complex was initiated in 1963 to obtain injury criteria for front seat passengers from experiments simulating frontal-type car accidents. Intact cadavers and dummies are used with impact velocities up to 30 miles per hour.

They are seated in conventional automobile seats with the feet on the floor or inclined toe board. Knee targets are oriented in about the same relative position, as the instrument panel in an automobile. While the main object is to study knee impacts, it is necessary to provide some means of stopping the subject after the knees hit. Since the center of gravity is well above the knee target, the subject would catapult over the target and strike other parts of the sled or building if not restrained. The injuries so incurred would limit the number of times each cadaver could be impacted and might mask the knee impact injuries. This problem is obviated by a chest target installed to stop the torso after the peak knee impact is reached.

Both knee targets and the chest targets are individually adjustable, and each includes a load cell, which measures triaxial forces. The target configuration can be varied from a flat, hard surface to a flat padded surface or to any desired shape and resiliency by attaching different targets to the load cell. The ultimate goal will be to evaluate enough different geometry and resiliency combinations to permit any design to be analyzed for injury potential by a combined theoretical and static experimental evaluation.

The initial results reported herein are based upon tests of one anthropomorphic dummy and six cadavers, using flat targets with surface conditions varying from the rigid bare metal to a semi-resilient padding three inches thick.[2]

Figure 6.2 shows the basic diagram for the location of the chest and knee targets as well as the test device, including the angle of each from the horizontal. Note the foot resting on the toe board and the distance of the ankle-bone above the floorboard. Note also the various lengths of the test device that must be adhered to for reproducibility of the tests.

The following is excerpted*:

Other target configurations to be investigated in this program include flat sheet metal of different thickness, single degree of curvature sheet metal of varying radii and thickness, sheet metal with compound curves, plastics of

* Excerpts from Reference 2. With permission from Wayne State University.

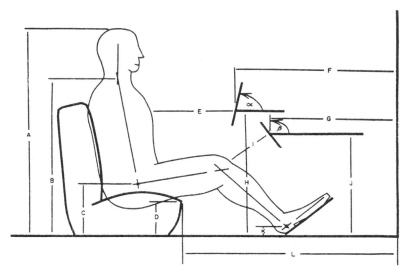

**Figure 6.2** Basic diagram for the location of the chest and knee targets.

various shapes and stiffness, and die casting. All of the studies will be made on "targets" rather than actual instrument panels so the experimental data can be compared with analytical data and extrapolated to new designs that will minimize injury. The forces to fracture vary from 1500 pounds to 2260 pounds, a finding which falls within the range of other investigators.[2]

Therefore, the investigator must be sure to inspect the lower instrument panel for areas of damage that may have caused a lesser injury to the occupant's knee or lower leg injury. The original lower panels were made of metal and the dents left by the occupant knees were readily apparent. The contour gauge from the tool kit is needed in this inspection.

The deformation can be measured for exact depth by placing the contour gauge over the dent and sliding the wires inward until they conform to the shape of the dent. This same procedure can be repeated for up to 360 degrees or until the investigator is satisfied that he/she has enough points to generate an accurate depth diagram of the dent. By using a computer-aided drafting (CAD) program, the data can be input, resulting in an accurate reproduction of the dent that matches the occupant's knee when in the seated position of the vehicle. The center of the dent is located and measurements are taken from a constant undamaged reference point such as the "A" or "B" pillar, the floor pan, or even the front edge of the seat.

Many of today's panels are made of plastic and usually fracture to some degree, depending on the severity of the impact. The fracturing of the panel acts to absorb a portion of the occupant's energy. If a deformed or fractured lower panel is not seen at the inspection, then once again the investigator must use his/her fingers as well as eyes.

Using a flashlight, he/she should shine the light different angles onto the lower instrument panel surface looking for smears of any type. These smears may come from a lower leg that may or may not be covered by some type of clothing. If there is no smear, then look for a pattern from the clothing that may have been impressed onto the plastic surface. This can be from jeans, stockings, slacks, or any other type of material. This pattern may be partially clear or may be brushed heavily into the surface. It must be remembered that these smears do not remain on the surfaces very long. If the vehicle is not covered, then the weather may erase these marks very quickly.

The horizontal distance from the seat to the lower panel can assist in determining which occupant was seated in what position at the time of the collision. It will be necessary to have the occupant who was in that seated position sit in an exemplar vehicle where the distances have been preset or the length of the lower and upper leg determined, then compare the lower leg length of the occupant with the distance from the back of the seat cushion to the lower instrument panel. These steps should yield fairly consistent results.

**Speedometer assemblies.**    The speedometer assembly is a necessary part of any vehicle. It tells the driver the speed of the vehicle at any point in time, but also has a second function, the odometer, which records the mileage of the vehicle. When inspecting a vehicle, it sometimes becomes apparent that the vehicle appears older or more used than its date of manufacture might suggest. A photograph of the odometer should verify any thoughts concerning the use or abuse of a vehicle.

With the increased use of electronics in today's vehicles the speedometer assembly is not observable without some additional work by the investigator. If the vehicle has not been in a fire, then the wiring should be intact. When preparing for an inspection, take a spare 12-V battery to the inspection site. Connect the spare battery to the accident vehicle and then photograph the odometer when the system has stabilized.

If it is possible for the investigator to bring his/her vehicle up close to the accident vehicle, he/she can connect the vehicle battery to the case vehicle battery by using battery cables, and then can proceed as before. Either way this gives an indication of the vehicle usage. Photograph 6.2 shows an older type of mechanical speedometer. Note the odometer reading is 9563 mi. It was once theorized that the speed of a vehicle at impact could be determined by the speedometer needle flexing against the inside surface of the unit and leaving a witness mark. Unfortunately, the person suggesting the theory did not realize that at impact the rear or front wheels may be lifted off the ground, thus allowing the wheels to run without a load, rotating the tires much faster,

**Photograph 6.2** An older type of mechanical speedometer.

and flexing the needle beyond the actual speed at impact when it leaves a witness mark on the inside surface of the unit.

**Glove boxes.**    The glove box is usually situated in the lower instrument panel on the passenger's side of the vehicle. It has a metal or plastic door and a locking device to keep it shut when the vehicle is moving or involved in a collision. A keyed system is used to lock it when the owners may want to store something in it.

Unfortunately, these locks do not always work. They may allow the glove box doors to come open during an impact, permitting the passenger to impact the edge of the door during the second collision with his/her knees.

## Steering Columns*

In 1959 General Motors developed the constant force absorber called the Invertube. It was made part of the steering shaft and was surrounded by a telescoping shift tube and a telescoping jacket. As the need for more collapse distance was demonstrated, the absorber was moved from the steering shaft to the jacket, a limiting connection was provided at the fire wall, a supporting breakaway connection was added at the instrument panel, gear shift tube, and steering shaft.

* Excerpt from Reference 3. With permission from General Motors Corportion.

The energy absorber was a slit and convoluted tube like a Japanese lantern, which was later modified to a mesh tube with multiple connections.

The original column had a force level, which was found to be sustainable, by the human chest without life-threatening injury. The collapse occurred over a 10-inch length of tube.

The next generation of design was basically a type of metal extrusion. The system still consisted of a tube within a tube but between the tubes was a set of ball bearings that were slightly larger than the space between the tubes, producing an interference fit. The number of ball bearings used as well as the tightness of the interference with the ball bearing worked to control the force level. The tubes slide along the ball bearings and were forced between the surfaces extruding the metal and absorbing the energy of the impact.[3]

Additional studies that were confirmed by accident investigations showed that a 10-in. length was not required, because the majority, if not all, of the impacts were contained within an 8 1/4-in. length of tube. This design has saved many drivers from severe and debilitating chest injuries. This system — called an energy absorbing (EA) steering column — worked well, acting as an additional restraint for the driver of the vehicle.

It must be remembered that the EA column works in conjunction with the lap and shoulder belt restraint system. The occupant does not strike the steering column at the same place when he/she is belted vs. when he/she is not belted. This means the EA column may not act as it was designed. When the occupant is belted, he/she comes down on the steering column in an almost axial direction, compressing the steering column and absorbing the energy of the driver at impact.

The unbelted driver rises up during the first stages of the impact; as a result, the driver has less downward force acting on the steering column assembly and more of a bending force, bending the steering column toward the instrument panel and having very little compression of the energy-absorbing portion of the steering column assembly. The occupant expends less energy during the steering wheel impact, leaving more energy to be absorbed by other components such as the restraint system. This system may be insufficient to bring the driver's injuries below a life-threatening level. Should the driver not be wearing a seat belt system he/she would be out of position too; the EA column has injured the out-of-position driver at the time of collision.

Measurements should be taken of the collapsed length of the steering column to determine its effectiveness as an energy absorber. The steering column is attached to the lower edge of the instrument panel. It continues down and through the floor pan and connects to the steering controls of the vehicle. Between the lower edge of the instrument panel and the floor pan is the section of the column that collapses. A plastic sheath that may or may not break off at impact covers this area of the column. If it is not broken, then remove it and measure the collapsed length between the floor pan and the edge of the lower instrument panel.

Remember, this EA column can collapse from the steering end if the damage extends to the steering controls where it would force the end of the steering column rearward into the passengers' compartment. An impact from the driver's chest or an impact to the steering gear pushing inward can yield the same results in terms of column compression.

The investigator must remember that the steering column is just a set of tubes attached to the steering mechanism at one end, and bolted to the lower instrument panel. This system is not ridged and as a result the steering wheel bounces up and down during the first two phases of the accident. Depending on the position of the steering column at the time of the collision, the steering wheel may cause chest and abdominal injuries. The EA steering column is bending sensitive, meaning it cannot collapse properly, absorbing energy when the total column is being forced upward and not being pushed downward, along its axial length, as it was designed to do.

Therefore, it is necessary for the investigator to remove the entire steering column from the vehicle, carefully marking its orientation. Then he/she determines if the column is bent by horizontally supporting both ends of the column and rotating it slowly. During this rotation the steering column may show any bending of its shaft. Photograph and measure the amount of bending.

Many times the investigator may be called on to determine who was driving the vehicle at the time of the initial collision. Analysis of the injuries of both front seat occupants can show the investigator which one has the least injuries in the chest area. This is a good indication that he/she was the driver of the vehicle.

## Steering Wheel Rims

The investigator may, from time to time, come across an accident vehicle in which the steering wheel rim is grossly deformed (i.e., the steering wheel rim has been bent so severely toward the front of the vehicle that the rims are almost touching the steering column itself). This almost always occurs with unbelted drivers.

*Commentary: I have heard and read that some investigators have reported that this type of rim deformation occurred from the driver applying his/her hands to the steering wheel rim and locking his/her elbows in place to prevent an impact with the steering wheel. Let us consider this situation. The average frontal impact imposes a force of approximately 3 to upward of 10 g on the vehicle and the body. This loading would be equivalent to a 200-lb man doing a push-up with between 600 and 2000 lb on his back.*

*Even the Olympic weight lifters could not do that, especially when you consider that the entire accident is over in 150 msec. There is no way any normal person could bend the steering wheel rim in this manner during an accident.*

The steering wheel has undergone a great many changes over the years in shape, design, material, and contours. Yet it is still made basically the same way: a steel core that is surrounded by plastic that may later be covered in other materials such as leather. The original design had the rim and the center of the wheel all in the same plane (i.e., there was no difference in height between the two upper surfaces). The next major change was a deep-dish design with the center hub lower than the rim by 4 in. or more. This came about because a minor collapse of the rim left the center hub protruding like a spear.

*Commentary: There were some steering column designs in the 1960s where the driver's end of the steering column was shaped like a point. After accident investigations were conducted and the problem with the pointed end of the steering column was discovered, the design was changed as quickly as possible.*

The center hub of the steering wheel, being only 3 or 4 in. in diameter, acted like a blunt spear and crushed or penetrated the chest of an unbelted driver. The belted driver fared somewhat better but still was impaled from time to time. Throughout the years, several different center pad designs were tried in an effort to spread the impact load over a wider area of the driver's chest, therefore decreasing the potential for a serious to life-threatening chest injury.

The steering wheel rim itself has also undergone many changes. Its circumference started out being totally round. The lower portion of the rim was then pushed radially toward the steering column, making the rim flatter on the lower side for more occupant room and reduced injury. Some manufacturers made the same modifications to the upper rim, giving the steering wheel rim the appearance of an overstuffed rectangle. With the increased use of power steering, the steering wheel did not have to be as large because of the reduced steering effort required of the driver. Thus, the steering wheel was decreased in size.

Several years ago the rim was designed with a flat surface toward the driver. The flat area is about 1/2 to 3/4 in. wide. With the increased use of lap and shoulder belts, the driver's face would impact the rim from time to time, causing facial bone fractures. This new surface was large enough to spread the load after the point contact with the small facial bones, minimizing (or in many cases eliminating) the fractures to the facial bones.

The type of steering wheel rim bending the investigator may see at vehicle inspections is usually due to the occupant's abdomen contacting the rim and bending it forward toward the front of the vehicle during the collision. This usually causes severe internal injuries to the driver. With the arrival of the driver's air bag supplemental restraint system, the steering wheel is again flat across the upper surface and the center of the hub and the rim are in the same plane. Now the steering wheel has a large air bag pad that prevents the spearing action by distributing the force of the impact over a wider area during a non-air bag displacement collision.

To determine the amount of deformation to the steering wheel rim, the investigator should make a cardboard circle of approximately 15 to 18 in. in diameter. The center of the circle is laid flat on the air bag container (or on the center of the hub in a non-air-bag-equipped vehicle), and the deformation distance is measured from the underside of the cardboard rim to the top of the steering wheel rim. The beginning and the end of the peripheral length of deformation are marked on the upper surface of the cardboard, along with the depth of the deformation. Once the position of the steering wheel is known at the time of the impact, the measured deformation then corresponds to the injuries sustained by the driver.

## Sun Visors

Both belted and unbelted drivers can and have impacted the sun visors and/or the front header of the vehicle. This usually occurs to the unbelted drivers as they rise up in the seat after impacting the lower instrument panel with their knees. This can occur to a tall belted driver in a small vehicle. The drivers' or passengers' heads can go upward and forward into the sun visors, which are padded or made of a cardboard and plastic material. It is necessary to check the depth and location of possible impacts to the sun visor. The damage is not usually evident to the naked eye; unless the investigator can feel for it, it may go unnoticed. This means that a light-to-moderate pressure of the fingertips along the surface facing the occupant allows the investigator to "feel" the dent or depression in the material surface.

Tissue smears or transfers are the best places to start looking for the damage. Why should the investigator be interested in the damage to a visor? The occupant may have had a closed head injury or a fractured cervical vertebra in the rear or posterior portion of the neck. Without being able to determine another location for a potential head impact site, within the interior of the vehicle, the sun visor dent is the positive point of contact for the injury.

If the occupant sustains a posterior neck fracture, his/her head has been forced rearward until the cervical bones are fractured. In the absence of a windshield impact or other possible site that would bend the head rearward, the sun visor dent is the most likely area of impact. Many times the occupant's head only grazes the sun visor leaving a smear and impacting the header area above the windshield. This impact may result in the same type of injury only more severe because of the rearward arching of the neck.

In the past, some investigators may have overlooked items that are or have been attached to the sun visor itself. These items — including garage door openers, sunglasses or glass cases, pens or pencils, or any type of item that can be attached to the edge of the visor — can prevent the softer sun visor surface from protecting the head at impact. When the head strikes the harder object, it acts as if it were struck by a hammer, causing severe or life-threatening conditions. A review of the medical records to determine if the head injury area has a peculiar mark, such as the case of the garage door opener, may verify the cause of injury.

## T-Tops, Moon Roofs, and Sunroofs

In approximately 1968, the sunroof was put into vehicles in the Detroit area on a commercial basis. The sunroof started out as a low-option item on medium-priced vehicles. The general driving public found this option easy to use and a lot more comfortable than a convertible. At about the same time there was a decline in the production and purchasing of the standard convertible. The time was right for a sunroof option to be sold by the original equipment manufacturer (OEM) companies instead of aftermarket firms. (This device was designed originally in Europe and brought to this country for use by aftermarket firms. One of these firms started a small plant and sold OEM manufacturers on the idea of this option on a limited basis.)

The sunroof has proved to be successful to this day. It was so successful that the OEM of manufacturers decided to move the option in-house. That means that instead of having it installed by a secondary supplier the device was installed by the manufacturer on the standard production line. Over the years several changes have been made to upgrade the design of the sunroof and these, too, have increased the usage of this option.

The original sunroof was a sliding steel panel that could be moved manually or electrically. The first changes in the design were to replace the sliding steel panel with a sliding glass panel. The glass was then tinted on the underside with various colors to complement the paint color of the vehicle. The tinting also decreased the amount of heat absorption inside the vehicle for the occupants' comfort. This change was dubbed the "moon roof" option.

Plastic, instead of glass panels was tried at various times but it was not able to comply with the necessary curvature of the road to the tumblehome of the vehicle. The largest design of a sunroof started at approximately the centerline of the driver and proceeded over to the centerline of the right front passenger. Its width was approximately 16 to 20 in. Due to the location, width, and opening of the sliding roof, the unbelted occupant would have difficulty in being ejected from such a small opening.

*Commentary: I have investigated approximately three cases of alleged occupant ejection through a sliding sunroof or a moon roof. In each case it was found that the occupant, either driver or passenger, had not been ejected through this opening.*

It is necessary for the investigator to combine the occupant's injuries with the possibility of an alleged ejection. Understanding the design of the sunroof option makes this possible. If an occupant were to be ejected through this opening, he/she would have to be pulled or pushed along the edges of the frame that holds the sunroof mechanism. These areas although rounded still have enough of an edge to tear the occupant's clothes and cause scratches to the body as it leaves the vehicle. In addition, the occupant may sustain other injuries from striking the exterior of the vehicle or the ground.

As an example, consider an occupant being ejected from and clearing the vehicle and then landing on a gravel shoulder. The injuries would include gravel being embedded into the hairline or facial tissue. Grass stains, weeds, or mud would be found on the occupant's clothing, hair, or other parts of his/her body. All these conditions must exist to assure the investigator that the occupant had truly been ejected.

The next generation of changes to the opening of the roof was to remove the glass entirely, giving the occupant more of a feel of a convertible without all the fuss and problems inherent in a convertible design. This new design was called a T-top. It consisted of two pieces of glass that were fitted between the door opening on the driver and passenger side of the vehicle. An "H"-shaped type-steel, spinelike structure was spot-welded between the front header and the side rails. A secondary structure was added just behind the "B" pillars for additional support. This entire structure held the two panels of glass in place to conform to the current shape of the roof.

The glass panels could only be removed when the vehicle was parked due to their weight and the procedure necessary to remove them. They were then stored in the trunk or rear hatch of the vehicle in the containers provided. This protected the glass and the aluminum side rail attached to the glass that replaced the original vehicle steel side rail. These glass panels were also tinted and had a reflective coating applied to reduce the sun loading on the vehicle in the occupants' compartment.

There have been alleged cases of occupants being ejected through a T-top roof. The investigator must provide detailed information on the possibility of an alleged ejection. The first information required is the action of the vehicle at the time of the alleged ejection. Several conditions must exist for an occupant to be ejected from a vehicle. First, the occupant must be unbelted, or the vehicle must be destroyed in such a manner during the collision that even the belted occupant can be ejected from the remaining portion of the vehicle. Second, there must be a significant movement of the occupant in an up-and-down as well as side-to-side manner. Third, there must be an opening within the occupant's compartment large enough to accommate the ejection of the occupant. Fourth, the position of the vehicle as well as the alleged ejected occupant must be known. Fifth, the injuries of the alleged ejected occupant must be available for review.

T-tops are held in place by mechanical devices. There were two types of fixtures used. A clamp-type fixture puts pressure between the T-top roof panel and the remainder of the side rails to hold the panel in position. The second type is a push rod that slides between the side rail of the T-top panel and the remainder of the original side rail. The second system is stronger and holds much better in collisions.

T-tops are installed on sport-type vehicles. The T-top installation reduces the structural rigidity of such vehicles in two ways: in fore and aft bending, and in twisting about the longitudinal axis. As a result of the reduced structural rigidity, such vehicles can displace or grossly loosen a panel when the vehicle is subjected to a twisting or bending motion just prior to a collision. Such a motion would consist of the vehicle going through a culvert of approximately 8 to 12 in. in depth at some angle other than 90 degrees to the culvert. As the vehicle goes down into the culvert, the front end is pushed upward against the rear end causing the bending movement. As the vehicle proceeds through the culvert, the front end is twisted into a clockwise manner where all the rear end is twisted in a contour clockwise manner. This twisting motion causes the sunroof panels to come free from the other connections to the remainder of the vehicle; and if the vehicle travels over bumps over the course of its travels, it can cause the panels to bounce free of the vehicle giving a clear opening for the occupant to be ejected under the proper circumstances.

## Rearview Mirrors

Rearview mirrors are attached to a bracket that may be bonded to the inside of the windshield glass by an adhesive. Vision studies have concluded that the position of the mirrors is the optimum one for the driver to see the traffic to the side and to the rear of the vehicle.

Of course, there are some blind spots but they can be minimized by the correct positioning of the inside rearview mirror in conjunction with the outside rearview mirrors. There have been numerous cases of impacts involving properly lap- and shoulder-belted occupants that have had a payout of the seat belt webbing that allowed them enough slack to impact the inside rearview mirror. This impact causes the molding surrounding the mirror to impact the inside annealed glass of the windshield, many times causing the inside glass to fracture. Depending on the severity of impact, the mirror itself may fracture and many times break the bracket off the inside glass. By positioning the inside rearview mirror that was broken free from the inside windshield glass against its location on the fractured glass, the investigator may determine how the mirror was broken off of its mounting. Interior photographs taken at the inspection can verify the mode and position of the fracture.

*Commentary: I had at least two cases where the impact of the driver's head to the inside rearview mirror resulted in a rounded corner imprint being embedded in the forehead of the driver. No one could figure out what caused the injury until we recovered the mirror and matched it up with the witness mark on the forehead. (Details solve cases. Never forget that!)*

## Seat Cushions and Seatbacks

There are seats that are very expensive made for strictly comfort. Some are made for the pseudo-racing crowd that holds the passenger in more securely on turns, and some are just plain but comfortable. The seats in today's vehicles are considerably different than those made just 5 years ago.

There are two methods of positioning the seats in a vehicle, power or manual. There is a new variation on the power seat. The driver's seat can now be ordered with a memory for multiple drivers' position. The driver can set the seat height, seatback angle, and cushion angle; once set, the driver then presses a button and the seat always returns to that position. There is sufficient memory to store the seat cushion and seatback position for a second driver.

This new option may come in handy at a vehicle inspection when it is necessary to determine by the position of the seat who was driving. The first step to be taken by the investigator is to mark, with a colored grease pencil, the location of the seat with respect to its position in the vehicle. Place a mark on the side of the seat cushion and on the step sill. Then move the seat forward and rearward to get the total length of seat movement, marking those as well.

This gives the location of the seat at the time of the accident with respect to the total movement of the seat, assuming that the emergency medical service (EMS) people did not move the vehicle seat or seatback during extrication when rendering aid to the injured occupant. If the vehicle contains the electronic seat memory storage, then press the button and see where the seat goes. If it moves to a new position, then press it again and see if it returns to the position just marked.

Check the police report to determine if there were other occupants in the rear seats at the time of the first collision. It is possible for an unbelted rear seat occupant to be thrown forward over the back of the front seats and impact the windshield and instrument panel. This can be determined by checking the back of the front seats for specific damage. This includes the seat being bent forward at a corner (or the whole back of the seat being bent), tissue smears, blood trails, or even ripped or torn seat material.

It is easy to determine whether or not the tears are fresh by comparing the color of the stuffing material sticking out against the original material. Many times there is a smear that looks like shoe polish, white, brown, or black. This finding is very important in rear-end impacts and is explained later in the chapter. Suffice it to say that it must be examined, noted on a sketch, and then photographed with a ruler next to it to show the approximate length of the mark.

The investigator may always have detailed information about the accident. It is his/her job to record every detail that is present at the scene as well as during the vehicle inspection that, in his/her eyes, cannot be easily explained as belonging to another accident or is not connected to this or any other accident.

Occupants may sometimes "submarine" underneath a lap belt during a collision. *Submarining* is defined in this context as the occupant sliding forward underneath the lap belt portion of the restraint system with the lap belt webbing resting above the pelvic girdle. This can lead to many serious soft tissue injuries because the seat belt webbing is pushing on the abdomen of the occupant. Many different methods have been tried to prevent this submarining.

One such method increases the lap belt angle with the horizontal, that is, the angle measured from the floor to a line running down the center of the lap belt webbing. This angle should be at least 45 degrees or higher, because it pushes down on the thighs of the occupant, holding him/her in place and back against the seat. Seat design has always been looked at as another possible method of reducing the submarining displacement. Basically the seats are designed so that the buttocks of the occupant are not allowed to drive down into the front portion of the seat where it could be far enough forward to allow submarining to occur; or allow the occupant to slide partially over the front of the seat cushion, but being kept from moving downward by the seat design and thus preventing the submarining action of the body during the collision. Many of the automobile manufacturers have developed special seat structures to prevent this sliding forward and under the seat belts in the event of a severe frontal impact.

Whichever way seats are designed, they all contain certain elements including structural frame members which are machined or stamped; and nonstructural materials such as springs, and cushioning material to provide load distribution and contour necessary for comfort. These materials absorb the transmission of forces through the seat structure.

As mentioned previously, there are adjustment mechanisms to accommodate the wide range of the human body from the smallest female to the largest male. The proper seat adjustment is a feature of comfort and also an important safety consideration both for the routine operation of the vehicle and for collision protection.

The seat anchorage is located between the adjustment mechanisms and the floor plan. They transfer forces between seat and the vehicle. Under static conditions these forces of compression, tension, and shear are transmitted from the seat to the floor. In a collision or under handling acceleration, the resulting forces are transmitted from the structure through the seat to the occupant.

In 1976 at the 20th Stapp Car Crash Conference, a paper was presented on an integrated safety seat. The research group modified a Volvo production seat with special support to the frame and protected hardware that included an integrated see-through head restraint, roof-anchored belts that traverse downward through the seat, built-in three-point inertia reels, back rest panels of deformable material, roof attachment inertia reels, and double seat tracks for positive transmission of forces. The use of the roof-attached systems removed the load from the fragile adjustment mechanisms to the stronger portion of the vehicle.

Unfortunately, it was 20 years before the system was put into a production vehicle, and then only portions of it were used. There are two vehicles on the market today with integrated seat belt systems on the driver's and right front passenger seat. Foreign manufacturers have done both.

It is better to have documented all the evidence found at the scene, even if it does not belong to the present accident, than to have missing data and to wish the inspection could be done over again.

## Headrests

Most if not all of today's vehicles are equipped with headrests. These devices were designed to prevent the occupant's head from hyperextending over the back of the seat, assuming the seatbacks do not deform and collapse. Non-adjustable headrests should reach the proper heights for the average driver, but they do not always.

Many years ago, a doctorial engineering dissertation showed the results of a controlled seatback with and without a headrest. An adjustable headrest must be raised up to the point where the portion of the head is just above its center of gravity. A person should then be able to withstand a 44-mi/h rear-end collision with no injuries. This is provided, of course, if his/her head is initially in contact with a flat, padded headrest, which is firmly attached to a rigid seatback. The dissertation showed that without a headrest, controlled seat back rotation reduces the severity of a given impact. This was demonstrated with instrumented anthropomorphic dummies and cadavers.

*Commentary: In the early 1970's there was a design for a pop-up head restraint that was similar to an air cushion. The problem was that the cushion did not have a charging or venting system, it was fully inflated at all times, and after impact the head was propelled forward almost as fast as it was pushed rearward. This design was eliminated as a potential solution for whiplash-type injuries.*

An OEM manufacturer has developed a new type of head restraint, which is activated during a rear-end collision to protect the occupant from incurring a whiplash-type injury. It is the author's understanding that this system moves the head restraint upward and forward toward the rear of the occupant's head, giving it support during the rearward motion of the occupant body during the collision.[4]

# Less Obvious Interior Deformation

The investigator has seen the obvious during the inspection — he/she must next look beyond that for the details. He/she has to use his/her fingers to probe the various components inside the vehicle.

## Moldings

Moldings are padded in luxury cars, so fingers must probe along the edges. If there a dent, it could have been made by one of the occupants during the impact.

The problem is determining if the damage was preexisting. Many times it is possible to match up a dent or deformed part with the trajectory and injury of the occupant, especially if there is fresh blood. If it is impossible to make such a determination, photograph it anyway. If it is later found to be done by some other cause than the collision, then it can be ignored. Nothing can be ignored at this stage of the investigation.

## Checklists

Checklists make the job easier for the on-scene investigator. One has been developed that can be used as a memory aide, as shown in Table 6.1. The investigator must take the checklist to the scene of the accident and actually put a check mark by each item. After everything has been checked off the list, he/she revisits the vehicle interior a final time, looking for the unusual

**Table 6.1    Investigators Checklist for Use at Vehicle Inspections**

Exterior

Minimum of 14 camera angles
Additional close-ups of damage
Dents, scrapes, and paint transfers
Missing components
Unusual or unexplained drainage

Interior: Frontal, Side, and Rear

Windshield bulge
Instrument panel damage
Sun visor and header damage
Door trim panel abrasions and dents
Seatback and cushion damage
Observe all interior surfaces for abrasions, cuts, dents, or other unexplained damage

that may not have appeared relevant at first glance. The investigator must use his/her eyes, hands, and nose to visualize how the damage occurred. He/she must put self in the vehicle and think through the possible scenarios. The investigation also must reject those scenarios that do not fit the physical evidence first and foremost.

The scenarios must fit as well as possible the witness statements when they are directly involved with the accident. The investigator/reconstructionist must truly believe that the scenario he/she has chosen is the best scenario that can be developed to fit with the physical and/or all evidence that has been presented to him/her. If the investigator believes otherwise, then he/she must continue to develop scenarios that relieve any doubts about any envisioned scenario. This thought process should result in a complete report of the damage that allows an accurate reconstruction of the accident.

# Types of Impacts as Related to Interior Deformation

## Side Impacts

The side of any vehicle is one of the weaker areas of a vehicle, due to the fact that there is very little space for energy-absorbing material. Side impacts can be generally defined as an impact between two vehicles that occur between common sides.

This definition can be further refined into one of the following: (1) an impact between two vehicles where the first vehicle strikes the second vehicle at some angle between −180 to +180 degrees; and (2) an impact where the vehicle slides sideways into a fixed object, such as a tree, utility pole, or other stationary structure.

In either event, the side of one or both of the vehicles is the primary area of the vehicle that is damaged. Vehicles involved in side impacts are without a doubt the most serious types of accident. Unlike the front of a vehicle that has from 1 to 3 ft of energy-absorbing material, the side of a vehicle at the passengers' compartment has less than 1 ft, usually 6 in. or less. Many if not all the components within that 6-in. space are not energy absorbing.

The unitized bodies used in almost all vehicles today many times allow more deformation than did the previous body-on-frame design. This possible increased deformation allows more penetration into the occupants' compartment. Because the vehicle body is unitized, one portion of it is dependent on another as a result of all being welded together to form the total body.

### Vehicle Posts

The occupant compartment of the vehicles is made up of a series of vertical posts that tie the roof into the floor pan and allow a space for the entry and exit of the occupants through the door opening between these spaces. Letters define each of these posts. The first post — called the "A" post — supports the front header, the front portion of the roof, the windshield, the front fender, the instrument panel, and the front door hinges.

The second post — called the "B" post — supports the middle portion of the roof, side headers, and ties the center of the floor pan to the doorsill and the roof. It also supports a portion of the locking mechanism for the front door and the hinges for the rear door if the vehicle is so equipped.

The third post is called the "C" post. Because the "A" "B" and "C" pillars or posts hold the roof and the floor pan together, any forces applied to these vertical structures can produce some action on the roof and the floor pan. In a two-door vehicle, the "C" post ties the roof and rear header to the rear quarter panel portion of the vehicle and provides areas for mounting the support of the deck or trunk and trunk lid. In a four-door vehicle, it serves all the same functions and supports a portion of the locking mechanism for the second door.

In station wagons and vans there is a fourth post that is called the "D" post. Because there is no external trunk on a station wagon, the "D" post supports the end of the rear quarter panels, the rear door with its hinges and locks, and the rear window mechanism.

Each of these posts also acts as a column to which are welded braces or fillets. These tie the various portions of the floor pan to the roof, making the vehicle a more stable structure.

## *Doors*

The doors are hung on the "A" and "B" posts. These doors are curved inward (called tumblehome) to match the location of the roof sheet metal. This decreases the aerodynamic drag on the vehicle. The door itself is made up of an outer and an inner sheet metal panel.

The inner panel is the skin that covers the inner workings of the door including the window mechanisms from the inside of the vehicle. The outer panel is welded to the inner sheet metal panel that together form a stable structure.

The inner sheet metal panel has many holes of various sizes that allow the line installer to hook up the side window glass to the regulator, door locks, radio speakers, and associated wiring. A plastic sheet is affixed to the inner panel with an adhesive to keep the water out of the vehicle (because rain and other water, such as that from a car wash, can travel between the inner and outer panels of the door). Fiberboard or plastic material that is covered with vinyl or leather material is then attached to the inner door sheet metal. Attached to this is the grab handle and/or armrest that is padded. These help to minimize the effects of the impacts to the lateral side of the human body.

Also included between the inner and outer door is a guard door beam. This beam was originally designed to prevent or minimize the intrusion into the occupants' compartment by another vehicle during a side impact, especially when the angle of impact is such that the corner of the bumper would act somewhat like a spear. This beam is made of much heavier gauge metal the majority of which are bent into a "W" shape to increase its stiffness. These beams have proved to be fairly successful over the years.

A standard crash test run by the automotive firms is called a moving barrier. This is where a 4- × 8-ft sheet of plywood is attached to the front of a large welded structure that resembles a vehicle chassis. The moving barrier is on four wheels and resembles the chassis of another vehicle with a broad front nose that is not deformable. The striking vehicle absorbs no energy; therefore, all the energy of impact is reflected back into the vehicle being struck. The moving barrier is wide enough to reach both the "A" and "B" posts. Thus, at impact the door itself is not struck without striking the posts. The post/door structure is much stronger and does not allow much penetration into the occupants' compartment.

Unfortunately, these types of impacts reflect only a small percentage of real-world accidents. In a typical side impact one of the posts takes the brunt of the impact. This causes an inward bending of the post.

### Vehicle Bodies

The body is a welded structure made up of many parts that all yield in varying amounts depending on the distance from the point of impact (POI) in the direction of the force. As the penetration of the compartment continues, the roof is pulled downward and inward into the compartment. The rocker panel, doorsill, and floor pan are being pulled upward and inward at the same time. When the posts, roof, and rocker panel are pulled inward, it is difficult to measure the amount of deformation.

The best measurement that can be taken is the depth of penetration at the severest point of the impact. If the opposite side of the vehicle does not have any induced damage, then it is possible for the investigator to use a set of measuring tapes to measure the distance to certain landmarks on the undeformed side of the vehicle. Using the undeformed front and rear bumpers as the starting and end points, place the tape measure parallel to the side of the structure, approximately 6 to 12 in. away from the nearest point, depending on how much room the investigator has to work in. Both vertical and horizontal measures are taken along the undeformed side of the vehicle at such places as the rear bumper, wheel axle, where the doors meet the posts, front fender, rear quarter panel, or any areas similar to the deformed area. Then by using the newly determined data, the investigator can set up his/her tape measure along the deformed side of the vehicle and determine the amount of crush or deformation along the entire length of the impact.

If the vehicle has induced damage to the opposite side to the vehicle, then the investigator must find an exemplar. He/she repeats the same procedure and then applies it to the impacted sides of the vehicle.

***Commentary***: *Photographs can be taken of the vehicle from the front, rear, and overhead. A second set of photographs is then taken of an exemplar vehicle from exactly the same positions. By using the negatives of both sets of photographs, the deformed vehicle can be superimposed on the exemplar vehicle and measurements can be taken in this manner. Great care must be taken when photographing both the vehicles to ensure that both sets of photographs are taken from the same position. This means the distance from each of the vehicles must be exactly the same in all three views. Detailed measurements must be taken of the distance from the camera to the vehicle in each photograph setup to ensure that all are correct.*

All the components that are being pulled inward into the compartment are now trying to take up the space the driver or passenger occupant is trying to occupy. Based on fundamental physics, no two objects can occupy the same space at the same time. The result, of course, is an increase in the number and severity of the injuries to the occupants that are on the nearside of the impact, that is those closest to the POI. The farside occupants are the ones who are the farthest away from the POI. The nearside occupant may continue to suffer moderate-to-severe or even life-threatening injuries until the automotive companies can increase the energy-absorbing capabilities of the side of a vehicle.

### Restraint Systems

Of course, the lap and shoulder belt restraint system is of lesser value to the nearside occupant because he/she is being impacted by the incoming door structure and the front of the impacting vehicle. The advent of the side impact air bag may prove to be beneficial to the occupant in this type of accident. Only continued accident investigation can prove or disprove the effectiveness of this new safety device. Insufficient numbers of vehicles with these systems onboard have been in an accident to produce any meaningful statistics, as of this point in time.

The farside occupant can benefit by the restraint system because it keeps him/her in place prior to and during the impact sequence. It also prevents the occupant from sliding into the other occupant, thereby preventing the second collision.

If both front seat occupants are in the vehicle and are unbelted, there is a great difference in the type and severity of the injuries between the two of them. The farside occupant, when belted, suffers very minor injuries. At most he/she sustains bruising. When unbelted, the farside occupant is thrown into the nearside occupant and suffers impacts such as head-to-head and/or shoulder-to-shoulder injuries. If there is a console between them, there may be rib or pelvic fractures along with other bruising. The nearside occupant may suffer considerably more injuries on the side of his/her body that is opposite the POI when the farside occupant is thrown into him/her.

Imagine the nearside occupant being slammed into the door panel and then a few milliseconds later the farside occupant strikes him/her with slightly lower energy than the original impact, depending on the energy absorption that has taken place. This phenomenon is even more prevalent in a rollover accident when the unbelted occupants are being tossed about and one lands on top of the other one. This topic is discussed further in a later section on rollovers.

### Instrument and Other Panels

The investigator must match up the injuries with the interior components that would most likely be in the path or trajectory of the occupants during the collision. He/she must look for evidence of skin and tissue smears on the inner door panel that would result in abrasions or tears to the skin of the occupant. Check for dents in the door panels as well as the trim that is used to cover the interfaces between the inner roof material and the door; and for missing components such as door handles and window cranks, and broken knobs from the radio or temperature control system.

Even cracked lenses on the instrument panel can be a source of injury to the occupant. Blood and tissue smears on the surface of any of these components are always an indication of occupant impact damage. The investigator must also check the position of the glass in the side window prior to impact. By placing a ruler between the edges of the wiping surface that wipes the glass as it moves up and down into the door, this can be easily done. If the glass is unbroken, the top of it can easily be seen. If it is broken, then he/she must determine the position of the glass at impact. Many times there are fragments of glass left in the window edge. This is sufficient evidence. There may also be fragments of tempered glass inside the vehicle. Check the other windows to see if they are broken.

If all else fails, then the interior trim door panel must be removed to see the location of the edge of the glass holder. This location reveals the position of the glass at the time of impact. The glass holder is positioned manually or by a electric motor. Several other areas to be checked for fragments of tempered glass include the upper edge of the door panel where it mates with the glass, the armrest, and the window hand crank (found in some nonelectric window vehicles). Some vehicles still do not have the interior door handles recessed. These can also be a source of injuries to hands or fingers even when recessed.

### Seatbacks

Many of today's vehicles have seatbacks that can be reclined. The handle for operating the seatback is located on the outboard side of the seat. There has been an occasion where in a side impact the incoming door material is pushed into the handle and then pushed upward releasing the front seatback latch. The seatback then falls rearward putting the occupant out of position if a second collision occurs, especially if it is a rearend impact. Side impacts require the investigator to closely examine the inner door trim panel to look for dents, scrapes, or even cuts in the material covering where it made contact with the seatback release handle.

Blood spatter and blood pooling also help the investigator to locate where and which occupants moved during and after the collision. These are then compared with the medical data of both the occupants.

Of course, photographs of the entire vehicle are necessary but in this case several special photographs and videotapes must be taken of the depth of penetration using the tape measures described previously, especially in the area of the door trim panel that pushed up against the seats. Remember, film is cheap compared with a second trip to look at the vehicle or the complete loss of the necessary photographs if the vehicle has been scrapped.

## Rear Impacts

Rear impacts can be fatal or they can be very minor; of course, they run the gamut in between these two extremes. Most vehicles have the trunk in the rear of the vehicle. This generally means a large open area with very little energy-absorbing capabilities. The quarter panels have an inner and outer surface but they are not very good absorbers, especially if the impact is above the rear floor/bumper area.

### *Bumpers*

To take full advantage of the energy-absorbing capabilities of the vehicle, the impact must be a bumper-to-bumper type of impact. If the impact area is greater than or less than half the height of the bumper, then an override or underride collision may take place.

Today's vehicles are designed with a relatively constant bumper height. This means that most vehicles under most braking situations impact each other's bumpers. These bumpers must meet the FMVSS standards for low-speed impacts. To accomplish this they have devices between the backside of the bumper and the floor pan. They are sometimes called PGMs, which is a trade name for the material used in some of them. The PGMs absorb energy by squeezing out a material into another chamber inside the device, thus absorbing the low energy of impact. After impact, the material returns to its original position.

The investigator can tell if a low-speed impact occurred by looking at the piston casing. During the stroking phase, the outside surface of the piston rubs against the collar, leaving scratch marks as a witness mark. An offset rear-end impact strokes one PGM more than the other and confirms the non-colinear impact. A rear-end impact to the open area of the trunk results in a great deal of deformation. This deformation must be documented as before with video and still cameras, but measurements must also be taken. A set of rods can be driven into the ground approximately 1 ft from the rear of the vehicle and a string tied between them. Measurements are to be taken from the string to the deformed portion of the vehicle.

There are computer programs that can use a series of deformation measurements to develop a barrier equivalent speed. These have not been found to be very accurate, but for the beginner in the field, they could prove to be a starting point for analysis. The investigator must always ensure that he/she obtains the maximum point of penetration as well as the width and length of the deformed area. Photographic documentation is necessary for the client, whether an insurance company or a lawyer.

Many of the smaller vehicles today are designed with a flexible nose fascia that has behind it a series of deformable materials that can absorb the energy of a minor, 5-mi/h impact. This is used instead of PGMs.

Inspection of the exterior plastic bumper surface may reveal many witness marks such as gouges, punctures, rips, and even minor-to-severe abrasions resulting from the bumper being ground down when sliding along the concrete road surface or a concrete barrier of a median. A detailed inspection of such abrasions tells the investigator the direction of grinding action; this is due to the fact that the plastic heats up during the grinding process and piles up on the last surface of the bumper to leave the concrete.

Speeds above approximately 15 mi/h cause a large deformation of the trunk area of the vehicle with very little energy absorption taking place. This means that the majority of the energy of impact is transferred to the occupants. They then feel the major force of the collision. After the trunk is collapsed, the only remaining components that absorb energy are the occupants' seats. All the seats in today's vehicle must meet FMVSS standards. These, however, are static tests or tests conducted at very slow-energy inputs.

### Seatbacks

Under dynamic conditions, the impact to a seat can increase by 1.2 to 1.5 times the original energy due to the dynamic input. Seatbacks cannot stand a dynamic rear-end collision above approximately 15 to 20 mi/h, in which case the seatback collapses in the rearward direction. The lap and shoulder belt restraint systems are of no value to the occupants in rear-end collisions. The seatback acts like a ramp launching the occupant in the rearward direction into the back seat or out the back window. The occupants slide from under both lap and shoulder belts during this type of collision. There have been occasions where the occupant's shoes may have been removed from the occupant's feet and are then held in place by the lap belt, but these are rare. When the ramping occurs, the occupants move headfirst in a rearward direction.

If the seatback has been lowered toward the rear seat, then the occupant strikes his/her head and/or neck on the upper portion rear seatback. Many times this results in a fractured neck. This can be fatal or result in some type of paralysis. If the seatback angle is approximately half way between the full up position and the full down position, the occupants can go partially or completely through the back window of the vehicle.

To determine how the occupants may have left the vehicle, the investigator must examine the rear seatback; the rear side trim panels, the surround moldings of the rear window opening, and the remainder of rear window area of the vehicle.

Hair strands have been found attached to the rear window molding and to the edges of any remaining glass pieces left in the window frame or on the seatback cushion. This happens because many times the deformed sheet metal of the trunk or deck lid is pushed upward toward the window area and catches the hair of the occupants as they pass out through the window. All these areas should be recorded by the investigator with a still camera and a videotape recorder, taking care to use a backdrop such as black cloth to ensure that the hair strands show up in the photographs and on the videotape. To increase the awareness of the strands of hair in the photograph, sticky red arrows can be placed on the surfaces next to the strands of hair as a means of bringing the attention of the viewer to their location. Both still photographs and videotape recordings must be taken from several different directions to show not only the location but also the length of hair and possibly the color. Many times an extreme close-up is required to show the color of hair against different colored backdrops.

Additional setup time was taken in each photograph to ensure that the strands of hair being photographed against a black or other suitable color background stand out from the rest of the lighter colored interior material. The strands of hair almost fill the full frame of the photograph. It is important that close-ups are taken that show the location detail, but not so close as to lose the portion of the vehicle where the hairs were found.

Other photographs should be taken from the extreme outside of the vehicle. Succeeding photographs should be taken closer and closer to the location of the hair strands so there is no doubt about the type, color, make, and model of the vehicle as well as the main area of the vehicle where hair strands are found. A close-up of the molding and then close-ups of the hair strands themselves should be taken. This way there can be no confusion as to where the hair strands were found when the vehicle was inspected. Measurements inside and outside the vehicle locating the hair and possible blood smears also assist in the reconstruction.

As the occupants slide up the seatback, their feet come up from the floor and are pulled along on top of the cloth material of the seat as well as the door trim panels and roof liner material. Shoe polish smears have been found on these areas of the interior portions of the vehicle. A record must be made of the location, length, and width of the mark as well as the color. This is then matched up against the shoes of the occupants.

Close examination of the sides, tops, and even underside of the shoes can confirm that they match the smears inside the vehicle and can allow the investigator to determine the direction of travel of the occupant during the collision. Remember that a witness mark may be left on the shoe as well as on the interior trim of the vehicle. Some portions of shoes may catch on the material of the seat and rip it (another witness mark for the investigator). Close examination usually reveals smears of shoe polish or rubber marks from the heels or soles.

It is necessary to measure the angle of the seatback as found at the vehicle inspection. Be sure to determine if the EMS units moved the seatbacks rearward to help extricate or manipulate the occupants before moving them.

The investigator must check the seatback release latch. This device could have easily been damaged during the rear-end impact. The seatback release is a sector gear that is released when the handle on the side of the seat is pulled up.

*Commentary: There has been a problem with many of the seatback sector gears over the past several years. They were not properly heat-treated. Some were too soft and as a result the teeth were worn down as the seat was moved back and forth over the gear. Some were not tempered properly, the teeth were too brittle, and they could be stripped off like popcorn during a rear-end collision.*

To determine the condition of the sector gear, it is necessary to partially disassemble the seat at the outside lower edge of the seatback. Whenever a disassembly process takes place, a video camera as well as a 35-mm camera must be used at each step during the disassembly operation to show that no illegal operations were done to the seat or the part during the process. The video cameras should be set up with both date and time for use of the camera. If both cannot be set on the screen at the same time, then just use the time, because it shows the continuous use of the camera during the disassembly operation.

## Rear Windows

Many times the rear window may have been broken out by the impact, but there have been those instances where the occupant's head fractures the window first before he/she exits the vehicle. The occupant may be partially ejected through the rear window when his/her head strikes the rear window holding it, while the occupant's body continues to move rearward causing a fracture of the cervical spine. The occupant may continue rearward and be completely ejected from the vehicle. Once the occupant leaves the vehicle, his/her chances of injuries increase dramatically, not only in frequency but also in severity.

Occupants have been found as far away as 100 ft from the vehicle. The environment outside of the vehicle is not forgiving if one considers trees, poles, metal signs, fire plugs, etc. If there is a lot of traffic on the road at the same time as the accident, there is a better than even chance the occupants can be run over by another vehicle.

## Rollovers

There are two types of rollovers: the helix or corkscrew and the barrel roll. The helix or corkscrew type of rollover is one in which the vehicle is moving forward and is rolling over at the same time. The barrel roll is one in which the vehicle rolls only along it longitudinal axis. The corkscrew type of rollover may start out as a helix, but the vehicle can and many times does turn sideways and ends up rolling like a barrel going downhill. In either case, a major portion of the vehicle is damaged in this type of accident and requires the investigator to spend a great deal more time at the vehicle and site inspection.

The first detail the on-scene investigator notices in either type of rollover is that one side of the vehicle has more crush or deformation than the other side. The side with the heavier damage is the side that hits the ground first after the vehicle starts its roll. This is because it has more kinetic energy on the first roll and this causes more damage to the exterior of the vehicle. In a helix-type rollover the "A" post is pushed rearward, giving the front windshield a smaller angle of slope. This deformation reduces the amount of occupant space available within the vehicle.

Federal standard 212 is a static rollover test. The body buck is bolted down to a platform and a 4 × 8 sheet of plywood attached to a hydraulic ram is placed against the "A" post at a specific angle. The pressure is applied and the "A" post and associated roof area are compressed to 5000 lb or 1 1/2 times the weight of the vehicle, whichever is smaller. When the pressure reaches 5000 lb, the test is completed. It is considered successful if the "A" post does not collapse more than 5 in. into the compartment.

In the real world, the occupants are not sitting in that position when the deformation occurs. The occupants' positions inside the vehicle are always lagging the roll of the vehicle. The vehicle strikes the ground and deforms before the occupants reach that same position. Depending on the location of the rollover, the investigator may observe both heavy dirt and grass impacted into various crevices of the vehicle or road abrasions over many areas of the vehicle. There are some cases where both types of damage are seen. These are the rollovers in the country where the vehicle starts the roll on the asphalt or concrete surface and ends up in a field next to the road.

In such a situation the investigator may find many areas of road abrasions that are not parallel to each other. The abrasions are going in several different directions. This is due to the movement of the vehicle between rolls where it changes direction, and therefore a different set of abrasion marks occur on a given surface that is not parallel to the original set of abrasion marks.

Because the road surface is uneven and so is the exterior of the vehicle, the vehicle may slide along until it strikes a pothole, bump, or some other irregularity in the road; or it may become caught on a door handle, a piece of chrome molding, or an edge of the bumper. Then it may flip over or rotate a quarter turn or several turns onto another surface of the vehicle and continue its slide.

The number of abraded areas and the depth of these areas tell the investigator how long the vehicle was on that particular surface and which abrasions came first. The longer and deeper the abrasions are, the more energy the vehicle had at that point in the slide. This would be early in the rollover.

The smaller the length and depth of the abrasions, the less time in contact with the road surface and the less energy expended in the sliding maneuvers of the vehicle. It is not always possible to determine which areas came first, but the investigator can put together enough of the puzzle to show what happened to the vehicle.

Clumps of dirt and grass wedged into the crevices of a vehicle can be matched up with the marks in the field and the investigator can develop a sketch showing the areas where the vehicle has rolled and/or tumbled over. If the area where the vehicle is sliding is a crop-free field or the lawn of a residential home, the vehicle may not roll over more than once; it just might continue to slide on that surface. The investigator must look at the witness marks in the field and match up the areas on the vehicle that contain the same material.

There have been occasions where a vehicle has slid along in a field, has struck a bump, then has begun to roll over end for end, and even has spun on a single point such as the grille opening panel or the rear of the vehicle. In such a case, it is again necessary to match the dirt and debris in the various areas of the vehicle with the witness marks in the field.

Ejections can occur during a rollover when the side or rear windows are broken out of the vehicle. This leaves an open area where the occupant can exit the vehicle. There are some cases where the windshield can be forced from its bonded surface, but this is rare. This usually can occur when the "A" post has been severely compromised and the windshield cannot stretch to maintain its bonding.

The windshield is stress cracked and may end up folding over onto itself at one of the major cracks and leave a gap for ejection of the occupant. There have been instances where an investigator has determined that the occupant was ejected from a vehicle with a special roof opening, such as a T-top or sliding sun roof or moon roof. In a sliding roof panel vehicle such as a sunroof or moon roof, it is almost impossible for this to happen.

The roof opening extends only to the center of the driver's and passenger's seated position. With both of these seats filled there is insufficient room for an occupant to be ejected. In a removable T-top roof-type vehicle, there is a larger opening and the opening is centered over the seats. Ejections may be possible but only under a certain set of conditions.

The investigator must be careful to determine if the ejected occupant has any witness marks on his/her head, shoulders, arms, or other body parts, in the form of long uneven scratches. There cannot be an ejection where the occupant is projected from the vehicle without touching some portion of the vehicle on the way out. It is also rare to have an ejection where the door was opened at impact. The double lock system that was added on the doors many years ago prevents this from happening unless the door is ripped from its hinges or a section of a vehicle is ripped away to expose the seated position.

If the unbelted occupants are not ejected, they undergo severe injuries as they are literally thrown about the vehicle. Consider a driver and right front passenger who is unbelted in a typical right-hand, side-to-side or barrel rollover. The vehicle may strike the ground with the left side of the vehicle first. Because the occupants are lagging behind the motion of the vehicle, they arrive at the point of impact after the deformation has occurred. The driver travels upward and to his/her left, striking the roof and/or the side header above the door. If there is a passenger in the right front seat, he/she travels over toward the driver.

Depending on the angle of impact, the right front passenger may go all the way over and impact the driver right side, or he/she may only go partially over to that side and strike the driver with his/her head. On the next roll both occupants may be slammed into the passenger's side of the vehicle with the driver following the right front passenger. Not only does the passenger become injured from impacting the interior of the vehicle on that side of the vehicle but also his/her injuries are exacerbated by the additional loading placed on his/her body by the second impact of the driver's body.

The back and forth movement as well as up and down motion of both occupants can continue through several rotations of the vehicle during the rollover process. The injuries that are sustained can be very serious and may be fatal. Belted occupants fare far better than nonbelted ones in rollovers. They are prevented from impacting the other occupant with the entire body. There may be some minimal contact, but it usually is not significant. In addition, the occupants are prevented from striking the interior of the vehicle, specifically the headliner. The restraint system keeps the occupants in their seats before, during, and after the collision.

***Commentary***: *There are those rare occasions where there may be a defect in the "A" post itself. In these cases, the post cross section is not sufficient to withstand the impact of the vehicle during a rollover phase of the accident. Static testing may not always reveal these defects. Dynamic testing has not been developed by any of the automobile companies or by the federal government. The on-scene investigator must be cognizant of the potential for a defect in the "A" post when investigating the vehicle. Clues to these potential problems would include the "A" post being collapsed severely, unusual bends in the "A" post at places other than the connection with the door, or poor or missing welds along the "A" post proper.*

## Smears and Blood Pooling

Smears and blood pooling are quite common in moderate-to-severe accidents. They can assist the investigator in determining the actions of the occupants during the crash sequence. This is especially important in rollover accidents. The blood and tissue smears show the direction of travel and the pooling shows the final resting place of the occupants within the vehicle. (Of course, this must be checked against the medical records.) Blood spatter is also helpful when the occupants are unbelted and the body is flailing around the inside of the vehicle.

When the investigator has documented all the easily identified evidence, it is necessary to reexamine the vehicle and the scene, with greater emphasis on the small, minor detail items they may have missed on the first round of inspections.

***Commentary:*** *In all rollover cases, the investigator must ensure that if water and mud have flooded the interior components of the vehicle, the mud is scraped away to look for any remainder of blood or tissue.*

## Comment on Restraint Systems

The restraint system of a vehicle is the first defense of the occupants to eliminate or at least mitigate their injuries. This topic, along with special restraint systems of today's vehicles, is discussed in great detail in Chapter 7.

## References

1. Patrick, L. M., Daniel, R. P., *Comparison of Standard and Experimental Windshields*, 8th Stapp Car Crash Conf. Wayne State University Press, Detroit, MI, 1966, 147, 150, 199, 204, and 217.

2. Kroell, C. K., Patrick, L. M., *A new Crash Simulator and Biomechanics Research Program*, 8th Stapp Car Crash Conf. Wayne State University Press, Detroit, MI, 1966, 199.

3. Marquis, D. P., Rasmusson, T., *Status of Energy Absorbing Steering Columns*, Proceedings of the General Motors Corporation Automotive Safety Seminar, July 11–12, 1968.

4. Additional information regarding the active head restraint can be obtained through the 1999 Saab automobile brochures at your local Saab dealer, or by logging onto the Internet at www.Saab.com.

# Restraining Systems 7

"I never guess. It is a shocking habit destructive to the logical faculty."
**Sherlock Holmes**
*The Sign of the Four*

## Standard Restraint Devices

The restraint systems in today's vehicles are the heart and soul of the occupant safety system. As previously alluded to, the restraint system keeps the occupants in their seats before, during, and after the collision. There are three types of restraint systems available on today's vehicles: a totally active system, semiactive or semipassive system, and totally passive system.

A totally active restraint system means that the occupant must actively connect the restraint system within the vehicle by inserting a buckle into a latch mechanism. A semiactive or semipassive system consists of a shoulder belt and sometimes the lap belt, which is activated by opening or closing the door. Opening the door pulls the belts away from the occupant and then lets them return to the occupant when the door is closed. The lap belt portion of the restraint system may or may not be engaged as the occupant would in a totally active system.

A totally passive system is generally considered to be an air bag system. Most restraint systems today use an active lap and shoulder belt system and a supplemental restraint system, which is the air bag system.

*Commentary: Several years ago some automobile manufacturers decided to use an air bag system only as the primary restraint system. That system as far as I know never came into widespread use in a production vehicle. Before the air bag only system, some European cars had a shoulder belt only restraint system. Accident analysis showed that the shoulder belt alone system produced severe if not fatal injuries. It primarily happened when the vehicle went into a clockwise spin. The driver was partially ejected through the driver's door. Because there was no lower restraint system such as a lap belt, the driver was often caught by the neck with the shoulder restraint system while the lower portion of the body was ejected out of the vehicle. There have been recorded cases of decapitation with this system.*

## Shoulder/Lap Belts

There is only one correct way to wear a lap and shoulder belt restraint system. The lap belt must be firmly placed below the top of the pelvic girdle and on the top of the upper surface of the thigh. The shoulder belt must cross over the chest, go between the point of the shoulder and the neck area, and extend down to the pelvic girdle.

*Commentary: Colonel John Paul Stapp was a pioneer in the field of aerospace medicine. His efforts have been regarded as the basic background for many life-saving devices used in the automotive and aerospace fields. He was among the first, if not the first, human to volunteer to ride a rocket sled at speeds of those of a pilot being ejected from a jet aircraft to determine the effects of wind blast on the human body. A series of tests had been conducted on live animals, but it came to the point in the program that more data were required and only a human volunteer could provide those data.*

*Stapp was strapped into the seat on the rocket sled with an Air Force harness and the seat belt angle used was 45 degrees. To this day that angle is still the angle most generally agreed on as the optimum angle to hold the occupant in his/her seat. The forces from the lap belt are spread between a downward force on the upper legs or femurs and a horizontal force being applied to the strongest bone in the human body, the pelvic girdle.*

*Stapp's work was so significant that a conference was named in his honor, the Stapp Car Crash Conference. It is held in approximately October of each year in different parts of the U.S. and has been attended by engineers and scientists from all over the world. It has become one of the major sources of basic research information in automotive safety.*

Photographs 7.1 and 7.2 show the old cinch-type lap belt latch system. This latch was found in a vehicle where the webbing had been torn in half. The latch then slides off the webbing itself. Note the diagonal bar inside of the latch. The webbing material is weaved around the bar. The bar itself sits in a slot, and when the end of the webbing is pulled, the bar and webbing work against each other to tighten the belt around the occupant and hold him/her securely in place. This system prevented the belt from rising up onto the abdomen of the occupant, thus preventing soft tissue or internal injuries.

**Photograph 7.1** The old cinch-type lap belt latch system.

**Photograph 7.2** The old cinch-type lap belt latch system.

Most vehicles built after the late 1980s use a latch, which slides easily up and down the length of the webbing. This system is commonly called the free-running loop system. This system does not allow the occupant to tighten or cinch the belt across the pelvic girdle. As a result the lap belt may ride up over the pelvic girdle into the soft abdominal region of the occupant. If the belt is allowed to stay in this position during the second collision of an accident, the occupant may sustain severe internal abdominal injuries. This is an incorrect position for the lap belt.

The shoulder belt must be positioned as previously described in order to prevent neck abrasions and other more serious injuries during the second collision. Many vehicles today allow the occupant to adjust the shoulder belt anchor position within specified limits so that the belt is properly aligned when connected to the buckle portion of the restraint system.

During a second collision, the occupants slide forward on the seats and into the restraint system, loading that system and applying forces to the human body. The application of these forces causes contusions or bruises to the occupant's body. These bruises and contusions are clear evidence marks to the investigator that the occupants were wearing the restraint system. In minor collisions these contusions are usually small and may not be recorded by the trauma physician or emergency medical technician (ETM) when treating the occupant after the collision at the scene or in the emergency room.

In addition to the occupants' contusions or bruising, there may be other clear indicators or witness marks such as stretch marks in the restraint system webbing. Webbing material is a man-made fiber. As the occupant loads the webbing, it is being pulled through the loop. The webbing material has approximately 9% stretch built into it. This means that the webbing can stretch up to 9% of its length when loaded by the occupant during a collision.

The stretching occurs because the webbing material is being held at its three anchor points in the vehicle — one either side of the seat and one on the "B" post — and is being locked in place at the latch plate as the occupant loads the system. The webbing must pass through a plastic-rimmed portion of the latch system. In doing so the loading process stretches the webbing material as it is being forced through the plastic opening. This heats the webbing material to the point where it begins to slightly melt and to break some of the strands of the webbing material.

Photographs 7.3 through 7.8 show the proper way to examine and photograph the restraint system webbing. Note that the webbing is completely pulled out from the retractor spool. A specified length is then photographed and that section of the webbing is released back onto the retractor spool. A second photograph is taken and the webbing is again released onto the spool.

**Photographs 7.3 through 7.8** The proper way to examine and photograph the restraint system webbing.

**Photograph 7.4** (Continued)

**Photograph 7.5** (Continued)

**Photograph 7.6** (Continued)

**Photograph 7.7** (Continued)

**Photograph 7.8** (Continued)

**Photographs 7.9 through 7.15** The reverse side of the webbing.

The process is repeated until the entire length of the belt on one side is examined and photographed. If any stretch marks were seen, then additional photographs should be taken with a close-up lens to see the actual marks. The same process is repeated for the other side of the webbing, because the investigator can never be sure where the stretch marks may be located.

Photographs 7.9 through 7.15 show the reverse side of the webbing using the same procedure as described previously. Note that each photograph has a card with the location of the restraint system, the length of webbing being recorded, and the side of the webbing being examined. This same procedure should be carried out for all restraint systems in the vehicle. If a restraint system is missing, then a special note is made on the inspection report and a photograph is taken of the bracketry that should have had the restraint system attached to it.

In addition to the webbing stretch marks, the free-running loop tongue can also be of assistance to the investigator. Photographs 7.16 through 7.18 are close-up views of the free-running loop. The webbing must pass over the plastic loop when being snapped into the buckle. The webbing passes through the plastic loop at an angle, due to the orientation of the system within the vehicle and the application to the occupant.

When the occupant loads the restraint system after the retractor has locked up, the webbing begins to stretch. As it is being pulled through the free-running loop, the heat and pressure leave a witness mark on the plastic material, as shown in Photographs 7.16 and 7.17. Note the lines that are at

**Photograph 7.10** (Continued)

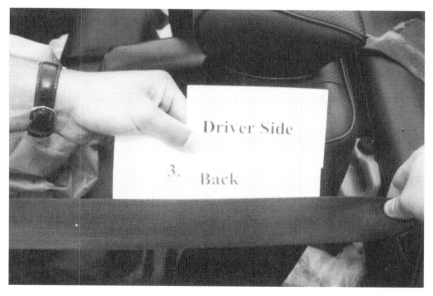

**Photograph 7.11** (Continued)

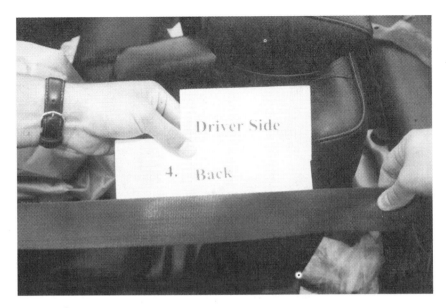

**Photograph 7.12** (Continued)

**Photograph 7.13** (Continued)

**Photograph 7.14** (Continued)

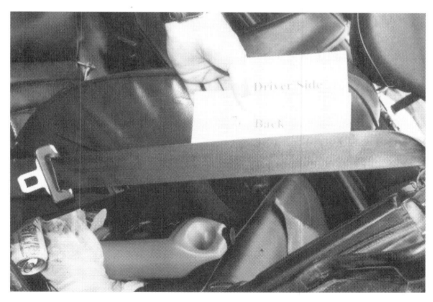

**Photograph 7.15** (Continued)

**Photographs 7.16 through 7.18** Close-up views of the free-running loop.

**Photograph 7.17** (Continued)

**Photograph 7.18** (Continued)

an angle to the direction of travel of the webbing. This is a clear indication that the occupant was wearing the restraint system at the time of the application of the stretch marks.

Photograph 7.18 shows the opposite side of the free-running loop. Notice the plastic surface is smooth and plain looking. This means that portion of the loop was not in contact with the webbing during the collision. The "D" ring, which is located on the "B" post, is also covered with plastic material and will usually have the same marks as the free-running loop. Many times the lap belt is held in place when the occupant rotates forward and prevents or minimizes the amount of movement of the webbing through the free-running loop. The investigator, to ensure that the information concerning the witness marks has been preserved, must photograph both of these components.

Photograph 7.19 shows a stretch mark on the webbing of the restraint system. See how it extends over only a portion of the webbing material and for only a short distance. Many times it is necessary to bring the webbing out into the light and to turn it in several different directions so that the camera can pick up the stretched strands of the webbing material. The photographer must work with the investigator to ensure that the webbing distortions are shown. This is the witness mark the investigator must look for during the vehicle inspection. It is an undisputable fact that the occupant was wearing the restraint system at the time of the collision.

**Photograph 7.19** A stretch mark on the webbing of the restraint system.

When the occupant claims to have been belted during the collision and the medical reports do not record the occupant's bruising and there are no witness marks on the belt webbing, then the investigator must look for other witness marks inside the vehicle such as stellar fractures on the windshield, dents to the lower instrument panel, deformation to the steering wheel rim, and/or deformation to the instrument panel upper surface. Of course, other witness marks such as blood, tissue smears, or other such signs along with the interior damage are clear indications the occupants were not belted.

Can occupants claim to have been belted at the time of the collision and have minor bruising, and the investigator find marks indicating they were unbelted? Yes! Under these conditions there had to be some type of failure of the restraint system. Restraint systems fail in a myriad of ways. The webbing can fail. A latch mechanism may fail. The anchors may fail, from the "B" pillars or from the floor pan. The retractor may fail in one of several ways, most of which are not of a permanent nature.

Webbing can fail in two ways:

1. The webbing itself can tear apart.
2. The webbing can be cut completely through with a knife or a piece of sharp metal during the collision.

There is a great deal of difference between the two when observed at the scene. Photographs 7.20 through 7.22 show webbing that has torn itself apart.

**Photographs 7.20 through 7.22** Webbing that has torn itself apart.

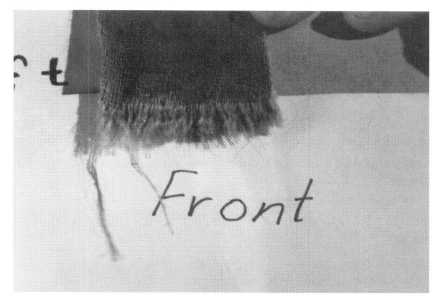

**Photograph 7.21** (Continued).

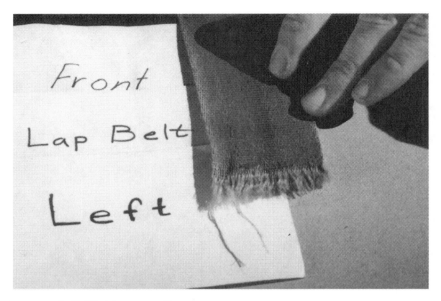

**Photograph 7.22** (Continued).

In other words, it has failed. A clean knife cut look has little or no ragged edges at the cut. If the cut is only partially through the webbing material, then it shows both a clean cut and a ragged edge.

Photographs 7.21 and 7.22 are close-ups of a piece of webbing in which the webbing material parted or ripped apart. Note the ragged edges. This is where the material began to stretch. Because the load was so great, the material had a flaw, or it aged due to use in the vehicle, it could not withstand the load, and the webbing material failed.

Several years ago some manufacturers changed production to a door-mounted "D" ring instead of a "B" post-mounted system. It used a system similar to a door latch with the round bar being caught by an opened mouth bracket mounted on the door frame. Photographs 7.23 through 7.25 show the results of a failure in that system.

When the occupant loaded the restraint system, it pulled on the webbing that pulled on the round bar caught in the bracket. In this case the bracket bent outward into the door opening, allowing the entire restraint system to slip out of the bracket and the occupant to strike the windshield and instrument panel. The three photographs show the bent bracket still in place. Note how the bracket is pulled up from the screws holding it in place. (Photographs 7.26 and 7.27 show a replacement bracket and round bar. Photograph 7.26 shows the combination, as it should go together. Photograph 7.27 shows the open side of the bracket.) As always, the opposite side of the vehicle should be photographed to see the wear on that system compared with the failed

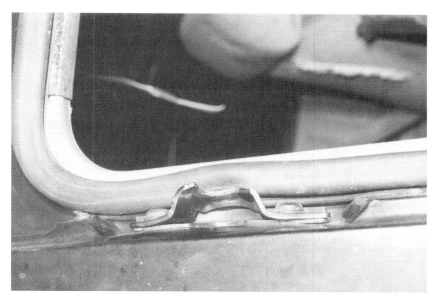

**Photographs 7.23 through 7.25** The results of a failure in a door-mounted "D" ring system.

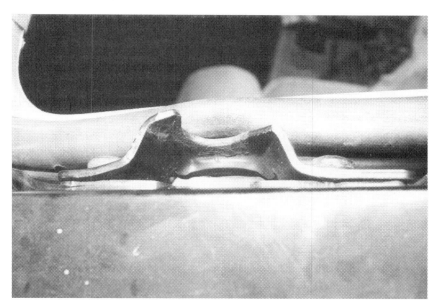

**Photograph 7.24** (Continued).

**Photograph 7.25** (Continued).

**Photographs 7.26 and 7.27**  A replacement bracket and round bar for the door-mounted "D" ring system.

one. Photographs 7.28 and 7.29 show the driver's side bracket. Note that there is some outward bending of the bracket, but not as severe as the failed system. The bright spot in the middle of the bracket is the wear spot from the round bar.

**Photograph 7.27** (Continued).

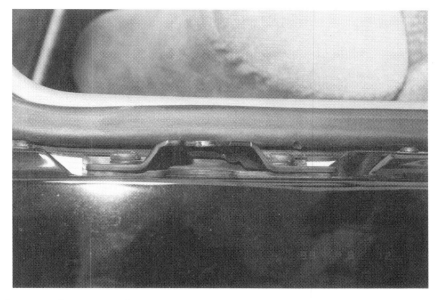

**Photographs 7.28 and 7.29** The driver's side bracket for the door mounted "D" ring system.

Many times the driver tells the on-scene investigator that he/she always wears his/her seat belt. One quick check is to look at the webbing itself, especially at the outside edges. Photographs 7.30 through 7.33 are a set of photographs taken of a very worn set of restraint systems. Webbing material does not go back through the various "D" rings and other attachments to the retractor in a straight line.

The edges of the webbing are always being rubbed up against the edges of the other components. That can only happen if the webbing is being pulled in and out of the retractor. This is a good indication of continual use of the restraint system. Another is the tongue of the free-running loop. If the belt system has been used for a period of time, the chrome finish is scratched and

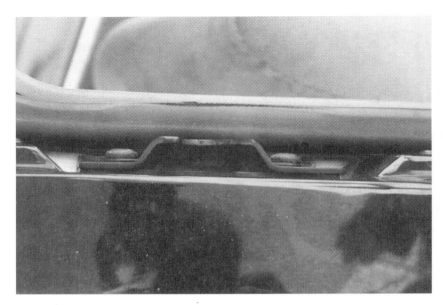

**Photograph 7.29** (Continued).

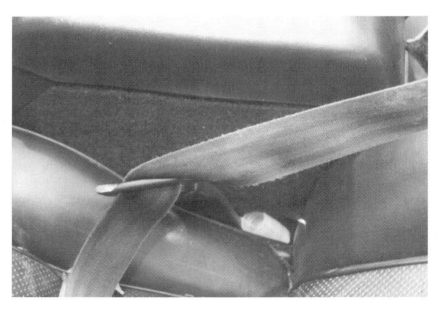

**Photographs 7.30 through 7.33** A set of photographs taken of a very worn set of restraint systems.

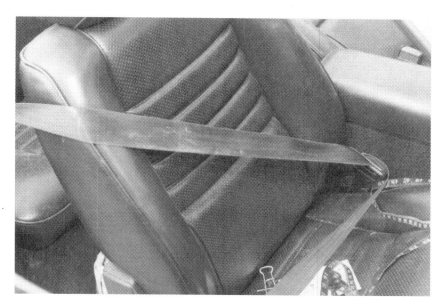

**Photograph 7.31** (Continued).

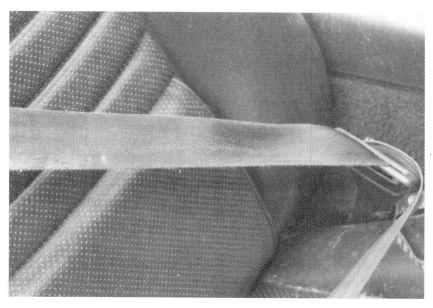

**Photograph 7.32** (Continued).

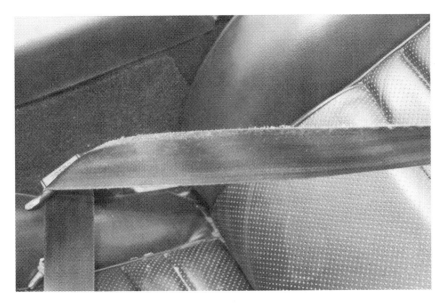

**Photograph 7.33** (Continued).

shows many wear spots. If the system has not been used, there are few wear spots and in many cases they are rusty.

As in all product design and development, there are new advances being made almost every day in the field of automotive safety. Within the past few years a new development has come onto the market with respect to the lap–shoulder belt restraint system. It is designated as a pretensioning device. A small charge is concealed in the assembly of the seat belt system, and at impact, the charge fires and pulls the seat belt tight around the occupant. This keeps the occupant in the seat and helps to minimize, and many times to eliminate, submarining of the occupant underneath the lap belt portion of the restraint system.

## Air Bags or Supplemental Systems

The man who is considered to be the father of the air bag is John W. Hetrick, an industrial engineer from Newport, Pennsylvania. He was awarded a U.S. Patent on August 18, 1953.[1]

He thought of the idea after a 1952 accident where he swerved his car and braked quickly to avoid an obstacle. Both he and his wife extended their arms to shield their daughter sitting in the center front position. Two weeks later, he submitted his plans to a patent attorney. Variations of the air bag have been around since that time. Sometimes it was called an air cushion. It has been tried in many different forms to act as a device to slow down the occupant during a second collision.

At one time, the air bag was considered the optimum restraint system. Many researchers thought it would replace the present lap and shoulder belt restraint system.

Accident investigations conducted over many years have shown that the air bag system must act in conjunction with not only the lap and shoulder belt restraint but also the energy-absorbing steering column and wheel, the padded instrument panel, and the padded knee bolsters. Therefore, it is now considered by the original equipment manufacturers to be a supplemental restraint system and is designated as such an all vehicles.

The air bag system consists of these basic components: a sensor for the detection and determination of crash severity; an inflator or energy source responsible for gas generation, and a bag to interact with the occupant and vehicle structure to provide signals to the sensor, support for the inflator, or bag and interior integrity for the occupants.

At the present time there are three air bag systems in most passenger cars: the driver's air bag system that is released from the interior of the steering wheel, the right front passenger air bag system that is released from the instrument panel above the glove box, and the side air bag that is released from the side of the seat and back cushion to protect the occupant in a side impact collision. There are usually two to four electromechanical sensors that are used to trigger the air bag system.

The first is mounted on the bumper system, the second is mounted at or near the front firewall, and the third is near the front seat of the vehicle. The air bags were basically designed to fire for frontal impacts only, ranging from 30 degrees left of center to 30 degrees right of center. There is a range of impact speeds at which the air bag systems operate. Below approximately 8 mi/h the air bag system does not fire, and between 8 and 17 mi/h the air bag systems may or may not fire. Above 17 mi/h the air bag is always supposed to fire, filling the bag with a gas to slow down the occupant and spread the load of the impact.

As with all new devices, there are specific problems associated with that injury-mitigating device. Air bags are filled with a gas that is hot as it inflates the bag, even though the gas is cooled and filtered; the hot surface of the bag has caused injuries to the face and arms of the occupants. There have been recorded cases of serious eye injuries from both the heat and the impact of the air bag against the occupant's face. Because the air bag system must operate for a wide range of occupants (fifth to ninety-fifth percentile), it is difficult to control the fill of gas into the bag. The smaller fifth percentile human in many cases (not in all) develops some type of minor injury. It must be remembered by the on-scene investigator that the air bag has panels to allow expulsion of the gas air mixture during compression by the occupant into the bag.

Photographs 7.34 to 7.37 show the driver's air bag position after it has been fired during a second collision. Note that the steering wheel rim has not been deformed; and there is no damage to the windshield, interior rearview mirror, or sun visors.

Other problems exist such as the crash-sensing criteria. This includes defining an impact threshold speed given a variety of crash conditions such as soft or hard impacts, and environmental conditions such as ambient temperatures and manufacturing tolerances.

Design thresholds must be evaluated with the other system components. As an example, a threshold can be set higher when the American public always wears seat belts when riding in a vehicle. Sensor placement is another area of concern as well as electromechanical vs. all electronic sensors. Each of these situations brings with it both positive and negative effects. Electronic sensors are smaller and more easily placed but electrical problems can occur; electromechanical systems are more reliable but are bulkier. Suffice it to say that a great deal of research money is being spent to develop the best system for the wide range of uses that an air bag must be put to in today's automobile.

**Photographs 7.34 to 7.37** The driver's air bag position after it has been fired during a second collision.

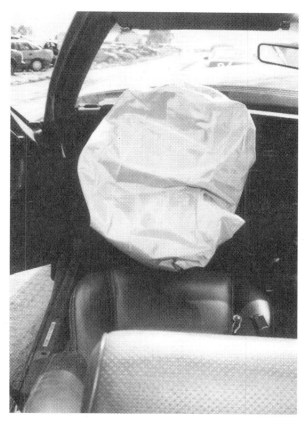

**Photograph 7.35** (Continued).

Starting in 1998, some model vehicles had a new supplemental restraint system installed; it is called the side impact air bag. These side impact air bags are usually mounted in the side of the front seats of the vehicle although some cars have mounted them in the door pillar above the window in the roof area.

One of the newest side impact air bag systems is designed to inflate first at the bottom to protect the occupant's rib cage at the point of impact between the door structure and the occupant; the top part of the air bag is then inflated to offer protection to the head.

The crash sensors trigger the gas inflator for the air bag in less than 5 msec after the collision begins. This requires a leading edge bag speed approaching 200 mi/h. To give some idea how fast 5 msec actually is, consider the fact that it takes 200 msec for the human eye to blink once; in other words, the sensor fires 40 times faster than the blink of an eye.

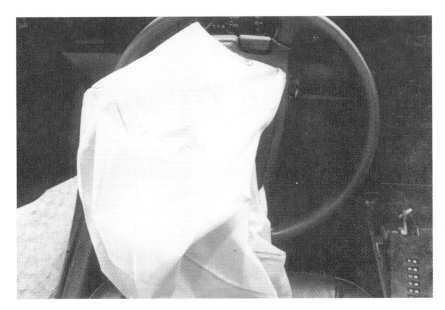

**Photograph 7.36** (Continued).

**Photograph 7.37** (Continued).

The purpose of the supplemental restraint system is to absorb energy but primarily to spread the load of impact over a larger area.

**Commentary:** *We have all been to the movies and seen the stuntmen perform falls from great heights. This is accomplished by using a very, very large air bag that has panels allowing the gas air mixture to escape, thereby slowly reducing the stuntman's velocity to zero. In each of the stunts the stuntman must make sure that he falls onto the air bag on his back. This ensures that the force per unit area being applied to his body is much smaller than if he were to land on his feet or any similar portion of its body.*

*There have been many recorded free falls of pilots whose parachute did not open. These men survived falls from great heights on large stacks of hay, in deep unpacked snow, or even on deeply plowed fields where the earth is still soft. In each case the men landed on their backs in a prone position reducing the force per unit area on their bodies.*

There have been other problems with supplemental restraint systems including the air bags not firing when they are supposed to or firing when they are not supposed to; the cover door on the system not opening completely, thereby forcing the bag to be released from its container in a very unusual manner and causing unnecessary injuries to the occupants; and the heat and speed of opening of the air bag causing injury to smaller occupants.

The air bag systems, just like the other occupant restraint systems, are devices that were developed to assist the occupants in a second collision. They work under a given range of conditions but are not a panacea for automobile accident injury prevention. The air bag or supplemental restraint system is a passive system, meaning it works without occupant intervention; the occupant restraint system, which is the lap and shoulder belt system, only works when the occupant actively engages one or more portions of the system.

## New Developments

Approximately 20 years ago webbing manufacturers were looking at a new material that could be woven into the webbing itself that would stretch at a predetermined level limiting the amount of force that the body would be subjected to under a collision situation. Within the last few months a manufacturer of seat belt systems has developed a new fiber that can be woven into the seat belt material that is tailored to work in conjunction with an air bag to slow and reduce a passenger's impact with an air bag during a collision. It is a synthetic fiber that is engineered for safety restraints and other managed energy applications. Webbing made with this fiber allows three separate actions to occur during a collision.

Initially, the webbing holds the occupants in position; then as the fibers relax as needed, they limit the forces imposed on the occupants, complementing the action of the air bag and allowing the occupants' bodies to decelerate. Finally, the fibers restrain the occupants, preventing impact with the instrument panel, steering wheel, or windshield. The manufacturer claims the new webbing material has such a resiliency that it works for a broad range of body types all the way from children to larger individuals. It also intends to use the new webbing material as a direct replacement for mechanical force limiters that are presently being used in about half of the cars in the U.S. This appears to be the latest engineering development that can work in conjunction with an air bag as opposed to a separate system as presently being used in today's automobiles.

At the present time, depending on the study involved, lap and shoulder belt systems are being used by somewhere between 50 and 75% of the population. These systems cannot work unless they are being used.

The accident investigator/reconstructionist must use his/her knowledge to educate the general driving public at every opportunity. When asked to speak before a local citizens group, service club, or professional group he/she must take the message that the driver is a part of the automobile–road–occupant problem. The automobiles and roads are being redesigned as necessary to prevent, if possible, the useless slaughter and maiming of the nation's population.

The occupants must be educated concerning the safety devices that have been built into the vehicle. A prime example is the automatic braking system (ABS) system. This was designed to prevent lock up of the brakes of the vehicle in an emergency braking situation. The American driving public generally does not know how the system functions.

In the past our drivers have been taught to pump the brakes during an emergency-braking maneuver to avoid brake lock up. The new ABS system requires that the driver does not pump the brakes, but keeps a constant pressure on the brake pedal to allow the electronic system to modulate the brakes, to prevent brake lock up, and to give a maximum braking effort.

Within the past year there have been several studies that show the new braking system is not being used properly and has not reduced the number or severity of emergency braking situations including collisions. Professional accident investigators and reconstructionists must all provide the world with the information gained through their work in this field.

Are there more air bags in the future? Work is being conducted on an air bag to reduce knee and femur injuries. Some work is even being done on roof-mounted air bags, principally for the rear occupants' head protection.

As long as accident investigators continue to find that there are problems with the safety devices in the vehicles, there will be research done to develop more and better devices to reduce and eliminate needless injuries on the country's highways.

## Restraint Devices for Special Occupants

The category of special restraining systems covers only a small percentage of the population, but they are the most important to many investigators: women and children.

### Pregnant Women

Restraints for pregnant women have often been a topic of discussion among the safety researchers across the world. There have been experimental studies to determine the mechanism of fetal and maternal injuries using different types of restraint systems. Studies with pregnant animals showed that in 11 of 18 cases using different types of restraint systems — including lap belts alone, forward facing, with two 3-point systems, forward facing, and two rearward facing — not *one* fetus survived an impact.

A series of experiments on three pregnant animals studied the prevention of fetal injury with the use of a new "net-type" restraint system. All animals were subjected to decelerations of over 40 *g*. The study using experimental animals showed that protection is available for the pregnant female.

One animal did not survive due to the inadvertent insertion of a needle into the lower edge of the placenta to place the catheter. The other two animals delivered healthy infants after going the full term of their pregnancies. No obvious injuries were noted in either mother or fetus. The results of the system looked promising. Unfortunately, no additional work was done either to determine its long-term effect or to bring it into production for the automotive driving public. At that time it was believed that a scaled-down version could possibly be used for a child in the toddler stage, but no further action was taken on this variation of the restraint system.

Researchers and field investigators/reconstructionists have always maintained that the lap belt should be worn as low as possible on the pelvic girdle so that the lower edge of the lap belt rests on of the muscles of the upper leg. The same can be said for pregnant women in the first and second stages of their pregnancies. Unfortunately, during the third stage this action does not work, because it is impossible to get the lap belt under the fundus. The investigator/reconstructionist when investigating accidents involving pregnant women must spend more time on the details of the webbing of the restraint system, to determine if the restraint system has been worn at the time of the collision. This method was reviewed earlier.

The investigator/reconstructionist must now review or have someone with medical knowledge review the medical data of the pregnant female driver to determine if there has been any bruising of the lower abdomen and upper thighs after the accident. If bruising is noted in any other location on the body, then the seat belt was improperly worn prior to the collision and may have been the cause of the fetal injury or death.

Additional injuries to the pregnant female driver such as thoracic or head injuries are an indication that the driver did not wear the restraint system at the time of the accident.

## Children

A suitable restraining device for children from the pre-toddler stage to the young adolescent age has always been a problem for automotive engineers, from the standpoint of not only comfort and safety for the children but also ease of entrance and egress for the parent who must put the children into the device.

Child restraints are basically divided into pre- and post-toddler types. The young adolescent can usually use the lap and shoulder belt system with the use of a booster seat. The pretoddler devices have had a great deal of experimental work conducted on them over the past 10 years. This type of work culls out the poorer designs and leaves the better designs in production for the safety of America's children.

Generally, the child seats are used in the front seat, but facing toward the rear. They are usually referred to as a rearward-facing child seats. At the present time all rearward-facing child seats appear to be working very well. The next step up for the child restraint system is a forward facing seat. Once again these child-seating systems have undergone experimental crash testing by the manufacturers' laboratories and the weaker systems have been discarded. The Insurance Institute for Highway Safety has conducted several in-depth studies on all types of child restraint systems and has once again culled out the poor performers in hopes of reducing the injuries to children.

The National Highway Traffic Safety Administration states that of the 479 children ages 5 to 9 killed in motor vehicles in 1997, 157 were probably too small for the seat belts to protect them. That is part of the problem with our younger yet larger and heavier population. These children are too big for the forward-facing seat systems and many of the booster seat systems are not generally available for the driving public to obtain information on their safety record as well as where to purchase these devices. Therefore, many parents today are putting their children into the standard lap and shoulder belt systems that come with the vehicle.

Unfortunately, these children who are too large for the forward-facing child seats are too small to use the standard lap and shoulder belt restraint systems; as a result they are more severely injured in an automobile crash because the standard restraint system does not protect them due to their size.

During his/her inspection, the investigator/reconstructionist must constantly be on the lookout for child restraint devices that were in an accident vehicle. The child restraint device must be inspected in depth along with the rest of the vehicle. The investigator must determine if the child restraint system has been properly attached to the existing restraint system in the vehicle. He/she must look for weakened component parts on the child restraint system, and worn or frayed seat belt webbing in the child restraint system or in the existing vehicle restraint system. Damaged child restraint components are also an indication of the child being thrown from the device during the collision.

*Commentary*: *The investigator/reconstructionist must always be ready for anything during the investigation and reconstruction of an accident. A child restraint accident can turn out to be a nightmare.*

*A child restraint system was used in the front seat of a vehicle that it did not fit into properly. As a result the restraint system did not work properly and the child was injured, or so it was thought after the initial inspection. Try as they might, they could not find anything wrong with the child restraint system. The opposing expert representing the manufacturer of the child restraint device requested to inspect, analyze, and verify that the device was indeed made by that company. Approximately 2 weeks later a letter was received from the client stating that the device that had been turned over to the opposing expert was not the one involved in the accident. The father of the child had, for some unknown reason, substituted a different child restraint system.*

*Further talks with the father who was driving the vehicle at the time of the inspection finally related to us that he had thrown out the original device, had gone to a junkyard, had found the device that he thought was similar to the one he was using, and said that it was the subject of the litigation.*

*The opposing expert told us they had discovered this by looking at the date of the manufacturer stamped on the product and it was made 2 months after the date of the accident. Therefore, they both knew it was the wrong device. In this case the investigator/reconstructionist did not do anything wrong.*

*The only fault found was that no one determined the manufacturer's information stamped into the plastic of the child restraint system. Had that been done, it would have hopefully found the father's mistake and saved a great deal of embarrassment.*

Once the child restraint device has been photographed and videotaped in place in the vehicle and the investigator/reconstructionist has completed a detailed inspection of the device, as best he/she can in its present position, the device must be removed from the vehicle. A thorough inspection should be done, once again looking for the components that could not be seen when the child restraint device was installed in the vehicle. Be sure to look for instructions that have been attached to it or to some surface of the device with respect to installing it in the vehicle.

Check to see that this device has been installed properly according to the manufacturer's instructions. If the instructions are not attached or adhered to the device, then check with the vehicle owner to determine if he/she still has the instructions that should have come with the unit when purchased.

The instructions should also delineate the way in which the child restraint device should be facing in the vehicle, forward or rearward; and also the restrictions, if any, on the type of vehicle in which it should be used. As an example, the device may not be usable in a pickup truck because of the distance from the seat to the instrument panel. It may be usable in a vehicle that only has a seat belt in the center position of the rear seat. These conditions must be determined during the process of the inspection of each restraint system.

## Converted Vehicles for the Handicapped

Since the U.S. Congress passed the Americans with Disabilities Act, there has been a change in the public's view of buildings and of automobiles. A considerable number of vehicles are on the road that have been converted for use by handicapped drivers. These conversions generally consist of vans that have been modified with either a higher roofline or a lower floor pan. The rear-opening doors or side-sliding doors have also been modified to accept a hydraulic–mechanical device, which can raise and lower the wheelchair of the handicapped driver. Once the driver is inside the vehicle, the platform used to raise the driver and wheelchair is pulled upward and inward and the doors automatically close.

The driver then must wheel himself/herself up to the driver's position and lock the wheelchair in place. These locking devices can lock the frame of the chair to a bolt or pin that has been fastened into the floor pan. The wheelchair may contain a lap belt system; generally, the restraint system of the vehicle has been modified to allow the handicapped driver to use it to hold himself/herself in the proper driving position once the wheelchair has been locked in place. The foot controls are modified by linkages to hand controls that the driver is taught to use.

These converted vans are very expensive and are usually kept for a long period of time by the handicapped individual. This means that the investigator/reconstructionist must be careful to fully investigate the maintenance of the van prior to the accident. This may include performing a detailed inspection of the braking system and the steering system to ensure that all components are actively working and have been properly maintained.

The wheelchair locking system must also undergo a detailed inspection. There are a variety of ways in which the wheelchair can be held in place; these include a pincher lock which encloses a high strengthen bolt or inserts into the floor pan that the wheelchair wheels roll into when reaching the proper driver position, or floor locks that hold the wheels in place. All these systems must be checked to ensure that they held that driver in place during the accident sequence. The same detailed analysis must be conducted on the webbing of the restraint system used in the vehicle. The analysis of the webbing is described earlier.

Some handicapped individuals are not able to drive a vehicle due to the severity of their handicap. In these cases a normal driver would then drive the vehicle, but the remainder of the vehicle is modified to allow the handicapped individual to enter and leave the confines of the van. These handicapped individuals must also be restrained inside the vehicle when it is moving. The investigator/reconstructionist must perform a detailed inspection of this restraint system including the wheelchair-locking device.

There have been some aftermarket manufacturers of these converted vans that place the handicapped passenger in a restraint system that is not parallel to the position of the normal driver and right front passenger. These handicapped passengers are forced to take the forward force impact as a lateral impact on their bodies. The wheelchair is not padded in the lateral directions, therefore resulting in serious if not life-threatening injuries to these handicapped passengers. The conscientious investigator/reconstructionist makes a thorough and detailed examination of a converted van with this type of arrangement to ensure that the handicapped passenger's restraint system offered the best protection for them in a forward force accident.

There is an additional problem with handicap-converted vans, and it has to do with a normal driver trying to move these vans into his/her own driveway or from the driveway to the street. There have been a few accidents of this nature and the investigator/reconstructionist faced with the situation must be extremely careful to determine if all the necessary equipment that was designed for use on the handicapped converted van is in place for the nonhandicapped driver.

*Commentary: A strange case was recently reviewed. A wife was moving her husband's handicap-converted van into the garage after washing it. She had driven the van on many other occasions prior to this one and felt confident in using it. She started forward into the garage and her husband was in a wheelchair in the parking space next to the van. For some reason the van shot forward and struck the husband in the wheelchair inflicting fatal injuries at the scene. It was discovered that a footrest was missing that would allow the nonhandicapped driver to rest the heel of his/her foot on it when driving the van. It was finally concluded that the wife did not use the proper pedal because she did not have a reference point from which to move her heel. She pushed on the gas pedal instead of the brake pedal, causing unnecessary acceleration of the van.*

There may be other types of special restraint systems being used in today's barrier-free world. The accident investigator/reconstructionist must be on the lookout during every inspection to ensure that he/she does not miss a special restraint system during his/her inspection of the vehicle.

## References

1. Hetrick, J. W., U.S. Patent, 1953.

# Vehicle and Occupant Accident Investigation Forms

# 8

"I am not retained by the police to supply their deficiencies."

**Sherlock Holmes**
*The Blue Carbuncle*

Recording the data at an inspection by the use of a video camera, a 35-mm still camera, and a tape recorder is the best way of documenting the accident vehicle. Many times, however, it is not possible to show on film or tape what is actually seen. A long-hand method is the use of standard reporting forms. Figure 8.1 contains standard forms. They have many advantages over a dictated tape recording in that the investigator can visualize the marked up areas of the vehicle. Another advantage is that long-hand forms eliminate the loss of photographs due to film lab or camera problems and they are a permanent record for the case file.

*Commentary: I have purposely left out a scene reporting form because there is no such thing as a standard scene. Each accident location is unique and requires that the investigator use his/her skills to accurately depict the area. (See Chapter 4 on scene investigation for a scene checklist and more details.)*

## Vehicle Data — Page 1

The vehicle data form on page 1 (Figure 8.1A) records the official information about the vehicle: make, model, year of manufacture, manufacturer's data plate with date of build, gross vehicle weight, body style from cars to tractor trailer, vehicle identification number (VIN), color, odometer reading, engine

**D. J. Van Kirk P.E. & Associates, Inc.**
**Forensic and Consulting Engineers**
**Accident Investigation Form**

VEHICLE DATA:

| MAKE: | | | | YEAR: | | | | |
|---|---|---|---|---|---|---|---|---|
| MODEL: | | | | | | | | |
| VIN: | | | | | | | | |
| MANUFACTURE DATE: | | | | GVWR: | | | | |
| BODY STYLE: | ( ) 4 DR   ( ) 2 DR   ( ) CONVERTIBLE   ( ) PICK-UP | | | | ( ) SPORT UTILITY | | | |
| | ( ) VAN   ( ) MOTORCYCLE   ( ) BICYCLE   ( ) TRACTOR/TRAILER | | | | | | | |
| | OTHER | | | | | | | |
| COLOR: | | | | | | | | |
| ODOMETER: | | | ( ) MILES | | ( ) KILOMETERS | | | |
| ENGINE: | | | | | ( ) TURBO / SUPERCHARGED | | | |
| ( ) AXIAL | ( ) TRANSVERSE | | | | | | | |
| TRANSMISSION: | ( ) AUTOMATIC | | ( ) MANUAL | | | - SPD | | |
| DRIVE AXLE: | ( ) FRONT | | ( ) REAR | | ( ) AWD / 4X4 | | | |

| WINDOWS: | WINSHIELD | LEFT | | RIGHT | | REAR | OTHER |
|---|---|---|---|---|---|---|---|
| | | FRONT | REAR | FRONT | REAR | | |
| UNDAMAGED | | | | | | | |
| BROKEN OUT | | | | | | | |
| CRACKED | | | | | | | |
| OUT OF PLACE | | | | | | | |
| HOLE(S) | | | | | | | |
| FIXED | | | | | | | |
| OPEN | | | | | | | |
| CLOSED | | | | | | | |
| IMPACT | | | | | | | |
| POST-CRASH | | | | | | | |

WINDOW NOTES:

| DOORS: | LEFT | | RIGHT | | REAR | OTHER |
|---|---|---|---|---|---|---|
| | FRONT | REAR | FRONT | REAR | | |
| OPERATIONAL | | | | | | |
| JAMMED SHUT | | | | | | |
| CUT/FORCED | | | | | | |
| CAME OPEN | | | | | | |
| REMOVED | | | | | | |

DOOR NOTES:

**Figure 8.1A** Standard accident investigation reporting forms: vehicle data.

size and direction in the engine compartment, type of transmission (manual; three-, four-, or five-speed, or automatic), and the location and number of drive axles.

The next section considers the condition of all the windows of the vehicle: from undamaged to holes; fixed, opened or closed; and damage due to impact or to postcrash such as might happen in a junkyard. There is a section marked "notes" for any unusual damage not cataloged. This might include "windshield removed by rescue squad and laid 10 ft down the road from the vehicle."

The final section on the page is for the all the doors of the vehicle. Again, the condition is rated from operational to removed. There is also a space for

**Van Kirk & Associates Accident Investigation Form**

TIRES:

| SIZE / BRAND: | | |
|---|---|---|
| FRONT | LEFT: | |
| | RIGHT: | |
| REAR | LEFT: | |
| | RIGHT: | |

| | | INFLATED: | | PUNCTURED: | | ON RIM BEAD: | |
|---|---|---|---|---|---|---|---|
| | | YES | NO | YES | NO | YES | NO |
| FRONT | LEFT: | | | | | | |
| | RIGHT: | | | | | | |
| REAR | LEFT: | | | | | | |
| | RIGHT: | | | | | | |

| WEAR: | | | | | | | |
|---|---|---|---|---|---|---|---|
| FRONT | LEFT: | | | | | | |
| | RIGHT: | | | | | | |
| REAR | LEFT: | | | | | | |
| | RIGHT: | | | | | | |

| DAMAGE: | | |
|---|---|---|
| FRONT | LEFT: | |
| | RIGHT: | |
| REAR | LEFT: | |
| | RIGHT: | |

TIRE NOTES:

**Figure 8.1B** Tire data.

notes, which could not be covered in the columns. This might include data such as "only the outer door panel had been removed during the crash."

# Tire Data — Page 2

The first section of page 2 (Figure 8.1B) is a column for the size and brand of each tire on the vehicle. The spare is not included because many new cars have a temporary spare. If there is a full-size spare, then make a note of it on the form. The reason for the tire sizes is that a vehicle does not operate properly if there are different size tires on it. In addition, there is also a problem when mixing steel-belted tires with bias ply tires.

The second section is to determine whether the tires were inflated, punctured, or still attached to the rim bead. The section marked inflated has to include the tire pressure, if the vehicle investigation is taken within a few months of the accident. Otherwise, the tires gradually lose air and the data are no longer useful. The section on punctured is for comparison with the

**Van Kirk & Associates Accident Investigation Form**

EXTERNAL DAMAGE SKETCHES

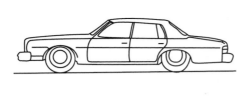

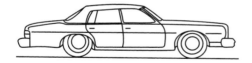
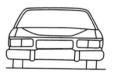

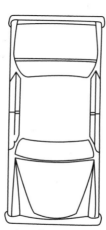

**Figure 8.1C** Exterior damage sketches.

on-scene photographs. The use of the section on rim beads is important because many of the tires do not stay on the bead if they are aired out at the collision and spun around until coming to rest.

The third section is for describing the wear of the tire. Usually it is a subjective evaluation unless wear bars are seen. Measurements taken of tread depth are not critical if there is any tread left. The last section is a space for the damage seen on each tire. This includes types of punctures, blowouts, cuts, abrasions, or other types of damage.

The section for tire notes can be used for additional comments or for sketches that been made to show some special aspect of the damage. (In one case, a sketch showed a grease cup driven into the hubcap when a tire and rim left the spindle.) This section should be coordinated with the still photographs to get a better idea of the tire problems as seen at the inspection. The wear patterns are recorded here, as well as any flat spots on the tread area, the sidewalls, and changes in the tire rims from scrapping on the roadbed during a sliding or rotating maneuver.

## Exterior Damage Sketches — Page 3

There are five views of a generic four-door passenger sedan (Figure 8.1C). No deliberate actions were taken to make the vehicle look like any special make or model. There are other pages for two doors, pickups, vans, and tractors such as cabovers as well as long nose. A special page is used for damage to trailers. Each view of the vehicle is supposed to be filled in by cross-hatching to show the areas of damage to the various areas of the vehicle.

The underside of the vehicle is not shown because many times it would be difficult either to turn the vehicle on its side or to lift it high enough to get photographs or sketch the damage. In addition, rolling the vehicle onto its side or top can induce other damage as well as exacerbate existing damage. Notes should be added to the vehicle sketch as well. These would include such items as window missing or rolled down, bumper missing, tires missing, and severe rusting including hole locations due to rust. Care should be taken to sketch the damage to the vehicle as accurately as possible. This is especially true in rollover cases. The amount of movement of the tumblehome in one direction or another is very important during the reconstruction phase of the accident report.

## Damage Measurements — Page 4

The upper portion of page 4 (Figure 8.1D) is a table for the measurements taken of the principal or initial damaged area of the vehicle. It asks for the

**Van Kirk & Associates Accident Investigation Form**

| DAMAGE MEASUREMENTS | | | | | | | |
|---|---|---|---|---|---|---|---|
| PDOF | CDC | | | | | | |
| Rollover | Turns | | Axis | | | | |
| Crush | Left-Right ( ) | | | Back-Front ( ) | | | D |
| Plane | C1 | C2 | C3 | C4 | C5 | C6 | |
| | | | | | | | |
| | | | | | | | |
| | | | | | | | |
| | | | | | | | |

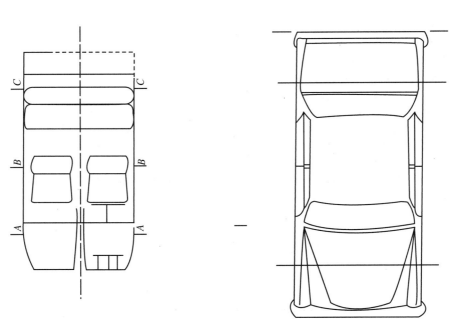

**Figure 8.1D** Damage measurements.

principal direction of force (PDOF) as well as the collision damage classification (CDC), where the direction of PDOF at point of impact (POI), vehicle deformation location, general type of collision, and damage scale are laid out by numbers and letters.

Consider the CDC 12FCEN6, for example. The first component, the number 12, refers to a clock direction system. The FCE component refers to "F" for frontal impact; "C" refers to specific horizontal area of the vehicle meaning center of the vehicle; and "E" refers to specific vertical areas on the vehicle, meaning everything below the beltline. The third component "N" designates a narrow object struck while the last component "6" refers to the damage scale. Chapter 10 on severity indices gives a complete description of the damage index and the principal direction of force.

The crush is then measured in six equal increments, starting from either the right- or left-hand side of the vehicle. There is room to include crush data at several different heights depending on the type of impact. These crush measurements can be used in a computer simulation program at a later date during the reconstruction

The lower half of page 4 (Figure 8.1D) shows the top view of the vehicle interior with the top and sides removed, and a normal top view of a generic vehicle. These are used to write down the changes in overall length of the vehicle and in the wheelbase. The view of the interior shows the location of the "A," "B," and "C" posts. Measurements are taken in both the X and Y direction to show the changes due to the collision. It is expected that the investigator will sketch in a reasonable facsimile of the damage.

## Occupant Area Intrusions — Page 5

Page 5 (Figure 8.1E) is dedicated to showing the damage to the occupants' compartment. Measurements can be taken but sketches here are mandatory because it is many times impossible to get inside the vehicle due to the exterior damage or to lack of enough room to focus the camera. The views shown include the fore and aft view of the front and rear seats, an overhead view of the seats, the floor pan; the steering wheel, and the location of the "A," "B," and "C" posts. There are also views of both the left and right side of the compartment. Again, sketches and dimensions are expected. This would also be the place to state if interior parts are missing such as the seats, and whether the seats have been loosened and/or removed and set back into the vehicle. Many times the steering wheel and column have been removed, the length of the energy-absorbing steering column is measured, and the parts are just thrown back into the vehicle.

**Van Kirk & Associates Accident Investigation Form**

OCCUPANT AREA INTRUSION

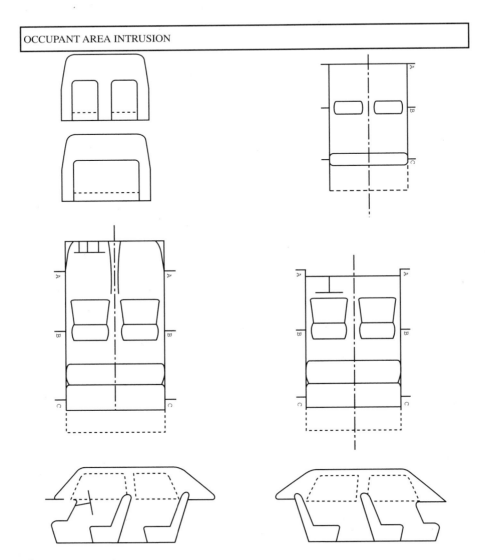

**Figure 8.1E** Left occupant area intrusions.

It must be remembered by the investigator that if permission is obtained prior to the starting litigation to remove and study any parts of the vehicle, the process should be recorded on videotape. The camera must be running during the entire procedure, with the time and a date shown in the frame of the camera. Location of the adjustable seats should also be recorded here as well as the position of the headrest and the adjustable seatback.

The investigator must bear in mind that the emergency medical service (EMS) people may have moved the seats, but dimensions still should be taken until all the information is obtained. Damage to the floor pan is also recorded here in both the $X$ and $Y$ directions.

## Internal Damage Sketches — Page 6

Page 6 (Figure 8.1F) was added when it was discovered that there was insufficient room on page 5 when there was a significant amount of damage to the interior of the vehicle. Again, dimensions and sketches are recorded of all the damage seen and felt by the investigator.

*Commentary: It is easy for an investigator to overlook damage on a vehicle that has been in a severe collision. At this point the prepared investigator can outshine his/her competition. He/she has come with a plan to start at a certain point on the vehicle and to continue moving around the vehicle until returning to the starting point. The same is done on the inside as well as the underside of the vehicle.*

*By following this type of plan little if any damage, witness marks, or missing parts can escape their inspection.*

## Interior Contacts — Page 7

Page 7 (Figure 8.1G) is sometimes referred to as a "flat room" drawing. The doors and roof are moved to obtain a flat view of the interior of the vehicle. The lower half of the page is a vertical view of the instrument panel, steering wheel, front windshield, and front doors folded outward. This is where the investigator marks down all the witness marks from the occupants' contacts inside the vehicle.

The location should be marked and the distance measured and recorded on the drawing. This would include "head stars" from impacts to the windshield by the occupants' heads, side window sliding contacts, marks on the interior door panels, dents to the instrument panel, sun visors, rear view mirror, and steering wheel. Detailed steering wheel damage is recorded on page 8 (Figure 8.1H). The investigator should not overlook any marks that he/she is not sure are from the occupants. It is better for him/her to record everything and later eliminate certain unnecessary details than to look foolish at a trial or deposition because he/she did not record that particular data point.

Van Kirk & Associates Accident Investigation Form

INTERNAL DAMAGE SKECTHES

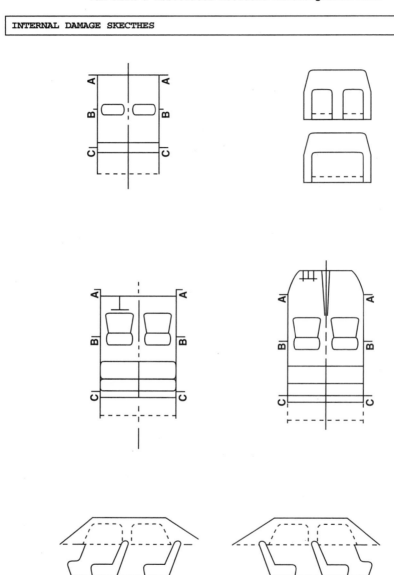

**Figure 8.1F** Internal damage sketches.

Van Kirk & Associates Accident Investigation Form

| INTERIOR CONTACTS |
|---|

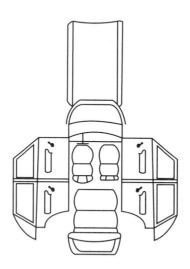

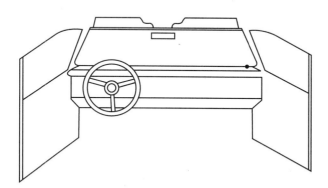

**Figure 8.1G** Interior contacts.

**Van Kirk & Associates Accident Investigation Form**

| INTERIOR: | | | | | | | | | |
|---|---|---|---|---|---|---|---|---|---|

| SEATS & HEADRESTS | | | | | STEERING COLUMN | | | | |
|---|---|---|---|---|---|---|---|---|---|
| | Front | | Back | | Fixed | | | | |
| | L | R | L | R | Tilt: | | | | |
| Bucket | | | | | dash ( ) | | | | |
| Bench | | | | | column ( ) | | | | |
| Adj. Base | | | | | Undeformed | | | | |
| Adj. Back | | | | | Amount | | | | |
| H/R avail. | | | | | Location | | | | |
| H/R adj. | | | | | | | | | |
| Undamaged | | | | | HUB MOVEMENT | | | | |
| Failure | | | | | none ( ) | Vert. | | Lat. | Long. |
| Deformation | | | | | 1 - 3 | | | | |
| Post-crash | | | | | 3 - 6 | | | | |
| | | | | | 6 - 12 | | | | |
| | | | | | 12 + | | | | |

Steering column diagram: A B C D (circle), L R (circle), UP LOW

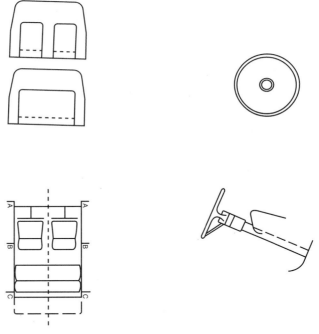

**Figure 8.1H** Interior seats, headrests, and steering wheel and column.

## Interior Seats, Headrests, and Steering Wheel and Column — Page 8

Detailed information on the seats and headrests is placed on page 8 (Figure 8.1H). This includes the types of seats, adjustability of the seat itself and the seatback, and the types of headrests available and if they can be adjusted, not only moved up and down but also rotated. Damage is then recorded but as to collision or postcollision at the scene or later at the storage or junkyard. Failures of any parts are recorded in detail. The steering column and steering wheel are handled in the same way. Is the column fixed, or tiltable, and is it still fixed to the dash panel?

It is necessary to determine the amount of deflection of the steering wheel rim. It is fairly easy to determine which is the upper edge of the steering wheel in today's vehicles. Make sure that the upper, lower, or sides of the wheel that are damaged are indicated. At the initial inspection the investigator may not have sufficient information to know if the vehicle was in a turn when it was struck head on causing rim damage at an unusual location. The hub movement is then recorded in the vertical, horizontal, and longitudinal planes.

A sketch is provided for the steering column compression change in length as well as any bending of the steering column that occurred at the second impact.

## Seat Belts and Air Bags — Page 9

Restraint systems today are almost exclusively a three-point design, which is a combination of lap belt and shoulder belt. The front seats of most if not all vehicles only have positions for two occupants. If the front seat allows for three occupants, then record that additional data under Notes at the bottom of page 9 (Figure 8.1I). The rear seat has positions for three occupants. The outboard seating positions have three point systems. The middle position has a lap belt only. The upper portion of this page is used to describe the type of restraint system using the code: "PD" for passive door mount, "PM" for passive motorized, "xxD" for passive belts that have been defeated by disconnecting the buckle, and "C" for cut during extraction.

The middle table is for the seat belt usage. It covers all six positions in the vehicle. The categories covered include loading or stretch marks on the webbing, usage marked on the police report, scratches on the buckle from usage, injury from the seat belts, hospital report of belt usage, and finally the opinion of the investigator if the belt was used. The last table is for the supplemental restraint system or air bags. There are only three categories. Were air bags available, were they deployed, and were they damaged before or after the impact? Only the front seating position is marked because no rear air bag systems were available at the time of this writing. The remainder is for notes.

Again, this is the point at which the investigator must apply his/her skills. He/she must note whether the webbing is worn or has been partially torn previous to the collision. This is usually easy to see from the color of the strands at the end of the tear or cut. Fresh cuts leave brighter colors. Looking for loading or stretch marks requires skill only learned on the job.

**Van Kirk & Associates Accident Investigation Form**

**SEATBELTS**

| | FRONT | | | REAR | | |
|---|---|---|---|---|---|---|
| | L | R | C | L | R | C |
| RETRACTABLE | | | | | | |
| LAP | | | | | | |
| SHOULDER | | | | | | |
| AVAILABLE | | | | | | |

Y = Yes
PD = PASSIVE DOOR MOUNT
PM = PASSIVE MOTORIZED
xxD = ABOVE PASSIVE BELTS HAVE BEEN DEFEATED BY DISCONNECTING THE BUCKLE
C = CUT DURING EXTRACATION

**SEATBELT USE**

| | FRONT | | | REAR | | |
|---|---|---|---|---|---|---|
| | L | R | C | L | R | C |
| LOADING | | | | | | |
| BUCKLE SCRATCHES | | | | | | |
| INJURY | | | | | | |
| POLICE REPORT | | | | | | |
| HOSPITAL | | | | | | |
| USED? | | | | | | |

**AIRBAG**

| | L FRONT | R FRONT |
|---|---|---|
| AVAILABLE | | |
| DEPLOYED | | |
| DAMAGED | | |

**NOTES:**

**Figure 8.1I** Seat belts and airbags.

The webbing material must be held up to the light and the belt turned at different angles until the broken strands are visible. Many times the fingers can feel these broken strands and then they can be photographed. The scratches on the buckle indicate that the occupant was a regular user of the seat belt system. It is a good indicator that the belt may have been worn. The notation on a police report is usually marked after talking to the occupants after the collision. It is possible that the police officer may have seen the occupants with the restraint system still in place but they usually arrive after or during the treatment by the emergency personnel.

Hospital data can again come from two sources. First, the injured party may tell the nurse or physician he/she was wearing a seat belt at the time of the collision. Second, a more positive method of assuring the seat belt was worn is evidence of localized contusions on the hip area, across the abdomen, and either on the chest wall or on the shoulder between the neck and the end of the shoulder.

The air bag data can be helpful in a front-end collision even if the air bag has not been deployed. The sensor system in the present air bags is not supposed to allow the bags to deploy at less than 8 mi/h. Between 8 and 15 mi/h the bags may or may not deploy. Above approximately 15 mi/h the air bags are supposed to always deploy. Off-angle frontal impacts of greater than 30 degrees from the centerline of the vehicle are not supposed to cause the air bag to inflate. Rear-end impacts do not deploy an air bag unless there is a second impact from the required direction above 8 mi/h or the bag is defective. Locations of blood, skin rub marks, powder, or other unusual marks must be measured and photographed on both the air bags and the seat belt webbing material.

## Occupant Information and Injury Data — Page 10

The upper portion of page 10 (Figure 8.1J) is used to list the personal data on the driver and all other passengers. It is advisable to obtain the occupants' ages, heights, and weights to determine how close they may have been sitting to the front of the vehicle.

The driving experience can be helpful in that a young driver or a mature driver may have problems when driving the vehicle. The young driver may have lack of experience in traffic situations as well as with the vehicle itself, and the mature driver may have health problems such as night blindness, very slow perception and reaction times, and muscular coordination. The occupants' injuries are then listed in order of severity.

## Soft Tissue Injuries — Page 11

All soft tissue injuries are marked on the "little man" drawings reproduced on page 11 (Figure 8.1K). This gives the investigator an idea of how the collision affected the occupants and if the injuries are consistent with the collision itself.

## Internal Injuries — Page 12

On page 12 (Figure 8.1L), a cutaway view is shown of the little man exposing the internal organs in the front and back of the body. Again, the injuries should be marked and comments made to the side showing the severity of each injury.

Van Kirk & Associates Accident Investigation Form

Patient Information

Hospital:_____

Age: _____    Sex: _____    Driving Experience:_____

Weight: _____lb   Height: _____ in    Seating Pos'n:_____

Other Occupants:   1:_____Pos'n:_____   Injury: _____

2:_____Pos'n:_____   Injury: _____

3:_____Pos'n:_____   Injury: _____

4:_____Pos'n:_____   Injury: _____

Patient Injuries (in order of severity):

1:_____

2:_____

3:_____

4:_____

5:_____

6:_____

7:_____

8:_____

9:_____

10:_____

11:_____

12:_____

Prior Disabilities:_____

_____

**Figure 8.1J** Occupant information and injury data.

The investigator must be careful to identify injuries from hospital or emergency room data only. If witness statement data are used, the investigator must describe from whom the data were received if not from a medical source.

## Skeletal Injuries — Page 13

On the chart on page 13 (Figure 8.1M) the location of all fractures or dislocations are marked. This includes all head injuries and loss of

Van Kirk & Associates Accident Investigation Form

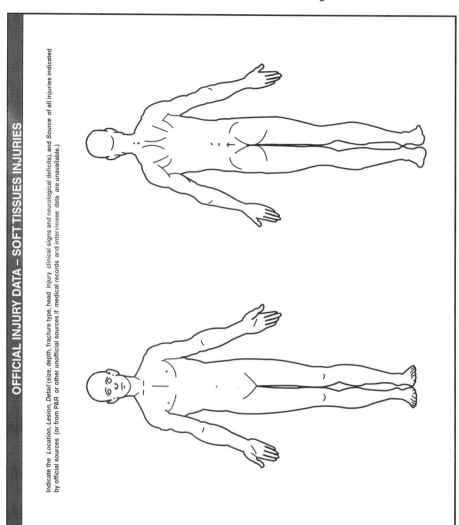

**Figure 8.1K** Soft tissue injuries.

consciousness data. Compound comminuted fractures as well as loss of appendages must also be listed and explained.

## Injury Mechanisms — Page 14

Page 14 (Figure 8.1N), in fact, should consist of several pages, one page for each occupant of the vehicle. The investigator can once again locate the

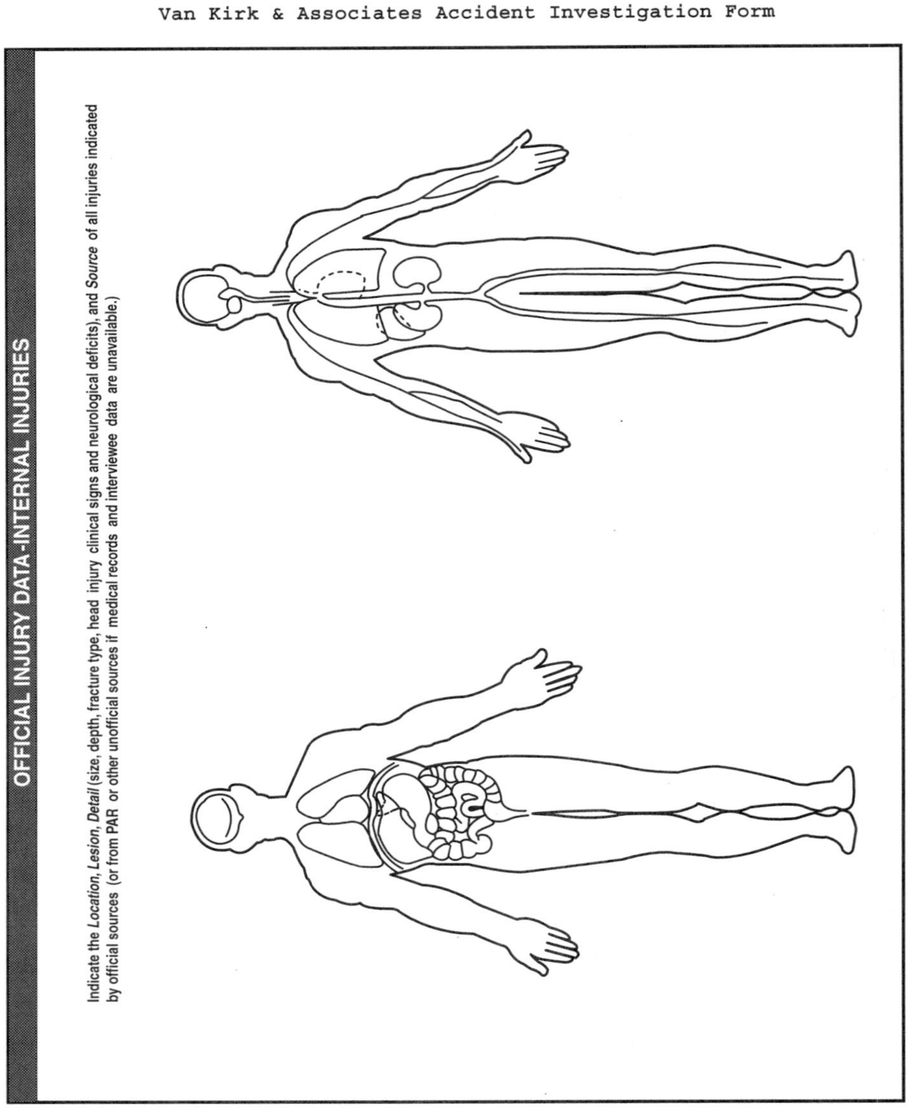

Van Kirk & Associates Accident Investigation Form

**Figure 8.1L** Internal injuries.

injuries and then add what component inside the vehicle caused the injury. Additional comments such as being trapped for a long period of time, which could bring about additional complications, must be recorded. The occupant being ejected and the cause of any injuries outside the vehicle also be noted.

Van Kirk & Associates Accident Investigation Form

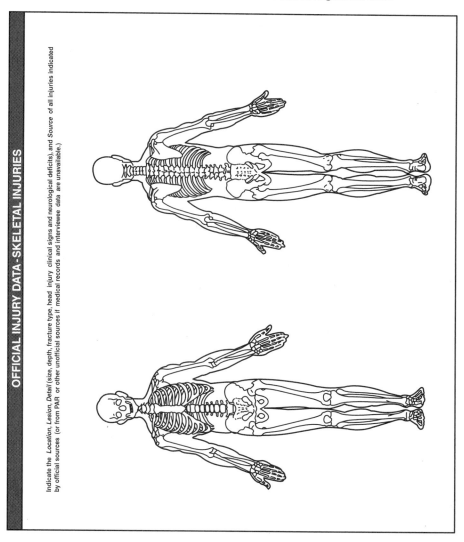

OFFICIAL INJURY DATA-SKELETAL INJURIES

Indicate the *Location, Lesion, Detail* (size, depth, fracture type, head injury clinical signs and neurological deficits), and *Source* of all injuries indicated by official sources (or from PAR or other unofficial sources if medical records and interviewee data are unavailable.)

**Figure 8.1M** Skeletal injuries.

## Notes and Injury Countermeasures — Page 15

Any notes or other data that do not fit into other categories are written on page 15 (blank page, not shown). These might include more occupants in the vehicle than seating positions.

**Van Kirk & Associates Accident Investigation Form**

| INJURY MECHANISM | | | |
|---|---|---|---|
| Position | Seatbelt | Ejected | Trapped |

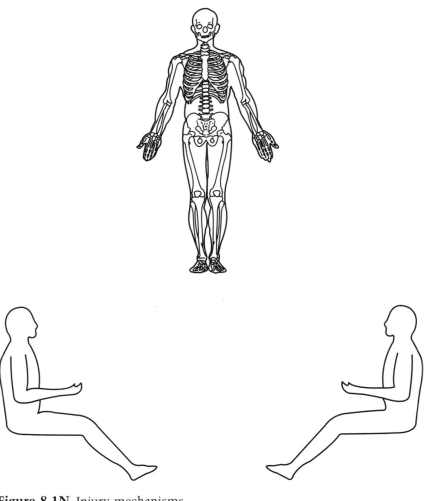

**Figure 8.1N** Injury mechanisms.

Baby seats or child seats that have been improperly attached to the vehicle restraint system or may have broken or become dislodged at impact, missing seat belts, missing window glass where the openings have been covered with plastic prior to the accident, and missing components or preexisting damage should also be listed.

There are some vehicles that have had additional equipment installed that did not come from the factory. This equipment should be listed and then who installed the equipment determined, especially if it may have played a part in the accident.

This form can be of great help to the investigator/reconstructionist when preparing for a deposition or a trial, in that it has a great many of the details necessary for the opinions to be given.

# Occupant Kinematics

# 9

"Singularity is almost invariably a clue."

**Sherlock Holmes**
*The Boscome Valley Mystery*

Kinematics is the study of the geometry of motion; it is used to relate displacement, velocity, acceleration, and time, without regard to the cause of the motion. Occupants in vehicles undergo motion whenever the vehicle they are riding in is in motion. The majority of the time the vehicle and the occupant are moving at the same velocity and direction. When the vehicle is accelerating or decelerating, the occupants do not move at the same velocity as the vehicle, hence, they are lagging behind the vehicle's motion and are moving in opposite directions until their relative motions are reduced to zero so that they are traveling together again. This difference in relative motions is usually small and they dampen out quickly.

There are large differences in relative motion that occur during a collision: when a vehicle comes to rest very quickly after striking a tree or another vehicle; when it abruptly changes directions on impact and spins around its vertical axis; or when it strikes another object and starts to spin about its lateral and/or longitudinal axis. In these cases the relative velocity and direction between the interior of the vehicle and the occupants are large, which results in injury when the occupants finally expend their energy and come to rest.

Why is it important to study the occupants' movements or kinematics? One reason is that the types and severities of these injuries can assist the reconstructionist in determining the motion of the vehicle prior to, during, and after the initial collision. In addition, knowing the kinematics of the occupants can assist in determining if the occupants were wearing their restraint systems, and in many cases which occupant was the driver of the vehicle at the time of the collision. The study of kinematics also helps to confirm the fact that the allegedly claimed injuries were actually sustained during the accident by matching up interior damage with occupants' injuries.

Before proceeding with the kinematics of the occupant, some background in basic anatomy is discussed. Anatomy has been defined as the study of the human body structure. The field of anatomy has two major divisions, microscopic and gross anatomy, which are covered in this chapter. Other areas include neuroanatomy, which is the study of the nervous system; embryology, the study of the development of the human body before birth; histology, a study of the tissues of the human body; and many other such divisions that need not be of concern at this time.

The medical community has developed a standardized orientation of the body, called the anatomic position, so that medical professionals the world over can understand the names and locations of the various body parts when discussing or reviewing medical data. In the anatomic position, the standing human body is facing forward with the palms of the hand outward. From this position, various directions are more clearly defined.

## Terminology Definitions

There are three axes or planes that are used to define areas of the human body. The $x$ direction goes from the front of the body to the rear of the body. The $y$ direction goes from one side to the other side of the body. The $z$ direction goes from the top to the bottom of the body. Therefore, there are three planes in which to describe the various portions of the human body.

The $x$, $y$ plane is parallel to the ground; the $y$, $z$ plane is parallel to the front of the body. The $z$, $x$ plane goes from the front to the rear of the body. Each of the three planes is perpendicular to the others.

    Median plane — a vertical plane through the center of the body and parallel to $x$, $z$ plane
    Sagittal planes — all planes parallel to medium plane
    Frontal coronal plane — any plane parallel to $y$, $z$ plane
    Transverse plane — any plane parallel to $x$, $y$ plane
    Medial direction — closer to the median plane
    Lateral direction — farther from the medium plane
    Ventral or anterior — toward the front of the body
    Dorsal or posterior — toward the back of the body
    Cranial or superior — toward or closer to the head
    Caudal or inferior — toward the tail or farther from the head
    Proximal — toward the body or root of the limb

Distal — farther from the body or root of the limb
Deep or internal — away from the surface or deeper to some other part
Superficial or external — toward the surface

In addition to the definitions for the planes of direction, certain anatomic terms for particular portions, or regions, of the body must also be defined.

| Anatomic Term | Body Term |
| --- | --- |
| Antibrachial | Foreman |
| Axilla | Armpit |
| Brachial | Shoulder to the elbow |
| Cervical | Neck |
| Cubital | Elbow |
| Epigastric | Above the stomach |
| Femoral | Thigh |
| Hypochondriac | Under the rib cage |
| Hypogastric | Below the stomach |
| Iliac (inquinal) | Over the hips |
| Lumbar | Small of the back |
| Pectoral | Anterior chest |
| Popliteal | Back of the knee |
| Thoracic | Chest |
| Umbilical | Naval |

# Basic Systems of the Human Body

Now that some of the terminology has been identified, the five basic systems of the human body are discussed: skeletal, muscular, nervous, cardiovascular, and visceral.

## Skeletal System

The skeleton consists of two elements: cartilage and bones. They function together to act as load-bearing elements and are defined as a framework of levers for lifting, moving, etc.; a protection of the very delicate internal organs; a source of production of red blood cells; and a medium for the storage of calcium.

The skeleton is divided into two major groups: the exoskeleton and the endoskeleton. The exoskeleton comprises parts that are not covered by tissue; these would include the toenails, fingernails, and teeth. The endoskeleton is the interior structure and can be divided into two groups: axial and appendicular. The axial portion consists of the head, neck, and trunk.

The appendicular consists of the extremities, which are attached to the trunk, the arms, and the legs.

The division can be broken down further to determine the composition of these groups. The axial portion of the skeleton consists of 87 bones. The head or skull contains 29 bones:

Cranial vault — 8
Facial — 14
Ear (ossicles) — 6
Neck/base of tongue (hyoid) — 1

The next major group is the vertebral column, which includes the Neck — 7 vertebra (cervical). The first is called the atlas. It controls our yes response. The second is called the axis. It controls the no response. The remainder of the vertebral column includes:

Thorax — 12 vertebra (chest)
Lumbar — 5 vertebra (lower back)
Sacrum — 5 fused bones (extreme lower back)
Coccyx — 4 fused bones (end of the spine)

Attached to the vertebral column is the rib cage, defined as follows:

Vertebro-sterno ribs — 14
Sternum — 1
Vertebro-costal ribs — 6
Verterbro ribs — 4

These are symmetrical on the midsagittal or median plane.

The appendicular portion of the skeleton contains the following:

Pectoral girdle

Clavicle — 2 (attaches the shoulders)
Scapula — 2 (attaches to the trunk or thorax)
Humerus — 2 (upper arm)
Radius — 2 (lower forearm)
Ulna — 2 (thumbside of forearm)

Hand

Carpus (wrist) — 8 + 8 = 16

Metacarpals — 10
Phalanges — 3 rows (10 from the wrist to the first knuckle, 8 from the first knuckle to the second knuckle, and 10 from the second knuckle to the end of the finger tip)

Pelvic girdle

Pelvic bones — 2
Femur — 2
Fibula — 2 (lateral)
Tibia — 2 (medial)

Ankle

Tarsus — 14
Metatarsus — 10
Phalanges — 3 rows (same positioning as in the hands)

Patella

Knee cap — 2

Bones serve different functions. The easiest method of classification of the various bones has been by shape, as follows:

Long bones (including the extremities, i.e., femur, humerus, etc.)
Short bones (including the ankle or wrist, i.e., tarsus, metacarpals)
Flat bones (such as the ribs and the scapula)
Irregular bones (such as the clavicle)

Flat bones are characterized as having thin plates of compact bone separated by thin sponge-like bony spaces. Long bones consist of three parts: the diaphysis and two epiphyses, one at each end. The cartilage is defined as a tough resilient connective tissue, which forms fibrous cells and a gel-like matrix.

Whenever one bone joins with another, there is always a joint between the two. There are two types of joints in the human body:

Fixed, no movement synarthroses (fibrous joints) — sutures in the skull
Extensive or freely movable diathroses (synovial) — elbow, knees, fingers, etc.

In addition, there are only three basic types of joint movements. These are:

Gliding — vertebral column, sterno-clavicular joint
Angular — ball and socket, pivot, hinge-elbow, atlanto-axial joint, shoulder, and hip
Rotating — wrist, shoulder, hip

Angular joint movements are defined as being in extension or flexion, such as the head and neck complex, or in the case of the arms or legs:

Abduction — moving away from the body
Adduction — moving toward the body

## Muscular System

The second system of the human body is the muscular system. The system working in conjunction with the skeletal system is responsible for all body movements.

Muscles are classified into three categories:

1. Skeletal (striated), voluntary — These muscles act with the bone system to control the motion of the body. Contraction and coincidental relaxation also fix joints or maintain balance.
2. Smooth, layers or sheets, intrinsic contractibility — These are used in forming the walls of organs and arteries, and allow peristalsis.
3. Cardiac, containing both striated and smooth muscle — This is the most important muscle system in the body.

Muscles also act to prevent overstretching of ligaments, to stabilize joint capsules, and to produce heat during the contraction phase of the muscle action. One end of the muscle is fixed and is called the origin. The other end is mobile and is called the insertion. Arteries, veins, and nerves are all bundled together on or near the muscle.

## Nervous System

The third and most important system besides the heart is the nervous system. The body's nervous system is divided into three groups:

1. Central — brain and spinal cord
2. Peripheral — cranial (motor and sensory), spinal, and peripheral nerves
3. Autonomic — regulates smooth muscle

## Central Nervous System

The central nervous system (CNS) consists of the brain, brain stem, and spinal cord. The brain is a large mass of nervous tissue with folds on the surface. In general, it is covered with gray matter called the cortex. The interior is white, except in the brain stem where it is mixed in color (reticular formation). The brain functions as a center for motor and sensory activities.

The motor functions are electrical impulses sent outward from the brain that, when called on, activate the muscle and produce motion of the appendages. The sensory functions are in all incoming impulses to the brain, which in turn are evaluated, classified, and reacted on by the brain.

The midsagittal section shows three areas of the brain of interest in this text:

1. Diencephalon — instrumental in producing cerebral spinal fluid (CSF)
2. Medulla oblongata — vital centers for heart rate and respiration
3. Cerebellum — regulation of body movement and posture

The meninges is composed of the protective layers over the central nervous system. It consists of these three layers:

1. Outer layer — dura mater — next to the skull and envelopes the whole CNS
2. Intermediate — arachroid — thin membrane, separated from the dura by small space, subdural space.
3. Inner layer — pia mater — thin membrane, the subarachnoid space being larger than the subdural space and being filled with cerebral spinal fluid (CSF)

The brain has a required blood supply and cannot function after loss of blood supply for more than 3 or 4 min. The spinal cord is made of white and gray matter that is interchanged from the brain.

## Peripheral Nervous System

The peripheral nervous system consists of fibers that go to the skeletal muscles to produce motion.

1. Efferent fibers — also go to smooth muscles for fixation.
2. Afferent fibers — come from the nerve endings in the skin and skeletal muscles (sensory);
   Afferent fibers — receptors in the viscera

3. Cranial nervous — (12 pairs, motor, sensory, and autonomic) — control the organs in the head and neck

4. Spinal nerves — efferent, ventral, motor response; efferent, dorsal, sensory response; autonomic, fibers from the ventral root at the thoracic, upper lumbar, and sacral levels

### *Autonomic Nervous System*

The autonomic nervous system contains two sets of nerve bundles: the sympathetic system that is commonly called the fight or flight reaction and the parasympathetic system that controls the inhibitory motion (i.e., metabolism, digestion, excretion, etc.).

## Cardiovascular System

This system is the most important system in the body. The heart is the main pump and the circulatory blood system is its pipeline. This system feeds oxygen and nutrients to the entire body; if it stops, the entire system breaks down.

The vascular system contains two separate and distinct circulatory systems:

1. Pulmonary circulation
2. Systemic circulation

The pulmonary system transfers the blood to the lungs for oxygenation before going to the systemic system. The systemic system transfers the blood to all the parts of the body including the heart itself. The blood is pumped simultaneously through both the pulmonary and systemic systems by the heart.

The heart is divided into four chambers: right atrium, left atrium, right ventricle, and left ventricle. A valve separates each pair of chambers. The one-way tricuspid valve separates the right atrium from the right ventricle.

The mitral valve separates the left atrium from the left ventricle. The blood enters the heart via the vena cava into the right atrium and passes through the one-way tricuspid valve into the right ventricle, which passes the blood out through the pulmonary valve into the pulmonary artery to the lungs. The oxygen-rich blood returns from the lungs, enters the left atrium through the pulmonary vein, then goes through the mitral valve to the left ventricle, and passes out through the aortic valve and through the aorta to the rest of the body.

Arteries carry the oxygen-rich blood to the rest of the body and keep bifurcating until it reaches arterioles. The smallest are the capillaries. Arterioles have smooth muscles, which control the flow of blood to the capillaries.

Larger veins have one-way valves allowing flow toward the heart. There are no valves in the veins from the brain.

## Visceral System

The visceral system consists of the internal organs, which are contained within the thorax and the abdomen. These four subsystems make up the visceral system:

1. Respiratory — trachea, lungs, pleura, and alveolar sacs
2. Digestive — closed mechanical system from the lips to the anus including the stomach, small intestine, and large intestine
3. Urogenital — maintenance of ionic balance in the blood, and also the fluid volume of the body
4. Endocrine — ductless glands secreting hormones directly into the stream of blood; include the thyroid, pancreas, and supra renal

# Anthropomorphic Dummies

The automobile companies and many of their suppliers use these devices to test individual components for each of the various vehicles they manufacture. They are called anthropomorphic dummies or test devices, meaning they have human form and characteristics. They come in three adult sizes: 5th, 50th, and 95th percentile. The 5th percentile means that there is only 5% of the population smaller than this test device represents. The 95th percentile means that there is only 5% of the population larger than this test device. Of course, the 50th percentile represents the median of the population. These dummies were designed to cover the greatest range of population of the human race. The exterior coverings of these devices are made of synthetic materials. Steel, brass, or aluminum make up the internal components.

The test devices have specific locations within various body cavities for the placement of instrumentation such as accelerometers, load cells, and pressure transducers to measure the resultant forces being applied. In recent years the anthropomorphic test device manufacturers have also developed a 3-year-old and a 6-year-old test device that are used to represent child occupants.

To ensure that each vehicle manufacturer would be testing to the same guidelines the Society of Automotive Engineers (SAE) developed a standard that describes in detail the purpose of the device, its general description, and each component or segment requirements. A table lists the anthropomorphic data required for each test subject. The use of the highly sophisticated test devices has saved countless lives in the on-going world of automobile safety.

In addition, SAE has developed high speed film analysis guides for dynamic studies of these test subjects during controlled crash studies. This standard describes, among other things, the location of specific targets to be placed on the test device or human volunteer to obtain repeatability between testing and/or research facilities.

These standards can be found in any technical library. They are listed as SAE recommended practices. Each carries a "J" number, which is used to locate it. "J 963" covers the anthropomorphic test device for dynamic testing.

A considerable amount of research has been conducted over many years at various universities and government facilities on the human volunteers, live animals, and cadavers. These data, although many years old, are the basis for many of the standards that are in place today with respect to human tolerance to impact of the human body. This information is presented as a background for investigators/reconstructionists to pique their interest and to assist them if the need arises in possibly approximating a change in velocity or a potential deceleration value that may have caused the injury to the occupant of the accident being investigated and/or reconstructed. More detailed and updated information is available through the various professional societies, and those interested in pursuing this should spend time on the Internet or in the technical library of their local university.

## Impact Acceleration

The acceleration environment covers a wide spectrum and has many variables. These include:

1. Duration of acceleration
2. Rate of onset
3. Magnitude of acceleration
4. Direction of the acceleration

What effects does this environment produce on the human body?

- Mechanical injury — fracture of the skeleton or rupture of internal organs.
- Physiological injury — (red out) — Bradycardia
- Psychophysical injury — loss of task performance, loss of visual acuity, loss of vestibular reactions

To better understand the effects of impact acceleration, consider the effect of one direction at a time on the human body.

# Linear Acceleration

A great deal of research has been conducted by the U.S. Air Force in this field and, as usual, this branch of the military service has created its own terminology.

## Positive Direction Coordinates

The Air Force considers the airplane to be a stable platform when it is in the air, just as the automobile engineer considers the automobile to be stable when it is being driven down the road. The automotive engineer also considers the $x$ direction as positive when going toward the front of the vehicle. This is true for the Air Force positive direction. The $y$ direction is considered positive when going to the right, and when looking down on top the vehicle; this is true both in the aerospace and in the automotive fields. The difference between the two fields of terminology lies in the $z$ direction. The automotive engineer considers the positive $z$ direction to be upward from the road through the roof of the vehicle. The aerospace engineer considers the $z$ direction to be positive, coming down from the top of the plane toward the earth. In addition, the aerospace engineer has added terminology for both the physiology and the displacement of the test subject during the test procedure. The investigator/reconstructionist can look up this terminology at any technical library if he/she is interested.

## Rotational Directional Coordinates

Roll is defined as the rotational direction around the $x$-axis. Pitch is defined as the rotational direction about the $y$-axis. Yaw is the rotational direction about the $z$-axis.

The duration of impact acceleration has been defined as that which occurs in less than 0.2 sec, or 200 msec.

***Commentary****: You have no doubt heard the expression "it happened in the wink of an eye." The average human eyewink takes 200 msec. The average 30 mi/h barrier crash takes approximately 150 msec. Therefore, if you would truly blink you would miss the impact.*

An older classification, which is still used by some researchers, is as follows:

- Impact or abrupt acceleration — 0 to 2.0 sec
- Brief acceleration — 2.1 to 10.0 sec
- Long-term acceleration — 10.1 to 60.0 sec
- Prolonged acceleration — over 60.0 sec

A complex system of forces acts on the body that greatly influences the body's tolerance to impact; among these are the type of protection given the body, the velocity at impact, and the position of the body.

How was research conducted to obtain data on impact injury?

- Human volunteers — tested below the tolerance level
- Automotive and aircraft accident data — estimate of injuries
- Live animals — tested above the tolerance level, soft tissue injury
- Cadavers — skeletal injuries only
- Mathematical models — statistical variations

## Caudocephaled Acceleration $(+G_x)$

This type of acceleration occurs during an ejection from an airplane. In 1941, a patent was applied for an ejection seat for a German airplane. The major injury resulting from such ejections was a crushing injury to the anterior portion of a vertebra. Anterior fractures usually occur in the area between T-8 and T-12 or T-12 and L-5. Most fractures have occurred at T-12. The thrust angle from the ejection seat can vary between 0 and 18 degrees and the upward direction.

## Actual Incidences of Vertebral Injury

Military physicians examining Navy and Air Force pilots after ejection from airplanes have recorded all the known cases. All fractures occurred between T-8 and L-5. The most common occurred at T-12.

It was determined that 62% of the injuries occurred because the pilot went through the canopy or of improper posture. Another study found after examining 729 cases of Air Force pilot ejections that the body position was a significant factor — especially the "D" ring, used on some jets. Once the problem was clinically confirmed as improper body position, it remained to verify the problem experimentally.

## Experimental Studies

A 1962 study described a vertical accelerator that would simulate the acceleration and rate of acceleration (jerk) of an airplane ejection. It delivered 50 g at an onset rate of 3000 g/sec, with the payload of 300 lb. This ramp-type function when plotted alongside the strain gauge read out from the vertebrae showed increasing strain several milliseconds after the function reached its level values.

A later study (1969) showed that a second peak actually existed that did not show up in the first study. It was the second peak that actually caused the vertebral fracture, and was discovered when an additional strain gauge was applied to the anterior surface of the individual vertebra. Inclining the ejection seat rearward 10 degrees minimized the anterior fracture. This changed the direction of loading on the spine and considerably reduced the frequency of vertebral fractures.

Many occupants involved in automobile accidents may claim that they sustained a vertebral fracture during the accident. It is fairly impossible to develop this type of injury without a large load being applied to the spine. In an automobile there could be an impact to the head or the buttocks that could produce a vertebral injury anywhere along the spine but it would be associated with the impact.

## Impact Acceleration to the Lower Limbs

Most of the information on impact tolerance of bones has been obtained from studies of automobile, airplane crashes, or impacts from free falls.

A definitive study of impact to the pelvis and femurs was conducted in 1966. Intact cadavers were placed on an automobile seat, and impact forces were applied to the patella — along the femoral axis — trying to simulate an automobile accident while measuring the load to the knee–thigh–hip complex. Ten cadavers were tested; forces applied to the right hip ranged from 950 to 3850 lb; forces applied to the left hip varied from 1400 to 2650 lbs; fractures of the hip occurred at 1900, 2550, and 3850 lb.

In the same series of tests, impacts to the right knee produced supra-condylar fractures from 950 to 1650 lb; and neck fractures of the femur occurred at 1500 lb. Impacts to the left knee resulted in a fracture to the head and neck of the femur at 1400 lb through a bone screw. Supracondylar femoral fractures occurred at 1650, 2250, and 2650 lb. Fractures of the patella also occurred when striking unpadded flat surfaces from 1500 lb to 2150 lb.

Human volunteers also carried out an unprecedented experiment. Impacts were applied to the knee, through voluntary muscular activity by striking the same surface used by the cadaver, with 800 to 1000 lbs. being tolerated with only minor pain to each knee.

Pedestrian impacts represent 38% of all accident victims. Injuries to the lower extremities are most frequent in accidents of the vehicle occupants; and especially of these impacts to the lower extremities, 38.3% are fractures.

A paper presented in 1973 conveyed the following data. Impacts to the tibia were carried out on cadavers 123 days postmortem (fresh). The impact region ranged from the head of the tibia down to the distal end. Peak cadaver age was approximately 75 years. Two cylinders were used as the impacting structure. One was 8.5 in. in diameter and the other was 5.7 in. in diameter.

These cylinders were chosen to simulate bumpers. A total of 200 cadavers were impacted at the tibia at impact speeds varying between 4 and 8 msec.

Fractures occurred at 4 m/sec with a force of 1000 newtons (N, or 224.85 lb of force).

The 5.7-in. diameter impacts underproduced a 50% frequency of fractures for impacts of 7.1 m/sec with a fracture force of 4300 (966.9 lb of force). The 8.5 in.-diameter impacts recorded values of 6.3 m/sec and 3300 N. The resulting injuries were noted as 64% moderate and 34% severe, and one case was considered dangerous by the Automotive Crash Injury Research (ACIR) scale.

In another paper presented at the 1973 Stapp Conference, a researcher tried to determine if 7560 N (1700 lb of force) was a realistic femur load criteria for both short and long duration impacts. The conclusion: 1700 lb of force was realistic for impacts in the range of 30 to 50 m/sec while the human femur can withstand higher loads for shorter durations.

*Commentary*: *It was believed at the time that the muscle tension in the human body resists the impact force, thus allowing for a much more severe impact than that which occurs in the cadaver.*

*The researcher neglected the fact that the majority of accidents occur to occupants who were not aware that they were being involved in an accident and therefore could not increase the tension in their legs prior to the impact. Despite an attempt to develop a correlation between the anthropomorphic dummy and the human cadaver, the conclusions are rather clouded, other than the fact that the dummy's dynamic properties are not characteristic of the human upper leg that attenuates input forces.*

However, a direct application of data from cadavers to dummies cannot be made due to a lack of mechanical equivalents in the knee impact resonance of existing dummies.

## Impact Acceleration to the Head and Face

Impact studies to the human head have been the basis for research at many universities, and private industry and government agencies for the past 30 years. Researchers at Wayne State University were among the earliest advocates for the use of human cadavers to study impacts to the head in conjunction with clinical observations from patients suffering from closed head injuries. It is generally true that almost 70% of all medical cases show that a mild-to-moderate concussion accompanies a linear skull fracture when the head strikes a flat hard surface. This does not imply that concussion, even serious and fatal, cannot occur without fractures, or that fractures do not occur without concussion. Therefore, it is generally conceded that in the majority of cases the same blow produces linear skull fractures and concussions.

The problem of depressed and perforated fractures does not need to be a concern in this discussion because the production of these traumas is due to the application of high-velocity energy with a blunt or pointed object. This is a failure of the skull in the area where the energy is applied.

Concussion is defined as an immediate posttraumatic unconsciousness due to an involvement of the brain stem centers, and in the human is associated with pallor and a shocklike state. Therefore, the problem with head impacts is not the fracture of the skull bone but the battering of the brain inside the cranial cavity, which is the major concern.

There are two basic schools of thought on how concussion is produced in the human brain. The National Institutes of Health claims documentary evidence that concussion is produced strictly by rotating the head. Wayne State University researchers have held that the head must undergo only a pure translational motion to produce concussion.

The basis for producing a concussion in experimental work, using a cadaver, is the linear skull fracture. Therefore, a great deal of research has been conducted to determine at what energy or force level this fracture can be produced. The rate at which forces are applied to the body is important because the body can support a greater load or force without breaking if it is slowly instead of suddenly applied. The duration of load and whether it is applied steadily in an incremental or repetitive manner also influence the behavior of the body.

When a force is suddenly applied, as by a blow or an impact, the energy involved must be considered because the ability of the body to absorb or store energy is an important factor in determining if failure (fracture) occurs. From the viewpoint of mechanics, it is more correct to speak of the energy of a blow than the force of a blow. Force and energy are two different phenomena and cannot be compared directly with one another. A force is measured in pounds or kilograms while energy is measured in inch pounds per cubic inch or kilogram centimeters per cubic centimeter.

The mechanical behavior of the intact cadaver head has been studied by high-speed motion pictures (500 frames per second and higher) and with accelerometers mounted on the occiput. Linear fractures were obtained with peak impact accelerations of:

| $g$ | sec |
|-----|-----|
| 337 | 0.01125 |
| 555 | 0.00903 |
| 644 | 0.00488 |
| 724 | 0.00338 |

A noted neurosurgeon and his colleagues have concentrated on the mechanism of brain injury itself. The acceleration and intracranial pressure were recorded in over 100 animals. It was found that the magnitude of the acceleration was not directly related to the concussive effect, but the time duration appeared to have the pronounced influence on the degree of injury produced. It was concluded that the concussive effect is characterized by an involvement of the brain stem centers; and if severe enough, actual tearing of tissue may occur in these regions.

Others at Wayne State University concentrated on determining the level at which the human head could sustain a closed head injury without impairment. In the classic experiment on the vertical accelerator, cadavers were dropped on their heads onto a 300-lb steel plate. The cadavers were dropped from heights of 32 to 36 in. to produce a linear skull fracture.

Comparison of these tests with those previously mentioned resulted in the establishment of a 28-in. drop height as the concussive injury level. This results in a velocity of 12/sec and an effective acceleration of 112 $g$ with a 4-msec duration. To be conservative, the value of 80 $g$ was suggested for a duration of no more than 3 msec as the value to which the unprotected head could sustain an impact and still survive without permanent injury.

## Facial Impact Acceleration

The skeletal structure of the human face is the weakest portion of the skeletal system. Work has been conducted in this area to determine the strength of the bones under impact.

One test used a rotary hammer to strike a seated cadaver at various impactor weights and various locations on the face to obtain the following:

Zygoma fracture — 324 to 978 lb
Frontal bone — 1410 lb

## Impact Acceleration to the Neck

The human neck is a structure composed of the cervical vertebral column, the hyoid bone, and a large mass of muscles. This structure has received the least amount of biomechanics research. This has been attributed to the fact that the neck has been usually considered along with the head in conducting any research.

Experiments were conducted on volunteers on a horizontal accelerator. These men were strapped in place in every conceivable manner with the head and neck complex free to move under acceleration. Special mounts were devised for each volunteer's mouth, head, and neck. Each man was accelerated to his tolerance level. Peak accelerations were recorded by the mouth accelerometers up to 4.78 $g$ with only slight cervical strain.

A dissertation from Wayne State University concluded:

1. Tensing of the neck muscles prior to a rear-end impact reduces the possibility of neck injury.

2. With or without a headrest, controlled seatback collapse reduces the severity of impact.
3. With the head in contact with a flat headrest and seatback rigid, a 44-mi/h rear end collision can be withstood with little discomfort.

## Impact Acceleration to the Chest

Besides the human head, the chest or thorax is the next area that has had the most research conducted on it. The thorax is composed of the rib cage, heart, lungs, bronchus, and associated vascular systems.

Heart injuries are divided into two general classes:

1. Complete destruction of the localized area of muscle occurs such as blowout injuries of the various chambers of the heart.
2. Impacts, which produce localized damage in the myocardium, may develop as a scar or can produce softening and subsequent rupture.

Aortic injury resulting from blunt trauma to the thorax commonly takes the form of partial or complete tearing of the ascending aorta immediately above the heart, or the descending aorta at the isthmus of the great vessels. The mechanism most frequently cited for this injury is the increased intra-aortic pressure due to the compression of the heart between the sternum and the spinal column.

There have also been reported injuries to the bronchus. They usually stretch at right angles to the trachea. Lung injuries due to blunt trauma result in lung punctures from fractured ribs. These ribs turn inward and puncture the lungs, resulting in the lungs filling with fluid or blood (pneumothorax or hemothorax). The lungs, even partially filling with fluid, do not allow the exchange of oxygen into the bloodstream and the victim either dies from hypoxia (lack of oxygen) or suffocates in his/her own blood.

One study established the value of chest impact with cadavers and a 6-in. diameter load cell covered by approximately 1 in. of padding. The cadavers were then impacted by the 6-in. padded load cell at speeds ranging from 10 to 19.5 mi/h. The maximum chest loads ranged from 365 to 1850 lb. The highest load resulted in linear fractures of the right sixth and seventh ribs in the midaxillary (from under the arm to the waist) line.

Some human volunteer work has been conducted using a self-pulling mechanism. By using the same padded load cell, the volunteer would pull the device against his/her chest until no longer able to continue. The maximum load developed was 400 lb. When the padding was removed, the load dropped to 300 lbs. This was mostly due to the sharp edges of the 6-in. diameter circular plate.

Static force–deflection work on cadavers has shown that rib fractures occurred at about 550 lb. and 1.8 in. of chest deflection. Dynamic thoracic stiffness has been calculated at approximately 1000 lb/in. up to a level of 900 lb.

# Longitudinal Acceleration ($+g_x$ and $-g_x$)

## Forward Acceleration ($+g_x$)

The advent of the jet aircraft forced aerospace medicine into the realm of the unknown: human tolerance to deceleration from high-speed aircraft. The Air Force undertook this research and in the early 1950s constructed a rocket sled on a 2000-ft track with an aircraft-type seat mounted to it (at Holman Air Force Base, Alamogordo, New Mexico).

A total of 19 experimental runs were conducted using human volunteers, who wore a full restraint system that consisted of a 3 in. wide chest belt and an inverted "V" crotch belt tied down over both legs. The $g$'s sustained were from 10 to 35. The rate of onset was 500 to 1200 $g$/sec, with a pulse duration of 0.15 to 0.42 sec.

The highest peak $g$ run was number 113 — the sled peak $g$ reached 3.6 $g$ with the rate of onset of 1150 $g$/sec. The human volunteers complained of tenderness in the lower back after the run. To get a higher level of onset rate, experimental animals had to be used. It must be remembered that the animals used have an entirely different skeletal and visceral system than man and no direct correlations can be made to the higher levels of $g$ recorded by the animals.

# Backward Acceleration ($-g_x$)

Forward-facing subjects were used, $-g_x$ deceleration mode, with 22 experiments being conducted on chimpanzees at Holman Air Force Base. The results ranged from 40 to 96 $g$; and the injuries ranged from superficial trauma to shock, temporary paralysis of either or both hands, abdominal distension, and absence of peristalsis. Recovery took a few hours to a few days.

In the early 1950s, 54 humans were subjected to deceleration at Edwards Air Force Base. One subject was fully restrained but the head was unrestrained. He underwent 32 $g$ at 1150 $g$/sec for 0.15 sec. He sustained spots in his vision with pinching at the thighs. During a second run using a triangular-shaped pulse, he underwent 45.4 $g$ at 282 $g$/sec. He sustained petechial hemorrhage in the retina of the eye, with conjunctival (bulbar) hemorrhage. This is considered to be the ultimate whole body deceleration when fully restrained in a negative $g_x$ direction.

## General Physiological Effects

A series of low g levels tests were conducted to determine the body's physiological effects to deceleration, the g level range from 15 to 25. Mechanically there were no injuries. Shock — the major area of concern — usually resulted in collapse of the peripheral venous system. This results in a fast pulse with a drop in blood pressure 15 to 30 sec postimpact. Lower rates of onset resulted in bradycardia, slow pulse rate, stimulation of the vagus nerve, and in general a slowdown of body functions. Neurologically the subjects appeared dazed and euphoric.

## Lap Belt Injuries in Aircraft and Automotive Accidents

A 1958 article reported that Holman Air Force Base had conducted tests on human volunteers at different ranges and durations of acceleration.

Therefore, the following can be concluded:

- These results are not applicable to either automotive or aircraft accidents; the g readings are too low and the time duration is too short.
- Automotive accidents at 30 mi/h take 50 to 150 msec or longer and reach 30 g or better.

## Occupant Injuries

Occupants can be injured in an automobile accident in a great many ways. Injuries to occupants who are not wearing their lap and shoulder belt restraint systems during a collision are discussed earlier. Depending on the severity of the collision, these injuries can range from minor to fatal. Occupants can also be injured in an automobile collision when they are wearing their lap and shoulder belt restraint systems and the vehicle collapses around and on top of them.

Lap and shoulder belt restraint systems are not a panacea for the reduction or elimination of occupant injuries. These restraint systems work in conjunction with the energy-absorbing capabilities that have been designed into the vehicle. Human volunteers subjected to decelerations approaching those of an automobile collision have survived such testing by the proper use of restraint systems.

This means that the restraint system furnished by the automobile manufacturer must be used properly for it to function in the manner in which it was designed. When these restraint systems are not placed properly on the occupant's body prior to a collision, then the occupant's body will sustain restraint system-induced injuries.

Many abdominal organ can be injured depending on the seat belt position. If the lap belt is placed too high on the abdomen that is above the pelvic girdle, then there is corresponding injury to an abdominal organ. The mechanisms of such injuries are direct compression, shear, torque, or some combination. Small intestines are also vulnerable. Torso flexion can cause injury to the duodenum and the pancreas.

A high belt placement that can result from the occupant submarining under the lap belt portion of the restraint system can result in spleenic injuries, the compression fracture of the lumbar vertebrae, and a tension fracture of the vertebral posterior process. When the occupant submarines under the lap belt portion of the restraint system, he/she provides a different point for the upper body to rotate above during the collision. The normal rotation point would be about the hips or head of the femur. Because the lap belt portion of the restraint system is now pressing into the soft abdomen, the upper portion of the torso rotates forward and causes the fracture of the vertebral column in approximately the T-12 to L-5 area.

What work is being done to reduce and possibly eliminate injuries induced by restraint systems? Experimental studies have been and will continue to be conducted into the mechanisms of injury and the testing of new and innovative restraint systems. The air bag was an outgrowth of such experimental work. How is the work being conducted?

## Cadaver Experiments

Cadavers have been used for many years to show skeletal structural failures in studies with and without restraint systems. They have never been used for soft tissue injury analysis. Cadaver testing has been used throughout the world by many different organizations including the automotive field. This work has proved effective, but does not always correlate with the injuries to the "live" passenger.

## Anthropomorphic Dummies

There has been a great deal of study, experimentation, and development of new generations of anthropomorphic dummies in the past 20 years. With each new generation the dummies' responses to impact more closely resemble those of the human body. There are some drawbacks such as corroboration of skeletal fractures, which do not occur when using dummies. Their greatest promise is the repeatability from comparison testing of restraint systems, body segment loading, and verification of mathematical models.

## Large Animal Experiments

There is only one method for the biomechanics expert and accident recon-structionist to study soft tissue injury in the laboratory and that is by the use of live animals. Volunteers only provide data up to the onset of human tolerance or the point of minimal injuries, cadavers only show the results of skeletal damage, and soft tissue injuries can only be done with live animals. Original testing conducted by the Air Force used bears in some of these tests but discarded them because of the handling problem and the comparison of their anatomy with the human anatomy. Baboons have been used by many test facilities for the determination of the effectiveness of restraint systems because their anatomy is closer to that of the human.

Work conducted on baboons using devices such as a lap belt only, a shoulder belt only, and the lap and shoulder belt combination have provided the following conclusions:

- Experiments with a single diagonal shoulder belt showed it was not a sufficient restraint system. It produces shoulder and chest fractures along with upper abdomen and thoracic internal organ injuries.
- Lap and shoulder belt combinations with all anchors fixed to the floor produce a vertical downward force that pushes the occupant farther into the seat and could contribute to the submarining problem.
- When using a three-point system with the diagonal belt attached to the center of the lap belt, the other end attached to the door pillar, and the lap belts anchored to the floor, an upward pull exerted on the lap belt during impact, definitely contributing to submarining.
- When all three anchors are mounted to the floor, then twisting of the torso produces an improper lap belt angle with the horizontal.

## Actual Injury Reports

Experimentation and comparison testing was fine under controlled condi-tions but the researchers, manufacturers, and medical personnel were inter-ested in what was happening in the real world. Accident investigation studies were conducted on a larger scale to try and understand how the interaction between the restraint systems and the vehicle were working during a collision.

After investigating 27,000 accidents involving the Volvo vehicle, research-ers concluded that the three-point restraint system used in their vehicles had:

- Reduced the frequency of injury
- Prevented ejection
- Recorded only minor injuries if any at all

Early research work conducted on three baboons at 30 $g$ with only a single diagonal belt showed that all animals had fatal neck or chest injuries. Therefore, laboratory evidence shows that the shoulder belt only system is not the restraint system of choice. It can induce severe upper body injuries on an area of the human body that anatomical cannot take the loading of a collision. The pelvic girdle is the strongest bone in the human body and therefore must assume the largest load-carrying capability.

# Lateral Acceleration (+$g_y$ and –$g_y$)

Most reports concerning injuries in automobile accidents appear to trace the sustained injuries to the restraint systems. However, medical people, many of whom are unaware of the mechanics of automotive impacts, have reported most of the data.

## Lateral Impacts — Animal Experiments, Lap Belt Only

Experiments conducted on baboons yielded the startling conclusion that accelerations in the lateral direction were much more severe than in the forward direction. Injuries included ruptured bladder, severed uterus, and cervical spine fracture with complete dislocation of the atlanto-occipital joint, spinal cord transection, and pancreatic hemorrhaging.

## Anthropomorphic Dummy Experiments

There has been extensive work for several years with the use of the new hybrid III dummy for lateral impact protection. Additional information can be obtained through the SAE publications or the Stapp Car Crash Conference proceedings.

## Volunteer Experiments — Full Restraint

Volunteer experiments were conducted in the $g_y$ direction. Minor complaints were noted from 50% of the volunteers. The $g_y$ of 6.25 $g$ produced a stiff neck, sore hips, and fainting; $g_y$ of 9.00 $g$ produced a lateral flexion of greater than 30 degrees. Tests were stopped because it was felt that the level of human tolerance had been reached.

## Combination Lap and Shoulder Belt

Approximately 52 volunteers were subjected to 87 runs in the –$g_y$ direction: 4.47 to 11.6 $g$ at 90 to 220-msec duration. Again, there were no serious injuries but minor complaints were noted from 60% of the volunteers.

Side impact structural crashworthiness presents a difficult design problem because of the limited crush available and the side geometry and structural design of the automobile. The occupant is typically situated closer to the impact region than in any other collision mode.

Beyond the collision aspect, the total traffic system survivability often referred to as vehicle aggressiveness must be considered. This term is defined as the potential for the vehicle to inflict death or serious injury to an occupant of a struck vehicle. Because there is less protection for the occupant in a side impact the problem becomes more acute.

The National Safety Council reports that approximately 6000 people are killed every year from injuries sustained in side impact collisions. The severity of such collisions with respect to their relative frequency is shown by the fact that only 6.5% of all injury-producing accidents involve the side of the car, while 22.9% of those accidents were regarded as severe. In contrast, there is a 59% involvement for the front of the car, with only 9.5% being regarded as severe.

Injuries to the body were of one type, direct damage to an organ. A limited number of investigations has confirmed these results; in addition, unbelted occupants run a higher risk of being ejected during a side impact. Intrusion is the major problem in side impacts.

It is impossible to cover all the experimentation and new literature being published each year in technical societies around the world. Those investigators and reconstructionists interested in pursuing their chosen profession should find time to obtain this additional literature for their office libraries.

## Summary

The data presented on the previous pages are only examples of where the information was obtained to determine what is called human tolerance to impact. This is the level at which the automobile component designs must absorb energy to prevent or at least mitigate serious to life-threatening injuries.

The more detailed information the investigator/reconstructionist has in his/her possession the more complete and accurate the investigation and later the reconstruction can be. As stated at the beginning of this chapter, knowing the injuries an occupant sustained during a collision can assist the investigator/reconstructionist to better determine the movement of the vehicle during the crash phase.

# Accident Reconstruction ## 10

"When you have eliminated the impossible, whatever remains, however improbable, must be the truth."
**Sherlock Holmes**
*The Sign of the Four*

As stated earlier, many people assume that accident *investigation* and *reconstruction* mean the same thing. They are as different as day and night, but they are closely related. The *investigator* observes or studies by close examination and also preserves and documents the evidence found. The *reconstructionist* must take the evidence along with all the other data from various sources and rebuild the accident a microsecond at a time.

## How to Become an Accident Reconstructionist

Some law enforcement agencies do have criteria for accident reconstructionists. Police officers who have attended a police academy or a community college that has within its curricula up to several hours of investigation techniques — such as use of measuring tapes, scene drawings, and information gathering from the principals and the witnesses — may be deemed reconstructionists by their respective departments.

In other agencies, officers may assist senior officers from their own departments who are considered qualified accident reconstructionists, thus becoming reconstructionists within the department. Many departments may instead call in a state trooper who has been qualified by the state police as a reconstructionist. This is usually how the road patrol officer gets his/her training unless his/her department has sufficient funds to send him/her to one of the recognized accident reconstructionist schools across the country.

There are several schools of formal education that private individuals may attend, and others that only allow police officers in attendance. These courses are usually taken over several weeks and sometimes years and cover specialty subjects such as lamp filament analysis, truck tire data, semi-tractor driving, etc.

As mentioned earlier, the Institute of Police Technology and Management (IPTM) at the University of North Florida in Jacksonville has both accident investigation and reconstruction courses (see Chapter 2). Most IPTM training programs are available for delivery on-site to a police agency or a group of police agencies. The Traffic Accident Reconstruction course is an 80-h course and requires that the student attend the IPTM Advanced Accident Investigation course.

As discussed previously, the University of California at Riverside has several traffic accident investigation and reconstruction programs (see Chapter 2). The Advanced Traffic Accident Reconstruction Training Institute consists of 200 h of course work that includes the 80 h from the Accident Investigation Institute. Electives include reconstruction of automobile accidents involving pedestrians or bicycles, staged traffic accidents, speed determination from crush analysis, and commercial vehicle accident reconstruction.

As mentioned earlier, the oldest established formal training school is Northwestern University Traffic Institute (NUTI) in Chicago (see Chapter 2). Courses include accident reconstruction and I and II, computerized traffic accident reconstruction I, II, III, and IV, using the commercial program EDCRASH. In addition, the institute offers specialized courses such as reconstruction of leaving the scene and pedestrian collisions, heavy vehicle crash reconstruction, accident scene mapping with total stations, and computer-aided drawing and measuring at the scenes of traffic accidents. The NUTI also sells textbooks and other course material for individual study.

As stated previously, there have been several organizations such as the National Association of Professional Accident Reconstructionists, (NAPARS), and the American Council of Traffic Accident Reconstructionists (ACTAR), that offer courses for a fee. At the end of the course an examination is given; If passed, the student is certified as an accident reconstructionist through that particular organization. Each of these organizations has some ties to the police in the form of retired officers or some sponsorship of the members where they can use their membership as a means to being active in a professional association for their departments.

As discussed earlier, the Society of Automotive Engineers (SAE) has a subcommittee called the Accident Investigation and Reconstruction Procedures Committee. See Chapter 2 for details.

## How is a Reconstructionist Defined?

*Webster's New Universal Unabridged Dictionary* defines a reconstructionist, "As a person who builds up from remaining parts and other evidence, an image of what something was in its original and complete form." Notice that the definition states, "builds up from remaining parts, and other evidence… an image of what something was… ." It does not say, "*recreate.*" It is impossible to recreate even the simplest of accidents.

For example, consider two vehicles coming off the production line, both with the same make and model, the same options, colors, etc. They are identical in every way, or so it would seem. Weighing the two vehicles shows a difference of a few hundred pounds.

This does not seem too important when considering the difference is probably less than 10% of the total weight. What must be remembered is that these vehicles are mass-produced. They are *not* identical. The body welds are not in the same place; some may even be missing. Other components are in slightly different locations in the vehicles. There are over 15,000 parts in a car. Each one is slightly different, but within the working tolerance necessary for the vehicle to operate effectively, not necessarily identically. Therefore, if these two vehicles were crashed into a solid concrete and steel barrier, they would have different crash signatures. Different parts of the vehicle would react differently under the stress of a collision.

The crash signature is a graph of the deceleration or velocity of the vehicle with respect to time. The peaks and valleys on the graphs may occur at different times and with different magnitudes. Therefore, even under the best of controlled conditions, it is impossible to recreate the accident. It is the task of the reconstructionist to develop a scenario or story of the collision sequence that best fits the damaged vehicles (remaining parts), and data found at the scene as well as witness statements and depositions (evidence).

## How to go about Starting the Reconstruction

Assume for the moment that the reconstructionist has not done the investigation of an accident. Most reconstructionists have a checklist of information that they require to start their analysis. It may include most or all the following:

- All photographs taken at the scene by the police or any other agency or interested parties such as the plaintiff or their families (color photographs required; color photocopies to start the initial analysis)

- Copies of the photographs of the vehicles taken at the scene or at a later date by the police or any other interested parties
- Copies of the police reports including all supplemental sheets and fatal squad reports if the accident victim is a fatality
- Copies of all witness statements taken by the police or any private agency such as an insurance adjustor or private investigator
- Copies of all reports and diagrams by the police or other agencies including calculations and data used to produce those calculations
- Copies of all depositions
- Copies of all medical data, primarily those of the emergency medical service (EMS) units and the hospital emergency room personnel
- Copies of the autopsy reports if applicable
- Copies of all fire department visits to the scene, or any other public agency such as first responders
- Copies of all accident simulation computer programs used to determine the direction, speed, and angle of approach and departure from the collision including all data that were inputted into the computer program
- Copies of all TV station or independent videotapes taken at the scene or at a later time concerning the accident victims, scenes, or others involved
- Copies of all newspaper clippings that were written about the accident, people, scene, or vehicles
- Clothes the accident victims were wearing at the time of the accident
- Weather reports from the local National Oceanic and Atmospheric Administration (NOAA) office or state department of agriculture
- Request an inspection of both vehicles and the accident site

Not all these items are required for all accident cases, but this is a good checklist that can be customized as required.

Additional data are required depending on the type of case to be analyzed. If a commercial truck or a city vehicle, or city property is involved, then the following is needed:

- Copies of all maintenance requests for each vehicle
- Copies of all accidents in which the vehicle was involved in
- Copies of all the drivers' professional and personal driving records
- Drivers' normal route, drivers' route on the day of the accident
- Inspection of the vehicle involved
- Inspection of the accident site

If the case involves a product defect then an additional set of information is required including:

- All drawings of the product area of concern involving any changes made to the drawings since the original design
- All test data from any and all types of tests that had been conducted on the product as it was released for sale
- Copies of all customer complaints concerning the problem
- Copies of all previous litigation concerning the product
- Any product change requests that were initiated at the production level to complete the production cycle
- All federal, state, or local test requirements, the results of all the testing done for compliance
- All sign-off compliance sheets for the testing that meet the required standards
- Copies of all the production process sheets for fabricating the product
- Copies of all manuals pertinent to the product, including the owner's manual, repair manuals, and any specialized manuals
- Copies of all service bulletins sent to the distributor of final point of sales and service for product updates due to potential or determined product failures
- Copies of all federal, state, or local recall campaigns conducted by the company either voluntarily or compulsorily

It must be remembered that much of the preceding information is requested through the client. It may take time, sometimes up to several months for the information to become available to the reconstructionist. Therefore, he/she must begin the investigation based on a hypothesis or theory of liability. It is his/her job to prove or disprove the hypothesis from a reconstructionist's standpoint.

## Sample Case

As an example, consider the case in which the hypothesis states that the occupants were belted, but the injuries they received in the collision were of such magnitude, severity, and locations that it would indicate that they were not belted. In this case, the reconstructionist assumes the occupants were belted and proceeds to find evidence to prove or disprove the hypothesis. He/she starts with inspections of the vehicles involved and the scene.

The vehicle inspections are detailed and include all the various views described earlier and all the necessary close-ups to show the extent of the damage. This includes the depth as well as severity of each area.

Many times the reconstructionist has to augment the photographs taken earlier depending on how much time was allotted to him/her at the first inspection. Perhaps the necessary equipment was not available to lift the vehicle safely to allow an under-vehicle inspection or the opposing side would not allow such an inspection without a court order. Attempting to raise a vehicle that has been severely damaged can cause more damage to the vehicle, can destroy existing damage, or can injure the parties trying to find if the necessary information exists. The use of a hi-lo is the worst possible way to lift a vehicle. Most operators are not trained in the proper use of the equipment and do not care what damage they cause to the vehicle because it is damaged already. Tow trucks do a better job, but usually cannot lift the vehicle sufficiently to allow for a satisfactory inspection. Safety is difficult to ensure with this type of lift, but it may be all that is available. If at all possible, have the vehicle placed on a trailer and hauled to a garage where it can be placed on a hoist to be safely held in place for a complete, thorough, and safe inspection.

There are occasions when it is virtually impossible to move the vehicle due to distance, location, or expenses. In these situations, another solution is possible. Roll the vehicle over on its least damaged side so that the underside is exposed for inspection. This operation must be done carefully and with much planning so that the existing damage is not destroyed or masked and other damage is not induced. Bracing must be provided to prevent the vehicle from completely rolling over. Lines must also be provided to allow the vehicle to roll gently onto its side on the soft ground. This is the second safest method and can be done safely in a salvage yard. Remember that film is cheap compared with not getting the necessary picture of that one single component that is crucial to the case. Take more pictures than necessary to ensure that everything on the vehicle has been covered.

Completely photographing the vehicle seems to be misunderstood by some investigators and reconstructionists. For some unknown reason, they only take pictures of the damaged portions of the vehicle, or what they perceive to be the damaged areas. If the entire vehicle has not been viewed underneath as well as in the trunk and in the engine compartment, the job has not been done adequately. Take pictures of the entire vehicle, damaged or undamaged, to prove, for example, that there was no damage to that area of the vehicle.

In a courtroom it is very difficult to explain to a jury under cross-examination that no pictures were taken of the undamaged parts of the vehicle when the reconstructionist still had film left in the camera before leaving the inspection, but the opposing expert got under the vehicle and found a part that was fractured and was the key to the entire reconstruction.

The scene inspections must also be as detailed as possible. An electronic measuring device such as a Nikon or Sokkia total station should be used if at all possible to accurately determine the location of all the landmarks at the scene. These landmarks include buildings, driveways, sidewalks, street signs, traffic lights, streetlights, cracks in the asphalt or cement roadway, and anything and everything that can yield a picture of the scene on the day of the accident (except the accident vehicles and debris).

It must be asked Why was this not done initially? It was, but not to the degree that the reconstructionist needs. Why such detail? The reconstructionist usually does not do the investigation. Therefore, the investigator should do what he/she thinks is necessary at the time, depending on the way he/she has seen the collision or what he/she has been told concerning the collision. Is it possible that these conclusions are incorrect? Most certainly! The investigator has taken his/her measurements and photographs, and has completed his/her report. His/her job is done; now the reconstructionist must put these pieces of the puzzle together to actually determine to the best of his/her ability what occurred immediately prior to, during, and just after the collision. He/she does this through the information he/she has or will obtain. He/she adds to it expertise on how vehicles operate and what their kinematics are during a collision, uses his/her mathematical and graphic skills, and develops his/her scenario of the event.

First the reconstructionist must gather all the possible information on everything involved in the accident. His/her next step would be to obtain the EMS and emergency room records of the occupants. If he/she cannot interrupt them, he/she must depend on a member of his/her staff or an outside consultant to outline the location and severity of each injury.

Assume that the injuries tend to indicate the occupants may have been unbelted, but they do not strictly coincide with a truly unbelted scenario. He/she needs additional information — it is now brainstorming time. If the occupants were truly belted, then their injuries would have been mitigated or less severe; however, if the seat belt system that would prevent such injuries failed or only partially failed, then it is possible the medical data would look like it does now. What parts of the belt system could fail or partially fail and produce such injuries? The webbing was intact so that is eliminated; the latch and buckle system was working; that leaves the retractor.

At this point the reconstructionist requests from the client certain types of information concerning the seat belt retractor. This request is called production of specific documents and questions or interrogatories, and it is a good idea for the reconstructionist to write out in specific terms exactly what information is needed. The client would then put these requests in the proper legal form. There is a minimum of about 30 days for the opposing side to provide answers. In some jurisdictions the time allotted for answers can be greater than 30 days. Unfortunately, these deadlines are not always met so several requests may have to be made before the information is obtained.

During this waiting period the reconstructionist should review his/her inspections and other information already received, looking for additional details that may lead to other data or directions. The most logical area to pursue next might be the scene drawing, done to scale. He/she can start with the scene data collected by the investigator. Many times there are discrepancies between the original investigator's data and the electronic data, which the reconstructionist has collected. This is the point at which these differences must be dealt with. The electronic data taken at the scene must be considered the prime or base data for the drawing.

All other data are secondary and are used only as a backup to the electronic data. These data are not destroyed but are used to show the differences. A second or overlay drawing is made using the original data. Then the discrepancies are easily shown when the overlay is placed over the base drawing. These overlays must be kept along with the other data, because they may ultimately be the key to the hypothesis. The base drawing must show the buildings, driveways, traffic lights, streetlights, and all other data that were collected at the detailed inspection. (See the chapter on scene drawings.)

Overlay drawings are then made for the various situations. As an example, consider there may have been three witnesses to the accident. There must be a separate overlay for the witness claimed position on the road, the direction of travel, the type of vehicle, and the line of sight up to the collision. There should be a separate overlay for the vehicles at the point of rest and the point of impact that the reconstructionist determines, as well as one thast may have been done by the on-scene investigator.

Finally, there must be a separate overlay for the theory of the accident. There may be more than one accident scenario at the early stages of the accident. These may be dismissed as the reconstructionist develops and receives more information. Some of this can be done prior to receiving the depositions of the individuals involved; the remainder is completed as the data are reviewed and incorporated into a scenario.

Many times it is necessary to develop sketches, such as sport utility vehicles (SUVs) or trucks, for use on the computer-aided design (CAD) drawings that do not exist in the file. There are commercial programs available that have a wire frame drawing of almost every type of vehicle. The costs of these programs depend on how much the reconstructionists want to spend per vehicle. The cost is dependent on the fidelity of the reproduction. Remember that the vehicle is being placed on a roadway that is 10 to 12 ft wide and the scene being depicted may cover upward to 500 ft. This shrinks the vehicle down to the size of a match head and almost all the details are lost at this scale. Some reconstructionists are capable of developing their own models that show sufficient detail for the scale drawing, even on a scale of 1 to 10.

**Commentary**: *There is one commercial program available that allows the user to take a photograph of the requested vehicle. The image is scanned into the computer and digitized, picking points from various changes in shape. The data are then saved in one of several different graphic images for use in various graphic programs.*

The same is true of various icons such as pedestrians from overhead views, motorcycles, and bicycles. If construction sites are involved, then it is necessary to develop that type of equipment also. These icons add a lot to a drawing and are especially helpful in the depositions, but more so in the trial.

The extensive use of measurements and photographs taken at the scene has been discussed previously. These are used during the development of the scale drawing. Many times the on-scene investigator takes measurements of the scene that are not accurate. Because the scene has been cleared by the time the reconstructionist is called into the case, it is impossible for him/her to check these measurements to determine their accuracy. The photographs taken at the scene are used by the reconstructionist to place the vehicles at the same location instead of depending on the measurements that are known to be incorrect when compared with the on-scene photographs.

The question asked by the beginning reconstructionist is, "How are they used?" Remember the discussion concerning photographs of all streetlights, traffic lights, sidewalks, and even cracks in the asphalt or concrete road surface. These detailed photographs taken by the reconstructionist are then compared with the photographs taken at the scene. The positions of the vehicles and other evidence such as gouges, skid marks, debris from the impact between the vehicles, blood smears, blood pooling, and other pertinent data are then determined from these comparisons. The measurements taken by the reconstructionist allow him/her to apply those to the on-scene photographs using comparisons to scaling. This means that if a tire of a vehicle is close to a curb and the on-scene measurements depict the tire being on top the sidewalk, there is no doubt that the on-scene measurement is incorrect. The reconstructionist, however, knows the width of the sidewalk at the point where the tire is located; he/she can then scale the photograph and by a ratio and proportion determine the distance the tire is actually from the curb. This method has been used many times to successfully locate vehicles and other evidence when all other methods have failed. Uneven road surfaces create cracks and crevices that make excellent landmarks by which to locate vehicles and other evidence.

There is always a time lag as the reconstructionist waits for depositions to be taken of the involved parties, including the witnesses to the scene. In some cases in which the reconstructionist is called into the case after a majority of information has been obtained, the time lag to receive the information is greatly reduced but the review time is increased when several hundred pages of depositions are dropped on his/her desk.

It is the task of the reconstructionist to review the mountain of paper and glean from it information that is consistent with the facts of the accident, bearing in mind the laws of physics concerning the movements of the vehicles, the medical information of the injured occupants, and the road and traffic conditions, as well as traffic lights and any line of sight problems that may exist. Notes are usually taken during the review process to highlight important information, either negative or positive, meaning it agrees with the facts of an accident or it does not. These notes also act as refreshers when preparing for depositions and trials. It may be necessary from time to time to consult the medical data for additional information to confirm or refute the statements made by the various parties. If this information is not available in the material on hand, then additional information is requested. This could include charting details, nursing notes, and consultations by other doctors. At this point, the details must be sought.

*Commentary: EMS and emergency room records do not always indicate all the complaints of the injured occupant of the vehicle at the time of the original examination. There are many good reasons why this happens (e.g., bruises and contusions are not significant when compared with a severely bleeding injury, the patient may not be conscious or cannot describe his/her injuries, or the major injuries are life threatening and need immediate attention). Minor injuries are cared for after the major problems have been addressed. The reconstructionist must bear this in mind and continue digging deeper into the routine nursing details for more detailed information.*

In this particular accident, the reconstructionist saw that there was mention on the nursing notes of small bruises on the lower abdomen below the iliac crest where the seat belt would be properly placed prior to the accident. This is a witness mark of the belts even though they were of a small or minor nature. There was also a note that a small, angular-shaped mark on the forehead of the driver was healing well.

Review of the driver's deposition indicated that there was a loss of consciousness but no memory of impact with any interior component. A review of the vehicle inspection photographs showed that the inside rearview mirror was pushed up against the windshield until there was a small fracture of the inside glass only. Examination of the rubber covering of the mirror revealed it had an angular shape, but there was no residue such as tissue transfer or blood. The mirror was removed and taken to the driver's home. The mirror was fitted to the forehead and the corner fit exactly. One problem solved.

In addition, seat belt bruising found in the medical charts indicated that the belt was in use for a short period of time. Examination of the belts indicated that they were intact after the accident. They were not fractured, ripped, torn, or cut. It would appear that the belts should have held the occupant in place and on the seat during the entire collision.

The reconstructionist continued asking questions of himself/herself and reviewing the data he/she had accumulated looking for the one piece of information that might answer his/her question. Not finding what he/she needed he/she requested more data about the entire seat belt system. One of the components was a retractor that winds the belts back onto the spool when not in use. Could the retractor hold and then momentarily release and then hold again? More digging showed that the review of the requests for information indicated that there was a problem with the retractor velocity sensitivity weight bob. The shaft holding it was too thin and it would swing back and forth so rapidly that it would override its position, springing backward, releasing the webbing for a few milliseconds, and allowing it to play out; the results gave the occupant enough slack to move forward on the seat and to strike the forehead on the inside rearview mirror, leaving a witness mark and causing the head injury. Thus, the hypothesis had been proved true. The occupant was belted and was injured due to a failure of the seat belt retractor system. A report was written, and the case closed.

## What was Learned?

From this hypothetical case, it was learned that extensive pictures paid off. The reconstructionist should continue asking questions and digging for details until the information is found or it is not available, and should follow the leads where they take him/her. It is better to tell the client as soon as the reconstructionist is sure that there is no case based on the present theory, than to wait until a later date. It saves the client money and indicates that the reconstructionist is honest and will not continue to work on the case expending his/her money or trying to develop evidence to support his/her theory if it does not exist. Many times the reconstructionist finds information that could change the entire direction of the case.

As an example, he/she may find that there was a problem with the traffic lights, there may have been a sewer backup leaving excessive water on the road, or other vehicles may have been involved that were not detected until the present time. Any of these could prompt the client to bring in a third party. This should be considered at all times. Helping the client to reconsider his/her theory of liability or to increase its scope should always be in the back of the mind of the reconstructionist. Following these examples can result in many callbacks from those clients who now are sure that they can depend on the reconstructionist and the firm to provide independent unbiased information and opinions.

## What Was Required to Solve the Case?

This case appears to have been solved rather easily. That is far from the truth. It required an extensive amount of digging for details that were not readily available. It required that the reconstructionist use his/her skills of analysis and deductive reasoning to determine what the possibilities were that would present the evidence that was not clear-cut. This type of case is more the rule than the exception. At first glance, the evidence leads the investigator to a false conclusion. In-depth analysis of the material and a basic knowledge of occupant kinematics and vehicle movements led the reconstructionist along a different path, which proved to be correct because it was verified by the details found in the additional material that was requested.

## What Happens When Details are Insufficient to Prove the Hypothesis?

When there are insufficient details to prove the hypothesis, the reconstructionist then proceeds as Sherlock Holmes suggests at the beginning of this chapter. "When you have eliminated the impossible, whatever remains, however improbable, must be the truth." The reconstructionist must look at every possible scenario and find data to eliminate them or to render them as a frivolous answer to the problem. In doing this he/she is taking the negative approach, that is, all other possibilities have been eliminated and the remaining answer, which cannot be proved and looks improbable, must be the truth. There is no other answer.

This type of solution is very difficult to prove to the satisfaction of the opposing counsel. The reconstructionist must bear in mind that most people are taught or develop the habit of thinking deductively. Inductive reasoning is much more difficult and requires the user to think many times in the abstract, bearing in mind that the answer found is not the proof but is the elimination of a position in the realm of the possibility. When presenting this kind of proof at a deposition or a trial, the reconstructionist must be very thoroughly acquainted with all aspects of the case so that the opposing counsel cannot find a weakness if it exists. He/she must be able to find alternative methods of presenting the same data in a different manner. This requires a lot of preparation but eliminates any loopholes that are a weakness in the analysis. If the evidence points to this type of negative solution and the reconstructionist's analysis cannot discover any weakness, then it is his/her duty to convince the opposing counsel and a jury that his/her solution is the only possible explanation, however improbable.

# Severity Indices

# 11

"My name is Sherlock Holmes. It is my business to know what other people don't."

**Sherlock Holmes**
*The Blue Carbuncle*

This book was written for a broad spectrum of investigators and reconstructionists. This includes researchers in government, private, and academic sectors. Insurance companies, risk managers, and medical organizations such as the Department of Public Health are taking a closer look at the need for accident investigation. These groups are interested in comparing large amounts of data that can statistically show a trend in automobile crashworthiness and occupant safety, effectiveness of new safety equipment, and crashworthiness and pedestrian design of today's vehicles vs. those of 5 or even 10 years ago. To carry out such studies, it is necessary that a means be devised to compare vehicle damage from accident reports in Oregon with those accidents reported in Florida.

An index was needed to classify occupant injuries so that all researchers as well as any individual could compare data from all medical locations across the country. This chapter is devoted to a short history of how the Collision Damage Index and the Abbreviated Injury Scale were developed.

***Commentary:*** *After a study of light aircraft accidents conducted by the pioneering efforts of Hugh DeHaven at Cornell Aeronautical Laboratories, he and a small group of police officers turned their attention to automobile accident studies and the world of automotive accident investigation and reconstruction was born.*

In the late 1960s many researchers and individuals worked diligently toward developing both a vehicle collision index and a medical severity index.

The first vehicle deformation index was developed and administered by the National Safety Council.

## Traffic Accident Data Index

The Traffic Accident Data (TAD) index[1] is the first collision index designed for a limited purpose by the TAD Project that was administered by the National Safety Council. The purpose of the TAD scale is to enable a researcher to compare large amounts of accident data and to make them more usable for people in the field of accident investigation.

Excerpts from Reference 1* state,

> There are a limited number of ways to study crashes. The first is staged crashes in which dummies, cadavers, or volunteers are used and large amounts of detail and great precision are obtained at a high cost per crash. A second method is the accident investigation team in which a larger number of cases are studied at the scene, and the cost per case is usually less than half of the staged crash system. There is less detail, but actual or real life events are studied at the scene. Another method is the Cornell Laboratories Automotive Crash Injury Research-type projects in which rather specialized data are obtained on a reasonably large number of cases at a relatively small cost. The last sources of information are the official records of automobile crashes, which are collected by the millions at a very reasonable cost. Information is generated on each of these vehicles, and if the data can be made usable for certain purposes, then there is a rather large sample available.
>
> In any study of crash injury involving a statistical series, there is a need for control variables. These can include where the car was struck, what sort of object it struck, and how hard it was hit. Various estimates of the "hardness-of-the-hit" are used. Sometimes the criterion is estimated dollar damage to the car. Another indicator of crash severity is speed reported by the on-scene officer. Both of these estimates are often held in low regard. Amount of crash-produced car deformation is another indicator of accident severity.
>
> The TAD project is searching for a way to enable the Investigator at the scene to produce a usable indication of car deformation. Now, the Cornell – ACIR project accomplishes this by receiving and rating photographs of the crash damage. In view of this, a manual has been developed which depicts automobiles struck in various places and with various degrees of resulting deformation. One page in this manual depicts front and side views of cars that struck something like a utility pole, producing concentrated damage on the front of the car. The first photograph shows a little damage. The next photograph shows a good deal more, and the final photograph shows quite a bit of damage.

---

* Excerpts from Reference 1. With permission of the author.

By using these three photographs and defining rating categories at each end of the scale and also in between the photographs, the ability to classify on a 7-point scale is achieved. The manual contains 12 pages, each depicting a common type of crash damage. Thus, the TAD damage-rating manual was conceived and put on paper, completing the first step.

## Scale Validation

Crash investigation teams that study severe cases pile up ratings at the severe end of the scale. When the scale is applied to all accidents reported in a given area, it was found that most cases accumulate at the low end of the scale. Both situations show that the present TAD scale does not accommodate a sufficient range.

The scale should have known interval properties. Researchers need to know whether a scale value of 5 is really more than a 4, and if it is, whether the distance from 5 to 4 is the same as the distance from 4 to 3.

One concern is the reliability with which different raters use the scale on the same cars. Another is the interval properties of the TAD scale. Scaling studies showed that the TAD scale is probably unnecessarily limited by being confined to a 7-point scale. Information in the pictures would probably justify a 10-point scale.

An important justification for the scaling procedure is seen when scale photos have to be revised. Someday the cars in the present photos will be out-of-date, and there will be a need to replace a photograph of an older car with a photograph of a newer car. Doing so will change the scale.

The success of the deformation index lies in the sharpness of its correlation with the injury. If there are two candidate scales, one should look at the relationship between values on the scales and injury. The better scale should show that within any deformation category, the injury variance should be less than the other scale. Several scales were being evaluated at that time for the sole purpose of assisting the Investigator at the scene to have an equivalent rating system.

The next step in the development of the vehicle deformation index occurred in 1968. Prior to that time several independent researchers were working on a deformation index for their own use. These groups were brought together as an ad hoc committee to collaborate on a scale that all researchers could use.

## Vehicle Deformation Index

The following material is excerpted from Reference 2*:

---

* Excerpts from Reference 2. With permission of the author.

In 1968 at the Eleventh Stapp Car Crash Conference, an Ad Hoc Committee for a Vehicle Deformation Index was formed from several authors who had presented papers on both vehicle deformation and medical injury indices. Originally, the group included in its scope an interest in a collision medical index.

This impromptu meeting led to a formalized conference in January 1969. The interested parties were then divided into two groups. Under John D. States, M.D. a subcommittee was organized to develop a medical index. With Kenneth Stonex acting as the liaison between the U.S. automobile industry, a group was formed to develop a deformation index.

In five subsequent meetings during 1968 and 1969, the following was accomplished:

1. It was decided to use the composite index developed for the "G.M. Form" as an interim General Medical Index, since this index was a synthesis of most of the systems currently in use and was based on the Cornell and UCLA Index.
2. It was further decided to ask the American Medical Association to develop a Specific Trauma Medical Index.... under the direction of Harold A. Fenner, Jr., M.D.
3. The medical and engineering members of the Ad Hoc Committee considered the TAD scale. This scale was used as a guide in formulating the Vehicle Deformation Index (D.I.). In April 1969 the committee met, voted upon and accepted the Index.
4. One further step remains, (i.e., to collate photographic examples of major collision types and to publish the Deformation Index in booklet form).

## Requirements for a Deformation Index

A partial listing of the more pertinent requirements used to develop the Index follows.

The Deformation Index should:

a. Be applicable to vehicles manufactured internationally and must accurately describe vehicles of both large and small size
b. Be capable of describing a scalar factor of relative deformation for current differences in vehicle structure and for vehicle construction changes
c. Describe the direction of principal force at point of impact
d. Describe the impact deformation in terms of area location on the vehicle (i.e., horizontally and vertically)
e. Consider the total magnitude or scale of deformation from fender scraping to crushed destruction, even though two-thirds to three-fourths of all collisions are relatively minor
f. Be independent of injury bias
g. Be capable of describing a multiple impact by multiple use of the Index

h.  Consider the object struck and the multiple effects of rollover, fire, and submersion
i.  Be flexible so that new factors can be added without requiring retrospective change
j.  Be capable of electronic computation

It was decided to define the Deformation Index as an index rather than a deformation scale.

Within the context of our discussion, a scale is defined as "a progressive graduated series," "a graded system from lowest to highest," "a series of spaces or lines." The word "index" is defined as an "indicator" or "a ratio or other number derived from a series of observations and used as an indicator or measure of a certain condition."

The Deformation Index contains both a vectorial representation of impact direction and impact magnitude; further, it contains a detailed description of vehicle impact location.

Therefore, the use of the term index is appropriate since the alphanumeric descriptor that has been developed is based on a series of observations and is used to indicate a distinct condition of impact direction, deformation location, and damage level.

## Description of the Vehicle Deformation Index

The Deformation Index is comprised of four components:

1.  Direction of principal force at point of impact
2.  Vehicle deformation location
3.  General type of collision
4.  Damage scale

The original Index was designed for mainframe computer uses at that time and required seven columns on a standard IBM card.

As an example, consider that we have a single car collision at moderate speed directly into a telephone pole less than 16 inches in diameter. The Deformation Index for our example is 12FCEN6.

The first component, the number 12, refers to a clock direction system. The next component, the FCE refer to "F" frontal impact and "C" and "E" refer to specific horizontal and vertical areas on the vehicle, The third component "N" designates a narrow object struck while the last component "6" refers to the damage scale.

With this example in mind we can analyze the Deformation Index in detail.

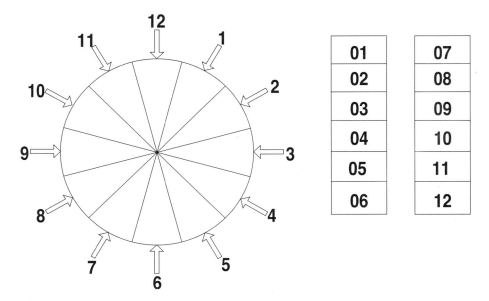

**Figure 11.1** A standard clock system to indicate the direction of principal force during the impact. (From Siegel, A. W., Vehicle Deformation Index: A Report from the International Ad Hoc Committee for Collision Deformation and Trauma Indices, in *Proc. Collision Investigation Methodology Symp.*, sponsored by the U.S. Department of Transportation, National Highway Safety Bureau, Washington, D.C., Automobile Manufacturers Assoc., Detroit, MI, 1969. With permission of the author.)

1.  Direction of principal force, first and second digit positions. As seen in Figure 11.1, a standard clock system is used to indicate the direction of principal force during the impact. The clock is figuratively superimposed at the point of impact with the 6 to 12 o'clock axis on the longitudinal or long axis of the vehicle, and the direction of principal force is then read. For all single event collisions, this procedure is quite simple. For a multiple collision event (e.g., a side impact to the vehicle by another vehicle and then the vehicle striking a lamp post), the procedure would require a primary Index and a secondary Index with, of course, different directional components and areas of damage.

*Commentary*: *Note that the single digits are displayed as double digits for both the old punch card and computer use (i.e., use 01 instead of 1 and so forth until the number 10 is reached).*

The complexities introduced by rollover collisions are simplified when one considers two principal types of rollover collisions.

Type I    Rollover without secondary collision
Type II   Rollover with secondary collision (e.g., vaulting, striking a tree, pole, wall, etc.)

The direction component for Type I rollover collisions may be taken as the initial direction of roll. Type I rollover collisions may have both a primary and secondary D. I. With a small amount of usage and experience the procedure becomes a simple routine. In the example above, the frontal impact was in the 12 o'clock direction.

2. Vehicle deformation location
   a. General Deformation, third digit position. The principal parts of the vehicle affected by the collision are listed with their code letter. Figure 11.2 describes the second component of the Deformation Index: "Principal part of car affected."

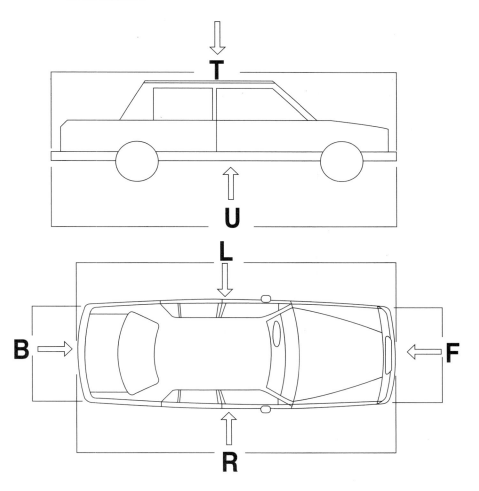

**Figure 11.2** The second component of the Deformation Index. (Redrawn from Siegel, A. W., Reference 2.)

*Commentary: Note that this first digit describes only the general areas of the vehicle that have been deformed.*

*This is basically for sorting purposes and gives the reconstructionist a general idea of the damaged area before continuing the search for more detailed information.*

"An attempt has been made to choose the code letters for their descriptive simplicity. However, the last code letter "X" or "Unclassifiable" needs some explanation.

Although infrequent, there are collisions in which a vehicle has been grossly crushed and deformed (e.g., vehicle to train collision, falling long distances off roadways, and so forth). The "X" code should be used for these massively deformed cases when the primary codes are not appropriate. In the above example the first letter of the second component was "F" for frontal impact.

In order to accurately describe the damage sustained by a vehicle, one needs to classify the damage location on a grid pattern basis. The Index was designed to account for both horizontal and vertical areas of damage by the fourth and fifth digit positions.

b. Specific horizontal location of damage, fourth digit position. The specific horizontal portions of the vehicle affected by collision are listed below with their code letters. Figure 11.3 describes the second letter code of the second component of the Index, the fourth digit location.

D  Distributed damage
L  Left front or rear damage
C  Center front or rear damage
R  Right front or rear damage
F  Side left front or side right front damage
P  Passenger compartment, left or right damage
B  Side left rear or side right rear damage
Y  The combination of side front (F) and passenger compartment (P), F + P or left front or rear (L) and center front or rear (C), L + C damage.
Z- The combination of side rear (B) and passenger compartment (P), B + P or right front or rear (R) and center front or rear (C), R + C damage.

*Commentary: These damage locations shown are for direct impact areas and not induced damage locations. As an example, consider the left front impact to the left front fender. The digit would still be an F, but the front end grille opening panel, headlights, and even bumper would be damaged due to induced damage. It has been the practice in the past not to include induced damage in the coding system.*

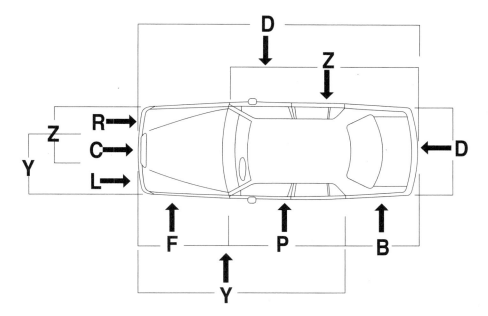

**Figure 11.3** The second letter code of the second component of the Deformation Index. (Redrawn from Siegel, A. W., Reference 2.)

    c.  Specific vertical location of damage, fifth digit position. The specific vertical portions of the vehicle affected by the collision are listed below with their code letters. Figure 11.4 describes the third letter code of the second component of the Index:

A  All, complete vertical damage
H  Top of frame to top roof damage
E  Everything below beltline damage
G  Beltline to roof or greenhouse damage
M  Middle (top of frame to beltline) damage
L  Low (below top of frame) damage

3.  General type of collision, sixth digit position. The third component of the Index is a general description of the type of collision. Figure 11.5 lists these components with their codes.
    The distinction for wide or narrow objects struck was arbitrarily chosen to be 16 inches because most power poles are 16 inches or less. Submersion should only be considered where a decided hazard to the occupants is present.

4.  Damage Scale, seventh digit position. The damage scale ranges front number one to nine. The TAD (Traffic Accident Data Project, National Safety Council) has a range of one to seven.

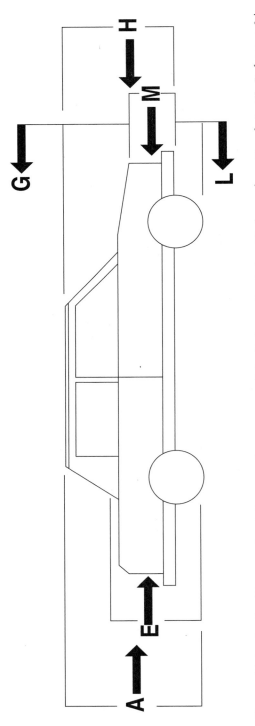

**Figure 11.4** The third letter code of the second component of the Deformation Index. (Redrawn from Siegel, A. W., Reference 2.)

W    WIDE OBJECT IMPACT (GREATER THAN 16" DIAMETER)

N    NARROW OBJECT IMPACT (DIAMETER OF 16" OR LESS)

S    SIDE SWIPE

O    ROLLOVER (INCLUDES ROLLING ON TO SIDE)

F    FIRE ONLY

Y    FIRE WITH IMPACT

Z    SUBMERSION (WHERE WATER PRESENTS A

        HAZARD TO OCCUPANTS)

**Figure 11.5** General types of collisions with codes. (From Siegel, A. W., Vehicle Deformation Index: A Report from the International Ad Hoc Committee for Collision Deformation and Trauma Indices, in *Proc. Collision Investigation Methodology Symp.*, sponsored by the U.S. Department of Transportation, National Highway Safety Bureau, Washington, D.C., Automobile Manufacturers Assoc., Detroit, MI, 1969. With permission of the author.)

The (TAD) scale has excellent design but does not have the completeness required by certain data users and researchers. Further, it has the limitation of not including higher speed impacts. The damage scale used in the Vehicle Deformation Index incorporates a scale of nine to overcome the latter disadvantage and also incorporating the more accurate description of damage location and impact direction.

Figure 11.6 diagrammatically represents the increasing amount of deformation for a frontal impact and for a side impact. Currently, members of the Ad Hoc Committee are compiling photographs of actual collisions, with appropriate description these will be arranged in a booklet form. These photographs will be displayed against the one to nine scale so as to clarify the level of damage.

## Conclusion

We have discussed an Index for describing vehicle deformation. Although primarily designed for automobile collisions, the Index is applicable with a location modifier to truck or bus collisions. Further, the Index may be applied to any size vehicle, domestic or import, for it relates to direction of impact, location of deformation, and to relative damage as a function of pre-impact size.[2]

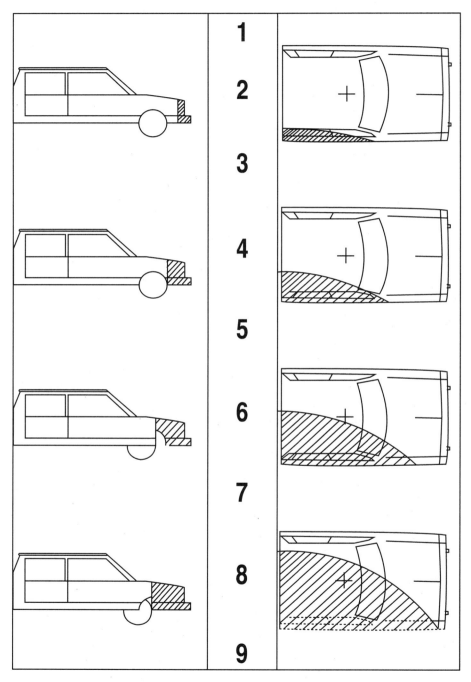

**Figure 11.6** Diagrammatic representation of the increasing amount of deformation for a frontal impact and side impact. (Redrawn from Siegel, A. W., Reference 2.)

There were several injury scales in use, but there was no singular medical injury scale that all researchers and clinicians could agree on at this time. The following is a review of existing scales up to 1969 and is excerpted from Reference 3*

# Development of a Medically Acceptable Injury Scale

## A Review of the Present Scales

Scales now in use can be classified into three groups, administrative, clinical, and research.

Foremost among the administrative Scales is the International Statistical Classification of Diseases, Injuries, and Causes of Death. This system utilizes a code (F Code and N Code) denoting the external causes, the nature of the injury, and body area involved. The severity is not coded but inferred.

Other Administrative codes list the most serious injury and are used for statistical records. Generally these are classed as no injury, nonfatal, fatal. The criteria to denote injury varies considerably (requiring medical attention, time lost from work, bed confinement for varying periods, etc.). Some even go to "any bodily harm received in a motor vehicle accidents." Fatalities are also classified in various ways ranging from death resulting 12 months after the accident to as recent as 1 hour after the accident.

The Civil Aeronautics Board in the United States and Road Research Laboratory in Great Britain use a slightly more elaborate scale. All the above scales have limited research use, due to the great span between classes of injury.

Clinical scales are coming into more widespread use and will see much more general use in the future. Several excellent ones are in existence. Surgical Research Teams of the U.S. Army in 1956 assigned points for various injuries.

The APGAR Scale is used in evaluating newborn infants. Dr. Keggi of Yale has recently developed an excellent scale for use in emergency care. Arizona State has also developed "SIMBOL" rating scale. All of the above scales utilize clinical signs such as degree of consciousness, skin color, pulse, respiratory rates, etc. A numerical value is assigned to each clinical condition and totaled, thus indicating the severity of the patient's reaction to injury.

DeHaven and his associates developed the first Research Injury Scale in conjunction with a study of light aircraft accidents in 1943. Since this time minor modifications have evolved but the basic format remains and is the basis of the American Medical Association Tissue Damage Scale.

Most research classifications are based on estimates of severity and threat to life. Ryan and Garrett of Cornell developed a "Quantitative Scale

---

* Excerpts from Reference 3. With permission of the author.

of Impact Injury" in 1968, which is excellent. Three criteria were used to rank injury: (1) force levels to produce, (2) danger to life, and (3) time to resume normal activities. Lange and Van Kirk of Wayne State developed a weighted injury scale and are in the process of developing a vehicle damage scale.

Dr. Eric Campbell of the Traffic Injury Research of Canada has developed an excellent tissue damage record utilizing a computerized form, which anatomically locates the injury and its severity. I believe this to be a major advancement in tissue damage classification and anticipated it would be the basis of the development of a fresh approach to the problem. Unfortunately Dr. Campbell was unable to be present and elaborate on this system at the Detroit meeting in June 1969.

There is considerable variance in the present scales in use. None of the present scales includes burns. (Table 11.1) illustrates the various rankings possible of the same injuries utilizing six different indices in common use in 1969. None of the present scales include burns.

**Table 11.1   Various Rankings Possible of Some Injuries Utilizing Six Different Indices in Common Use**

| | 1 | 2 | 3 | 4 | 5 | 6 |
|---|---|---|---|---|---|---|
| Laceration foreman exposing muscle | Moderate 3 (1–4) | Severe 4 (1–6) | Minor 1 (1–4) | Moderate 2 (1–4) | Severe 3 (1–3) | Minor 1 (1–5) |
| Skull fracture undisplaced | Moderate 3 | Severe 4 | Minor 1 | Serious 3 | Severe 3 | Moderate 2 |
| Mandible fracture with displacement | Moderate 3 | Not classified 0 | Very severe 4 | Serious 3 | Severe 3 | Severe 2 |
| Rupture, stomach | Dangerous 4 | Critical 6 | Very Severe 4 | Life threatening 4 | Severe 3 | Critical 5 |
| Rupture, kidney | Dangerous 4 | Critical 6 | Very Severe 4 | Life threatening 4 | Severe 3 | Severe 4 |
| Unconsciousness, 30 min | Moderate 3 | Severe dangerous to life 4 | Severe 3 | Serious 3 | Severe 3 | Severe 3 |
| Compression fracture L-1 | Moderate 3 | Serious dangerous to life 5 | Very severe 3 | Serious 3 | Severe 3 | Severe 3 |

From Fenner, H. A., Development of a Medically Acceptable Injury Scale, in *Proc. Collision Investigation Methodology Symp.*, sponsored by U.S. Department of Transportation, National Highway Safety Bureau, Washington, D.C., Automobile Manufacturers Assoc., Detroit, MI, 1969. With permission.

At the same time the vehicle index was being developed, and the Ad Hoc committee headed by Dr. John States was at work in coalescing and adding to existing medical injury scales.

## American Medical Association Abbreviated Injury Scale

After the impromptu meeting of October 1968, Dr. States and the ad hoc committee of Society of Automotive Engineers (SAE) initiated work on the development of both an Abbreviated Injury Scale and a Comprehensive Research Injury Scale. Preliminary meetings were held in January and May 1969. In June 1969 representatives of the automotive industry and the medical profession met in Detroit to discuss common objectives and the method to be used in reaching a decision on reclassification.

Several shortcomings were noted. The engineering profession thought it very important that seated height be obtained if at all possible; also knee height, tibial and femoral length were also thought desirable. After much discussion it was felt if height, weight, as well as distance between anterior superior iliac spine to knee joint line and to medial malleolus were obtained, seated height could be calculated.

The various specialty groups [listed as follows] were then asked to list all injuries within their specialties both commonly and rarely seen by them in their treatment of automobile trauma, then rank these injuries on a 1 to 10 scale as to estimated amount of force required to produce the injury, threat to life, treatment period, permanent impairment, and frequency. This worked out quite satisfactorily giving a representative scaling of each condition — some difficulties were encountered, of course, but generally scaling worked out quite well using 1 as most minor, 10 as major, and 5 as moderate. Each man then rescaled these in each specialty as to severity and threat to life on a 1–5 scale. This then was compiled and a resultant American Medical Association Abbreviated Injury Scale formed (Figures 11.7 through 11.11).

### Specialities Represented

| | |
|---|---|
| General surgery | Orthopedic surgery |
| Plastic surgery | Otolaryngology |
| Neurosurgery | Obstetrics and gynecology |
| Cardiology | Ophthalmology |
| Thoracic surgery | |

***Commentary:*** *The Abbreviated Injury Scale (AIS) has six levels of injuries ranging from no injury to four categories of fatal. The severity codes range from 0 to 9. As the type and severity of injuries increase so does the severity code. The police codes are included for reference.*

| Injury Category | Description | Severity Code | Police Code |
|---|---|---|---|
| No Injury | None | Zero | O or D |
| MINOR | **General**<br>Aches all over.<br>Minor Lacerations<br>All first degree or small second or third degree burns<br><br>**Head and Neck**<br>Cerebral injury with headache; dizziness no loss of consciousness.<br>"Whiplash" complaint with no anatomical or radiological evidence.<br>Abrasions and contusions of Ocular apparatus (lids, conjunctiva, cornea, uveal, injuries); vitreous or retinal hemorrhage.<br>Fracture of the nose.<br><br>**Chest**<br>Muscle ache or chest wall stiffness.<br><br>**Abdominal**<br>Muscle ache; seat belt abrasions; etc.<br><br>**Extremities**<br>Minor sprains and fractures and/or dislocations of digits. | 1 | C |

**Figures 11.7 through 11.11** The American Medical Association Abbreviated Injury Scale. (From Fenner, H. A., Development of a Medically Acceptable Injury Scale, in *Proc. Collision Investigation Methodology Symp.*, sponsored by U.S. Department of Transportation, National Highway Safety Bureau, Washington, D.C., Automobile Manufacturers Assoc., Detroit, MI, 1969.)

Within the various specialties there was surprisingly very little problem in scaling with the exception of minor differences in opinion which were easily solved. The neurosurgical classification was the most difficult. Of neurosurgeons queried, all believed the term "concussion" should be eliminated, primarily due to lack of definition. Cerebral trauma was the preferred term; all also agreed that skull fracture had no relation to cerebral injury and so each grouping so states, "with or without skull fracture."

The group was about evenly split as to using the period of unconsciousness or the period of posttraumatic amnesia (PTA) as an indication of the severity of cerebral trauma. Hence, both were listed. I feel upon the statements of several in-depth investigators that PTA is more indicative. There was no disagreement regarding the minor or critical classification. The period of unconsciousness delineating moderate cerebral injury from severe was changed from the commonly used 5-minute period to a 15-minute period as a good deal of support is in the literature indicating a much worse prognosis if the period of unconsciousness exceeds 15 minutes. This time

| Injury Category | Description | Severity Code | Police Code |
|---|---|---|---|
| MODERATE | General<br><br>Extensive contusions; abrasions; large lacerations; avulsions (less than 3 inches wide).<br>10 -20% body surface 2 degree or 3 degree burns.<br><br>Head and Neck<br><br>Cerebral injury with or without skull fracture, less than 15 minutes unconsciousness; no post traumatic amnesia.<br>Undisplaced skull or facial fractures.<br>Compound fracture of the nose.<br>Lacerations of the eye and appendages; retinal detachment.<br>Disfiguring lacerations.<br>"Whiplash" - severe complaints with anatomical or radiological evidence.<br><br>Chest<br><br>Simple rib or sternal fractures.<br>Major contusions of chest wall without hemo or pneumothorax, or respiratory embarrassment.<br><br>Abdominal<br><br>Major contusion of abdominal wall.<br><br>Extremities<br><br>Compound fracture of digits.<br>Undisplaced long bone or pelvic fractures.<br>Major sprains of major joints. | 2 | B |

**Figure 11.8** (Continued)

interval was used as a cut-off point. The 15-minute to more-than-24-hour span was purposefully left quite loose to cover age span and individual variance. In general, agreement of unconsciousness over 24 hours placed the patient in the critical category.

In the development of the Comprehensive Research Injury Scale it was decided to keep all rating on a 1–5 scale so some correlation between various ratings could be maintained. A 3 in any of the scales represents the halfway point.

The American Medical Association Research Injury Scale is certainly no panacea. It was developed from the basic scale of DeHaven and the many modifications of various investigators. It represents what I believe to be the most knowledgeable, multidisciplined approach to injury classification and

| Injury Category | Description | Severity Code | Police Code |
|---|---|---|---|
| SEVERE (Not life-threatening) | **General**<br><br>Extensive contusions; abrasions; large lacerations exceeding involvement of two extremities, or large avulsions (greater than 3" wide).<br>20 -30% body surface 2 degree or 3 degree burns.<br><br>**Head and Neck**<br><br>Cerebral injury with or without skull fracture, with unconsciousness more than 15 minutes; without severe neurological signs; brief post-traumatic amnesia (less than 3 hours).<br>Displaced closed skull fractures without unconsciousness or other signs of intracranial injury.<br>Loss of eye, or avulsion of optic nerve.<br>Displaced facial bone fractures, or those with antral or orbital involvement.<br>Cervical spine fractures without cord damage.<br><br>**Chest**<br><br>Multiple rib fractures without respiratory embarrassment.<br>Hemo or pneumothorax.<br>Rupture of diaphragm<br>Lung contusion.<br>Thoracic spine fracture without neuro-involvement.<br><br>**Abdominal**<br><br>Contusion of abdominal organs.<br>Extraperitoneal bladder rupture.<br>Retroperitoneal hemorrhage.<br>Avulsion of ureter.<br>Laceration of urethra.<br>Lumbar spine fractures without neurological involvement.<br><br>**Extremities**<br><br>Displaced simple long bone fractures, and/or multiple hand and foot fractures.<br>Single open long bone fractures.<br>Pelvic fracture with displacement.<br>Dislocation of major joints.<br>Multiple amputations of digits.<br>Lacerations of the major nerves or vessels of extremities. | 3 | A |

**Figure 11.9** (Continued)

it is my hope it will be used by collision investigators throughout the world to ease comparison of data.

General use of the Comprehensive Research Injury Scale will allow detailed comparison of data from different sources as well as leading to clinical data on human tolerances when compared with vehicle damage scales. Evaluation of the federal standards can be more readily accomplished,

| Injury Category | Description | Severity Code | Police Code |
|---|---|---|---|
| SEVERE ( life-threatening, survival probable) | **General**<br><br>Severe lacerations and/or avulsions with dangerous hemorrhage.<br>30-50% body surface 2 degree or 3 degree burns.<br><br>**Head and Neck**<br><br>Cerebral injury with or without skull fracture, with unconsciousness more than 15 minutes;  with definite abnormal neurological signs; post-traumatic amnesia 3 -12 hours.<br>Compound skull fracture.<br><br>**Chest**<br><br>Open chest wounds; flail chest; pneumomediastinum; myocardial contusion without circulatory embarrassment; pericardial injuries.<br>Thoracic spine fracture with paraplegia.<br><br>**Abdominal**<br><br>Minor laceration of intra-abdominal contents (to include. ruptured spleen, kidney, and injuries to tail of pancreas).<br>Intraperitoneal bladder rupture.<br>Avulsion of the genitals.<br>Lumber spine fractures with paraplegia.<br><br>**Extremities**<br><br>Multiple closed long-bone fractures with paraplegia.<br>Amputations of limbs.. | 4 | A |

**Figure 11.10** (Continued)

comparison of varied treatment regimes and some indication of the effectiveness of the retrieval, and of medical and hospital care reflected.

## Injury Scale Uses

I have been asked to comment on the various uses of an accurate injury/severity scale. In our varied interests I feel we have perhaps overlooked our objectives. Foremost is to reduce injury and death due to automotive collisions. Presently there is no significant way improved collision performance can be determined. Ultimately we should come up with two numbers, one indicating the degree of vehicle damage, another indicating

| Injury Category | Description | Severity Code | Police Code |
|---|---|---|---|
| SEVERE (survival uncertain) | **General**<br><br>Over 50% body surface 2 degree or 3 degree burns.<br><br>**Head and Neck**<br><br>Cerebral injury with or without skull fracture, with unconsciousness more than 24 hours; post-traumatic amnesia more than 12 hours; intracranial hemorrhage; signs of increased intracranial pressure (decreasing state of consciousness, bradycardia under 60, progressive rise in blood pressure or progressive pupil inequality).<br>Cervical spine injury with quadriplegia.<br>Major airway obstruction.<br><br>**Chest**<br><br>Chest injuries with respiratory embarrassment (laceration of trachea, hemomediastinum etc.)<br>Aortic laceration<br>Myocardial rupture or contusion with circulatory embarrassment.<br><br>**Abdominal**<br><br>Rupture, avulsion or severe laceration of intra-abdominal vessels or organs, except kidney, spleen or ureter.<br><br>**Extremities**<br><br>Multiple open limb fractures. | 5 | A |
| FATAL within 24 hours | Fatal lesions of single region of body, plus injuries of other body regions of severity Code 3 or less. | 6 | K |
| FATAL (within 24 hours) | Fatal lesions of single region of body, plus injuries of other body regions of severity Code 4 or 5. | 7 | K |
| FATAL | 2 fatal lesions in 2 body regions | 8 | K |
| FATAL | 3 or more fatal injuries | 9 | K |

**Figure 11.11** (Continued)

the degree of occupant injury. If then, with a consistent degree of vehicle damage, and a decrease in the degree of occupant injury, we will know if we are in the right ballpark. It is hoped that by standardizing both a collision severity scale and an injury severity index, it will be possible to evaluate the effectiveness of design changes.[3]

How are injury scales determined? There are many injury scales as we have seen previously; each was developed on a specific basis or for a specific program. The following is excerpted from a paper that describes the basis for an injury scale*.[4]

# A Detailed Injury Scale for Accident Investigation

In an effort to attach more meaning to the cause of an injury during an automobile collision, professional accident analysts have devised various injury index severity codes by which a label or value has been placed on human pain and suffering. On the surface it may appear to be a morbid or rather objective way of judging the value of human life; but, this is the only path open to the engineering–medical team if they are to obtain the necessary information to determine human tolerance to impact.

The most quoted and used "degree of injury scale" was developed by ACIR of Cornell. It uses simple keywords or phrases to guide the analyst in assessing the overall severity of gross body injury. The scale ranges in four steps from minor to fatal-type injuries and has been used by many investigators for statistical studies. This scale has also served as the basis of other codes but again only as a guide.

An injury criterion has been developed to estimate injury hazard. It is primarily used for head impact design work and is based on integration of the area under the acceleration–time curve with the value of acceleration raised to 2.5 power. This value is the inverse slope of the Wayne State University human tolerance curve. A moderate amount of correlation has been shown for this criterion.

## Definition of Detailed Injury Criteria

Approximately 3 years ago, Wayne State University embarked on a two-phase program to determine human tolerance to impact for a special type accident. Phase 1 of the program is the investigation of forward force accidents in the Metropolitan Detroit area in which interior deformations can be accurately measured and photographed. In many cases the interior components were removed and taken to the laboratory for more extensive study. Very minor to severe accidents are used, but only when the exact cause of injury can be determined from the deformed interior components.

A comprehensive and detailed injury criteria was needed for two reasons: (1) available injury scales did not provide fine enough increments between areas of gross bodily injury; and (2) the investigation was not to be used on a large sample of accidents, but only a small number of cases, which are analyzed in depth. Table 11.2 shows the degree of injury criteria,

---

* Excerpts from Reference 4. With permission of the author.

**Table 11.2  Degree of Injury Criteria**

| Weighting | Severity Code | Description |
|---|---|---|
| 1 | $A_0$ Minor | No hospitalization — Abrasions, contusions, fracture of nasal bones, and lacerations without enough loss of blood to cause physiological damage or necessitate transfusion |
| 2 | $A_1$ Minor | Hospitalization — For reasons other than injuries; that is, no means of care in vicinity, at home or otherwise; age of patient; medical history (diabetic shock, insulin shock, etc.) |
| 4 | $A_2$ Minor | Hospitalization — Considered necessary for observation where patient's obvious injuries are minor, and no additional injuries are found during the observation period |
| 6 | $A_3$ Minor | Fracture of small bones of the hands and feet |
| 8 | $B_0$ Moderate | Cerebral concussion with loss of concussion for a short period (usually less than 1 h) with or without injuries |
| 10 | $B_1$ Moderate | Hospitalization for repair of severe facial wounds |
| 12 | $C_0$ Moderately severe | Cerebral concussion with loss of consciousness for a period greater than 1 h without residual signs or symptoms and/or fractured patella, fracture of the long bones of extremities, dislocation of major joints, fractured ribs without pneumothorax, fractured facial bones — excluding nasal bones, fracture of frontal sinus, and extensive lacerations; operative procedure necessary, other than emergency room including postoperative hospitalization |
| 14 | $C_1$ Moderate severe | Same injury as listed above but with complications; that is, pregnancy, pneumo-, or hemothorax |
| 16 | $D_0$ Severe | Extended loss of consciousness; compound fractures of long bones; multiple fractures of extremities; crushing injuries to the chest; skull fracture-X-ray and symptoms, temporary loss of consciousness; multiple facial fractures; fractured vertebra(e); cardiac confusion, fractured pelvis without bladder involvement |
| 18 | $D_1$ Severe | Ruptured spleen, liver, mesenteric tear, perforated colon, etc. |
| 20 | $E_0$ Critical | Shock, multiple comminuted, compound fractures of the long bones; fracture of the pelvis with bladder involvement; skull fracture with extended periods of unconsciousness |
| 22 | $E_1$ Critical | Unconsciousness extending to state of coma |
| 24 | $F_0$ Fatal | Immediate |
| 26 | $F_1$ Fatal | Traceable to the accident |

From Van Kirk, D. J. and Lange, W. A., Detailed Injury Scale for Accident Investigation, in *Proc. 12th Stapp Car Crash Conf.*, Society of Automotive Engineers, New York, 1968. With permission.

which has evolved from this study. It is highly flexible and can be changed by the investigating team if it does not cover a special or particular type injury.

Class A defines the minor emergency room treatments where no hospitalization is required, or where hospitalization is necessary because of extenuating circumstances as described in subsections $A_1$ and $A_2$.* The type of case used to develop this first Class involves a 1965 Mustang, which struck another vehicle in an offset type head-on collision. Both vehicles were estimated to be traveling at between 25 and 30 mph. The 22-year-old male driver sustained a fracture of the central upper incisors and abrasions of both elbows from the steering wheel rim. The steering wheel was deformed and incurred 0.99 in. of deformation from the teeth and 3.33 in. from the elbows and abdomen. The driver was not wearing a seat belt and recovered uneventfully.

Class B is the so-called moderate type injury where hospitalization is required for a few days up to a week, but usually no surgery or only minor repair work is necessary as described in subsection $B_1$

A 1964 Plymouth sedan struck another vehicle in an offset type head-on collision. Both vehicles were estimated to be traveling at 35 mph. The 17-year-old male driver was unconscious for only a few moments. He also sustained a fractured left lower incisor, laceration of both the upper and lower lips, and a large left frontal-occipital laceration to the scalp through the temporalis muscle and into the hairline. The steering wheel had 2.88 in. of the upper portion and was caused by teeth, lips, and chest. The lower deformation of 6.28 in. was caused by abdomen. There were knee dents near the steering column but no knee injuries were recorded. He was not wearing a seat belt and recovered uneventfully.

Class C describes the moderate to severe type injury where surgical procedures are required for repair of skeletal damage. It also covers postoperative hospitalization.

Subsection $C_1$ defines the area for complications arising from the primary injuries where hospitalization is required for longer than a week, but not extended periods. Up to this point the injuries have not been considered as dangerous to life.

A 1965 Ford sedan driven by 52-year-old man who sustained a class C type injury. The vehicle was traveling at approximately 35 mph when it struck a utility pole. The driver suffered three fractured ribs on the right side, a fractured right hand at the wrist, and a bruised right thumb. The steering wheel had a deformation of 5.43 in. at the right spoke. The broken right spoke was due to the right hand and both caused the rib fracture. Knee dents were observed but no injury was reported. The driver did not wear a seat belt and recovered uneventfully.

* See Table 11.2

Class D describes the severe type injury, which is not considered dangerous to life, if treated promptly; and includes most intra-abdominal injuries. This class usually requires extended postoperative hospitalization.

A 1966 Chevrolet sedan struck another vehicle in an offset type head-on collision producing a class D type injury. Both vehicles were estimated to be traveling at between 40 and 50 mph.

The driver, a 71-year-old female, suffered a fractured lower sternum complicated later during her recovery by pneumonitis at the base of both lungs. The deformed steering wheel upper rim was deformed 1.34 in. by the occupant's forehead, which was bruised. The abdomen caused the lower rim deformation of 3.63 in. The occupant *was belted.*

Class E injuries are the most critical and always considered dangerous to life. Hospital and operative requirements cannot be clearly defined but are usually quite extensive.

A 1965 Mustang struck a moving train. The vehicle was traveling between 60 and 70 mph. This accident produced a class E type occupant injury. The 25-year-old male driver sustained a concussion; laceration of scalp, tongue, right arm, and knee; fractures of both clavicles, right fibula, and tibia; contusion of right kidney, sternum, and right elbow; along with pleural effusion. The grossly deformed steering wheel had a deformation of 11.33 in. at its maximum. The wrap-around effect of the arms on the wheel caused the clavicle fractures. The header caused the concussion. Several knee dents were noted but no injuries reported.

Class F represents a highly specialized group of fatal accidents in which are included only cases where the cause of death is known or can be traced directly to the accident. This excludes many cases, where the bodily injury and interior deformation were so severe that the cause and effect could not be determined.

A 1962 Chevrolet sedan with an 18-year-old male driver struck a tree at an estimated speed of 50 mph. The driver was dead on arrival at the hospital with multiple facial fractures and lacerations, fractured sternum, and a probable broken neck (that is, blood found in the spinal fluid). The entire steering column was driven into occupant's compartment due to the type impact.

## Accident Data

At present, there are over 1700 frontal-force accidents under investigation including both rural and urban types. Of these, 330 cases have been analyzed in depth. There were 422 occupants involved.

(Figure 11.12) is a bar graph showing the number of injuries for the leading causes of injuries in forward force accidents (data taken from accident files of Wayne State University).

These data include only front seat occupants, which were not wearing seat belts. Occupants who were ejected or partially ejected from the vehicle

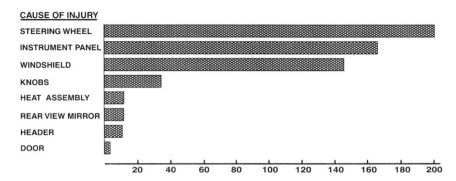

**Figure 11.12** Number of injuries for leading causes of injuries for forward force accidents (1960 and later cars). (From Van Kirk, D. J., and Lange, W. A., Detailed Injury Scale for Accident Investigation in *Proc. 12th Stapp Car Crash Conf.*, Society of Automotive Engineers, New York, 1968. With permission.)

upon impact are not included since the exact cause of the injury could not be determined. In many cases the occupant is injured in more than one body area; therefore, each injury is included. Cases where there has been minor bodily injury but no interior deformation have been eliminated since these do not allow data for human tolerance. Phase I of the program is aimed at investigating only injury-producing accidents, but many accidents occur each day where the occupants are restrained sufficiently to prevent injury from interior components. These, of course, are not included since they do not produce interior deformations.

The steering column leads the way as the major cause of injury, followed by the instrument panel and windshield. The number of lone driver cases is almost four times that of the driver and passenger accidents. Since only a relatively few energy absorbing steering column accidents have been obtained, no judgment can be made at this time regarding its effectiveness in reducing injury.

Many types of injury-weighting factors have been devised to add "realism" to the injury scale. This, in effect, gives the critical-fatal type more importance. (Figure 11.13) shows the injury score for leading causes of injury in forward force accidents. The weighting system used here is a (1-2-4-6-8-10). See (Table 11.2) for the exact assignment of weighting numbers to the class of occupant injury. The value for each cause was obtained by adding the weights, and dividing by the number of injured occupants for each cause. This graph differs from (Figure 11.12) in that only the major injury sustained by the occupant is used. In comparing (Figures 11.12 and 11.13) it is interesting to note that the order for the three leading causes has not changed. The only change that takes place is the case of rear view mirrors, which moved from sixth to fourth place.

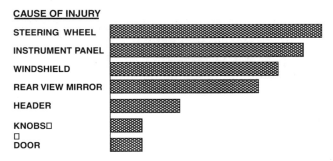

**Figure 11.13** Injury score for leading causes of injury for forward force accidents (1960 and later cars). (From Van Kirk, D. J. and Lange, W. A., Detailed Injury Scale for Accident Investigation, in *Proc. 12th Stapp Car Crash Conf.*, Society of Automotive Engineers, New York, 1968. With permission.)

## Conclusions

1. The proposed injury criteria can be used by the engineering medical team to accurately classify occupants' injuries.
2. Using this criteria and data obtained from phase II of the program, an accurate force-injury index can be developed for each gross body area in terms of the required force to produce any given injury.
3. After the index is completed, the investigator will be able to use the deformed interior components as transducers to predict the severity of the accident.
4. The automotive industry will then have at hand human tolerance data, based on past performance of interior components. These will enable the engineer to design better energy-absorbing components to reduce bodily injury further.

## Discussion

The previously described injury index is based upon the injuries and possible complications an occupant sustains during an automobile accident. Armed with these data and measured interior deformations, the accident investigator must determine exactly what occurred inside the vehicle during the "second" collision. Included in this reconstruction are many other factors, which are not pertinent to this study, but must be taken into account. These include age, condition of health, type of clothing worn, interior spacing, seated height and weight, trajectory of vehicle prior to accident, and its motion during the accident. The proposed injury index and its associated weighting system have tried to include as many of these as possible with the various subdivisions under each main class of injury. Each injury which occurs to a gross body area adds to the overall injury picture;

that is, an occupant who strikes his knees on the dashboard prior to impacting the steering wheel with his chest will reduce his kinetic energy by the amount necessary to deform the dashboard, therefore sustaining a milder chest injury.

It is clearly seen, therefore, that the injury criteria were devised for the sole purpose of aiding in determining the force necessary to produce an injury during an automobile accident.[4]

# References

1. Campbell, B. J., Rouse, W., and Gendre, F., The Traffic Accident Data Project Scale, *Proc. Collision Investigation Methodology Symp.*, sponsored by U. S. Department of Transportation, National Highway Safety Bureau, Washington, D.C., Automobile Manufacturers Assoc., Detroit, MI, 1969.

2. Siegel, A. W., Vehicle Deformation Index: A Report from the International Ad Hoc Committee for Collision Deformation and Trauma Indices, *Proc. Collision Investigation Methodology Symp.*, sponsored by U. S. Department of Transportation, National Highway Safety Bureau, Washington, D.C., Automobile Manufacturers Assoc., Detroit, MI, 1969.

3. Fenner, H. A., Development of a Medically Acceptable Injury Scale, *Proc. Collision Investigation Methodology Symp.*, sponsored by U.S. Department of Transportation, National Highway Safety Bureau, Washington, D.C., Automobile Manufacturers Assoc., Detroit, MI, 1969.

4. Van Kirk, D. J. and Lange, W. A., Detailed Injury Scale for Accident Investigation, *Proc. 12th Stapp Car Crash Conf.*, Society of Automotive Engineers, New York, 1968.

# Motorcycle Accidents

# 12

"Detection is or ought to be, an exact science"
**Sherlock Holmes**
*The Sign of the Four*

Motorcycle accidents occur at a rate almost three times that of automobile accidents, on a per mile basis. The average motorcycle travels less than 2,000 mi/year, while the average car, bus, or truck travels more than 10,000 mi/year. Then why are there more motorcycle accidents than other vehicular accidents? If all other factors are considered as being equal, the number of accidents should be a function of the number of miles driven.[1]

Statistics also show that there are 20 times more fatalities in motorcycle accidents than in other vehicular accidents. Examination of the motorcycle accident vs. the other vehicular accidents shows that the motorcyclist must expend his/her energy by impacting another fixed object such as a car, tree, or pole, or must impact or slide along the ground until all his/her kinetic energy has been dissipated. In other vehicular accidents the vehicles are designed to absorb energy, thus preventing it from being transferred to the occupants of the vehicle. In addition, the occupants are restrained in such a manner as to absorb an additional amount of energy, thus reducing their kinetic energy to a level below that which causes life-threatening injuries.

## Factors Involved

In motorcycle accidents the drivers of the other vehicles generally indicate that they did not see the motorcycle coming at them or crossing in front of their field of vision. This can be attributed to several factors.

## Size of Vehicles

The first is the size of the motorcycle vs. the size of any other vehicle on the road. Vehicular drivers can lose sight of the motorcycle or be blocked by the "A" post of their vehicles. This is especially true if the motorcycle is 100 ft or more away from the vehicle, and its profile is so small that it is lost as the vehicular driver rotates his/her head from side to side to check for oncoming traffic. The law was changed several years ago making it mandatory that motorcycle headlights be on at all times. It was hoped to minimize if not eliminate the vehicular drivers' vision problems. Accident statistics have shown that this new law did not make much difference.

*Comments: The latest change to motorcycle headlight systems has been to add dual headlights. Accident investigation will prove their worth in the future.*

## Headlights and Taillights

The second factor involves the headlights and/or taillights of the motorcycle. Any other vehicle approaching a car or truck can see two headlights, one on each side of the vehicle. The distance between these headlights increases as the vehicle comes closer to the car or truck. It is difficult enough to determine the velocity of an approaching vehicle by trying to use the surrounding landmarks, let alone to evaluate the change in the distance between the headlights of the oncoming car. Many, if not most, drivers have not been trained in this manner or have not taken the time to train themselves in this respect. Therefore, many accidents occur when a vehicle turns out into approaching traffic assuming that the approaching vehicle is farther away than the driver estimated when starting the maneuver.

Consider the motorcycle that has only a single headlight as it approaches a driver sitting at a stop sign or traffic light waiting to turn across the path of the oncoming motorcycle. Does the vehicular driver consider the single headlight as that of a car or truck with one burned-out headlight or as that of a motorcycle? In the daytime it may be possible to distinguish between a single light on a motorcycle and a vehicle with a burned-out headlight, but during the nighttime it is virtually impossible to make this distinction. Therefore, a misjudgment of the velocity of the oncoming vehicle can happen quite easily.

# Details to be Investigated

The investigation of a motorcycle accident requires much more detailed analysis at the scene than does a normal car-to-car or vehicle collision. As stated previously, most motorcycles are not seen by the vehicle that strikes them or that they strike. Therefore, the motorcycle is more likely the one to try some type of maneuver to remove itself from the path of the collision vehicle.

## Braking System of Motorcycle

The on-scene investigator/reconstructionist must also remember that the braking systems on motorcycles are different than those of standard automobiles. The larger touring bikes have a proportional valve that develops a greater percentage of force on the rear brake system than on the front brakes. The front hand brake is still used but the foot brake can stop the motorcycle by itself. The lighter bikes do not have this feature and therefore the novice motorcyclist may overapply the front brake and may cause the motorcycle to tip headfirst over onto the roadbed. It is also easy for the motorcycle to sway during a skid, lending a wave or curve to the rear wheel skid mark.

Most motorcyclists sparingly apply the front hand brake, due to the potential for a front tip over of the motorcycle. In addition, today's motorcyclists have taken an approved course and have an endorsement on their driver's license to operate a motorcycle. Therefore, they have been trained to "lay the bike down" when they believe that they cannot stop the bike in time or maneuver out of the way of a potential collision.

## Witness Marks at Accident Site

Thus the on-scene investigator/reconstructionist must spend an extra amount of time on the details of the scene, which may include an area where the motorcycle was "laid down." These details should include skid marks from the front and/or rear of the motorcycle tires, gouge and scratch marks from the tire rims, and also various mechanical components of the motorcycle — such as the oil filter cover, foot pegs, exhaust covers, crash bars, handlebars, or even the instrument package — if the motorcycle tumbles and slides along to its point of rest.

These gouges and scratch marks may vary in depth as well as in length along the surface of the roadbed. Many times the investigator finds the gouges and scratch marks in more than one direction. This is an indication that the bike has either tumbled from one side of the machine to the other side, or has rotated about a foot peg or other metal portion of the machine, thereby changing its center of balance and causing a different component of the machine to create gouge or scratch marks in the roadbed.

## Witness Marks on Motorcycle

Of course, a detailed examination of the motorcycle itself is also necessary to confirm that witness marks match the scratch and gouge marks on the roadbed and that both sides of the machine may have been involved.

The depths of the witness marks on the machine are an indicator of a match up with the deeper gouge marks or scratches that are on the roadbed. The more material that has been worn off the motorcycle, the deeper the gouge or scratches are. Heavier, stiffer materials such as the crash bars on the side of the engine generally make the deepest gouges.

Surface scratches on the roadbed are usually done by broader lighter surfaces such as the oil filter cover or chain covers. The direction of the marks on the machine itself is also an indication of the movement of the motorcycle during the accident after it has been laid down or has fallen over onto the roadbed and continued to slide along to its resting point. These marks can be horizontal or parallel to the ground, or can be at any angle and between the horizontal and vertical (from the tires to the seat). Photograph these marks from a wide angle to a close-up view placing an adjustable scale in each photograph that allows the angle of the marks to be read in the photographs.

Remember that the angle of the witness marks dictates the direction of the motorcycle movement. As an example, vertical scratch marks on the machine would indicate that the motorcycle was sliding either with the tires first or with the seat first. To confirm this check the sides of the tires for vertical rub marks as well as the sides of the seats for the same type of damage.

## Measurement of Angle of Impact

If there are scratch marks on the machine at some angle between the horizontal and vertical, the investigator can determine the angle of the motorcycle with respect to the ground that would produce these marks by doing the steps discussed next.

Lay a yardstick or yellow tape longitudinally along a roadbed. Determine the angle of the scratch marks on the machine and place the machine on the roadbed so that the scratch marks line up with the yardstick or yellow tape. Photograph the motorcycle in this position, making sure that the yardstick or yellow tape are very evident in the photograph.

In this manner all the angles of the various scratch marks on both sides of the machine can be determined by using the same process as described previously. Once all the various scratch mark directions have been determined and photographed, the investigator/reconstructionist can then match up those scratch marks on the machine with the gouges and scratch marks on the roadbed. This step allows him/her to determine exactly the positions that the motorcycle underwent during its slide to its point of rest.

## Oil Trail

If the motorcycle is struck prior to being laid down or thrown down, there will be a trail of oil a foot or so after the impact to the final resting point of the motorcycle. This is an additional indicator of the path of the motor-cycle after the collision.

## Determination of the Motorcyclist's Point of Impact

The next step to be investigated thoroughly is the POI of the motorcycle rider with the ground. If the cyclist laid the bike down and was smart enough to wear leather pants or Levi jeans, then there may be a witness mark on the concrete surface where the leather or Levi material has been rubbed into or on top of the surface itself.

If there was a collision with the vehicle first and the rider was ejected over the vehicle, then there may be only a small area of potential witness marks that the rider may have left when striking the ground. If the rider has any type of jacket on when he/she strikes the ground, there may be some of the fiber or colors on the surface of the roadbed. If the rider chose not to wear a heavy outer garment, then there may be blood spatters or a trail of blood from the point of impact to the point of rest.

## Motorcyclist's Helmet

Finally, a check must be made of the motorcyclist's helmet. The majority of helmets in use today are made of some form of polycarbonate with an impregnated color. This color usually leaves a trace on the roadbed surface. The helmet itself must be examined for a fractured outer surface as well as compression dents in the inner foam surface. Motorcycle helmet exterior shells are designed to fracture, absorbing the energy of impact in conjunction with the compression of the inner foam surface. The type and depth of fracture are an indication of the kinetic energy of the cyclist after being ejected from the motorcycle itself. The depth of compression of the inner surface is an indication of the forces that were applied to the head at the time of the impact of the helmet with the roadbed or other fixed object after ejection.

Many times helmets only show a variety of scratches in more than one direction. The on-scene investigator/reconstructionist must determine if any of these marks were preexisting. If they can be shown not to have existed prior to the contact with the fixed object, then once again the investigator can show the different directions that the rider underwent during the sliding phase of the accident.

## Inspection of Inoperative or Deformed Motorcycle Components

It would be prudent for the on-scene investigator/reconstructionist to check on the steering, brakes, headlights, and taillights of the motorcycle during his/her inspection, assuming that all these components are intact.

*Commentary: There are some motorcycles that have a special switch added to the headlight and taillight system so that the lights could be turned off while the motorcycle was in motion, allowing the battery to charge.*

The brake pads are easy to check on most motorcycles today by a visual inspection for the thickness of the pad. Generally speaking, the biggest problem with motorcycle maintenance is either lack of brake fluid or inoperative headlights for one reason or another.

The determination of the direction of impact of a motorcycle is easily seen by the deformation of the front steering wheel. A direct head-on impact compresses the front wheel rim very similar to a vehicle tire and wheel rim striking a curb, except it is much broader and deeper depending on the velocity at impact.

Many motorcycle manufacturers today use an aluminum rim instead of the old spoke rims that were used on bicycles. As a result, the rims deform quite similarly to the aluminum wheel rims on cars. If the impact is a sideswipe, then the center hub of the wheel is pushed in the direction of the impact. As an example if the front bumper strikes the right side of the motorcycle at the front wheel, the hub is pushed to the left.

As in vehicular accidents, the motorcycle accident details are found in the deformation of the machine as well as the evidence left on the roadbed. The problem is that there is not as much machine deformation and witness mark evidence left on the roadbed for the on-scene investigator/reconstructionist to analyze. That is why much more attention to detail must be adhered to when inspecting such scenes.

The machine deformation can take the form of direct impacts, scratches from sliding, and punctures into the tires or other components — all the way to a total destruction of the machine where it may not even be possible to determine the manufacturer without a manufacturer's plate. These details when analyzed, as discussed in the early chapters, can lead the investigator/reconstructionist to the most likely and optimum reconstruction of the accident.

## Determination of Velocity of Motorcycle at Impact by Alternative Method

It is always a problem to try and determine the velocity at which a motorcycle struck or was struck by a vehicle. There has been some research done on determining the velocity of a motorcycle at impact by the amount of damage sustained in the collision. The reader should consult the Society of Automotive Engineers (SAE) for relevant papers. Most of the work conducted was done at right angles, which is fairly common in motorcycle accidents.

However, there are still a great many accidents where the cycle is struck or strikes a vehicle at some angle other than 90 degrees.

One method that is extremely useful for determining velocity of a motorcycle at impact is described by Collins.[2] Consider the rider or driver of the motorcycle as a cannonball being shot out of a cannon at the time of the impact. First, it must be determined that the rider did not strike any other object except the handlebars or the gas tank on the bike when he/she exited the machine. By reviewing the injuries of the rider's abdomen, upper arms and wrists, and upper and lower legs, some additional assessment of the velocity or energy lost can be made. Depending on the angle the cyclist leaves the machine, he/she may try to use his/her arms as a restraint system by locking or keeping the arms and wrist as stiff as possible to stay in the seat. This can cause fractures of the wrist, elbows, and upper and lower arms. If the cyclist strikes the handlebars or the gas tank he/she can cause injuries to the lower parts of his/her body ranging from minor bruising to severe fractures and internal injuries.

Consultation of biomechanics texts on human tolerance can provide some guidelines for assuming the velocity lost due to these initial impacts. The distance between the point at which the rider left the bike and the point where he/she initially struck the ground as well as his/her final resting point must be determined by the investigator/reconstructionist. Many times a rider strikes the ground and then rolls or slides to a complete stop. Both positions should be known or determined. The calculation can yield the velocity of the motorcycle driver at the time he/she leaves the bike, using the following procedure.

As in all cannonball problems, the investigator/reconstructionist must know several variables before the problem can be solved. In general, to determine the velocity as the projectile leaves the cannon, the angle at which it was launched, and the location of the launch (i.e., above or below the final resting point and the distance to the resting point) need to be determined. Because it is difficult to determine the angle that the rider left the machine, the investigator/reconstructionist can work backward by assuming the apogee (maximum altitude) of the driver. Collins[2] states, "… that in the absence of eye witnesses a range of 5 to 7 ft is appropriate."

It is obvious but it must be mentioned that a motorcycle rider is not as smooth or aerodynamically designed as a cannonball. This is especially true when the cyclist is being propelled through the air with the limbs akimbo. Therefore, there is a certain amount of wind drag while the motorcycle rider is being airborne. At velocities below 25 mi/h Collins[2] claims that wind drag can be ignored; above those velocities he provides a table of correction factors for the two different apogee heights.

When the cannonball motorcyclist is launched into space after the collision, each of them rises to the maximum height (apogee) and then falls back to earth. Cannonballs usually explode on impact, but motorcycle riders may stay where they land if the earth is soft enough or they may roll or slide along the surface until they expend the remainder of their energy and finally come to rest.

By assuming that the seated motorcyclist has an average center of gravity of 3 ft above the ground, the distance he/she rises in the air $\Delta H$ is the apogee height $H_0$ minus 3 ft. Then the time to rise to its maximum height is given by the formula:

$$T_1 = [(2 \cdot \Delta H)/g]^{1/2} \tag{12.1}$$

where $T_1$ is the time to rise in seconds; $\Delta H$ is the rise distance in feet, and $g$ is the acceleration of gravity, 32.2 ft/sec/sec.

During this same time period the rider travels a distance $S_1$ over the ground given by:

$$S_1 = 1.47 \cdot V_E \cdot T_1 \tag{12.2}$$

where $S_1$ is in feet and $V_E$ is the rider's launch velocity in miles per hour.

Once the motorcycle rider reaches his/her maximum height and gravity takes over, he/she then begins to fall to the earth.

Due to wind drag and gravity the rise and return to the earth do not follow the same path. The time to fall from apogee is given by the following formula:

$$T_2 = [(2 \cdot H_0)/g]^{1/2} \tag{12.3}$$

where $T_2$ is the time to fall to the earth in seconds. During this time the rider travels a distance $S_2$ over the ground, which is given by the following:

$$S_2 = 1.47 \cdot V_E \cdot T_2 \tag{12.4}$$

The distance the rider then travels along the ground $S_3$ while rolling and sliding to rest is given by this equation:

$$S_3 = [(V^2_E)/(30 \cdot \mu)] \tag{12.5}$$

where $\mu$ is the ejected rider's coefficient of friction.

The total distance the rider travels from launch, hopefully the point of impact, to the point of rest is simply the summation of the distances traveled through the air and over the ground:

$$S_T = S_1 + S_2 + S_3 \qquad (12.6)$$

The values for $S_1$, $S_2$, and $S_3$ are known, so just substitute the values and obtain the following:

$$S_T = (1.47 \cdot V_E \cdot T_1) + (1.47 \cdot V_E \cdot T_2) + ([(V^2_E)/(30 \cdot \mu)] \qquad (12.7)$$

Notice, however, that Equation 12.7 contains three unknowns, the launch velocity and the times of the rise and the fall of the rider in space.

Substitute the equations for $T_1$ and $T_2$ and then combine terms to arrive at an equation where all the unknowns are on the right side. Starting with the base equation gives:

$$S_T = (1.47 \cdot V_E \cdot T_1) + (1.47 \cdot V_E \cdot T_2) + ([(V^2_E)/(30 \cdot \mu)] \qquad (12.8)$$

Now by substitution the following equation in its raw form is

$$S_T = (1.47 \cdot V_E \cdot [(2 \cdot \Delta H)/g]^{1/2}) + (1.47 \cdot V_E \cdot [(2 \cdot H_0)/g]^{1/2})$$
$$+ ([(V^2_E)/(30 \cdot \mu)] \qquad (12.9)$$

Plugging in the value for $g = 32.2$ ft/sec/sec gives:

$$St = (1.47 \cdot V_E \cdot [2 \cdot \Delta H/(32.2)]^{1/2}) + (1.47 \cdot V_E \cdot [2 \cdot H_0/(32.2)]^{1/2}$$
$$+ ([V^2_E)/(30 \cdot \mu) \qquad (12.10)$$

Separate the constants out from under the square root sign as follows:

$$St = (1.47 \cdot V_E \cdot [(2)^{1/2} \cdot (\Delta H)^{1/2}/(32.2)^{1/2}]$$
$$+ (1.47 \cdot V_E \cdot [(2)^{1/2} \cdot (H_0)^{1/2}/(32.2)^{1/2}]$$
$$+ ([V^2_E)/(30 \cdot \mu) \qquad (12.11)$$

By expanding terms in Equation 12.11, the following is obtained:

$$St = (1.47 \cdot V_E \cdot [1.414 \cdot (\Delta H)/(5.67)] +$$

$$+ (1.47 \cdot V_E \cdot [1.414 \cdot (H_0)^{1/2}/(5.67)]$$

$$+ ([V^2_E)/(30 \cdot \mu) \tag{12.12}$$

By combining constants:

$$St = (2.078 \cdot V_E \cdot [(\Delta H)/(5.67)] + (2.078 \cdot V_E \cdot [(H_0)^{1/2}/(5.67)]$$

$$+ ([V^2_E)/(30 \cdot \mu) \tag{12.13}$$

Combining terms so there are only constants in the denominator gives:

$$St = (V_E \cdot [(\Delta H)/(2.72)] + (V_E \cdot [(H_0)^{1/2}/(2.72)]$$

$$+ ([V^2_E)/(30 \cdot \mu) \tag{12.14}$$

Only one unknown remains, the velocity of the object as it exits. Unfortunately, it looks cumbersome but it is rather easy to use.

Apply an iteration process by which scientific approximation is used for the velocity, and do the math to see how close it comes to the known value of the distance traveled $St$. If the approximation is too high or too low, then try another and continue until getting as close to $St$ as desired in terms of accuracy.

An example helps to show the process. A motorcycle was traveling down a highway at approximately 40 mi/h when a vehicle made a running stop at a stop sign, did not see the cyclist approaching from the left, there was a collision with the motorcyclist striking the left front fender of the vehicle and flying over the handlebars without contact to it or the gas tank, and landed on the ground 45 ft away after skidding 5 ft. Use Equation 12.14 and make the following assumptions.

Assume the apogee of the rider is 5 ft and the coefficient of friction for the rider sliding on the ground is 1.2.

$$\Delta H = H_0 - 3 \tag{12.15}$$

therefore

$$5 - 3 = 2$$

As a starting point consider the velocity $V_E = 40$ mi/h. By asserting this value into Equation 12.14, the following can be obtained:

$$St = (40 \cdot [(2)^{1/2}/(2.72)]) + (40 \cdot [(5)^{1/2}/(2.72)])$$

$$+ ([40^2]/(30 \cdot 1.2) \tag{12.16}$$

$$St = 20.79 + 32.88 + 44.44 \tag{12.17}$$

$$St = 98.11 \text{ ft}$$

However, the known measured distance for the first POR at the unknown exit velocity was 45 ft. Therefore, the assumed value is too high for the exit velocity. Thus, try a lower value of 30 mi/h.

By plugging in the new value of 30 mi/h the following equation can be obtained:

$$St = (30 \cdot [(2)^{1/2}/(2.72)]) + (30 \cdot [(5)^{1/2}/(2.72)])$$

$$+ ([30^2]/(30 \cdot 1.2) \tag{12.18}$$

$$St = 15.60 + 24.66 + 25 = 65.26 \text{ ft}$$

This outcome is still higher that the measured distance; therefore, another value for the exit velocity must be assumed. Assume 25 mi/h and obtain the following equation:

$$St = (25 \cdot [(2)^{1/2}/(2.72)]) + (25 \cdot [(5)^{1/2}/(2.72)])$$

$$+ ([25^2]/(30 \cdot 1.2) \tag{12.19}$$

Combining terms gives the following:

$$St = 12.99 + 20.55 + 17.36 = 50.90 \text{ ft}$$

Once again, this is higher than the measured distance of 45 ft. Again assume a value for the exit velocity of 23 mi/h. By plugging these values into Equation 12.14 the following is obtained:

$$St = (23 \cdot [(2)^{1/2}/(2.72)]) + (23 \cdot [(5)^{1/2}/(2.72)])$$

$$+ ([23^2]/(30 \cdot 1.2) \tag{12.20}$$

Combining terms gives:

$$St = 11.99 + 18.91 + 14.69 = 45.6 \text{ ft}$$

This value is very close to the measured value. It is actually close enough but if the investigators/reconstructionists wish to continue the iteration process, they can obtain a closer value but not necessarily a more accurate one.

*Commentary: This method works very well and is quite accurate. The accuracy is dependent on the number of iterations and the requirements of the case under investigation.*

# References

1. Noon, R., *Introduction to Forensic Engineering*, CRC Press, Boca Raton, FL, 1992.
2. Collins, J. C., *Accident Reconstruction*, Charles C Thomas, Springfield, IL, 1979.

# Pedestrian Accidents

# 13

"I am a believer in the genius loci"

**Sherlock Holmes**
*The Valley of Fear*

Pedestrian accidents are unique. This type of collision pits a 4000-lb vehicle against a human pedestrian weighing an average between 90 and 250 lb. It does not take a professional investigator/reconstructionist to determine the outcome of such a collision; the human pedestrian always loses.

## Details to be Determined

The details of this type of accident are extremely important, more so than a car-to-car collision.

### Direct Impacts from Front of Vehicle

The disturbance of any dust on the outside surface of the vehicle all the way from the bumper to the top of the vehicle and down to the truck deck lid are of paramount importance in the investigation. This disturbance is a path that the pedestrian most likely took during his/her travel over the outside surface of the vehicle. Dents and other metal depressions indicate points of contact between the pedestrian and the vehicle. Blood spatter or other anatomic material found on, or embedded into, various components of the vehicle are details that must be photographed, measured, and recorded on videotape.

313

Imprints on the bumper from the pedestrian's clothing, for example, the weave of jeans or other types of trousers such as twill, leave distinctive marks and patterns on today's soft bumper fascia.

### Pattern of Injury to Pedestrian

The investigator must also look at the pattern of injury to the pedestrian to determine points of impact on the vehicle vs. points of impact on the pedestrian. As an example, pedestrians generally wear rubber or leather-soled shoes; the pedestrians' weight acts downward on the shoes and provides a friction force between the shoes and the highway. If a pedestrian is walking across the street and has been struck on his/her left side, his/her knee may buckle in such a manner as to conform to the shape of the bumper.

The friction force between the pedestrian's shoe and the street partially holds the shoe in place at the bottom of his/her foot while the vehicle is pushing forward at his/her knee level. This causes a fracture of the lower leg bones and causes the pedestrian to rotate about their center of gravity to his/her left on top of the hood or farther up on the vehicle depending on the velocity of impact. There is a weight transfer from the right foot to the left foot preventing, in most cases, a fracture of the right foot, which is farther forward of the vehicle bumper and is behind the initial impact.

The manner in which the pedestrian rotates onto and over the vehicle and lands on the roadbed, the gravel shoulder, or possibly even on a grassy surface is another significant area that must by necessity require a detailed analysis.

### Determining Pedestrian Rotation

The investigator must have knowledge of the front shape of today's automobiles to understand the possible trajectory of the pedestrian during his/her flight onto and over the vehicle. For the last 20 years, automobile manufacturers have been designing into each new vehicle an aerodynamic softening of all the surfaces, but especially the front end to reduce the wind drag and to increase the gasoline mileage of the vehicle. This aerodynamic design is based on rounded corners and surfaces to allow a smoother flow of the air over these surfaces. With smoother air flow there is less drag and hence more aerodynamic flow and better gas mileage. In addition to the rounded surfaces, the front of the vehicles has been tapered into a wedge shape, again to allow smoother flow of air.

The shape of the front of the vehicle has a great deal to do with the trajectory of the pedestrian after impact. The higher the front of the vehicle the less chances are that the pedestrian will be rotated on top of the hood. With the reduced height of the front of the vehicle there is more of a scooping effect similar to that of a cowcatcher on the front of a train. This effect literally rotates the pedestrian rearward, and onto the hood or top of the vehicle instead of impacting him/her with a blunt front end of the vehicle.

*Commentary: Pedestrian accidents are very messy. By that I mean they usually are very bloody and in almost all cases are fatal. Several years ago, a case was reported in the local newspaper. A pedestrian was struck by the blunt front end of a large luxury vehicle. The vehicle had a very square hood and grille. Because the height of the hood of the vehicle was several feet above the ground at impact, and the upper edge was very square, the impact literally caused a separation of the pedestrian's body between the rib cage and the pelvic girdle, with the lower half staying on the grill of the vehicle and the upper half being propelled rearward through the front windshield and onto the front seat. A series of preliminary pedestrian-to-vehicle impacts was conducted at the Biomechanics Research Lab of Wayne State University in the late 1960s. A cadaver was used with and without shoes. Without shoes it was shown that there was very little if any frictional force between the foot of the cadaver and the concrete floor. As a result, the cadaver was thrown upward onto the hood and many times completely over the vehicle. In the experiments using shoes, X-rays showed fractures of the lower leg long bones as seen at on-scene investigations.*

Almost all vehicle hoods are sloped from the center to the left and right sides of the vehicle. This sloping affects the motion of the pedestrian as it rotates from a standing position to a somewhat horizontal position and lands on the hood. Because of the slope of the hood, the pedestrian's body moves either to the right or to the left depending on the initial point of contact between the vehicle and the pedestrian. The higher the speeds at impact the farther rearward the pedestrian may land on the upper surface of the vehicle.

Several papers have been published by the Society of Automotive Engineers (SAE) indicating that at approximately 40 mi/h the pedestrian may land near the base of the windshield or into the windshield itself. This is usually the first contact point. Depending on the type of clothing worn by the pedestrian, it is possible he/she may stay in that position, roll over the top of the vehicle, or slide off to one side. Leather coats or other fabrics that have a sticky-type surface may hinder the pedestrian from sliding very far across the surface of the hood. The new smoother type surfaces such as ski jackets allow the pedestrians to slide more easily off the vehicle surface.

## Impacts to Vehicle Windshield

When impact occurs into a windshield, there is fracture of the exterior and most likely interior glass of the windshield. If the pedestrian's head strikes the windshield, it may leave hair, tissue, and blood on the surface of the glass as well as in between the glass fragments at the point of fracture. The on-scene investigator must photograph these details as soon as possible because they disappear quickly due to rain or snow.

If possible, the on-scene investigator should contact the emergency medical technician (EMT) at the scene or the emergency room technician and have them check for glass particles in the hair/scalp of the pedestrian victim. This can verify the contact point on the vehicle with a particular location of injury on the pedestrian.

## Dents in Vehicle Exterior

The same would be true with a large dent in the hood. A request should be made to check for injury, primarily bruising, to the pedestrian's upper body, such as a shoulder or elbow, as well as the hips and knees. Today's automobiles must meet a specific standard bumper height above the ground. The vehicle bumper causes impact to a pedestrian's lower leg. Matching the height of the leg fracture above the bottom of the bumper with the known height of that particular bumper can verify the impact point.

Thus far, direct impacts from the front of the vehicle to the pedestrian have been discussed.

## Sideswipe Type of Impact

There is a second type of vehicle pedestrian impact, which is a sideswipe-type impact. In this particular case the pedestrian is not impacted by the front bumper but instead is struck by the side of the vehicle. This is done by the pedestrian walking into the side of the vehicle or as the vehicle is turning into the pedestrian. These types of impacts are difficult for the on-scene investigator, because they do not leave as much evidence as the frontal-type impact.

## Comparison of Vehicle Exterior Surfaces

At the beginning of this chapter the dust on the surface of the vehicle is mentioned. Unless the vehicle has been freshly washed prior to impact with the pedestrian, there are varying degrees of surface dust and dirt on the horizontal as well as the vertical surfaces. The dust is disturbed in a swipe-type pattern from front to rear of the vehicle. This is the best clue for the on-scene investigator.

In addition, there may be some types of scratching of the painted surface due to the pedestrian's clothes. These could include zippers, buttons, or any type of decorative material that is on the outside of the pedestrian's jacket or coat. The on-scene investigator can request the outer garments worn by the pedestrian at the time of the accident from the police, funeral home, or family. A meticulous inspection of these garments can show worn or torn spots at the same height above the ground as the swipe/smears of the dust on the accident vehicle.

## Rearview Mirrors

The only other exterior object that may be of help to the investigator is the outside rearview mirrors. These mirrors are all aerodynamically shaped with the semipointed surface facing the front of the vehicle. These mirrors may cause severe injury and in many cases fatal injury to a pedestrian in a sideswipe-type accident, depending on the location of the impact and the physical size of the pedestrian.

*Commentary: Visualize a pedestrian impact case in which a 9-year-old boy was sideswiped by a van and the outside rearview mirror struck the young boy in the head, causing a fatal injury.*

*Examination of the NFL sports jacket he was wearing that night showed a rubbing away of the slick jacket material surface over the flaps and over the zippers used on the upper pockets.*

*There was some question concerning whether or not the hood of the jacket was up on the boy's head. Opposing counsel suggested that the hood was up and as a result the young boy did not see the van approaching. Close examination of the interior of the hood of the jacket showed no blood stains whatsoever, even though a head impact of this type would have resulted in a great loss of blood, therefore proving the vehicle did strike the boy and the hood of the jacket did not play a part in the accident itself.*

A third type of pedestrian accident is claimed to have occurred but the author puts no stock in it based on the physics of the situation. The contention was that a pedestrian ran into the side of a bus and in some magical way ended up under the wheels of the vehicle. The author has never found this to be true, let alone possible. The only way he believes that this could occur would be if the pedestrian were running toward the bus and either stumbled or fell forward, grazing the side of the vehicle and then rolling forward as the bus was turning and drove over the body of the victim.

If the pedestrian is standing, in a normal walking or running position, it is impossible for that individual to strike the vehicle and then bounce off and roll underneath the wheels. The trajectory motion would be away from the vehicle, not toward it.

*Commentary: A recent bus-to-pedestrian impact claimed that a pedestrian was chasing the bus and then fell under the rear wheels, causing her demise.*

*A detailed investigation at the scene showed that the pedestrian had to cross over at least one curb and navigate around several potholes that were close to the curb. The bus was turning to the right at the time the pedestrian was approaching from the rear.*

*Our examination showed that the pedestrian fell into either a pothole or over the curb and then landed far enough forward that the left rear bus wheels ran over her as the bus was turning the corner.*

# Determination of Pedestrian's Walking or Running Speed

Determination of the walking or running speed of a pedestrian is extremely difficult. There are many research papers published by both the engineering and the human factor communities that have tried to determine these speeds for a variety of age groups of individuals. The only problem with using these data is that the pedestrian involved in the accident may not fit into one of these groups.

As an example, a 60-year-old man in one of the studies may have performed very well. In an accident case the man may have had arthritis, an injured leg or hip, poor reaction times, or even poor eyesight. These may or may not have been taken into account during the studies. Suffice it to say that the use of such tables can be a starting point for the mathematics of the situation. However, be sure to use a range of values for such speeds to include the possibility of any inherent physical disabilities that may be known at the time the calculations are made. Once again, it is necessary to contact the relatives of the pedestrian, if it is a fatal accident, and to determine if any such disabilities did indeed exist at the time of the accident.

# Determination of Distance Pedestrian is Thrown

Based on the author's experience, most drivers relate to the on-scene investigator that the pedestrian came out of nowhere and they never had a chance to see him/her before impact. This can be confirmed easily by determining the distance the pedestrian was thrown from the point of impact. There have been several methods used by different reconstructionists over the years to determine the vehicle speed at the time the pedestrian was struck. Only a few of them are discussed in this text.

In Chapter 12 on motorcycle accident reconstruction, work done by Collins[1] is discussed. He uses a method called the "cannonball." Collins assumes the height of the center of the motorcyclist and then projects him to an approximate height of 5 to 7 ft. Knowing the distance the motorcyclist landed at impact and the height or apogee of the trajectory, he can determine the velocity with which the motorcyclist left the motorcycle at impact. This same principle can be applied to a pedestrian accident.

From anthropomorphic data the center of gravity of standing individuals can be determined. The impact point on the vehicle can also be measured, and the center of gravity apogee from that impact point can then be assumed. Next the resting point of the pedestrian can be located from the police reports. The point of impact must be determined with respect to the roadway of the pedestrian with the vehicle. Once this is known the investigator can calculate the velocity of the vehicle at the point of impact by the "thrown distance" of the pedestrian. The system is accurate within a few miles per hour. It is likely that every reconstructionist who delves into the theory of pedestrian/vehicle interaction has developed or is using 1 of 20 or so other methods devised by other reconstructionists since the early 1970s. Only a few of those are mentioned in this chapter. Each of the systems of equations reviewed contains a throw distance and a sight distance from the point of impact of the pedestrian with the vehicle.

## Determination of Impact Velocity

Limpert,[2] in his book titled *Motor Vehicle Accident Reconstruction and Analysis*, developed a formula for solving the impact velocity of a vehicle based on a known throw distance. The equation, however, is to be used when the vehicle was breaking before impact. He claims a reliability of plus or minus 2.5 mi/h. Neither the source nor the derivation of the formula is described in his book.

In 1989, Northwestern University[3] developed a pedestrian formula for vehicle velocity for use with large trucks and vans or generally blunt front-end vehicles. The limitation was that the leading edge of the front of the vehicle must be higher than the center of gravity of the pedestrian.

Eubanks,[4] a member of the American Council of Traffic Accident Reconstructionists (ACTAR), has formalized a method in his book, *Pedestrian Accident Reconstruction and Litigation*, similar to the one the author has used from time to time in pedestrian–vehicular accidents. It considers the throw distance of the pedestrian to include not only the point of impact but also the time and distance that the pedestrian may be sliding on the upper surfaces of the vehicle — hood, windshield, or roof. The trajectory itself includes the time and distance that the pedestrian leaves the vehicle until initial contact with the ground, and until coming to rest by sliding or rolling along the surface of the ground. In this manner the entire movement of the pedestrian is accounted for, which can give a more accurate analysis and calculation for the impact velocity by the vehicle to the pedestrian. The only limitations to this process that the author has found are the assumptions that need to be made for coefficient of friction of the pedestrian sliding or rolling on the surface of the vehicle as well as landing or rolling on the ground.

Once the pedestrian is sliding or rolling on the hood of the vehicle he/she can leave certain witness marks such as scratches, gouges, or even dents. The experienced investigator/reconstructionist develops a sense of values to use for the coefficient of friction based on the amount of damage seen on the vehicle. An example is light scratches without any depth, or the absence of dents which would indicate a low coefficient of friction such as 0.1 to 0.3. A large dent in the hood, or a fractured windshield with the glass being pushed inward several inches would indicate a higher coefficient of friction such as 0.7 to 0.8.

Most reconstructionists use a coefficient of friction for the pedestrian sliding along a highway or grassy surface of 0.7 to 1.2. The reason for this higher coefficient of friction is the clothing worn by the pedestrian may snag and catch on the highway, slowing down the pedestrian much faster than on a painted surface such as the hood of the vehicle. The remainder of the analysis for the pedestrian's throw distance is similar to what is discussed in this chapter and in Chapter 12. It is left to the reader's discretion to develop them at leisure or to purchase any of the books discussed here.

## Witness Statements

As stated at the beginning of this chapter, pedestrian accidents are very messy, not only because of the terrible injuries sustained by the pedestrians but also because of the lack of evidence to assist the investigator/reconstructionist in his/her work. In many cases the amount of information such as witness statements may be overwhelming to say the least. Most likely there are not two of them who will give the same statement. This is where the skills of the investigator/reconstructionist must take over. Many statements can be thrown out because they are preposterous; others are easily seen to be made to help the pedestrian instead of giving an accurate account of what happened at the scene. A scale drawing of the scene showing the point of impact and the point rest of both vehicle and pedestrian along with the locations of the various witnesses can go along way to help separate the somewhat accurate statements from the completely misleading statements. Remember, it is the job of the investigator/reconstructionist to develop the best scenario from the hard evidence found at the scene or uncovered at a later date with respect to the pedestrian's injuries.

Witness statements are a secondary source of information. If the facts presented as the witness sees them do not match the hard evidence from the scene, then they must be discarded. As stated previously, the information found at the scene, from the vehicle, and in this case from the pedestrian should be the majority of the evidence necessary to develop an accurate scenario of the accident for reconstruction purposes. Any other data uncovered should either confirm or refute, if possible, the evidence found at the scene.

*Commentary:* *A single vehicle-to-pedestrian accident is in many cases dif-*
*ficult to reconstruct. When multiple vehicles strike a pedestrian, the situation*
*becomes very difficult, unless by a thorough examination and detailed analysis*
*of the scene and the data found, there is sufficient evidence for reconstruction.*

*Several years ago a young man was crossing a five-lane highway, the center*
*lane being used for turning into the high school, when he was struck from the*
*rear by a van and then struck the second time by an approaching vehicle from*
*the other direction. This case is indeed unusual and points out to the investiga-*
*tor/reconstructionist what a thorough and detailed investigation can produce.*

*The young man was wearing a backpack with a large thick shoulder pad.*
*The backpack was slung over one shoulder while resting on his back. It was*
*possible to separate the two impacts by the impressions of the backpack into the*
*young man's back from the large thick shoulder pad. In addition, being impacted*
*from the rear, he left a large impression of the backpack in the hood of the van.*
*He had fractures of the posterior rib cage as well as fractures of both lower legs*
*from the rear at the height of the bumper. The second impact occurred less than*
*15 msec after the first impact. When the pedestrian was laying on the ground*
*with his head over the yellow line into the oncoming traffic lane, the oncoming*
*car caught the head of the young man with the lower part of the bumper fascia.*
*A destructive fracture of the human skull was caused with blood and brain*
*matter being thrown into the wheel well and other undercarriage parts of the*
*vehicle. These two distinct patterns of injury with the associated evidence found*
*at the scene and from the photographs taken by the on-scene investigator were*
*sufficient to reconstruct the case and separate the two impacts.*

Remember what Sherlock Holmes said, "When you have eliminated the
impossible, what ever remains, however improbable, must be the truth."

# References

1. Collins, J. C., *Accident Reconstruction*, Charles C Thomas, Springfield, IL, 1979.

2. Limpert, R., *Motor Vehicle Accident Reconstruction and Cause Analysis*, Michie Co., Charlottesville, VA, 1989.

3. Northwestern University, Evanston, IL, 1989.

4. Eubanks, J. J., *Pedestrian Accident Reconstruction*, Lawyers & Judges Pub. Co., Tucson, AZ, 1994.

# Scale Drawings, Surrogates, Animations, and Computer Simulations in Preparing Exhibits

# 14

"It is, of course, a trifle, but there is nothing so important as trifles."

**Sherlock Holmes**
*The Man with the Twisted Lip*

## Developing Exhibits

Exhibits prepared for depositions and trials must convey to the observer the scenario of the accident. They must be able to stand on their own merits with little or no explanation. The essential ingredients in exhibits include photographs taken of the scene and/or vehicles involved in the collision, and scale drawings made from accurate measurements.

## Photographs

As an example, consider the photograph of the accident scene. If the street-lights were broken on the evening of the accident, a simple stick-on arrow pointing to the broken light highlights the area on the photograph that shows exactly what is being conveyed. In the same manner, highlight on a photo-graph the beginning, middle, and end of a vehicle's skid marks, rapid changes in direction of skids, or marks on a lawn or field. Vehicular photographs are treated in the same way, with dents, missing parts, paint transfers, etc. all being highlighted.

## Scale Drawings

It is crucial that the scale drawing of the scene be completed for use at both the deposition and the trial. The accident investigator/reconstructionist must remember that opposing counsel as well as the judge or jury may never have been to the scene of the accident and will not be familiar with the area. Therefore, it is his/her duty to show, to the best of his/her ability, the accident area; this would include commercial stores, telephone poles, traffic lights, stop signs, and all other easily identifiable landmarks that might help the tryer of facts to get a feeling for the accident scene.

Panoramic views of the scene can be lightly tacked to the scale drawing at the various compass points. These can act as an aid to the jury, especially if there are hills or curves just prior to the point of impact. Great care and precision must be used when developing the scale drawings. They must be done in one of two ways, either by an experienced draftsman or by the use of a computer-aided drafting (CAD) program. Freehand or semi-freehand drawings do not give the appearance of being a professional presentation. It sends the message that the expert could not take the time to make an adequate presentation for the tryer of fact. There are many low-priced computer programs that are available to assist the reconstructionist to develop a professional looking exhibit.

## Measurements

It is indispensable that detailed measurements be taken either by the on-scene investigator or later by the reconstructionist. In either case they must be done as soon as possible after the accident.

These measurements can be obtained by the use of paper, pencil, and measuring tape, or by a faster and more accurate method, the new electronic measuring devices. These electronic measuring devices are commonly called total stations and are very expensive, as much as $15,000 to $20,000. They are well worth the cost. A hundred different measurements can be taken in an hour and stored electronically. A computer program is supplied with the device that converts the electronically stored data into a CAD drawing. A decided advantage of the use of a total station is that a portable computer can be taken to the scene or even the vehicle inspection, and the data can be downloaded into the computer and then checked for accuracy before leaving the scene. In this way any missing or mislabeled data can be remeasured for a complete and accurate presentation. If the opposing attorney's expert questions the data, a list of the points that were taken by their coordinate locations can be printed out and they then can be checked by any method they would prefer to use.

A basic step in any reconstruction is to check the accuracy of the measurements taken at the scene by the on-scene investigator. Remember, the reconstructionist is dependent on the measurements to develop the necessary calculations and to complete the analysis of the accident scenario.

It may be possible to rely on the on-scene investigator's measurements by checking several of the major locations such as point of rest of all the vehicles involved; the width of the road, the width of the shoulder; the reference point or reference line depending on which is chosen; and other strategic points that may enter into the reconstruction such as trees, telephone poles, traffic lights, or other types of traffic devices. If these prove to be accurate, then the reconstructionist can use them without fear of having a problem later in developing his/her opinion.

One of the first questions asked during a trial cross-examination is, "Did you check the accuracy of the original measurements?" If the answer no, then the next logical question is, "If the measurements are incorrect then all the calculations that are based on them are incorrect, yes or no?" This is not the way to impress the judge or jury with your expertise. The investigator should save the embarrassment by taking a few extra minutes to check any measurements given to him/her prior to starting any calculations or the basic scene drawing.

Once the basic drawing is completed, then the reconstructionist must determine what and how many types of scenarios need to be portrayed. CAD drawings are generally designed with a layering system for drawing different pages. The base drawing should contain the main streets and necessary intersections with all the driveways; street corners; pedestrian crosswalks; fronts of any commercial buildings showing their entrances; traffic lights; stop signs; overhead lights; utility poles with identification numbers; and any parked vehicles or trucks, shrubberies, trees, fences, and other objects that may act as blind spots for pedestrians or drivers of vehicles. In addition, there should be labels placed on each street, giving direction if it is one way; names of the commercial businesses; addresses of houses if the accident occurred in a residential section of the city; and types of fences or bushes that may be acting as a blind spot to give the viewer of the drawing a mind's eye view of the object that he/she cannot see physically in the drawing. Traffic lights (either freestanding or overhead onto the street), stop signs, yield signs, fire hydrants, freestanding commercial signs, and low-growing trees that may block out a stop sign or a traffic light from the vision of a driver also must be labeled (see Figures 4.1 and 4.2).

A separate layer is then developed as a draftsman would on a new sheet of paper, showing a set of particular events that have occurred before, during, or after the collision. There should be an overlay for just the point of rest of all the vehicles, pedestrians, or other victims of the accident — including any components that have been deformed and thrown from the vehicle onto the roadbed or shoulders of the highway. Each component should be numbered and identified.

An additional overlay should include just the skid marks, yaw marks, gouges, scratches, vehicle fluids, blood stains, pools of blood, and any other elements that can be identified with this particular accident that leaked onto the roadbed during or after the accident.

From time to time an additional overlay is required showing just the on-scene investigator's measurements using his/her reference point as described in the report. When comparing the measurements, there may be a great discrepancy between those just taken and the on-scene investigator's measurements. Generally this occurs when the on-scene investigator is using tape measures and has to roll and unroll the tape to take a longer measurement. He/she may forget the number of times that the tape was used, therefore causing the dimensions to be off by the length of that particular tape measure. If there is a major discrepancy between the on-scene investigator's measurements and the reconstructionist's, then an overlay should be made showing each.

It may be necessary, just before the deposition or even the trial, to print these two layers as separate overlays so that the discrepancy can be displayed. When the correct dimensions are overlaid on the improper ones, the incongruities as they relate to the on-scene investigator's measurements or opposing expert's calculations can be pointed out as incorrect.

The reconstructionist should develop several additional layers of the accident scene when there are eye witnesses who relate a scenario that is completely different from the reconstruction. A layer can be used for each witness or one layer can include all witness statements in graphic form if it does not complicate the scene and make it so complex that it would be difficult to explain to the opposing counsel at deposition or to a jury at trial. Usually the eyewitness scenarios are placed on separate layers and shown one at a time during the deposition and/or trial, and a combination of all the witness scenarios are then printed showing them in total.

The reconstructionist must develop a sense of what the jury can see and understand when looking at a scale drawing that is approximately 20 × 30 in. Too much information on a drawing can be overwhelming for any observer, thus destroying the scenario the reconstructionist is trying to develop to confirm his/her opinion.

A special layer must be used for the reconstructionist's point of impact and subsequent movement of the vehicles. If multiple impacts occurred between more than one vehicle or a vehicle and a fixed object, then a separate layer is necessary for each multiple impact or specialized movement of the collision vehicles. Then these separate layers are printed as a single layer for demonstration purposes at the deposition or trial testimony.

When all the calculations have been completed, it is obligatory to develop another layer for the scenario opinion. It should include such details as the perception and reaction times of one or both drivers in a multiple car accident, the various possible positions of either or both vehicles prior to the collision (if there are preimpact maneuvers), and during the collision so that the drawing shows the vehicles arriving at the point of rest in a manner that does not violate the laws of physics. If the drawing does not become too cluttered in showing the movement of either or both vehicles during this scenario, these details can be placed on a single drawing. However, it is generally better to place them on separate overlay drawings and then to lay one on top of another during the deposition or trial testimony. It is easier to control and to show the tryer of fact each situation separately, and then they can be combined when the testimony is being brought to a conclusion.

## Surrogates

Surrogates can be very helpful to a reconstructionist when trying to visualize the movement of the occupants inside the vehicle. A surrogate is something that serves as a substitute. The best method is the use of another human being of roughly the same stature as the occupant. That way there is no confusion as with the weight and height issue.

The accident reconstructionist is faced with a major problem when he/she enters a courtroom. He/she must convert the stacks of paper, diagrams, photographs, and videotape collected over the past few years from many different sources, into a viable image that must be portrayed in the mind's eye of a judge and a jury. The myriad jumble of equations and technical jargon increases his/her difficulty because he/she does not know or cannot even gauge the level of technical comprehension of the judge and jury.

Photographs and two- or three-dimensional models have helped to show the results of the collision both inside and outside the vehicle, but describing in some manner the trajectory of the occupant is still left up to the reconstructionist. Photographing surrogates in the accident vehicle after posing them in possible trajectory positions is the most effective manner. This allows the reconstructionist to try out several different scenarios with respect to the movement of the occupants during the collision sequence.

Photographs 14.1 and 14.2 show a posed surrogate in the drivers' side of a vehicle that was involved in a rollover accident. The "A" post on the driver's side collapsed, trapping the driver's head and left arm outside the vehicle during the rollover sequence. This, of course, resulted in severe injuries to the driver. The two photographs show the most likely position of the head and the left arm at some period after the rollover action started. Due

**Photograph 14.1** A posed surrogate in the driver's side of a vehicle.

**Photograph 14.2** A posed surrogate in the driver's side of a vehicle.

to the collapsed nature of the "A" post, there was very little room for the driver's head to reach that position after the "A" post collapsed. Therefore, the head and arm must have been outside the vehicle prior to the time that the vehicle rolled onto the left "A" post. There was no residual hair or tissue in any area of the door/window opening and no witness marks on the body showing that the head and arm squeezed out through the small opening after the collapse of the "A" post. Therefore, the only remaining possibility was the driver's body to move violently to the left while being lifted off the seat to allow the motion to carry it out the window.

***Commentary:*** *I have seen films of rollovers where the dummy occupant was completely thrown clear of the vehicle through the passenger's window during the rollover sequence. The dummy was partially ejected through the open window at the beginning of the rollover; as the vehicle continued its rollover, the dummy was caught underneath the roof and side of the vehicle. When the vehicle was completing its rollover, the occupant was thrown clear on the next roll before the vehicle came to rest on its four wheels.*

Photographs 14.3 through 14.8 are a series of photographs taken to show how the right front occupant of an early model sport utility vehicle (SUV), with a fiberglass camper-type top attached to the truck body, was ejected partially through the fiberglass opening behind the driver. The vehicle had been involved in a rollover accident and the fiberglass top was cracked and had pulled away from the attachments on top of the truck body.

In Photograph 14.3 the windshield shows the stress cracks from the rollover. Note how the driver's seat was pushed to the left and the seatback was forward of the rear camper top opening. A detailed examination of the area around the fiberglass opening on the driver's side showed red fibers from what appeared to be a sweater. A review of the police statements showed that only the right front occupant was wearing a red sweater. After reviewing the driver's seat, it was evident that it had been pushed to the left by an object other than a direct impact from outside the vehicle.

Photograph 14.4 shows another view, taken from the rear, with the right front surrogate's left hand pointing in the direction of the rear window opening in the fiberglass top. Photograph 14.5 is taken from the left rear quarter panel looking directly at the surrogate. Note the clear path directly from the right front seat to the opening in the fiberglass top. Photograph 14.6 was taken from the right rear side of the vehicle. Note the surrogate's head is out the opening and the left arm and upper right shoulder and neck area are in contact with the edges of the opening in the fiberglass top. This is where the red fibers from the sweater were found.

Photograph 14.7 was taken from the left rear side of the vehicle. The angle of the surrogate's body is not correct. It would be more horizontal during the rollover but was impossible to show in a still photograph.

**Photograph 14.3** Windshield stress cracks from a rollover.

**Photograph 14.4** The right front surrogate's left hand pointing in the direction of the rear window opening in the fiberglass top.

**Photograph 14.5**  The clear path directly from the right front seat to the opening in the fiberglass top.

Photograph 14.8 was taken from the rear but slightly to the left outside the vehicle. Note the white marks just above the right shoulder of the surrogate. These are cracks in the fiberglass top that were made when the occupant was being ejected from the vehicle. The upper opening of the fiberglass top is much more flexible than the lower section. The lower section is attached firmly to the truck body with a plate and screws. This makes it quite rigid when compared with the upper opening.

Surrogates have a use in accident reconstruction and work very well, as shown by the preceding sample case. They are inexpensive and can be completed in about a half day of work including the setup.

## Animations

Animations are the newest tools to be added to the reconstructionist's arsenal of equipment. Walt Disney did animation since the early 1920s. This required the expertise of an artist to develop the animation sequence frame by frame. While this process yielded an outstanding film presentation, it was very time-consuming and expensive. With the advent of the computer, animations have reached a new high.

Most or all of us are familiar with the *Star Wars* movies that contained a great deal of animation superimposed on film with live actors. These again

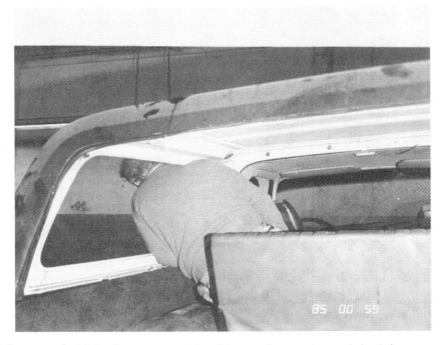

**Photograph 14.6** The surrogate's head is out the opening and the left arm and upper right shoulder and neck area are in contact with the edges of the opening in the fiberglass top.

**Photograph 14.7** The surrogate as taken from the left rear side of the vehicle.

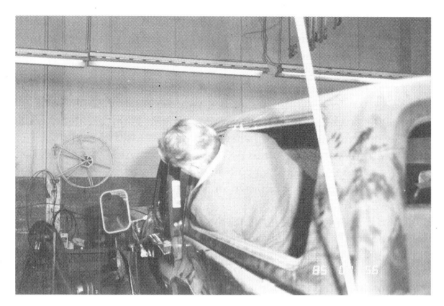

**Photograph 14.8** Cracks in the fiberglass top made by the occupant while being ejected.

were done in sophisticated laboratories by highly trained technicians and artists with a great deal of computer expertise. In the late 1980s and 1990s several companies with highly skilled computer programmers developed animation programs for the remainder of the population. It is now possible to render an entire commercial with animation that looks like it was shot live, on film. These, of course, are very expensive.

Accident reconstructionists in conjunction with their attorney clients have begun to use animation to show the tryer a fact the accident sequence instead of trying to paint a word picture or using scale drawings with a series of vehicle motions attached.

As in all technology, the degree of sophistication is dependent on the amount of money that can be expended to bring the realism of the scene to life. There are many commercial programs available that cover the wide spectrum of animation from the highly sophisticated to the everyday usable cartoon-type animations.

For accident reconstruction of more completed collisions, animations should be used. The animation camera can be placed inside as well as outside the vehicle and at any angle desired. Of course, this does not come without a penalty — the increased cost. Animations can cost from a few thousand to upward of $20,000. This is due to the complexity, creativity, and labor-intensive work involved. The client must decide if it is worth the expense to produce such an animation video. Remember, the reconstructionist is part of a team that is headed by the client. It must be a mutual decision based on a number of factors that all the team may not be privy to. Therefore, the client should be informed of the reconstructionist's progress and any ideas he/she has to make their joint presentations better and easy to understand in the deposition and at the trial.

The reconstructionist must consider, after he/she has completed his/her reconstruction and has developed his/her opinion, if the accident sequence should be animated to bolster his/her opinion and assist the tryer of fact in understanding this opinion. At this point the reconstructionist has two choices.

The first choice is to go to a commercial studio or an individual who is highly proficient in use of animation for technical presentations and to explain step by step what the accident sequence should do and what it should look like when completed. He/she can take along photographs of the scene as well as the vehicles involved to show the animator what the vehicles looked like prior to and after the collision. This is extremely difficult in that most commercial studios employ many artistic animators who do not understand the motion that the vehicles must undertake during the sequence of the collision and their trajectories as thet come to rest. It is very difficult to try and explain these motions to a nonmechanically inclined individual. The second choice is for the reconstructionist to purchase a commercial program, take a course in the use of the program, and then animate the accident sequence himself/herself.

*Commentary: This is the method that I have found most useful. After working with several animators I have found that they were more interested in developing the scenario from an artistic standpoint as opposed to an engineering standpoint that was required for use in a deposition or trial. Newly graduated engineers have extensive computer backgrounds in today's college curricula and therefore are usually well versed in the many useful programs of a computer. These young men and women can be sent to a local training facility to learn the basics of animation programming and with time and practice develop into very good computer animators.*

It also is possible to videotape the accident scene and to insert it into the computer program and then lay the animation sequence on top of the live action, adding a distinct degree of authenticity to the animation. This saves time because the entire scene does not have to be constructed from scratch. The whole scene would consist of buildings, trees, pedestrians, and other vehicles. The actual scene on tape saves the client money and looks better in the long run.

The reconstructionist/animator must remember that the actions of all the vehicles in the sequence are to be smooth and plausible without any jerky movements during the trajectory of the vehicle before or after the collision.

Once the reconstructionist/animator has completed the animation sequence, it must then be shown to the attorney client to ensure that it not only covers his/her opinion but also includes all the information the attorney client wishes to bring forth for presentation to the tryer of fact. Any adjustments or changes, additions of close-up scenes, scenes from different angles, and slow motion sequences are completed at this time. Interior scenes can also be developed showing the injuries sustained by the occupant during the accident. These sequences can be very life-like and the animation/engineer must be careful not to include too much blood and gore because the jurors can object and the reconstructionist may lose his/her edge with them. The reconstructionist must then develop a script that he/she can use during his/her deposition and/or trial to ensure that the opinions reflected in the animation are covered. Remember that the animation tape, just as with the photographs, remains with the firm. Copies can be made for all parties concerned but the original should never leave the hands of the reconstructionist. It is possible that some individual may change the animation without his/her knowledge. It is unlikely but possible. Do not give anyone the opportunity to do so.

As stated in the first portion of this chapter with the accident simulation program, the animation programs are just another tool to be used by the reconstructionist to assist him/her in bringing forth his/her opinions in a more clear and concise manner to the opposing counsel at deposition and to the tryer of fact at a trial if necessary.

These tools are not intended to replace the deductive reasoning powers of the reconstructionist. Indeed they may need to be enhanced, as more details are required of his/her opinion in the accident scenario to produce a simulation or an animation of the accident sequence. The use of these tools may assist the reconstructionist to bring his/her opinion of the accident sequence into sharper focus with the additional details provided by these computer programs.

Remember, the animation cannot be constructed before the opinion is completed. The animation is the reconstructionist's opinion put into motion. It represents his/her thinking and reasoning based on the information that has been made available to him/her. Every movement of the vehicle on the roadway and the occupant inside the vehicle must have been determined prior to the animation even being started. If the reconstructionist has not developed each of these movements, then the animator cannot create them on the animation sequence.

## Computer Simulations

In the 1970s a computer accident simulation program was written for use on mainframe computers. The automobile companies wanted a method to test new safety devices to determine their performance before committing to hardware development. It was soon discovered that these programs could be modified to simulate a vehicular accident, such as a single car into a fixed object or a car-to-car or truck-type accident.

In the early 1980s this program was redeveloped for use on personal computers (PCs). There are several versions of this program commercially available for use by an individual or a firm. To the author's knowledge, never having analyzed the code of these programs, they are based on the conservation of linear momentum equation.

These programs have been found to be effective in two ways. First, they can lead the reconstructionist in a particular direction based on the facts that he/she may have available at the time of putting data into the program. Second, they can be used to check out the opposing expert's reconstruction based on the computer program and basic opinion of the vehicular accident when all the input data that were used by the opposing expert are supplied with his/her deposition.

It must be remembered that the computer simulation is only a tool to be used by the reconstructionist. *It is not a reenactment of the accident sequence.* These types of programs allow the investigator/reconstructionist to input a variety of information to perform what is called a "what if" scenario. The following information is only a portion of what can be changed:

- Wheelbase of the vehicle
- Weight of the vehicle not including the occupants
- Coefficient of friction of the tires to the road surface on which the vehicle is sliding
- Turning angle for the front wheels
- Rolling or sliding friction for each tire

A great many other data points can be used in the program to simulate the path of the vehicle and to have it reach the only known point on the accident scene, which is the point of rest of all the vehicles.

The investigator/reconstructionist may have to try to vary many of the variable data points to get the vehicle to move in the required direction, with the most likely rotation. These variables may include changes in initial velocity, initial angle of movement, and changes to the coefficient of friction on one side of the vehicle if it should end up sliding on a grass or snowy surface. Many of these programs include a graphic section in which a representation of the damage to the vehicle is developed and is shown for comparison to the actual depth and location of the damage on the vehicle. These can be very helpful when comparing them with the photographs taken by the on-scene investigator or at a later date by the reconstructionist.

*Commentary*: *I have seen a great many accident reconstruction reports in which there has been a computer simulation study conducted. In the majority of these cases the reconstructionist has based his/her entire opinion on the computer simulation, neglecting or completely forgetting the physical evidence found at the scene. There is no comparison to actual damage, to the location of the simulation point of rest to the actual point of rest, or even to any comments concerning the occupants' injuries and the principal direction of force necessary to produce them. Using computer simulations for evidence is wrong and does a disservice to the client.*

The computer simulation must be used only as a tool to point the reconstructionist in a specific direction by using a variety of data points that allow the output of the program to show how closely it would reach the point of rest of the vehicle as found at the scene. The program can indicate if it was necessary to have a steering input prior to impact, if one or more of the tires were locked up or yawing, or even if the driver had to brake prior to the impact to reach the point of rest. These are all indicators that must be checked against the actual physical evidence before a complete opinion can be rendered.

A variety of commercial programs is available from the very expensive to the rather inexpensive, depending on the needs and budget of the investigator. It is up to the investigator/reconstructionist to determine which one is best suited for his/her particular needs.

At the same time, the reconstructionist must determine and be aware of the limitations of each of the programs that he/she is considering. If a particular accident vehicle that is under study has undergone a rollover, be sure to find out before purchasing if the program can simulate a rollover accident with the damage that would have been sustained in that case. Another program requirement might be that the vehicle should have all four tires in contact with the ground all times. This is not always possible in the real world. Consider, for example, a side impact with a bullet vehicle penetrating the struck vehicle with such velocity that it pierces deeply into the side of the struck vehicle, forcing the front wheels of the bullet vehicle to leave the ground as both vehicles (now totally engaged) rotate to a point of rest. The results of the simulation may not be accurate after the maximum point of engagement, and the vehicles may never reach the same point of rest as in the actual case because the amount of friction slowing the vehicles down is reduced.

Some programs are also available for occupant kinematics. Once again before purchase, determine the data that are required of the program. Also spend time determining the limitations of the program to ensure that it can perform what is needed.

Remember, the reconstructionist submits a final report with the scale drawing of the simulation superimposed on the scene scale drawing, and also the input data used to develop that simulation. The opposing expert then analyzes that input data to determine if they were properly used.

As an example, consider a vehicle that is skidding with all four tires locked up. Unfortunately, the data show that the front two tires are locked up with a coefficient of friction of 1.0 while the two rear tires have a coefficient of friction of 0.10, which is just rolling friction. This is an obvious error, which should not have been allowed to happen, and which could eliminate the opinion from the case. This, of course, does not bode well for the reconstructionist; as the word of his/her poor reconstruction moves along the grapevine of attorneys, he/she may see the number of cases decrease.

Remember, computer simulations are only tools to be used by the reconstructionist when preparing his/her scenario of the accident opinion for his/her client. Total dependence on the computer or any of its programs usually results in poor performance.

## Conclusions

Experience using exhibits comes with developing and using them at depositions and trials. The one overriding fact that the investigator/reconstructionist must bear in mind is that the exhibit must be simple, easy to understand, and not cluttered with too much information. It is very easy to overlook an exhibit with too much information, which does not assist the tryer of fact in rendering an opinion. Information overload, especially during a technical presentation, can occur without the investigator/reconstructionist knowing when or why it happened.

Exhibits are a necessary part of any deposition or trial. "A picture is worth a thousand words" has never been truer. Never speak when a photograph, diagram, or drawing can make a point better than trying to say it. The basic rule of thumb is to keep it simple; keep it accurate; and use as much everyday language as possible when preparing a deposition, or making the presentation to the opposing counsel or to the tryer of fact at a trial. This requires some showmanship and presentation skills that can be learned through public speaking courses that are quicker than on-the-job training by going through multiple depositions in trials. Remember, the reconstructionist must be professional and prepared because his/her client and opposing client are dependent on his/her presentation.

# Mathematical Analysis 15

"Circumstantial evidence is a very tricky thing."

**Sherlock Holmes**
*The Boscombe Valley Mystery*

In every phase of physics or engineering it is necessary at one point or another to develop some mathematical equations of various relationships. In this chapter those equations and relationships needed for use in investigation/reconstruction are developed.

Because in automobile accidents the motion of the vehicle is usually in a linear or straight line, this type of motion is now discussed. If the motion followed a curve, it would be described as curvilinear motion. When there is straight-line motion at a steady rate, it is called uniform linear motion. The motion of any vehicle can be studied by observing it carefully over a period of time and then measuring what it undergoes every second. If this motion is uniform, that means the distances traversed are found to be equal. To have uniform linear motion there must be equal displacement along the same straight line during equal intervals of time, however brief these intervals may be.

Motion is not always linear or uniform. A falling body has been observed to travel faster as it approaches the earth. As mentioned earlier, the car reaches uniform motion only after starting from rest and later loses uniform motion when the brakes are applied.

The velocity of a vehicle in uniform linear motion can be defined as the distance that the vehicle travels divided by the time it took to travel that distance. The equation form gives the following:

$$\text{Velocity} = \text{distance/time traveled}$$

or

$$V = S/T \qquad\qquad (15.1)$$

where $V$ is the velocity of the vehicle, $S$ is the distance traveled, and $T$ is the time that it took to travel the distance.

From the facts stated earlier, there is equal distance traveled in equal intervals of time when the ratio of $S$ to $T$ remains constant; and a vehicle that has uniform linear motion has constant velocity. Velocity, of course, can be expressed in feet per second, centimeters per second, or meters per second. In this chapter feet per second or miles per hour are used; conversions to metric units are readily available and the reader is left to perform any desired conversions.

Velocity is a vector quantity that means it has direction as well as magnitude and requires that when velocities are to be added they must be done so by vector addition. This is usually done by the parallelogram method or by the polygon method. Either way these vector quantities can be added in more than one plane; the polygon method is most preferable when adding more than two vectors.

The velocity of a vehicle often changes from moment to moment, such as a passenger bus repeatedly starting from rest, speeding up, slowing down, and stopping. The average velocity of this bus would be the total distance traveled divided by the elapsed time to travel that distance. If the distance traveled is considered as getting shorter and shorter, then the elapsed time becomes progressively smaller and smaller and the resultant velocity is restricted to a correspondingly short portion of the entire distance traveled.

When the distance traveled and the time are taken in smaller and smaller portions, an infinitesimal amount is reached. Then the velocity of that vehicle for the particular instance selected is called the instantaneous velocity. In the special case where a vehicle has uniform linear motion, it has the same instantaneous velocity at every instant, and its average velocity is the same as its constant velocity.

When discussing the purchase of a new car, every vehicle owner describes how fast his/her new vehicle can get away from a traffic light. By this he/she means how quickly the vehicle can gain velocity, which is technically called the acceleration. As an example, if a vehicle starting from a traffic light reaches a velocity of 4 ft/sec by the end of 1 sec and then gains an additional 4 ft/sec during the next second and so on, the vehicle is said to have an acceleration of 4 ft/se.

**Commentary:** *The acceleration of the vehicle is defined as the change of its velocity during any interval of time divided by the duration of that interval.*

If $V_o$ is the initial velocity of a vehicle at the beginning of a time period and $V_f$ is its final velocity at the end of that period, the new change in velocity is $V_f - V_o$; and if this change occurs in a time interval $t$, the average acceleration of the vehicle over that time interval is average acceleration = final velocity minus a new initial velocity divided by the time interval.

In equation form:

$$a = (V_f - V_o)/t \tag{15.2}$$

Defined precisely, acceleration is the time rate of change of velocity when acceleration is constant; its instantaneous values are all alike and is the same as the average acceleration.

## Linear Motion with Constant Acceleration

There are four equations that show the relationship between initial velocity, final velocity, distance traveled, and acceleration, in terms of linear motion with constant acceleration.

**Equation one** — The first equation comes from the definition of acceleration, Equation 15.2. By rearranging the terms, the following can be obtained:

$$V_f = V_o + a \cdot t \tag{15.3}$$

**Equation two** — The second equation is an expression for the distance traveled of the vehicle in terms of its initial velocity, its final velocity, and the elapsed time. Because the change of velocity during the time interval $t$ is uniform, the average velocity is the mean of the velocity at the beginning and end of the time interval, namely, $V_i$ and $V_f$, respectively. Therefore, the average velocity is

$$Vav = (V_o + V_f)/2 \tag{15.4}$$

but only where the acceleration is constant.

Then the distance traveled during that interval is the product of the average velocity and the duration of that interval. By substituting terms, the following equation is

$$S = [V_o + V_f]/2] \cdot T \tag{15.5}$$

**Equation three** — The third equation also gives the distance traveled of the moving vehicle but expresses it in terms of the initial velocity, acceleration, and time. By substituting terms, the following equation is obtained:

$$S = [V_o + (V_o + at)]/2]/t \qquad (15.6)$$

or

$$S = V_o t + (1/2)\text{a} \cdot t^2 \qquad (15.7)$$

**Equation four** — The fourth equation is obtained from the first and second by eliminating the time interval $t$.

$$V_f = V_o^2 + 2 \cdot a \cdot s \qquad (15.8)$$

These equations can be used in many different ways and in many different combinations for solutions to investigation/reconstruction problems.

Appendix 15.1 is an equation workbook with examples for various types of problems that can be expected when reconstructing an accident. These equations were developed using a mathematical computer program. There are several such programs, which are available commercially, and the reader can investigate them for their own purposes.

## Definition of Terms

Before examining each of these special equations it is necessary to define a few terms that are used in these various equations.

### Perception and Reaction Time

*Perception and reaction (P&R) time* is the time it takes for the driver to perform a simple act in a vehicle, the simplest act being applying the brake pedal or turning the steering wheel to avoid an accident. Human factor professionals have carried out extensive studies on the perception and reaction times of the human individual.

To break down these studies into their simplest terms we must understand *perception* — the ability of the individual to perceive an action about to take place, or taking place on the highway in front of him/her. The perception of this action leads him/her to some type of *reaction*; this could be a brake application or turning the steering wheel to move the vehicle out of the line of the action taking place in front of the driver. The driver of today's modern vehicles is faced with a myriad of problems when driving on superhighways or in congested and overcrowded city streets. His/her senses are overloaded by an enormous amount of information every second he/she is driving his vehicle.

As an example, during city driving the driver is faced with traffic signs that are many times confusing in terms of street names, directions, or information about detours, especially when he/she is a visitor to that city. Also, there are traffic signals that are sometimes hidden by the neon signs of a commercial business. They may be placed in unusual locations or half hidden by local business improvements such as tree planting (which, by the way, are usually not pruned). In addition, drivers are inundated with blaring horns, loud music from passing vehicles, and other vehicles that are constantly pulling away from the curbs or trying to get over to the curb to park.

With all this overload of information, the driver is expected to be able to perceive a situation such as a pedestrian darting out from between parked cars at the curb, or a car pulling in front of him/her and stopping quickly to let off a passenger. When he/she does perceive this situation, the driver must now look in his/her mirrors to judge the surrounding traffic before deciding to apply brakes or to steer the vehicle away from the pedestrian or the stopped vehicle. On expressways or superhighways, vehicles travel at much higher velocities and decisions must be made more quickly and at a greater distance before the perceived event to prevent a collision.

Many years ago a human factor study was conducted on young well-trained and well-developed Air Force pilots to determine their perception and reaction times. These young men were given a battery of tests covering all types of situations. In each of these tests their perception times and reaction times were recorded. It was found that the best times for both perception and reaction to any situation were approximately 3/4 sec for each, for a total of 1.5 sec. Bear in mind that these were highly trained and highly developed young men involved in these studies. The average American driver does not come anywhere close to those Air Force pilots in terms of training or development. Add to this the fact that as people age their perception and reaction times increase; that is, it takes longer for them to make these decisions and to perform the necessary actions.

Additional human factor testing has shown that the average adult's perception and reaction time can range from 2 sec to as high as 7 or 10 sec, depending on the particular situation he/she may be involved with, his/her age, the information he/she is being given at a particular point in time, the weather conditions, and even the condition of the vehicle. It is impossible for the reconstructionist to know the perception/reaction time of one or both drivers in the collision being investigated/reconstructed. Therefore, it is necessary to give both drivers the benefit of the doubt and give them the best perception and reaction times available.

*Commentary: The Departments of Transportation in many states adhere to a national organization that supplies information on the design of highways, traffic lights, signs, and all other information necessary to design and maintain the state's highways. One section of the book discusses perception and reaction time. It assumes that 2.0 sec is the best perception and reaction time for a driver when designing various aspects of the highway system.*

Most reconstructionists use a range of values for perception and reaction time. Generally the range is 1.5 to 2.0 sec. This is a fairly standard practice in the field.

*Commentary: When considering air brake systems on articulated vehicles such as tractor trailers, the air brake systems add an additional 0.5 sec to the reaction time because of the compressibility of the air and the release of air in the line.*

## Coefficient of Friction

The *coefficient of friction* is the force of resistance every object in the world has when coming in contact with another object. That coefficient of friction is dependent on the material make up of the two bodies undergoing contact. A steel wheel such as a railroad wheel in contact with a railroad track has a very small coefficient of friction, because both surfaces are similar and both surfaces are smooth. The rougher the two surfaces are in contact with one another, the higher the coefficient of friction.

As an example, consider pulling a concrete block along a concrete roadway. It is difficult because the coefficient of friction is very high. Take that same concrete block and pull it on a frozen pond; it now becomes very easy to pull along. The road surface is very rough and so is a concrete block, the frozen pond is smooth even though the concrete block; is rough and therefore the block moves much easier on the smoother surface.

There are many different types of tires used on today's automobiles as well as many different types of internal construction and varieties of rubber. Once again, it is difficult for the reconstructionist to determine the coefficient of friction for each of these tires on each of the various types of highway surfaces in use today. One type of highway is new concrete, another is the concrete surface that has been worn down from constant travel by trucks and other vehicles over a long period of time. The rough surface of the concrete has become smooth as a result of the interaction between the tire and the surface of the road; as a result there is a lower coefficient of friction than when the concrete was new and rough.

Another very common surface is the asphalt road. A new asphalt roadbed is rough and has a high coefficient of friction. With heavy traffic use of that same highway for several years the surface once again becomes smooth, resulting in a lower coefficient of friction. Then, of course, consider gravel roads, which are rough and as the gravel itself is pushed to the side of the road, the road becomes smoother as the other aggregates are pounded firm by the constant action of vehicle tires on the road surface. A different type is the asphalt road that has a chip seal on top of it. It is a very rough road surface and as the oils come to the surface it becomes smoother. Finally, there are dirt roads, which are sprayed in many cases with oil to hold down the dust. The combination of dust and oil hardens, however, making the roadbed very slick in both summer and winter, resulting in a low coefficient of friction.

Every statics and dynamics engineering text, especially those in the civil engineering field, can provide tables of coefficient of friction values for tires on new, worn, and smooth concrete and on asphalt surfaces. In addition, they have values for wet road surfaces as well as ice, deep snow, and packed snow. Some even show values for grass, dirt, and mud.

*Commentary*: *Another problem for the reconstructionist is the timing of when he/she becomes involved in an accident. This can range from a few weeks to several months.*

*A problem results from the extended time period with respect to the coefficient of friction on the roadway. There are several conditions that can change the coefficient of friction over time. First, there are differences in the weather conditions, summer vs. winter, and spring vs. fall. Second is the temperature of the roadway at the time of the accident vs. the temperature on the day the investigation takes place. Third is the condition of the roadway; with the passage of time each roadway deteriorates and the coefficient of friction decreases therefore the road becomes smoother. Finally, foreign materials on the roadbed at the time of the accident or at the time of the inspection can change the coefficient of friction.*

*For example, was there sand on the road or had there been a recent rain? Was there gravel from a side road sprayed across the surface itself? All these must be taken into account if the reconstructionist is going to try to use a specific value based on what he/she has seen in his/her inspection several months after the accident.*

*This is extremely difficult and unless the on-scene photographs show a very smooth or a new roadbed, use a range of values between 0.5 and 0.8 for the coefficient of friction. These values work in most situations.*

## Drag Factor

There is another term that is being used by on-scene investigators when trying to determine the coefficient of friction of the road on which the accident occurred. It is called the *drag factor* of the roadbed.

For instance, the investigator has in his/her vehicle about a one third portion of a standard vehicle tire. This portion of a tire has been filled with concrete and weighs approximately 20 to 50 lb depending on the tire size. An eyebolt has been inserted into the concrete before it dried and hardened. The investigator then attaches a scale (commonly called a fish scale) to the eyebolt and drags it along the surface of the highway, supposedly where the accident occurred. *This system does not work.*

The weighted tire does not react like the air-filled tire on the vehicle during the accident in many different respects. In a collision, the vehicle tires, when locked up, are no longer rotating; they are only skidding along on the surface of the roadbed. This skidding action causes the tires to heat up and in so doing yields a different coefficient of friction than that of a cement-filled cold tire. Yes, the tire is being dragged along the surface of the roadbed, but the values being recorded are not consistent with what the accident vehicle underwent prior to the actual collision. Consider also what has been suggested previously: the differences in the rubber of the tire as well as the construction of the tire compared with the drag tire, which the investigator knows nothing about, being used by the on-scene investigator.

Is there a better way? When looking at all the factors involved in determining the coefficient of friction, it is almost impossible to determine a method of obtaining this value at the scene. Consider the temperature of the road, the temperature of the tires, gravel or sand on the road, bald tires, poor alignment of the tires, and, of course, the tire pressure (over- or underinflated). We have not even included weather problems such as rain, snow, mud, ice, or hard-packed snow; nor the problem of the manner in which the tire is being dragged across the road surface.

The scale that is inserted into the eyebolt must be parallel to the roadbed surface when being dragged or the scale can yield a false reading dependent on the angle at which it is being dragged. As an example, consider the scale at 45 degrees to the horizontal. The reading will only be 70.7% of the actual value. If the tire is only approximately one third of the actual height of the full tire, that means the tire puller must be within a foot of the ground when pulling. Many investigators do not bother with this trifling fact when performing a drag test.

The closest method to the actual collision that has been used is to obtain an exemplar vehicle, that is, the same make, model, year, and accessories as the collision vehicle. Next make sure it has the same tires and same weight as the accident vehicle, and then find a day that has similar weather conditions and use the same time of day to perform a skid test using the exemplar vehicle.

Even this method has problems because the total weight of the accident vehicle cannot be accurately determined even if it is weighed after the accident, because many parts, components, and vehicle fluids have been lost at the accident scene. Therefore, the investigator/reconstructionist is forced into using a range of values consistent with the weather conditions on the day the accident occurred.

As an example, on a calm, dry day with a smooth road surface a coefficient of friction value might be between 0.6 and 0.8. On a rainy day on a smooth road the values might be 0.3 to 0.6. The expert reconstructing the accident has the most knowledge to make the best estimate of these variables. His/her estimates must be backed up by certain data such as the weather report for the few days before the accident as well as the conditions on the day of the accident. Data from the local newspaper, witnesses, and police reports (and possibly television coverage) on the same day would act as backup information for his/her decision.

## A Detailed Description of Figure 15.1

An example of the use of Equation 15.80 (see page 382) in a simple one-direction, rear-end collision is given next. Figure 15.1 shows the complete vehicle-to-vehicle rear-end impact. Figure 15.1A shows the preimpact skid distance and velocity for vehicle 1 prior to initial impact.

### Problem One

Problem one finds the velocity of a moving vehicle that collides with another vehicle moving in the same direction (rear-end collision).

### *Step One*

Calculate the postimpact velocity of both the vehicles. Figure 15.1C shows the postimpact between vehicle 1 and vehicle 2.

The variables needed are:

$$V_3 = \text{postimpacts of vehicle 1 in miles per hour}$$

$$S_3 = \text{postimpact skid distance of a vehicle 1 in feet}$$

$$\mu = \text{coefficient of friction of the roadbed}$$

Assume that the postimpact skid distance $S_3$ is 50 ft, and $\mu$ is 0.60. Use this skid equation to obtain the following:

$$V_3 = (30 \cdot S_3 \cdot \mu)^{1/2} \qquad (15.9)$$

Plugging in the assumed values gives:

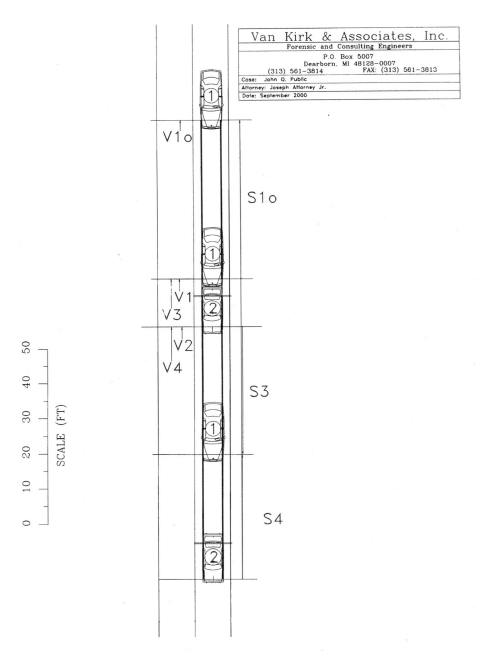

**Figure 15.1** The complete vehicle-to-vehicle rear-end impact.

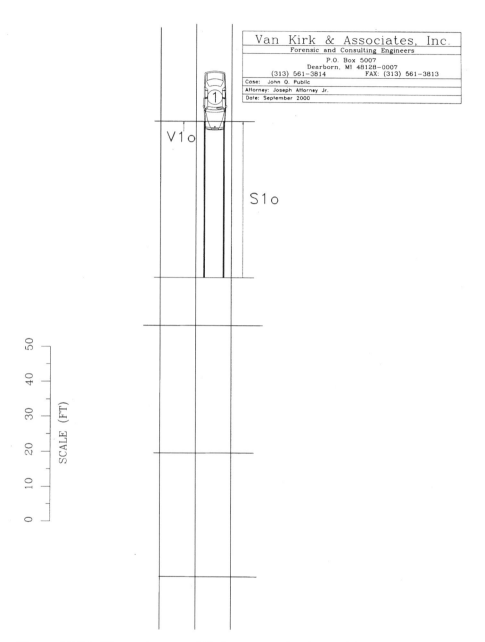

**Figure 15.1A** The preimpact skid distance and velocity for vehicle 1 prior to initial impact.

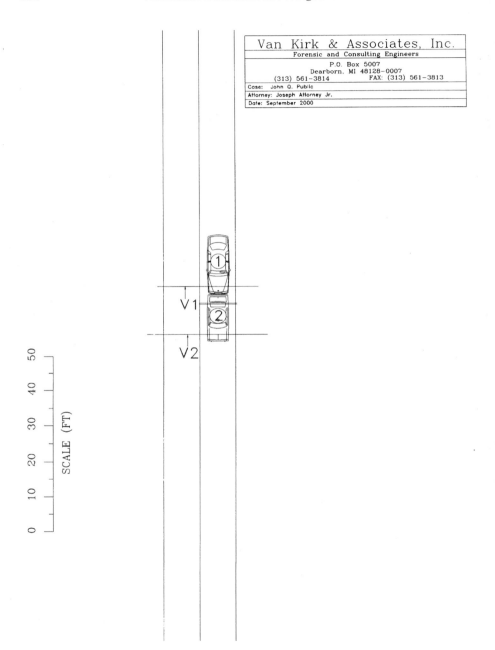

**Figure 15.1B** The initial impact between vehicle 1 and vehicle 2.

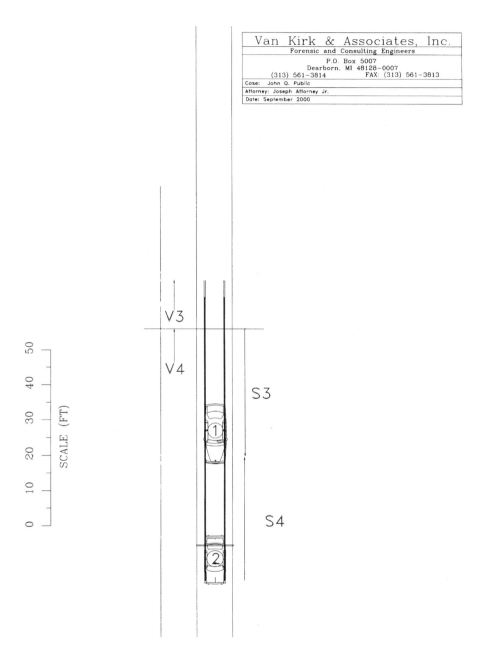

**Figure 15.1C** The postimpact skid distance and velocity for vehicle 1 and vehicle 2.

$$V_3 = (30 \cdot 50 \cdot 0.60)^{1/2} \tag{15.10}$$

Solve the equation to obtain:

$$V_3 = 30.00 \text{ mi/h}$$

Solving for the postimpact velocity $V_4$ of the other vehicle in the same manner gives:

$$V_4 = (30 \cdot 80 \cdot 0.60)^{1/2} \tag{15.11}$$

Then solve Equation 15.11 to obtain:

$$V_4 = 38.00 \text{ mi/h}$$

The postimpact velocity of $V_3$ and $V_4$ has now been calculated for the two vehicles. Next either assume or have some previous knowledge of the preimpact velocity of the second vehicle. With this example, assume the preimpact velocity $V_2 = 30$ mi/h. Also determine the weights of the two vehicles, $W_1 = 3500$ and $W_2 = 2500$ lb.

### Step Two
Calculate vehicle 1 velocity at time of impact. Figure 15.1B shows the preimpact skid distance and velocity for vehicle 1 and vehicle 2. Return to the equation that solved for the preimpact velocity $V_1$ of the first vehicle to obtain the following:

$$V_1 = \{V_3 + [(W_2)/(W_1)] \cdot V_4\} - [(W_2)/(W_1)] \cdot V_2 \tag{15.12}$$

Substitute the assumed and calculated values to obtain:

$$V_1 = \{30.0 \cdot [(2500)/(3500)] \cdot 38.00\} - [(2500)/(3500)] \cdot 30.0 \tag{15.13}$$

$$V_1 = \{30.0 + [(0.7142)] \cdot 38.00\} - [(0.7142) \cdot 30.0] \tag{15.14}$$

$$V_1 = \{30.00 + 27.142\} - [21.428] \tag{15.15}$$

$$V_1 = \{57.142\} - [21.428] \tag{15.16}$$

or

$$V_1 = 35.714 \text{ mi/h}$$

This is the preimpact velocity of vehicle 1.

Also assume that in this example vehicle 1 was skidding prior to impacting vehicle 2. The skid length $S_{1o}$ is 40 ft and the coefficient of friction is 0.70.

Because of the need for dealing totally with velocity, the two postimpact skid velocities and the velocity lost during this skidding phase of vehicle 1 are used to determine the preimpact velocity of vehicle 1. This is done by squaring the two velocities and then taking the square root of both as follows:

$$V_{1o} = [(V_{skid})^2 + (V_1)^2]^{1/2} \qquad (15.17)$$

The skid equation can give the velocity lost during the initial skids of the first vehicle.

$$(V_{skid})^2 = 30 \cdot S_{1o} \cdot \mu \qquad (15.18)$$

or

$$V_{skid} = (30 \cdot S_{1o} \cdot \mu)^{1/2} \qquad (15.19)$$

Substitute this in the original collision for the velocity of vehicle 1 at the start of the initial skid to obtain the following:

$$V_{1o} = [(30 \cdot S_{1o} \cdot \mu) + (V_1)^2]^{1/2} \qquad (15.20)$$

Substituting the values in Equation 15.20 yields:

$$V_{1o} = [(30 \cdot 40 \cdot 0.7) + (38.00)^2]^{1/2} \qquad (15.21)$$

$$V_{1o} = [840 + 1444]^{1/2} \qquad (15.22)$$

$$V_{1o} = 47.791 \text{ mi/h}$$

This is the velocity of vehicle 1 at the beginning of the initial skid mark.

## A Detailed Description of Figure 15.2

### Problem Two

Determine the velocity of vehicles that collide at right angles to each other. Figure 15.2 shows the vehicle-to-vehicle collision and the final resting points of the two vehicles. Note the postimpact directions and angles.

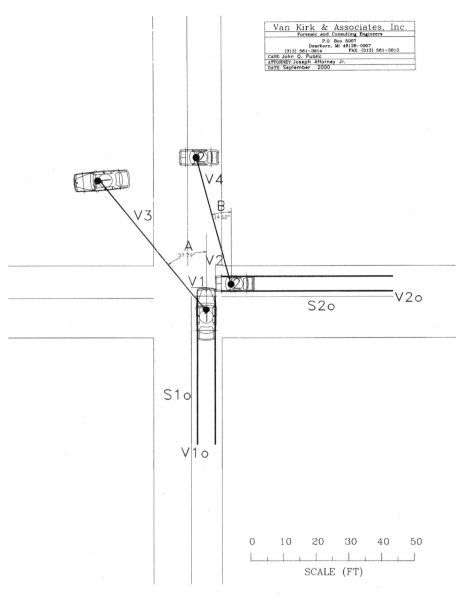

**Figure 15.2** The angle between the center of gravity of the vehicle at the point of impact and at the point of rest.

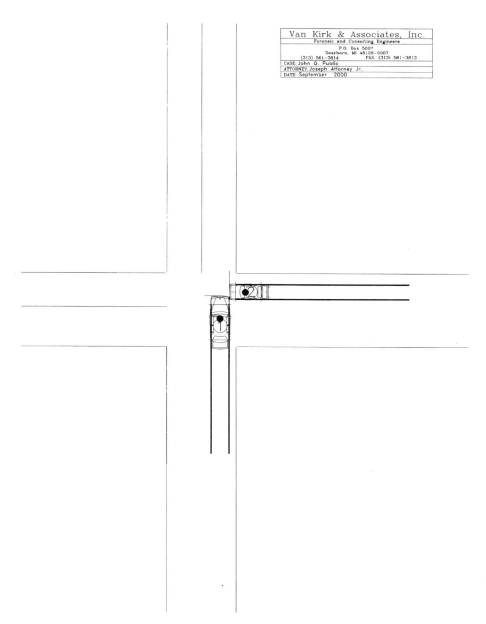

Van Kirk & Associates, Inc.
Forensic and Consulting Engineers
P.O. Box 5007
Dearborn, MI 48128-0007
(313) 561-3814          FAX: (313) 561-3813
CASE: John Q. Public
ATTORNEY: Joseph Attorney Jr.
DATE: September   2000

**Figure 15.2A**  The point of impact at the intersection.

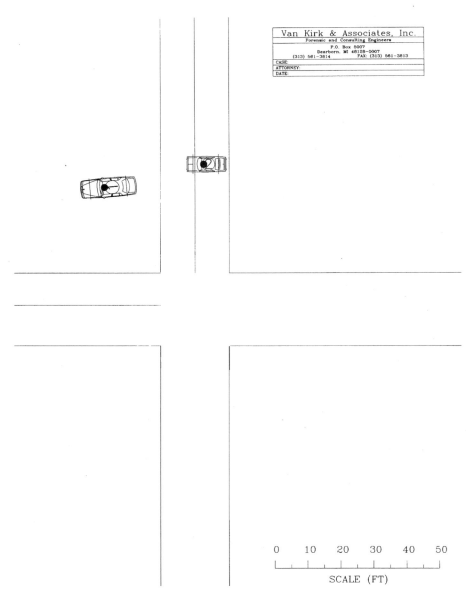

**Figure 15.2B** The vehicles at rest.

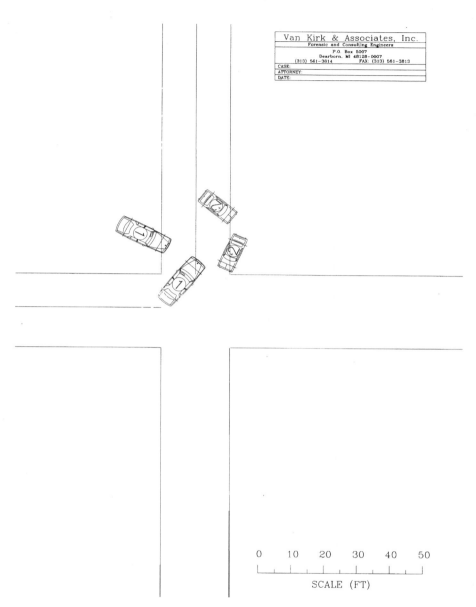

**Figure 15.2C** The rotation of the vehicles from point of impact to point of rest.

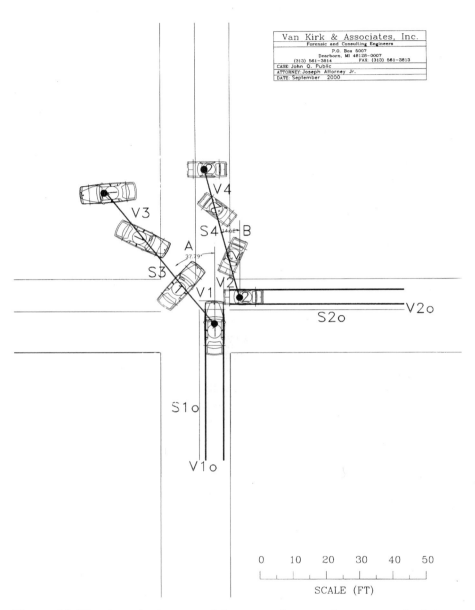

**Figure 15.2D** The vehicles rotated from initial point of contact to final point of rest.

In the previous example, a straight-line situation was examined in which both vehicles were moving in the same direction and in the same lane, and then collided and stayed in the same lane and direction after impact.

Most accidents occur at some angle other than straight into one another. Therefore, consider the next example. Two vehicles enter an intersection at approximately the same time and collide with one another at an approximately 90-degree angle. The coefficient of friction is either assumed or measured to be 0.75. Figure 15.2A shows the point of impact at the intersection.

The driver in vehicle 1 saw the impact about to take place and left preimpact skid marks of 50 ft. The first vehicle was struck by vehicle 2 in the right front fender and rotated 40 ft to the left and forward of the point of impact. The distance that vehicle 1 rotated to the point of rest was measured from the center of gravity of the vehicle at the point of impact to the center of gravity of the vehicle at rest. Vehicle 1 weighed 4250 lb.

Vehicle 2 struck vehicle 1 with its left front fender and left preimpact skid marks of 20 ft. It left a postimpact skidding distance while rotating to the right and slightly above the point of impact of 50 ft, again as measured between the center of gravity of the initial and final resting points of vehicle 2. Figure 15.2B shows the vehicles at rest; vehicle 2 weighed 3100 lb.

## Exercises

1. Calculate the velocity of vehicle 1 and vehicle 2 at impact.
2. Calculate the preimpact velocity of vehicle 1 and vehicle 2, $V_1$, $V_2$.

**Step one.**    Calculate the velocity of both vehicles after impact, $V_3$, $V_4$. Use skid Equation 15.9 to complete this first calculation:

$$V_3 = (30 \cdot S_3 \cdot \mu)^{1/2} \tag{15.23}$$

Plug in the values for the distance skidded by vehicle 1 and the coefficient of friction to obtain the following:

$$V_3 = (30 \cdot 40 \cdot 0.75)^{1/2} \tag{15.24}$$

$$V_3 = (900)^{1/2} \tag{15.25}$$

$$V_3 = 30 \text{ mi/h postimpact velocity of vehicle 1}$$

The same calculation is carried out for the postimpact velocity of vehicle 2:

$$V_4 = (30 \cdot S_4 \cdot \mu)^{1/2} \tag{15.26}$$

Plug in the values to obtain the following:

$$V_4 = (30 \cdot 50 \cdot 0.75)^{1/2} \tag{15.27}$$

$$V_4 = (1125)^{1/2} \tag{15.28}$$

or

$$V_4 = 33.54 \text{ mi/h postimpact velocity of vehicle 2}$$

Figure 15.2D shows that each vehicle rotated from its initial point of contact to its final resting point. This assumes that the tires of the vehicles were in constant contact with the roadbed at all times. The distance traveled from the point of impact to the point of rest for both vehicles is considerably longer when considering the rotational distance the vehicle would undergo as opposed to a straight-line distance.

**Commentary:** *Many vehicles when rotating unload the trailing set of tires during the rotation. This reduces the resistance of the tires with the concrete road surface so that the vehicle is not being slowed down as much as it was previously when all four tires were in contact with the roadbed. This is very similar to a straight-line-braking situation where only two tires are skidding instead of four.*

It is almost impossible to determine the number of rotations a vehicle underwent from the point impact to the point of rest. Therefore, it would be impossible to plot the rotation of the vehicle and measure the exact distance that the vehicle rotated during the postcollision phase. By using the measurement from the center of gravity of the vehicle at the point of impact to the center of gravity of the vehicle at the point to rest, a minimum value for the amount of velocity and/or energy lost during the postimpact phase to the point of rest can be obtained. Figure 15.2C shows the rotation of the vehicles from point of impact to point of rest.

This minimum value must be explained to the client prior to the investigator/reconstructionist deposition or trial testimony. This value means that the vehicle had a higher velocity postimpact, but it is difficult if not impossible to determine how high it was.

Once the point of impact and the point the rest of both vehicles have been plotted on a scale drawing, then the angle between the center of gravity of the vehicle at the point of impact and at the point of rest can be measured, as shown on Figure 15.2. Angle A, the postimpact angle of vehicle 1, was measured at 37.79 degrees. Angle B, the postimpact angle of vehicle 2, was measured at 14.62 degrees.

The equation for the conservation of linear momentum is modified for this calculation because the angles between the impacts of the bodies are unique as compared with the original example. The vector velocity $V_3$ and $V_4$ must be resolved into its $x$ and $y$ components, as shown on Figure 15.2. Choose the long axis of vehicle 1 as the $x$ component and the lateral or transverse axis as the $y$ component. Because there cannot be two different coordinate systems between vehicle 1 and vehicle 2, the same axis designations are applied to vehicle 2. This means that the transverse axis of vehicle 2 is the $x$ component and the longitudinal axis is the $y$ component. Because the vectors have been resolved into their component parts, these component parts must be added to determine the preimpact velocity of each of the two vehicles. The $y$ components of both vehicle movements would not affect the $x$ component movements of either vehicle.

Therefore, the original conservation of linear momentum equation is modified as follows for finding $V_1$:

$$W_1 \, V_1 = (W_1 \cdot V_3 \cdot \text{Cos A}) + (W_2 \cdot V_4 \cdot \text{Cos B}) \tag{15.29}$$

Solve for $V_1$ to obtain the following:

$$V_1 = (V_3 \cdot \text{Cos A}) + [(W_2/W_1) \cdot (V_4 \cdot \text{Cos B})] \tag{15.30}$$

Substitute the measured and given values to obtain:

$$V_1 = (30 \cdot \text{Cos } 37.79) + [(3100/4250)(33.54 \cdot \text{Cos } 14.62)] \tag{15.31}$$

Filling in trigonometric information gives:

$$V_1 = (30 \cdot 0.790) + [(3100/4250)(33.54 \cdot 0.968)] \tag{15.32}$$

Combine like terms to get:

$$V_1 = (23.70) + [(0.729)(32.454)] \tag{15.33}$$

Complete the math to obtain:

$$V_1 = 47.37 \text{ mi/h preimpact velocity} \tag{15.34}$$

The original conservation of linear momentum equation is also modified as follows for finding $V_2$:

$$W_2 \, V_2 = (W_1 \cdot V_3 \cdot \text{Sin A}) + (W_2 \cdot V_4 \cdot \text{Sin B}) \qquad (15.35)$$

Solve for $V_2$:

$$V_2 = [(W_1/W_2) \cdot (V_3 \cdot \text{Sin A})] + (V_4 \cdot \text{Sin B}) \qquad (15.36)$$

Substitute the given and measured values:

$$V_2 = [(4250/3100) \cdot (30 \cdot 0.613)] + (33.54 \cdot 0.252) \qquad (15.37)$$

Combine terms to get:

$$V_2 = [(1.371) \cdot (18.39)] + (8.452) \qquad (15.38)$$

$$V_2 = 33.66 \text{ mph preimpact velocity} \qquad (15.39)$$

**Step two.** Calculate vehicle preskid velocity of $V_{1o}$ and $V_{2o}$. As discussed previously, the two postimpact skid velocities and the velocity lost during this skidding phase of vehicles 1 and 2 are used to determine the preimpact velocity of both vehicles. This is done by squaring the two velocities and then taking the square root of both.

$$V_{1o} = [(V_{\text{skid}})^2 + (V_1)^2]^{1/2} \qquad (15.40)$$

Calculate the velocity lost during the skid ($V_{\text{skid}}$) for both vehicles, by using the skid equation:

$$(V_{\text{skid}})^2 = 30 \cdot S_{\text{lo}} \cdot \mu \qquad (15.41)$$

or

$$V_{\text{skid}} = (30 \cdot S_{\text{lo}} \cdot \mu)^{1/2} \qquad (15.42)$$

Plug the skid equation into the total velocity equation to obtain:

$$V_{1o} = [((30 \cdot S_{\text{lo}} \cdot \mu)^{1/2})^2 + (V_1)^2]^{1/2} \qquad (15.43)$$

or

$$V_{1o} = [(30 \cdot S_{\text{lo}} \cdot \mu) + (V_1)^2]^{1/2} \qquad (15.44)$$

Plug in the given values to get:

$$V_{1o} = [(30 \cdot 50 \cdot 0.75) + (47.37)^2]^{1/2} \qquad (15.45)$$

Collect terms as follows:

$$V_{1o} = [(1125.0) + (2243.9)]^{1/2} \qquad (15.46)$$

or

$$V1o = [3368.9]^{1/2} \qquad (15.47)$$

The preskid velocity for vehicle 1 is:

$$V_{1o} = 58.04 \text{ mi/h} \qquad (15.48)$$

Perform the same calculations for vehicle 2 to obtain the following:

$$V_{2o} = [(30 \cdot S2o \cdot \mu) + (V_2)^2]^{1/2} \qquad (15.49)$$

$$V_{2o} = [(30 \cdot 20 \cdot 0.75) + (33.66)^2]^{1/2} \qquad (15.50)$$

Multiply and collect terms to get:

$$V_{2o} = [450 + (1133.0)]^{1/2} \qquad (15.51)$$

$V_{2o} = 39.79$ mph as the preskid velocity of vehicle 2

These are the basic equations that investigators/reconstructionists can use during the course of their investigations. If a deeper knowledge is required, any college textbook on engineering mechanics is recommended to the reader for perusal.

---

## Appendix 15.1  Equation Workbook

### A.  Distance Equations

I.    Distance traveled at a constant velocity (known velocity)

$S$ = distance traveled in feet
$v$ = velocity in mi/hr
$PR$ = perception and reaction time in seconds

Enter data here:          $v: = 34 \cdot$ mph
                          $PR: = 1.5 \cdot$ sec

Calculations: $S: = v \cdot PR$

Solution: $S = 74.800 \cdot \text{ft}$

II. Distance required to decelerate to any velocity when initial velocity and friction coefficient are known

Variables: $S$ = distance in feet
$V_o$ = initial velocity in mi/hr
$V_f$ = final velocity in mi/hr
$\mu$ = roadway coefficient of friction

Enter data here: $V_o: = 69 \cdot \text{mph}$
$V_f: = 60 \cdot \text{mph}$
$\mu: = 0.85$

Calculations: $a: = m: 32.2 \cdot \dfrac{\text{ft}}{\text{sec}^2}$

$a = 27.370 \cdot \text{ft} \cdot \text{sec}^{-2}$

$S: = \dfrac{(V_o^2) - (V_f^2)}{2 \cdot a}$

Solution: $S = 45.624 \cdot \text{ft}$

III. Distance required to decelerate to any velocity when initial velocity and deceleration are known

Variables: $S$ = distance in feet
$V$ = initial velocity in mph
$a$ = deceleration rate in ft/sec

Enter data here: $V: = 69 \cdot \text{mph}$

$a: = 27.37 \cdot \dfrac{\text{ft}}{\text{sec}^2}$

Calculations: $S: = \dfrac{V^2}{2 \cdot a}$

Solution: $S = 187.092 \cdot \text{ft}$

IV. Distance traveled each second during acceleration from any velocity

Variables: $S$ = distance
$V_o$ = initial velocity in mph
$t$ = time in seconds
$a$ = acceleration or deceleration rate

Enter data here:         $V_o = 30 \cdot$ (mph)

$a: = 4 \cdot \dfrac{\text{ft}}{\text{sec}^2}$

$t: = 1 \cdot \text{sec}$

Calculations:            $S: = (V_o \cdot t) + (0.5 \cdot a \cdot t^2)$

Solution:                $S = 46.000$ ft

## B. Velocity Equations

I.   Velocity at any point during deceleration

Variables:          $V_f =$ velocity at any point during deceleration (mph)
$V_o =$ initial speed when brakes where applied (mph)
$\mu =$ coefficient of sliding friction
$L =$ length of skid mark to point being measured (ft)

Enter values here:  $V_o = 69 \cdot$ mph
$m: = 0.85$
$L: = 45 \cdot$ ft

Calculations:       $a: = m \cdot 32.2 \cdot \dfrac{\text{ft}}{(\text{sec}^2)}$

$a = 27.370 \cdot \text{ft} \cdot \text{sec}^{-2}$

$V_f: = \sqrt{(V_o^2) - (2 \cdot a \cdot L)}$

Solution:           $V_f = 60.132 \cdot$ mph

II.  Velocity from skid marks when vehicle has partial braking capability

Variables:          $V =$ velocity at beginning of skid marks (mph)
$S =$ distance of skid (ft)
$\mu =$ coefficient of friction
$\eta =$ percentage of vehicle weight carried on wheels
having braking capability

Enter values here:  $S: = 56 \cdot$ ft
$\mu: = 0.65$
$\eta: = 0.75$

Calculations:       $V: = (\sqrt{\mu \cdot n \cdot S}) \cdot \sqrt{30 \cdot \dfrac{\text{ft}}{\text{sec}^2}}$

Solution:           $V = 101.200 \cdot \text{ft} \cdot \text{sec}^{-1}$

III.    Velocity calculation when continuous skid on different surfaces

    Variables:

$V$ = velocity (mph)
$S_1$ = skid distance on first surface (ft)
$S_2$ = skid distance on second surface (ft)
$\mu_1$ = coefficient of friction on first surface
$\mu_2$ = coefficient of friction on second surface

    Enter values here:

$S_1$: = 33
$S_2$: = 46
$\mu_1$: = .70
$\mu_2$: = .50

    Calculations:

$$V: = \sqrt{(\mu_1 \cdot S_1) + (\mu_2 \cdot S_2)} \cdot 5.477$$

    Solutions:

$V = 37.187$

IV.    Velocity calculation from skid marks with each side of vehicle on different surfaces

    Variables:

$V$ = velocity (mph)
$\mu_1$ = coefficient of friction for side 1 of vehicle
$\mu_2$ = coefficient of friction for side 2 of vehicle
$L$ = length of skid (ft)

    Enter data here:

$\mu_1$: = 0.65
$\mu_2$: 0.55
$L$: = 51

    Calculations:

$$V: = \sqrt{12 \cdot (\mu_1 + \mu_2) \cdot L}$$

    Solutions:

$V = 30.299$

V.    Velocity after acceleration from a stop over a known distance

    Variables:

$V$ = velocity (mph)
$a$ = acceleration rate (ft/sec/sec)
$S$ = distance (ft)

    Enter data here:

$$a: = 4 \cdot \frac{ft}{sec^2}$$

$s: = 8 \cdot ft$

    Calculations:

$$V: = \sqrt{2 \cdot a \cdot s}$$

    Solution:

$V = 5.455$ mph

VI. Velocity after acceleration from known speed and distance

Variables: $V_2$ = velocity after acceleration
$V_1$ = initial velocity (mph)
$a$ = acceleration rate
$S$ = distance traveled

Enter data here: $V_1: = 45 \cdot$ mph

$A: = 4 \cdot \dfrac{\text{ft}}{(\sec)^2}$

$S: = 500 \cdot$ ft

Calculations: $V_2: = \sqrt{V_1^2 + (2 \cdot a \cdot S)}$

Solution: $V_2 = 62.326$ mph

## C. Momentum Equations

I. Velocity of moving vehicle that collides with vehicle moving in same direction (rear-end collision)

Step 1 - Calculate postimpact velocity of both vehicles

Variables: $V_3$ = postimpact velocity of vehicle 1 (mph)
$S_3$ = postimpact skid distance of vehicle 1 (ft)
$m$ = coefficient of friction

Enter data here: $S_3: = 50$
$m: = 0.60$

Calculations: $V_3: = \sqrt{30} \cdot \sqrt{S_3 \cdot \mu}$

Solution: $V_3 = 30.000$

Step 2 - Calculate velocity of vehicle 1 at time of impact

Variables: $V_1$ = velocity of vehicle 1 at time of impact
$V_2$ = velocity of vehicle 2 at time of vehicle 1
$V_3$ = postimpact velocity of vehicle 1
$V_4$ = postimpact velocity of vehicle 2
$W_1$ = weight of vehicle 1 (lb)
$W_2$ = weight of vehicle 2 (lb)

Enter data here: $V_2: = 30.00$ mph
$V_3: = 30.00$ mph
$V_4: = 38$ mph
$W_1: = 3500$ lb
$W_2: = 2500$ lb

Calculations:          $V_1: = \left[ V_3 + \left( \frac{W_2}{W_1} \cdot V_4 \right) \right] - \left( \frac{W_2}{W_1} \cdot V_2 \right)$

$V_1 = 35.714$ mph

Step 3 - Calculate vehicle 1's velocity at the commencement of its initial skid marks

Variables:          $V_{1o}$ = velocity of vehicle 1 at commencement of initial skid mark

$S_{1o}$ = length of initial skid mark

$\mu$ = coefficient of friction

$V_1$ = impact velocity of vehicle 1

Enter data here:          $S_{1o}: = 45$

$\mu: = 0.60$

$V_1: = 36$

Calculations:          $V_{1o}: = \sqrt{30 \cdot S_{1o} \cdot \mu + V_1^2}$

Solution:          $V_{1o} = 45.891$

II.          Velocity of moving vehicle that collides with stopped vehicle

Step 1 - Calculate postimpact velocity of vehicle 1

Variables:          $V_3$ = postimpact velocity of vehicle 1 (mph)

$S_3$ = postimpact skid distance of vehicle 1, measured mass center

$\mu$ = coefficient of friction

Enter data here:          $S_3: = 20$

$\mu: = 0.70$

Calculations:          $V_3: = \sqrt{30} \cdot \sqrt{S_3 \cdot \mu}$

$V_3 = 20.494$

Step 2 - Calculate postimpact velocity of vehicle 2

Variables:          $V_4$ = postimpact velocity of vehicle 2

$S_4$ = postimpact skid distance of vehicle 2, measured mass

$\mu$ = coefficient of friction

Enter data here:          $S_4: = 80$

$m: = 0.70$

Calculations:          $V_4: = \sqrt{30} \cdot \sqrt{S_4 \cdot \mu}$

Solution:                     $V_4 = 40.988$

Step 3 - Calculate vehicle 1's impact velocity

Variables:                    $V_1$ = impact velocity of vehicle 1
                              $V_3$ = postimpact velocity of vehicle 1
                              $V_4$ = postimpact velocity of vehicle 2
                              $W_1$ = weight of vehicle 1
                              $W_2$ = weight of vehicle 2

Enter data here:              $V_3$: = 21 mph
                              $V_4$: = 22 mph
                              $W_2$: = 3000 lb
                              $W_1$: = 4000 lb

Calculations:                 $V_1: = V_3 + \left( \dfrac{W_2}{W_1} \cdot V_4 \right)$

Solution:                     $V_1 = 37.500$ mph

Step 4 - Calculate vehicle 1's velocity at commencement of its initial skid
        mark

Variables:                    $V_{1o}$ = velocity of vehicle 1 at the commencement of
                                  its initial skid mark
                              $S_{1o}$ = length of initial skid mark
                              $\mu$ = coefficient of friction
                              $V_1$ = vehicle 1's impact velocity

Enter date here:              $S_{1o}$: = 40 feet
                              $\mu$: = 0.70
                              $V_1$: = 38 mph

Calculations:                 $V_{1o}: = \sqrt{(30 \cdot S_{1o} \cdot \mu) + V_1^2}$

Solution:                     $V_{1o} = 47.791$ mph

III.  Velocity of two vehicles that collide at right angles to each other

Step 1 - Calculate the postimpact velocities of both vehicles

Variables:                    $V_3$ = postimpact velocity of vehicle 1 (mph)
                              $V_4$ = postimpact velocity of vehicle 2 (mph)
                              $S_3$ = postimpact skid distance of vehicle 1, measured
                                  mass center to mass center (ft)
                              $S_4$ = postimpact skid distance of vehicle 2, measured
                                  mass center to mass center (ft)
                              $\mu$ = coefficient of friction

Enter data here:         $S_3$: = 40 ft
                         μ: = 0.75
                         $S_4$: = 50 ft

Calculations:            $V_3$: = $\sqrt{30 \cdot S_3 \cdot \mu}$

                         $V_4$: = $\sqrt{30 \cdot S_4 \cdot \mu}$

Solution:                $V_3$ = 30,000 mph
                         $V_4$ = 33.541 mph

Step 2 - Calculate velocity of $V_1$ and $V_2$ at time of impact

Variables:               $V_1$ = velocity of vehicle 1 at time of impact
                         $V_2$ = velocity of vehicle 2 at time of impact
                         $V_3$ = postimpact velocity of vehicle 1
                         $V_4$ = postimpact velocity of vehicle 2
                         $W_1$ = weight of vehicle 1 (lb)
                         $W_2$ = weight of vehicle 2 (lb)
                         Angle A = postimpact angle of vehicle 1
                         Angle B = postimpact angle of vehicle 2

See Figure 15.2D for scene sketch

Enter data here:         $V_3$: = 30.00 mph
                         $V_4$: = 33.54 mph
                         $W_1$: = 4250 · lb
                         $W_2$: = 3100 · lb
                         A: = 37.79        cos(A): = 0.790
                         B: = 14.62        cos(B): = 0.968

Using the modified Linear Momentum Equation as follows:

Calculations:            $V_1 := \left( \dfrac{W_1}{W_2} \cdot V_3 \cdot \cos(A) \right) + \left( \dfrac{W_2}{W_1} \cdot V_4 \cdot \cos(B) \right)$

                         $V_1 := (V_3 \cdot \cos(A)) + \left( \dfrac{W_2}{W_1} \right) \cdot V_4 \cdot \cos(B)$

                         $V_1 := (30 \cdot 0.790) + \left( \dfrac{3100}{4250} \right) \cdot 33.54 \cdot 0.968$

Solution:                $V_1$: = 47.37 mph preimpact speed

Calculation:             $V_2 := \left( \dfrac{W_1}{W_2} \right) \cdot V_3 \cdot \sin(A) + (V_4 \cdot \sin(B))$

                         $V_2 := \left( \dfrac{4250}{3100} \right) \cdot 30 \cdot 0.613 + (33.54 \cdot 0.252)$

Solution:                $V_2$: = 33.66 mph preimpact velocity

Step 3 - Calculate both vehicles preskid velocities

Variables:            $V_{1o}$ = velocity of vehicle 1 at the start of initial skid
                          marks
                      $V_{2o}$ = velocity of vehicle 2 at the start of initial skid
                          marks
                      $S_{1o}$ = length of the initial skid mark for vehicle 1
                      $S_{2o}$ = length of skid mark for vehicle 2
                      $\mu$ = coefficient of friction
                      $V_1$ = impact velocity of vehicle 1
                      $V_2$ = impact velocity of vehicle 2

Enter data here:      $S_{1o}$: = 45
                      $\mu$: = 0.75
                      $S_{2o}$: = 20
                      $V_1$: = 47.37
                      $V_2$: = 33.66

Calculation:          $V_{1o}$: = $\sqrt{30 \cdot S_{1o} \cdot \mu + V_1^2}$

                      $V_{2o}$: = $\sqrt{30 \cdot S_{2o} \cdot \mu + V_2^2}$

Solutions:            $V_{1o}$: = 58.04 mph preskid velocity
                      $V_{2o}$ = 39.37 mph preskid velocity

---

# A Detailed Look at Appendix 15.1

## Section A — Distance Equations

### Problem One

Problem one is to determine the distance traveled at constant velocity (known velocity). The data required to be inputted is $S$ = the distance traveled in feet, $V$ = the velocity in miles per hour, and $PR$ = the perception and reaction time in seconds.

Assume the velocity $V$ is only equal to 34 mi/h (remember to convert miles per hour to feet per second) and the perception/reaction time is 1.5 sec; then use the equation:

$$S = V \cdot PR \tag{15.52}$$

and plug in the values to obtain:

$$S = 49.878 \cdot 1.5 \tag{15.53}$$

The solution is the distance

$$S = 74.817 \text{ ft} \qquad\qquad (15.54)$$

This seems like a very simple problem, but it is significant to the reconstructionist for a very specific calculation. This calculation is used when trying to determine how far a vehicle can travel, the distance traveled, during the time the driver is undergoing his/her perception and reaction time.

## Problem Two

Problem two is to determine the distance required to decelerate any velocity when the initial velocity and the coefficient of friction are known. The data required to be inputted include the initial velocity $V_o$ (in miles per hour), the final velocity $V_f$ (in miles per hour), and the deceleration $a$.

Assume the initial velocity $V_o = 69$ mi/h and the final velocity $V_f = 60$ mi/h, and the vehicle has all four tires locked up so they are not rotating; then the deceleration is strictly the coefficient of friction between the tires and the roadbed surface — $\mu = 0.85$, which is 85% of the deceleration $a$ or $a = 27.370$ ft/sec/sec. It must be remembered that miles per hour must be converted to feet per second before it can be used in this equation.

By using the equation:

$$S = [(V_o{}^2) - (V_f{}^2)]/2 \cdot a \qquad\qquad (15.55)$$

and by plugging in the values and changing miles per hour to feet per second, the following solution is obtained:

$$S = 45.624 \text{ ft} \qquad\qquad (15.56)$$

Again, a solution is obtained for a simple equation. However, its ramifications are important and can be used in the following way.

The skid distance can be determined if the initial velocity and the final velocity are known about a vehicle that the driver heavily braked but whose wheels did not skid.

The initial velocity may have been assumed from the witness statements or the driver's statement, and the final velocity may have been developed from the amount of deformation on the front of the vehicle at the collision. Many times the final velocity is zero, and therefore making the calculation is easier.

## Problem Three

Problem three is to determine the distance required to decelerate to any velocity when the initial velocity and deceleration are known. Input the initial velocity in miles per hour and the deceleration rate in feet per second. Assume the initial velocity $V_o$ = 69 mi/h, and the deceleration rate is 27.37 ft/sec/sec.

Using a variation of Equation 15.55 from problem number two, which is setting the final velocity to zero, gives the following equation:

$$S = V^2/(2 \cdot a) \tag{15.57}$$

The solution obtained is $S$ = 187.092 ft.

This equation could be used by the reconstructionist when trying to determine when the brake application occurred or if the initial velocity that may have been assumed is correct. Setting the final velocity to zero assumes that there is no collision.

If there is deformation of the vehicle, then the velocity is incorrect. Therefore, the reconstructionist knows that the driver must have been braking prior to the collision. By using this equation, the reconstructionist can track the vehicle from the point of collision back to the point of brake application. Then by using Equation 15.52, which gives the driver's P&R distance, he/she can locate the point where the vehicle first perceived the possibility of a collision.

### Problem Four

Problem four requires determination of the distance traveled each second during an acceleration or deceleration from any velocity. Once again, input the initial velocity in miles per hour, the time in seconds that the vehicle will be accelerating and either its acceleration or deceleration rate. Assume a velocity of 30 mi/h, a rate of deceleration of 4 ft/sec/sec at a time of only 1 sec.

By using Equation 15.7, which was developed at the beginning of this chapter, the following equation can be obtained:

$$S = (V_o \cdot t) + (0.5 \cdot a \cdot t^2) \tag{15.58}$$

with a solution of $S$ = 46.00 ft.

How can investigators/reconstructionists use this equation? Such an instance is any time a vehicle travels along a highway and the driver decides to accelerate around a slower vehicle like a semitruck. Unfortunately, the driver of the car does not know that there is another vehicle on the other side of the truck, accelerates around it, and ends up striking the unseen or hidden vehicle. This equation allows the reconstructionist to determine what distance was traveled at a constant acceleration rate when trying to pass the truck. There are other uses for such an equation but this is only one possibility being brought to the reader's attention.

## Section B — Velocity Equations

### Problem One

Problem one determines the velocity at any point during a vehicle's deceleration. For example, a vehicle is in a four-wheel skid, and is slowing down prior to turning. This equation allows the final velocity at the end of the skidding phase of the accident to be determined. What variables are needed to determine the final velocity?

The requirements include the initial velocity, which is 69 mi/h; the coefficient of friction, which is 0.85 and translates into a 27.370 ft/sec/sec deceleration; and, of course, the length of the skid marks ($L$), which is 45 ft. Then use the following equation:

$$V_f = [(V_o^2) - (2 \cdot a \cdot L)]^{1/2} \tag{15.59}$$

Plugging in the values gives the following solution:

$$V_f = 88.22 \text{ ft/sec or } 60.132 \text{ mi/h}$$

This means that the vehicle was in a four-wheel skid of 45 ft, and slowed down from 69.0 to 60.132 mi/h. This was not much of a slowdown for a skid length of approximately three car lengths.

This equation has been used many times and in variety of situations. The one that comes to mind is the instance in which a vehicle is braking with all four wheels and is skidding; just prior to the collision there is an absence of skid marks. For some reason the driver has released the brake pedal and the vehicle has continued forward to the collision. This equation allows the reconstructionist to determine the vehicle velocity at the end of the skid mark.

If there is a short distance between the skid mark and the collision, it can be assumed that the vehicle velocity is close to being constant from the end of the skid marks until the collision. Therefore, the value for vehicle velocity at the end of the skid mark would be the same as the velocity at impact.

Believe it or not, all vehicles are not maintained properly. Many drivers today only spend money on their vehicles when it is absolutely necessary. Many do not even check the brake fluid in the master cylinder at any time during the life of the vehicle. Today's modern vehicles have a split braking system which allows braking to only one set of brakes with one half of the master cylinder. The other section of the master cylinder controls the other set of brakes. Both halves of the master cylinder must be filled with fluid, and if and when there is a loss of such fluid in one half of the master cylinder, the other half of the master cylinder allows the driver to stop the vehicle, but it takes a longer distance to do so.

Many if not all vehicles on the road have self-adjusting brake shoes. When the vehicles back up, the brakes are adjusted to the proper tolerance of closeness to the shoes. When the shoes become too worn, then the adjuster cannot bring the shoes back within tolerance. When either of these conditions exists, the braking capability of the vehicle is reduced. The front brakes are designed so that they can handle approximately 60% of the braking load of the vehicle. This means that if a front wheel brake system has a loss of fluid or is not properly adjusted, then it cannot assist in the braking of the vehicle and the braking capacity is diminished by approximately 60% of its capability. If a rear brake system is in the same situation, then the vehicle braking capability is reduced by 40%. Many times at the scene of the accident it is impossible to determine if the braking system was operating on all four wheels. In that case a good approximation is a loss of 25% for each wheel that is not operating properly.

## Problem Two

Problem two determines velocity from skid marks when the vehicle has only partial braking capability. Assume the skid length is 56 ft, the coefficient of friction $(\mu)$ is 0.65, and only three wheels are braking. Also assume the percentage $(\eta)$ of vehicle weight carried on the wheels having braking capability is 0.75.

By using the following equation:

$$V = [(30 \cdot \mu \cdot \eta \cdot s)^{1/2}] \tag{15.60}$$

Then substitute the assumed values to obtain the following:

$$V = [(30 \cdot 0.65 \cdot 0.75 \cdot 56)^{1/2}] \tag{15.61}$$

$$V = 28.618 \text{ ft/sec}$$

To see an indication of the difference in using the actual value for the partial braking loss vs. the assumed value, go back and calculate the velocities using the actual number for $\eta$. If a rear wheel was not braking, then $\eta$ would be one half of the rear braking capability, which is approximately 20%. Therefore, $\eta$ would be 0.80 and $V = 29.56$ ft/sec, which is less than 1.0 mi/h difference or 3% error. If a front wheel was not braking, then $\eta$ would be 0.70 and $V = 27.64$ ft/sec, a difference of approximately 1.0 mi/h or a 3.3% error. This is a small difference when considering the error in determining the length of the skid marks on the pavement after the accident, and the coefficient of friction of the roadbed itself.

The previous equation is sometimes referred to as the skid equation. It must be remembered that the skid equation determines the velocity of the vehicle at the beginning of the skid.

The skid equation basically assumes that the vehicle has reached zero velocity at the end of the skid mark. Therefore, it is up to the reconstructionist to understand the shortcomings of this equation by knowing that the value represented by the calculation is only a partial solution to the problem if the vehicle has not reached zero velocity at the end of a skid and continues on its path to a collision. The skid equation is then only telling the reconstructionist that the value obtained from the equation is the velocity lost during the skidding of the vehicle. No other inference can be made from it.

It is very important for the reconstructionist to take the time and effort to determine exactly, if possible, the number of skid marks at the scene of the collision. The basic equation is derived on the assumption that all four wheels of the vehicle are skidding. If less than four wheels skidded, then a correction must be inserted into the skid equation to ensure a proper response.

As an example, consider the fact that the two rear wheels of a vehicle do not lock up; in other words, they are not skidding. Then the vehicle has lost approximately 50% of its braking capability when skidding and therefore requires a longer stopping distance from the same velocity.

This is extremely important when determining the preskid velocity of the vehicle. If the reconstructionist calculates a preimpact velocity of 40 mi/h based on the assumption that all four wheels were skidding and closely examines the roadbed to find only two skid marks, then the actual velocity is 26 mi/h. This is a vast difference and tarnishes the reputation of the reconstructionist in the eyes of his/her client and the judge or jury trying the case. By spending a little extra time at the collision site and checking for the details of the accident, simple blunders such as these can be easily overcome.

### Problem Three

Problem three determines velocity when continuous skids occur on different surfaces. This might happen, for example, when a vehicle goes into a skid from the concrete roadbed surface onto gravel or even a grass surface. How can the velocity lost during the skid be determined?

Assume the skid distance ($S_1$) on the first surface is 33 ft and the second skid distance ($S_2$) is 46 ft, with the coefficient of friction on the first surface being 0.7 and on the second surface being 0.5.

By modifying the skid equation the following equation can be obtained:

$$V = \{[(\mu_1 \cdot S_1) + (\mu_2 \cdot S_2)] \cdot (30)\}^{1/2} \qquad (15.62)$$

By inserting the assumed values the following is obtained:

$$V = \{[(0.7 \cdot 33) + (0.5 \cdot 46)] \cdot (30)\}^{1/2} \qquad (15.63)$$

or

$$V = 37.187 \text{ mi/h}$$

Once again, the calculation yields the loss of vehicle's velocity due to the skidding on multiple surfaces. If the vehicle had come to a stop at the end of this skid, then the final velocity would be zero and the preskid velocity would be 37.187 mi/h.

If the vehicle had continued toward a collision, a preskid velocity would be needed to determine the vehicle velocity at the time of the collision. Subtracting the 37.187 mi/h from the assumed value would result in the vehicle preimpact velocity, if the velocity lost in the collision were ignored.

## Problem Four

A vehicle many times may skid on two different surfaces with different sides of the vehicle. In other words, the right or passenger side of the vehicle may skid on a gravel shoulder, while the left or driver's side of the vehicle skids on the concrete or asphalt roadbed surface.

The following equation, again as a modification of the skid equation, can assist the reconstructionist in determining the velocity lost during the skid. Assume a coefficient of friction of 0.65 for side one of the vehicle, and 0.55, for side two. Assume also the length of the skid mark is 51 ft. By using the following modified skid equation the following is obtained:

$$V = [30 \cdot ((\mu_1 + \mu_2)/2) \cdot L]^{1/2} \qquad (15.64)$$

Substituting assumed values gives the following:

$$V = [30 \cdot ((0.65 + 0.55)/2) \cdot 51] \qquad (15.65)$$

$$V = 30.299 \text{ mi/h}$$

Once again, this equation is used when making the assumption that all four wheels are skidding. If the reconstructionist can determine that less than four wheels were skidding, then he/she must modify the equation again by inserting a proportional value for the loss of braking capability using the number of wheels that were not skidding.

## Problem Five

Problem five determines the velocity of a vehicle if its acceleration and the distance it has traveled is known or assumed. For example, if a vehicle is stopped at a traffic light waiting to make a left turn, or is stopped at a stop sign waiting for traffic to clear, it is necessary to determine the vehicle velocity over a certain distance that the particular vehicle can travel.

Assume that the vehicle has traveled 8 ft after starting from a stopped position, either at a traffic light or at a stop sign. Further assume that the vehicle also had an acceleration rate of 4 ft/sec/sec. By using the following equation, determine the velocity at the distance of 8 ft from the stopped position (remember that the acceleration value must be in feet per second):

$$V = (2 \cdot a \cdot s)^{1/2} \tag{15.66}$$

Substitute the assumed values to obtain the following:

$$V = (2 \cdot 4 \cdot 8)^{1/2} \tag{15.67}$$

$$V = 8 \text{ ft/sec or } 5.455 \text{ mi/h}$$

## Problem Six

Problem six determines the velocity after acceleration from a known velocity and distance. Assume the initial velocity $V_1$ is 45 mi/h, the acceleration rate is 4 ft/sec/sec, and the distance traveled is 500 ft. Determine a velocity $V_2$ after acceleration. Always remember that if the acceleration is in feet per second per second and there is no constant to convert the velocity from miles per hour to feet per second, then the miles per hour must be converted to feet per second before plugging that value into the equation.

$$V_2 = [(V_1)^2 + (2 \cdot a \cdot S)]^{1/2} \tag{15.68}$$

Plug in the assumed values to obtain the following equation:

$$V_2 = [(66)^2 + (2 \cdot 4 \cdot 500)]^{1/2} \tag{15.69}$$

Combine terms to obtain the following:

$$V_2 = 91.42 \text{ ft/sec or } 62.32 \text{ mi/h}$$

## Section C — Momentum Equations

The momentum of a whole body is defined as the product of its mass and its acceleration. This statement described mathematically gives:

$$F = ma \tag{15.70}$$

where acceleration can be expressed as the difference between the final velocity and the initial velocity divided by the time of the event:

$$a = (V_f - V_o)/t \tag{15.71}$$

This basically becomes Newton's second law of motion and is expressed as follows:

$$F = (m \cdot V_f - m \cdot V_o)/t \tag{15.72}$$

By rearranging the terms the following can be obtained:

$$Ft = (m \cdot V_f - m \cdot V_o) \tag{15.73}$$

where the product of force and time is called impulse. Because this is to be appled to a system of two more bodies where the resultant force acting on the system is zero, the system is said to be "isolated," therefore, the resultant force $F$ must equal zero. This means that the momentum of the system remains constant. Expressing in equation form gives:

$$m_f \cdot V_f = m_o \cdot V_o \tag{15.74}$$

This equation basically expresses the law of conservation of momentum, which states that the total momentum of an isolated system stays constant regardless of any interactions that may take place among its parts. The law of conservation of linear momentum is a useful tool for the investigator/reconstructionist, but it has drawbacks and problems as with using any tool.

In any two-car collision there are six variables. Five of those variables must be assumed, or the actual value must be calculated or known by some other means. Needed are the weights of both vehicles, the postimpact velocity of both vehicles and one of the two vehicle velocities at the time of impact.

The weights of both vehicles are usually easy to obtain. In some cases the police may weigh the vehicles after the collision. These figures are not always accurate due to the loss of components and/or fluids at the scene, but the loss of these at the accident scene may be negligible compared with the total weight of the vehicle. The on-scene investigator must determine this for himself/herself.

A second method is to take the weights from the registration slips of the vehicles. The weights of the occupants of the vehicle must also be taken into account especially when considering a van that would carry between 8 and 12 people. Many times those weights must be estimated from medical records, conversations with the occupants after the accident, or anthropomorphic data for the size and height of the occupant.

Another area where the investigator/reconstructionist might obtain vehicle weights is the sticker or manufacturer's plate that is inside every door of every vehicle made today. These stickers give the axle weight for both the front and rear axle. Finally, a method that has worked in the past is to call up a referral service that can supply, for a fee, the physical dimensions and weight of the vehicle. Be careful when using these data, because they may not contain the actual model with all the possible accessories that were on the collision vehicle.

The next two variables that need to be determined are the postimpact velocity of both vehicles. The most common method used is the skid equation. This equation requires that the vehicles have all their wheels locked up at the time of the collision to the time the vehicles come to rest. This is usually not the case: the vehicles may be sliding sideways, rotating, and moving in a forward or sideways direction; or they may be in a yaw.

If the vehicles are sliding sideways that means that only two of the four tires are actually sliding on the ground; the other two trailing tires would be partially unloaded in terms of vehicle weight and would not leave a sliding mark on the concrete or asphalt surface. In addition, these tires may be rotating to some degree, which changes the coefficient of friction with the roadbed, because the coefficient of friction is based on a skidding tire as opposed to a sliding tire.

Finally, the vehicle that is yawing is the worst case for determining the postimpact velocity. The reason for this is the fact that the tires may be rotating as fast as they are sliding sideways. This means that the coefficient of friction cannot be used as the basis for the amount of deceleration the vehicle can undergo during this maneuver. There are some reconstruction schools that teach the investigator/reconstructionist to estimate the percentage of coefficient of friction that can be attributed to the skidding action vs. the yawing action.

*Commentary: I have seen reports completed by investigators/reconstructionists who have assumed a coefficient of friction percentage from as low as 20% to as high as 80% of the full value. They do not include any explanation for the percentages that were chosen.*

*I have not yet seen any textbook or seminar speaker discuss the basis for such an assumption of coefficient of friction percentages. Instead of trying to convince the client or the opposing counsel that the percentage chosen is the proper percentage for the coefficient of friction, it would be easier to assume a full coefficient of friction and then state the maximum deceleration that the vehicle would undergo given those conditions. In addition, the distance traveled is a straight-line distance, which is less than the circular distance the vehicle is undergoing when it is yawing or rotating to its final resting point. Therefore, the time that the vehicle is under deceleration is shorter than the actual time. It may be possible to consider these two conditions to offset one another. Thus, an assumption of maximum wheel lock up for deceleration is the best choice for that particular situation.*

Therefore, it is possible to obtain a postimpact velocity for the two vehicles involved in a collision after they depart from the point of impact using certain assumptions based on fact and not on guesses.

The last two variables are the velocities of the two vehicles just prior to the point of impact. Determining these is difficult because a preimpact velocity for one vehicle cannot be obtained unless a preimpact velocity for the second vehicle is known or assumed. This may be very difficult in some situations. If the equation for coefficient of linear momentum is used, be sure to include all assumptions made concerning the postimpact velocity and the preimpact velocity for the various vehicles involved. In this way there can be no confusion concerning the reconstructionist's opinion on this particular accident. This is what he/she should strive for in all reconstructions, so as to eliminate any confusion in the manner or method of the reconstruction on the part of the person reading the report.

The basic equation for conservation of linear momentum can be stated as follows:

$$M_1 \cdot V_1 + M_2 \cdot V_2 = M_1 V_3 + M_2 V_3 \tag{15.75}$$

where $M_1$ represents the mass of the first vehicle and $M_2$ represents the mass of the second vehicle. The various velocities have already been explained. To use the weight, divide the mass $M$ by the constant $g$ to obtain the weight $W$. Therefore, the equation can be written as follows:

$$(M_1/g) \cdot V_1 + (M_2/g) + V_2 = (M_3/g) \cdot V_3 + (M_4/g) \cdot V_4 \tag{15.76}$$

The mass $M$ divided by $g$ = the weight $W$. Therefore, substitute this into Equation 15.76 to obtain the following equation:

$$(W_1) \cdot V_1 + (W_2) + V_2 = (W_1) \cdot V_3 + (W_2) \cdot V_4 \tag{15.77}$$

Assume that the velocity of the first vehicle $V_1$ is to be obtained. Transpose terms and solve for the velocity $V_1$ to obtain the equation that follows:

$$(W_1) \cdot V_1 = [(W_1) \cdot V_3 + (W_2) \cdot V_4] - [(W_2) \cdot V_2] \qquad (15.78)$$

Solving for $V_1$ gives:

$$V_1 = [V_3 + (W_2) \cdot V_4]/(W_1)] - [(W_2) \cdot V_2]/(W_1) \qquad (15.79)$$

By eliminating like terms, the final equation becomes:

$$V_1 = \{V_3 + [(W_2)/(W_1)] \cdot V_4\} - [(W_2)/(W_1)] \cdot V_2\} \qquad (15.80)$$

# Sources of Information

# 16

"It has long been an axiom of mine that the little things are infinitely the most important."

**Sherlock Holmes**
*A Case of Identity*

From time to time accident investigators and reconstructionists need additional sources of information to complete the analysis of their investigation and/or reconstruction. These sources of information can range from data to be used in the formation of final opinions to collaborating or checking with another expert to determine if a scenario is correct based on information available. It is a well-known fact that the more information the investigator or reconstructionist has to complete an analysis, the better the reconstruction can be.

## Weather Sources

Weather is a key factor in many accidents, especially in the winter when the weather conditions change almost hourly. The investigator or reconstructionist needs to know the weather conditions at the time of the accident to determine if the participants were correct in their statements and also to verify the police officer's report.

The best source is the National Oceanic Atmospheric Administration (NOAA) office in Washington, D.C., which collects the weather information from all the major airports in the U.S. They issue a folded four-page report each month that contains a great deal of information on a day-to-day basis of the monthly weather activities at a particular airport. The data are generally sent out 1 month after the activity. Any investigator/reconstructionist can obtain a subscription to this weather report by sending a nominal fee to the NOAA.

If the accident occurred in a rural area that may be located too far from a local or even regional airport, a second source is the agricultural station within that particular area of the state. There may be several in a state and their locations can be obtained from the local state agricultural department. The data are not as complete as the NOAA data, but can help with correlating the participants' information with the police report information.

Local newspapers always print the weather forecast on a day-to-day basis. If there is a dramatic change in the weather it is discussed in the next day's paper. To obtain weather information, contact the local newspaper, stop by its office and purchase a copy, or copy the paper from the day in question.

Public libraries are also a source of local and other major cities' weather reports. Other sources that would be helpful are local radio and television stations. They usually keep copies of news and weather reports on audio or videotape. These tapes usually can be purchased for a nominal fee by calling the station. Be sure to obtain the report that was given on the air, at or near the time of the accident.

## Meteorology Experts

Many times it is necessary for the investigator/reconstructionist to call on another expert to confirm a scenario during the accident sequence concerning such details as black ice formation, frost formation and timing, location of fog banks on the highways, and icing conditions on a specific point of a highway at a specific time. To be sure that the condition the investigator/reconstructionist believes was in part a cause of the accident, he/she may need to contact a meteorology expert. Most if not all major cities have at least one meteorologist working for a local radio or TV station. Call that radio or television station to be put in touch with such an expert.

*Commentary: I have found meteorology experts to be very professional and very helpful even when you may not know the exact terminology of the profession. They will take the time to explain fully what you require and how that information can be obtained if they do not have it readily available.*

As an example, consider a situation in the late fall or early winter. An accident has occurred and there is a hole in the windshield. The driver, the only occupant of the vehicle, has been injured. The inside of the windshield is covered with what appears to be frost. The contention of the on-scene investigator was that the occupant, while waiting for the ambulance to arrive, formed the frost by heavy breathing. The meteorologist can determine at what temperature a frost condition would occur from the temperature of the breath of the occupant and the outside temperature. Another example is the formation of black ice on any new asphalt surface. Black ice is a temporary condition and disappears with a moderate amount of heat from the sun. A meteorologist would be able to determine, given the weather conditions at the specific time and location of the accident, if black ice could have formed at that particular time and place.

## Vision and Lighting Experts

A driver's vision and the highway lighting conditions go hand in hand with respect to the driver's ability to see the road ahead.

It is common knowledge that as the human body ages there is a loss of visual acuity. Poor street lighting or the absence of street lighting altogether can have a dramatic effect on a driver's ability to perceive pedestrians, vehicles approaching, or even some aspects of the road itself. There are a great many books and technical papers available to the investigator/reconstructionist for review and information-gathering purposes on this topic.

This information, however, can become rather confusing if the investigator/reconstructionist is not sufficiently versed in the terminology of either of these technical fields. It would then be necessary to locate a suitable expert. If the investigator/reconstructionist lives close to any major city, there may be a college or university with individuals well versed in these fields. They can either act as experts for your clients, or they can explain the technologies of their particular fields so the investigators/reconstructionists can use the information themselves. If these sources are not available, there are many expert search services that can locate an expert witness in the locale of concern with the qualifications that may be required.

It would be best for the investigator/reconstructionist to call an expert first, to explain the background of the case, and then to describe his/her scenario of the accident involving vision, lighting, or both with respect to the sequence of events of the accident. Then he/she can judge whether the expert may be able to sufficiently help to provide the necessary information for the deposition and/or trial, or request the client to retain the other expert to give the best support to the case at hand.

## Vehicle Statistics

There are many reasons to obtain the statistics of a vehicle involved in an accident. The first, of course, would be to check the vehicle identification number (VIN) to determine if it matches the vehicle involved in the accident. It is rare that for one reason or another the VIN plate has been changed; or the same make, model, and color vehicle is in a salvage yard and the vehicles become confused. This allows the investigator/reconstructionist to check the police information and to verify that this in fact was the accident vehicle.

A second reason for obtaining the statistics of the vehicle is to be able to draw a sketch of a vehicle with the same overall length, width, and wheelbase to portray it on the detailed scale drawing used as an exhibit in the deposition or at trial.

This is especially helpful when using a scale of 1 to 10 or 1 to 20. The specific shape of the vehicle must be such that it would be easily recognized as the accident vehicle by a nonautomotive professional such as a judge or a juror.

Additional vehicle statistics are used to determine details such as break-over angle; this is the angle between the point at which the center of the tire touches the road and the driveway the vehicle is approaching, which might interfere with the vehicle's undercarriage. The statistics also yield the ground clearance at the lowest point of the vehicle. This allows the investigator/reconstructionist to determine which component of the underside of the vehicle would strike the ground first during a head-on impact. In the case of buses or trucks, the lowest point under the vehicle is used to determine if a pedestrian could be caught underneath the vehicle and could be dragged along as the vehicle was being driven down the road.

*Commentary: The worst case I have ever seen of a pedestrian being caught under a vehicle involved a woman who was thrown from a van after a sideswipe-type collision, and a second vehicle following the van started to run over the woman, and wedged her between the front bumper and the front tires, and dragged and rolled her along for 22 blocks.*

*This included passing through 12 different intersections with the road changing elevation by approximately 2 ft during the movement from one side of the intersection to the other. The driver of the vehicle never had an indication that he had been pushing this unfortunate pedestrian in front of his vehicle. Approximately 1 h later the driver was going to drive to a store for a take-out dinner and found the woman just forward of the bumper of his vehicle. He then called the police describing what he have found, assuming someone had put the body in front of his vehicle.*

Vehicle statistics are also used to determine the potential acceleration ability and braking capabilities of the vehicle. In addition, they describe the various components of the vehicle such as the type, load range, and size of tires used on the vehicle, and list the engine size, type of transmission (automatic or manual), and type and gearing of the rear axle, among other things. All these may become important to the investigator/reconstructionist as he/she proceeds to analyze the data available and to reconstruct the accident.

Much of this performance data can be found in automotive-oriented magazines such as *Car and Driver, Road and Track*, and others.

## Accident Intersection Data

Many state police agencies have developed a program that has copies of all reported accidents by cities, townships, and counties sent to the state police headquarters data information center. These data are coded by street, highway, or intersection; time of day and date; weather conditions; road conditions; direction of travel of both the vehicles; type of impact and severity of impact; occupants injured or killed; and maneuvers of the vehicle, i.e., turning right, left, or going straight through the intersection. The information is available for at least 5 years and sometimes longer.

Also, these data are generally used to determine if there is a problem with the roads or the intersections either by design or by maintenance, including such problems as bridge icing and road salting or sanding. Reports also may include the lighting at the location, and the number and type of traffic control devices.

Many county or city traffic improvement associations also have such data. These associations may use the information to determine frequency and severity of accidents, along with the usual other data to determine if there should be changes made in the design of the intersection, or in the traffic control devices. These associations are also an excellent source for information about the frequency of the accidents at a particular location in conjunction with the weather and road conditions during the specific time of year that the accident occurred.

## State Highway Department Photographs

Most state highway departments have a program of taking photographs of all state-built and -maintained highways every tenth of a mile or 528 ft. These photographs are very useful to the investigator/reconstructionist in determining not only the condition of the road prior to the accident but also any changes that may have been made to the road between the date of the photograph and the date of the accident. Information seen on these photographs includes potential blind areas from overgrowth of trees that are hiding stop signs, freestanding traffic signals, condition of the paved road surface, bumps and/or changes in the construction of the road, condition of the paved or unpaved shoulder areas, and many more details about the scene itself.

Furthermore, these photographs also include expressways and freeways. Road design dictates that there must be a clear area of at least 30 ft from the outside edge of the paved highway. This is to allow a driver who has been forced off the road to get sufficiently off the highway without being subjected to impacts with a tree or other man-made objects. This clear area is also useful to drivers of vehicles having an emergency on the road; they are able to get off the road, signal for help, change a flat tire, or maybe even repair the vehicle — again without being subjected to collision with another vehicle.

A 35-mm camera mounted in the center of a van takes the highway department photographs. The camera is attached to the odometer and exposes a single frame of film every 528 ft. This roll of film is then placed into the state highway department files and is held for use by those concerned. Copies of these photographs can be obtained by requesting documentation from these highway departments. The requester must be sure to ask for only those photographs he/she deems necessary prior to and after the location of the point of impact and the rest of the accident. Generally, a tenth of a mile prior to the impact and a tenth of a mile past the point of rest are good guidelines for the number of photographs that the investigator/reconstructionist might require. These photographs are in color and are usually very expensive.

## Construction Zone

Each and every highway construction project requires a construction drawing of precisely how the highways are to be built. As in all projects, the finished product does not always match the original drawings. Therefore, it behooves the accident investigator/reconstructionist to check the "as built" highway drawings from the highway department. Many times there are errors on the drawing or at the scene in the location of the sewers, sewer covers, placement of highway signs, traffic signals, and even locations of turnarounds and exit lanes.

Other regions the investigator/reconstructionist must investigate with respect to the state highway department drawings include the crown of the road, and areas where the road shifts from three lanes to two lanes to determine if the length of the shift lane is sufficient. In addition, he/she must look for the design width of the shoulders, the width of the paved shoulders, and/or the gravel shoulders up to the property lines. Each of these areas can assist the investigator's/reconstructionist's client in determining whether or not to add the state highway department into the civil proceedings.

A considerable number of accidents occur on or near the approach to a construction zone. To determine if these construction zones have been laid out properly, the investigator/reconstructionist must request the state engineers' drawings that lay out the closure of specific traffic lanes leading up to the start of the construction.

The American Association of State Highway and Transportation Officials (AASHTO) codes have specific standards that must be adhered to in developing these construction drawings. When the investigator/reconstructionist obtains these drawings from the state highway department, he/she will then locate each of the barrels and/or cones that have been specified by location and number. The location of the barrels and cones and other equipment in use at the site must be placed on the scale drawing on a separate overlay. In this manner, during a deposition and/or trial the reconstructionist is able to pull the overlay off the main drawing showing what the site would have been prior to the start of the construction and the problems the construction zone caused. The use of these state drawings as an addition to the reconstruction drawing provides an excellent overview of the new path of the vehicles during the construction. These new paths many times have built-in problems that are not apparent until they are brought to the fore by the reconstructionist.

*Commentary: In a recent construction case inference was made that a right-turn-on-red sign on the cross street entering a construction zone should have been removed. In addition, the cross street entered at an obtuse angle to the main road. This forced the driver to look over his left shoulder to see oncoming traffic.*

*In addition, the normal right-hand turn lane leaving the main street was blocked by the construction equipment and cones; therefore, the right-hand turn traffic was now proceeding down the normal right-hand through lane. The construction zone also closed off the through traffic across the main highway boulevard. Thus, the only way possible for the cross street traffic to cross the entire boulevard was to make a right-hand turn. The state highway engineers also left the first turnaround lane past the intersection open, and it was less than 300 ft from the cross street traffic.*

*Any cross street traffic wanting to proceed across the entire boulevard had to make a right turn to the turnaround lane, next make a left turn going the opposite direction on the main highway, cross three lanes of traffic on that highway, and then take another right-hand turn to continue in the original direction.*

*The one problem the state highway department did not foresee was that a motorcycle would be lost to the cross street traffic line of sight due to the right-hand turn lane being forced inward by one lane. In this particular case, the cross street driver looked at the oncoming traffic, saw what he thought was an opening in the traffic, proceeded to make a right-hand turn, and was struck from the rear by a motorcycle. The driver of the motorcycle flew over the handlebars and struck his head on the rear door of the sports utility vehicle (SUV). Had the right-hand turn sign been removed and the turnaround lane closed, this accident would never have happened because the cross traffic would have had to wait for a green traffic signal before starting its mandatory right turn, thus ensuring no hidden traffic and a potential accident. The turnaround lane being farther from the intersection would have given the cross street traffic more time to cross the three lanes to make another right turn to continue on the cross street and to eliminate another potential accident situation.*

*Therefore, the accident investigator/reconstructionist must always search for ways to minimize or eliminate the possibility of the original accident by not overlooking inherent problems that are almost always generated with what many believe to be the solution to the original problem.*

Many times the investigator/reconstructionist is given a set of on-scene photographs showing the accident having taken place at or near a state highway sign. These state highway signs are a good method by which the investigator/reconstructionist can locate the final resting point of an accident. They must, however, bear in mind that the location of these highway signs is not always accurate. Many times they may have been placed several feet from their original location. Once again, drawings of traffic signage can be obtained from the state highway department. These drawings show the original location of the state highway department signs. Unfortunately, there may have been other accidents in the same location as the accident under investigation that would require checking the state police accident logs or the state maintenance department to determine if a prior accident had occurred there.

If this has happened, another method may be of assistance to the investigator/reconstructionist when investigating the scene. State highway department signposts are driven into the ground and a second post is bolted to the post that has been driven into the ground. This is to hold down the costs of replacing signposts after an accident. The bolted posts break off much easier, allowing a second post and sign to be installed just by bolting them back onto the original driven post. Look for bent posts in the ground or the remains of bent posts if entire new signs have been installed.

## Power and Telephone Poles

Electrical power and telephone companies place wooden poles along highways for their use in delivering power and telephone services to the consumer. There are many of these posts erected in each community. To keep track of these posts by location and age, the companies have either stamped identification numbers right into the wood or have nailed a zinc-coated metallic tag to the post. Aluminum or steel posts usually have a tag installed on them. In cases where there is a possibility that the overhead street lights were not functioning on the night of an accident, it is possible for the investigator/reconstructionist during his/her on-scene investigation to copy each of these numbers from the posts. A request for documentation to view the power company or the telephone company layouts or listings can yield a drawing showing the location of these posts.

In addition, a reconstructionist should request a maintenance log for each of the posts that hold overhead lights in the accident area. The maintenance log indicates when the overhead lamps have been or will be changed. If the on-scene investigator has not taken photographs of the poor or missing traffic lighting conditions, the reconstructionist must do so at the scene in the evening at approximately the same time and date the accident occurred, if possible.

Once he/she has established the correct site and the direction the vehicles were traveling on the night of the accident, he/she must photograph not only the lights that may be missing or damaged but also how those affect the driver's ability to see oncoming traffic or pedestrians in the area where the lights are not working.

The same procedure must be used when photographing traffic lights in a particular area where the lights may have been hidden by overgrowth of trees, or which may have a smaller diameter than that required by the department of transportation for the road in that particular state. Both still photographs and videotape should be taken at all times.

These power and telephone poles also serve a second purpose with respect to the reconstructionist's scale drawing of the accident scene. Most of the time reconstructionists may not get involved in an accident until a few weeks or up to several months have passed. During that time period there may have been road construction, scenery changes such as trees being cut down or growing much larger than originally photographed, houses being built in the location, or even hedges planted or removed. Any of these may have been the original on-scene investigator's reference point.

The new reconstructionist visiting the site for the first time, trying to use the photographs taken several months prior to his/her involvement, cannot understand why he/she cannot find the original reference point. Electrical power and telephone poles are rarely changed, except when they are struck during an accident or need replacement for maintenance purposes. Therefore, it is necessary whenever possible to use an electrical power pole, a telephone exchange box, or a telephone pole as the original reference point when developing data for a detailed scale drawing.

When it is necessary to replace a pole, a second pole is located as close to the original as possible due to the power and electrical lines lengths. The ground around the pole requires several months, if not more than one growing season, for the clay or sand that has been pulled to the surface when drilling a hole to be replaced with grass or weeds. The clay around the base of the pole is a clear indication of a replacement due to an accident. These facts must be borne in mind by the investigator during an on-scene investigation.

## State Maintenance Records, Roads, and Trucks

All state highway departments keep maintenance records of the roads they maintain as well as the trucks they use to maintain those roads. Once again, a request to the state highway department for these documents can provide the reconstructionist with a plethora of information. Highway maintenance is very costly, especially salting and/or sanding of roads. Many accidents occur on state highways that have not been salted properly, or have not been salted in a reasonable length of time after the ice or snow has fallen. These highway maintenance logs show the number of trucks used on specific highways, the pounds or tons of salt or sand that have been used, and the hour and day of the accident.

Many times the outcome of an accident reconstruction is dictated by the fact that insufficient salting or sanding of the highway occurred when it should have been done by the state's own standards and specifications.

Maintenance of the state highway department trucks can also be an issue in some accidents. Requests should be made for their records for at least 2 to 3 years prior to the date of the accident. The reconstructionist should look for patterns of repairs of brakes, suspension systems, steering systems, engines, and lighting and ignition systems. Each of these patterns can indicate to the reconstructionist what work has been done and should have been done with respect to the involvement of the state truck in the accident.

As an example, consider a state highway department truck that slams into the rear and side of another vehicle as it is following a turnaround section of the highway. This would indicate one of two situations. Either the road was not salted or sanded properly or the brakes of the truck had failed. Both situations must be considered and looked into by the reconstructionist until one or the other can be disregarded.

## Aerial Photographs

When an accident scene covers a large area, it may be necessary to obtain an aerial view of the accident scene. If it occurs within a major city, then it is usually possible to obtain an aerial view that was taken by the city for its own purposes. These are generally very good and show good detail of the streets, buildings, and other major landmarks.

If the accident occurred outside of a major city, it may be necessary to hire an aerial photographer to get photographs that are needed. Generally speaking, aerial photographs should be 500 and 1000 ft above the area of interest. Make sure the aerial photographer knows that the camera lens must be parallel to the earth when taking the photograph, and that the height at which the photograph was taken also must be marked.

These aerial photographs are helpful when an accident occurs such as a long police chase where it would be impossible or it may take an inordinate amount of time to obtain the data by paper and pencil or even electronic means. In addition, the photographs are also useful when determining the route of emergency vehicles such as emergency medical service (EMS) trucks, and fire and ambulance vehicles when they are involved in a collision.

The photographs also assist with plotting the intended route of a participant prior to an accident. This information allows the reconstructionist to determine if it was possible for the accident participant to proceed as described in his/her statement or deposition. These statements are not always compatible with the route on an aerial map.

*Commentary: Aerial photographs of a site were used in Alaska where the accident involved a snowmobile and a truck with a snowplow. Of course, there were no streets, but there were paths that were used as streets between the various buildings and the major streets in the town. The aerial map was very helpful in showing the potential movement of both vehicles prior to the impact. On that particular area map, there were not only power lines and communication lines but also drinking water pipes aboveground because of the depth of the frost line in Alaska.*

## Vehicle Information

Those investigators/reconstructionists who get involved in litigation involving the automobile companies need to know the jargon of the automobile designers and/or engineers when requesting certain documentation for review.

### Full Size Body in White Drawings

These drawings are made by the body layout specialists to show the positions of the 5th, 50th, and 95th percentile anthropomorphic dummies in their normal seating positions for all seating positions in the vehicle. The drawings indicate to the investigator/reconstructionist the amount of the headroom clearance that the occupant would have during a forward force impact. Anchor positions for all the lap and shoulder belts used and the locations of the inner door panels and the tumblehome of the vehicle are also shown.

These details are important when determining the distance from the occupant's head to the side glass windows in the front and rear seating positions, and the position of the armrest with respect to the vulnerable internal organs of the occupant in case of a side impact.

The request for these documents must be very precise with respect to the year, make, and model of the particular vehicle involved in the collision. Otherwise, the request can be denied as being too overly broad in its scope. A great deal more information is revealed by these drawings. It is up to the investigator/reconstructionist to determine how much of this information is necessary for the reconstruction.

## Preproduction Defect Reports

This is the report in which many automobile companies list the problems that have been seen and need resolution on the preproduction run of vehicles that have not been fixed prior to the date of the full production of the vehicle. This information may be important from the standpoint that all vehicles may not have been repaired prior to the time that the deficiency was found on the preproduction run. The vehicle under investigation may contain this deficiency and would assist the client in determining the manufacturing or design product defect.

## Warranty Reports

Every manufacturer of every product — automotive or consumer — has a warranty reporting system. Its purpose is to help manufacturers improve their products as well as repair design or manufacturing defects. The accident investigator/reconstructionist involved in any type of product analysis needs to know the warranty history of that particular product and the potential or existing product defects.

Many of these defects may have been repaired on an as-required basis, or at the request of the customer, if he/she knows the repair is available at the dealer where the item was purchased. The consumer who is unaware of these defects can be using the product in a manner in which it was designed to be used and can still end up with a serious injury. By knowing the warranty history, the investigator/reconstructionist can assist the client in determining the product defect.

## Customer Service Bulletins

Most, if not all, manufacturers from time to time issue a service or technical bulletin to its dealers, or in some cases to the consumer, concerning problems with their products. Depending on the source and severity of the problem, these bulletins may be available to the general public. Technical bulletins are generally sent to dealers only. This is usually due to the technical nature of the necessary repair, best understood by trained technicians.

Technical and/or service bulletins are, and have become, very important to the reconstructionist. These bulletins describe the problem and the designated fix for the problem as determined by the design and/or manufacturing engineers.

Once again, the owner of the vehicle or product may not have knowledge that such a problem exists, especially if it is not considered safety related. This information can be requested from the manufacturer through a request for production of documents, but many times it is available through the Internet at various Web sites of the manufacturer or watchdog associations such as the Insurance Institute for Highway Safety. This institute publishes a monthly bulletin with such information.

## Recall Campaigns

For several years now the general public has heard the term *recall* for all types of products. These recalls can include everything from automobiles to hot water heaters.

*Commentary: A few years ago, hot water heater manufacturers used plastic tube inserts at the entrance to the hot water line. With time this plastic tube disintegrated, allowing the broken pieces to enter the hot water system of the clothes washer. These pieces ended up clogging the filter in the hot water hose that goes to the laundry machine. As a result there was very little input of water into the machine, necessitating a call to the repairman. A local repairman mounted a recall campaign with several of his colleagues and the manufacturers are now replacing these hot water tubes.*

Recall campaigns in the automotive industry are usually conducted by the National Highway Transportation Safety Agency in Washington, D.C., after a series of complaints has been received from owners of the particular automobile involved with the problem. These recall campaigns, done voluntarily by the manufacturers, are very expensive and can tarnish their images with their customers. Companies do not look forward to this type of information becoming known to the public.

Therefore, recall data can be very difficult to obtain. However, the investigator/reconstructionist needs to know about this information if he/she is working in the automotive field. Extensive use of the Web and other such sources of information can provide the data necessary for use in assisting the reconstructionist's client.

## Endurance Testing

Many, if not all, products on the market today are tested in a variety of ways. Many have to meet standards from different organizations for use by the consumer. These tests are mandatory and must be completed before sale of the product. All manufacturers may not do endurance testing, which involves the product being subjected to normal use for an extended period of time. This time period may be governed by the designers' determination of the extended normal use of the product. Testing may also be conducted to determine the exact extent of the product life.

Many times these are called product life tests. Manufacturers use these data to determine product changes or development of new products for consumer use. The investigator/reconstructionist can use this information to determine if the defect found at the inspection of the vehicle is in any way related to the endurance of the vehicle. This information is obtained through request for production of documents.

## Laboratory Testing

To ensure that the complete vehicle can meet all standards imposed on the manufacturer, it is necessary to test the components of the product in the laboratory for compliance prior to installation. This method is more economical than crash testing an entire vehicle and leads to better designed and manufactured components. If the reconstructionist determines that there is a defect in a particular component, then it behooves him/her to request from the manufacturer the laboratory testing data of that particular component along with the full-scale testing of the vehicle. Be sure to request the test setup, the test procedure, the raw data, the completed test reports, and all before and after photographic material.

## Federal Motor Vehicle Safety Standards Test Results

The National Highway Transportation Safety Agency requires a significant number of tests to be conducted on today's vehicles before they are sold to the general public. The description of these tests can be found in the CPR title 49 issued by the Department of Transportation.

Each vehicle manufacturer must show compliance with each individual standard. This is done by signing a compliance document and placing it on file with the government. There is a required period of time that the manufacturer must keep these documents in its files. Therefore, the investigator/reconstructionist can obtain copies for his/her perusal after the lawsuit has been filed with the court and while discovery is ongoing. The request is made in the usual manner.

## Barrier Crash Tests

One of the major tests conducted by the vehicle manufacturer is called a barrier crash test. It can be conducted with or without instrumented anthropomorphic dummies as occupants and use of experimental or preproduction components. The crash tests are photographed both by high-speed motion picture film and by 35-mm still photographs. Then a significant number of data points are recorded on electromagnetic tape and transferred to paper for review by the test and design engineers.

These data can be very important to the reconstructionist because they show the trajectory of the occupants during the head-on barrier crash, and the crush characteristics of the various interior and exterior components.

*Commentary: In my professional career, one case stands out in which the crash film was extremely important. A small vehicle was rear ended by a larger vehicle in an offset rear-end impact. The impact was to the left rear of the small vehicle, causing a severe deformation to that side of the vehicle. This pushed the rear seat interior trim panel forward toward the front of the vehicle. This dislodged a small interior steel trim molding that was used to cover the gap between the headliner and the interior door area. The steel molding was pushed forward, rotated laterally halfway across the vehicle, and ended up lodged between the driver's seat and the console with the end pointing upward toward the rear of the driver's head. The driver was pitched rearward, then forward, and rearward again; on the second rearward movement the area of the rear of the occupant's head that meets the neck was pushed down on top of the edge of the steel molding, piercing the skull and the brain and resulting in a fatal injury.*

*A request was made for the rear-end barrier crash tests conducted by the vehicle manufacturer and an analysis of those tests. One test in particular showed that the same molding had been displaced when the testing was conducted in the manufacturer's facility. This discovery was a turning point in the case.*

There are many different tests conducted by the manufacturer and they generally include a head-on barrier crash, an angled barrier crash either right or left, a moving barrier crash to the rear and to either one or both sides of the vehicle, and a rollover test, just to name a few. When requesting these data, be sure to request the high-speed films, the photographic stills, the raw data, the finished report, and the test procedures as outlined by the test facility.

## Independent Agencies

There are independent agencies and consultants that do accident investigations for the automobile manufacturers. These individuals may do the work on behalf of the manufacturer or by contract with some other organization.

Review periodic journals or magazines devoted to accident investigation or reconstruction for lists of these various organizations.

The investigator/reconstructionist who is willing to study and learn as he/she practices the craft should take time to read and study these periodicals. Many of these journals carry lists of recall campaigns, product defects, notes from specific or unusual accidents, and new techniques and equipment used in accident investigation. Also, never underestimate the use of the Internet in locating these details from individual consultants or agencies.

The National Transportation Safety Agency conducts crash testing of its own each year on various model vehicles to determine if they meet the Federal Motor Vehicle Safety Standards (FMVSS). Independent testing laboratories or organizations conduct these tests and the data are available to the general public. Make use of these data whenever possible because they are another source of information to assist the reconstructionist and client.

## Database Analysis

Several organizations collect accident information data and store them in a database for use in developing statistics of every known type. The usefulness of this information is evident by the widespread development of this type of database. The medical community has used it to determine the type and severity of injuries in vehicle accidents. These data help medical personnel develop fast response systems such as in the use of helicopters in medical emergency situations.

Insurance companies also use this information to compare the damage to different types of vehicles for repair costs. Undoubtedly this also comes into play when setting the insurance rates for various types of vehicles.

Researchers use database analysis in a variety of ways. Comparisons have been made between model years to determine the effects of various safety devices that were added to the vehicles during the intervening years. This necessarily involves both the type and severity of injuries the occupants sustained in the same type of crashes. Work has been done comparing the use of seat belts alone with seat belts and an air bag system in the vehicle. This can be very useful to any investigator with his/her particular investigation in trying to analyze if the use of an air bag would have assisted the occupant.

## Medical and Scientific Journals

The investigator/reconstructionist who may be involved with occupant kinematics and associated injuries may be interested in these types of journals. The National Safety Council has a large data bank of accident information. It includes products, plant safety, and vehicle information.

Membership is a requirement for the council to search its database for any information on a particular product or other data. The council also publishes a yearly journal covering accident information on deaths and injuries of the American public from all sources starting with disease and going all the way through to death by natural causes; and on injuries in vehicular accidents in the workplace, or in the home. This information may become useful in certain situations of a particular reconstruction with respect to statistics necessary to develop a particular scenario. The investigator/reconstructionist should consult such professional organizations as the Society of Automotive Engineers, the American Association for Automotive Medicine, the American Medical Association, and medical journals specific to a particular area of the body that may have been injured in the specific accident being investigated.

*Comment: I have found the journal entitled Trauma to be very useful over the years, especially when looking at back issues that many times contain specific references to injuries sustained in vehicular collisions. The local medical school library is an excellent source of these journals. The Internet has a specific location where searches can be conducted for information, along with case studies on what they may be consider to be unusual medical injuries.*

## Data Research Companies

There are companies today that specialize in collection of information from all fields of endeavor. Many times the reconstructionist may be involved in determining if the vehicle manufacturer has complied with the FMVSS standards. There are several companies in Washington, D.C., that collect data concerning the responses of the automobile companies to proposed legislation on new standards by the federal government. These responses can sometimes lead the reconstructionist to a certain scenario concerning a defect in the vehicle that was involved in the accident. The cost of such information must be weighed against the severity of the injury before a request is made to these organizations for the particular data.

## Human Factor Data

From time to time it may be necessary for the investigator/reconstructionist to obtain certain data about the occupant with respect to what is specifically known as human factors. These could include physical size such as height, weight, and particular lengths of certain portions of the body, namely the lower limbs and upper arms. In some cases the seated height may be necessary to determine if the occupant of a vehicle could reach a particular component that was damaged during a collision.

There may be other data that the investigator is interested in determining such as the muscle strength of a particular size of an occupant — the pulling, lifting, reach, head size, foot and hand size, and grip strength. A great deal of this information has been made available through the SAE recommended practices or standards. There is a new cooperative effort between members of the automobile industry as well as the clothing and other industries that cater to consumer needs, to determine the physical size of the adult population in the world today. This effort may require several years before its completion but it is the best study that has been made in the past several years. Its effects could be far reaching in all aspects of human life, considering that the average size of the adult male in the U.S. has been growing approximately 1 in. every 10 years. This could mean larger vehicles, larger clothes, and different style furniture for the home and the workplace. The human factor experts need to study the data for the interaction of man and environment to determine if they are working on the best situations to avoid injuries to themselves due to the changes in the size of the American population.

There are other standards that different types of investigators/reconstructionists may be involved with in their particular practice. These could include the Occupational Safety and Health Agency (OSHA). These standards govern the workplace and equipment for personal safety. Each state also has its own occupational safety and health agency with standards that can be purchased by the accident investigator/reconstructionist for personal use.

The Building Owners and Construction Association, BOCA, standards have been adopted by most U.S. cities. The standards govern not only the commercial building but also residential construction. They include electrical, fire, and construction techniques and design standards for buildings built in many U.S. cities. Those reconstructionists involved in accidents on commercial or residential property find this a very useful source of information.

# Trade Associations

There is a trade association for every industry in the U.S. today. Many of these industries have specialized trade associations for a particular portion of their industry. These associations publish guidelines or recommended practices for business in their industry.

These guidelines and recommended practices are useful for the reconstructionist to determine if the particular product he/she is investigating meets those particular industry requirements. The information is available in the form of bulletins or other pamphlets in each of these associations.

*Commentary*: *As an example, information was required for a particular case involving an asphalt highway. I found the trade association and requested information concerning the construction of asphalt highways and was inundated with about 2 in. of information. Sometimes you get more than you ask for or can use.*

## Professional Associations

There is a professional organization or association for each group of individuals working in government or industry today. Associations within associations are for specific groups of people who believe it is necessary to associate with professionals working in their highly specialized fields of endeavor. These associations can be very helpful to the reconstructionist looking for experts who can assist in particular analysis and reconstruction. In addition, reference books in any public library list both trade and professional associations in the U.S. and in some cases international addresses may be available.

*Commentary*: *I once had a case where there were several pieces of wood embedded into the crevices of the damaged vehicle. The site inspection showed fresh marks on both the wooden telephone pole as well as several different types of trees in the area. I was unable to determine on a visual examination if this wood was from any of the trees or the telephone poles. A contact with the forester's professional association led me to a local expert who reviewed the wooden samples from the vehicle and determined that the vehicle had impacted both the telephone pole and several of the trees. This information assisted me in completing the path of the vehicle during its rolling and tumbling before it came to rest.*

Do not hesitate to seek out new sources of information whenever the need arises. The reconstructionist may be surprised and pleased at what is found.

# Deposition and Courtroom Appearance

# 17

"As a rule, the more bizarre a thing is the less mysterious it proves to be."
**Sherlock Holmes**
*The Redheaded League*

In 1981, a panel of communications experts met at the American Academy of Forensic Sciences meeting to discuss the topic of "Effective Expert Testimony." The author of this text has not found any other articles as clear as the ones presented at this meeting for assisting the expert to effectively communicate his/her opinion in a deposition or in a court of law. When the author of this text disagrees with some areas of thinking expressed in the articles, he describes those disagreements under the various sections.

The first article gives the investigator/reconstructionist some solid basic information on how and when to use videotape effectively.

## Expert Witness and Use of Videotape Recordings[1]

Excerpts from Reference 1 follow\*:

> A couple of years ago I gave a presentation to a group of communication researchers and lawyers on videotape research. At that time, videotaping was experimental and not a widely accepted procedure for recording depositions, lineups, and taping of full trials. That particular group was interested in research methods and results. They were especially interested in

\* Reprinted with permission from Reference 1, copyright American Society for Testing and Materials, 100 Barr Harbor Drive, West Conshohocken, PA 19428.

how juries reacted to the use of videotape in the courtroom when the entire trial was taped, or videotape was simply used for depositions. I believe that members of the American Academy of Forensic Sciences would be primarily interested in the best ways to persuade a jury, and the best ways to express expertise to assist jurors in understanding some aspects of a case. Videotape is becoming a more popular method for achieving these goals.

I would therefore like to summarize briefly some of the research on the use of videotape in the courtroom and also to summarize some legal issues involved. Finally, I would like to center on some of the specific uses of videotape for the expert witness. My interest in this area developed in the early 1970s. I was involved with research on jury decision making and created a videotape stimulus to test various factors that might affect that process. The effect of the following variables on decision making was studied: six versus twelve member juries, physical attractiveness, and litigant sex differences. I thought the area of most interest to the symposium participants would be the reactions to the use of videotape in the courtroom.

Some readers may be familiar with many advantages of using videotapes, particularly with depositions. Perhaps you have been deposed through videotape because transportation costs or time restraints prohibited your attendance at the trial. Also, if a witness was very ill the witness's deposition might have been videotaped and then played back at trial. In a recent court decision, *Chandler v. Florida [11]*, the Supreme Court of the United States held that a state may experiment with radio, television, and still photography in the courtroom, in criminal trials in spite of the defendants' objections. This case has encouraged the use of videotape technology.

***Commentary***: *Note that this article was written in 1983.*

## Major Studies

Various communication researchers have explored juror reaction to the use of videotape and particularly how witness credibility is affected by using videotape. There was a major study done at Michigan State University studying live versus videotape trials, and black and white versus color videotape trials. The Michigan State team also studied the deletion of inadmissible material in videotape trials, and the editing techniques for deleting such evidence. Detecting witness deception in videotape presentations and production techniques were also studied.

*The Brigham Young University Law Review Vol. 2, 1975 [5]* issue included an excellent discussion of the BYU research in this area. Basically, what the Michigan State study concluded was that their findings failed to show that the *use of videotape trial materials produced any negative effects on juror response.* I think this conclusion is very significant as far as expert witnesses are concerned. One suggestion is that the use of videotape may make something more real to jurors than just discussion or the use of photographs.

*Commentary: I believe the use of videotape by an expert witness is much better than the attorney and one of his/her staff reading the deposition to the jury. The reason is that the expert witness modulates his/her voice and annunciates words when expressing an opinion much better than another person who has never seen the expert or heard his/her opinion given in the context of a deposition or trial testimony.*

## Expert Witness's Use of Videotape

Real or demonstrative evidence represents an attempt to supplement the witnesses' descriptions of things with actual portrayals of the subject matter. Videotape is considered real or demonstrative evidence and should be considered for use by expert witnesses.

In the expert witness's presentation one needs to clarify for the jurors the basic statements you are trying to communicate. Some of these statements tend to be very complicated, and although there may be a very careful and competent explanation, the use of additional techniques tends to enhance credibility and clarity.

*Commentary: I agree that the presentation by the expert witness must, by virtue of its technicality be communicated on a non-technical level to the jury or tryer of fact. Therefore, the expert witness must use common everyday language to make his/her point clear and concise to the jury. As an example, consider the idea of the coefficient of friction. Over the years I have developed a procedure, during the trial, by which I take a common ordinary eraser and draw it across the surface of the table. I then draw it across a small piece of smooth plastic, pointing to the amount of rubber left on the table vs. the amount left on the plastic surface. This would be equivalent to a tire stopping on a normal concrete surface vs. a smooth slick surface, which would be equivalent to a tire stopping on a grassy or even icy or snowy road. Thus this demonstrates the coefficient of friction is dependent on the two surfaces that come in contact with one another.*

Videotape has been used by expert witnesses to depict a day in the life of paraplegics, to show the difficulty of handling such simple tasks as bodily elimination. Simply describing the problem would not be as descriptive as a videotape portrayal.

In another example related to me by a lawyer, a wing fell off of an airplane and was found three miles away. The problem here was to show that the wing of the plane's structure was of sound design, and to demonstrate the relationship between that and the accident. What the lawyer did with the videotape in this situation, working with the expert witness and the videotape expert, was to show at various times and from various camera angles that the person flying the plane had to be exceeding the indicated structural possibilities for this airplane. Those who are experts in this technical area will understand that even more fully than I do, but from a juror's point of view it meant that they could see what had to happen in order for the wing to fall off.

An accident liability trial provides another example of the use of videotape. A man fell off a retractable four-wheel ladder. It was a three-step ladder, and the problem was to show whether the retractable wheels of the ladder were a defect in design. The expert witness discovered that when the ladder was pulled toward the person and then pushed away, the back wheels lined up and the ladder wheels did not retract fast enough as the ladder moved. What the videotape technician decided in talking with both the lawyer and the expert witness was that they needed to use a stuntman. The warning here is that taped evidence must not look too theatrical. Audiovisual techniques have generally not been allowed in court for this very reason.

*Commentary: I never allow a videotape in court that has a soundtrack on it. There are several reasons for this; primarily it is to eliminate the extraneous noise that is always prevalent at an inspection.*

*This could include traffic, other investigators discussing their points of view in a low voice, the cameraman giving instructions on pointing to a specific object or portion of a vehicle, or even the attorneys discussing some aspect of the case behind the cameraman but still within audio range of the camera's microphone. The use of a plug in the exterior microphone jack will eliminate this potential problem for the expert.*

*Another instance when I prefer no audio track on the videotape is during the deposition or trial testimony. I point out various aspects of the inspection of the scene or vehicle to the attorneys and/or jurors that I believe are important to the opinion being rendered. Extraneous voices in the background would only hinder the presentation and make it more difficult for the jury to concentrate on my remarks.*

## Pros and Cons of Videotape

What are the problems and the benefits in using videotape techniques? One problem is that care must be taken to guard against a "blood-and-guts" presentation. Some courts have not allowed the use of certain videotaping because of its sensationalism. This could occur in the "day in the life of" videotapes if discretion is not used. For instance, as mentioned above, it could be unpleasant to watch someone performing bathroom functions, and there are ways of videotaping this process so that it is not offensive. One final consideration is that the videotape must not perplex the jury. The objective is that it assist rather than confuse the jurors.

Basically, then, my major premise has been that the use of videotape may be an effective and beneficial way of enhancing credibility and clarifying issues. There are many examples of its successful use. The things that I have suggested may be done in many cases without great expense. Admittedly it is a controversial technique, but I would suggest that the expert witness discuss the use of videotape with the attorney involved in the case. A videotape expert might also be consulted. The expert witness seeks to clarify issues for the jury and videotape may assist in this effort.

***Commentary:*** *It is almost mandatory today for an expert witness to use videotape as well as still photographs. A color photograph only shows one particular point of a vehicle at a time, the front view instead of a side view instead of a rear view. Videotape can show the entire front of the vehicle while zooming into various damaged aspects of that portion of the vehicle.*

*As an example, the video photographer would take an overall view of the vehicle to establish its identity, would zoom into the windshield to show the fractures of the glass, zoom out and zoom in again to the front grille and headlight damage, and finally zoom in to show damage to the front bumper. All these views can be taken from the same position and maintain that the damage was to the front of the vehicle.*

*Still photographs establish the vehicle and are better used to show the details of fractured and bent metal as close ups. Better lighting can be used too, and more detail can be shown in a still photograph as opposed to close-up videotape view, which usually does not show as much detail.*

The second article deals with nonverbal communication, commonly known as body language. This process virtually goes unnoticed in the courtroom but is very powerful in the eyes of the jury or the tryer of fact. The judge, attorneys, and expert witness can in some cases change the outcome of a trial with their body language.

## Nonverbal Communication in Expert Testimony[2]

Excerpts from Reference 2 follow*:

> I want to talk about two large areas and, so you will know where I am going, I want to give you a little road map. First, I want to tell you about my research in nonverbal communication in the courtroom and, second, I want to share with you a day in the life of a communication consultant assisting a law firm in trial preparation. Specifically, I will isolate the work I do in preparing an expert witness to be effective during the trial. My purpose is

---

* Reprinted with permission from Reference 2, copyright American Society for Testing and Materials, 100 Barr Harbor Drive, West Conshohoken, PA 19428.

to try to help you be most effective. How can you as an expert witness be most effective? I have structured my entire paper to answer that question. But before I get to that answer, let me first share with you how I became interested and involved in the area of courtroom communication research. When I started my quest I wanted to answer the question. What is it that makes an expert witness credible? I discovered that scholars before me had found that there were many things involved in what our field calls source credibility.

In another paper, Professor Ken Serreno from the University of Southern California will identify the major components of source credibility of the expert witness. Unfortunately, research in this area has not explored the role that nonverbal communication can play in the determination of source credibility. Thus I found myself breaking new ground.

Kalven and Zeisel in their famous study on the American jury reported judges and juries were in agreement on the verdict 75% of the time. They used this statistic to suggest that this demonstrates that the jury understood the cases they were hearing most of the time. My observation of courtroom trials led me to suspect that the judge was indicating nonverbally how he felt about witnesses, each side's case, and so forth, and I suspected that some of the time the jury was influenced by these nonverbal indications and merely followed the judge. Of course this is a very difficult speculation to prove.

As an initial step, I hypothesized that if I could film the testimony of a witness and have the judge respond nonverbally both positively and negatively toward the witness in full sight of the jurors, I predicted that his or her credibility would go up or down depending on the judge's nonverbal behavior. *My findings confirmed my hypothesis.*

In assisting the trial preparation process, I first read all the depositions and interrogatories in the case so I have a good idea of the large picture and the major issues involved. With respect to choosing a jury, I prepare a profile of the ideal juror we are looking for and, from the jury pool list, we grade each prospective juror on various scales. In addition, I also will assist the witnesses in preparing their testimony. We put the witnesses on videotape and let them see themselves. We try to isolate their strengths and weaknesses on a communication level. Similarly we also videotape the attorneys making the opening and closing. Next I go to the trial and assist in the selection of the jury.

After the jury is seated, I observe the trial, in particular the jurors and their individual reactions toward particular witnesses. At the end of each day I give the attorneys a report on what happened in the courtroom from a communication perspective. We try to reinforce positive reaction and clarify any possible contradictions or confusing elements in our case and try to act as a shadow juror. But one of the most interesting parts of this process is how I assist expert witnesses in being most effective.

## Pretrial Preparation

The first thing we are looking for with the expert witness is that they be prepared. The first thing we do is brief the experts on the facts in the case. What is the full lay of our presentation? What are the issues? What are we trying to prove? Now, if you are called upon to be an expert witness, I suggest that you demand that information. Yes, demand to know it.

*Commentary: The expert should be prepared long before the trial itself. He/she must be prepared for the deposition and this of course would carry over to the trial. The attorney might be aware of certain facts from the opposing expert, which he/she may want you as his/her expert to clarify or announce if they are incorrect. Other than that the expert must be ready with all the facts that are needed to perform the reconstruction and to render an opinion long before the trial date itself.*

*It is interesting to note that I have on occasion refused to testify because I was not given full access to all the information I felt I was entitled to as the expert in the case. I agree wholeheartedly with Mr. Miller in that respect.*

*The attorney may walk away from the trial untarnished even if he/she loses but the expert may indeed lose credibility with other attorneys and judges. Remember, the details are the most important factors in the case. If the expert cannot see all the information, he/she may not be able to determine if the information being withheld contains any details that might be necessary for completion of his/her analysis and opinions.*

For those of you that have gone to trial and been "hung out to dry" because you were not told everything that was going on in the case, you will appreciate my suggestion. Extensive pretrial preparation will increase your effectiveness.

## Physical Appearance

The physical appearance of the experts, how they appear, and the color and kind of suit they wear is of great interest to the communication researcher. Additionally, we try to isolate on videotape any nervous habits or distractions that might distract the experts from their presentation so they can see them. The book *Dress for Success* by Molloy offers many helpful tips on effective dress.

*Commentary: Again, Mr. Miller and I agree on the appearance of the expert at trial. Mr. Molloy's book is very good and it will help the novice and expert in preparing for the courtroom. I would add the following: many men belong to a fraternal or social or even civic organizations, which they are very proud of. Unfortunately, the jurors may not agree with your choice of organizations. Therefore, I would suggest that any lapel pins, rings, or other distinguishing jewelry or ornaments that serve to demonstrate the symbol of that organization should not be worn in the courtroom. It must be remembered that you are acting for your client and for his/her client.*

*If the judge or jury takes a dislike to you as the expert because of another organization you belong to instead of listening to your expert opinion, you have done your client a disservice.*

## Establishing Qualifications

The first thing we do with expert witnesses is emphasize their expertise and so we ask for their qualifications; I would recommend to you that you not be humble. Share any and everything you can with your trial attorney. Presenting your qualifications is how the trial attorney can make you more credible in the eyes of the juror. The first thing that he probably will ask about are your qualifications as an expert. Now as hard as it may be to believe, I have met some modest expert witnesses whose arms I had to twist in order to get more information and data out of them.

Let me give you some idea of the things you should talk about. You should mention your education, any postdoctoral training, your work experience, any publications you have written, articles, and any professional societies you belong to. Most important is your expertness when it comes to the issue that you are going to be testifying about. Also, I think it is very critical that the attorney go through your qualifications with you and present them in open testimony. You may hear the other attorney say, "Your honor, I will stipulate that this witness is qualified." Do not let this stop your attorney from asking questions about your qualifications. It is important that the jury hear all those books and articles you have written. You want them to know that you are an expert because that is your power. The more expertise the jury perceives you possess, the more likely it will be that they will be persuaded by your testimony. Attention to physical appearance and establishing your qualifications will increase your effectiveness.

***Commentary:*** *When the client advises me that we are about to go to trial, I prepare a special document called a direct testimony. This document gives a synopsis of my education; any additional courses or seminars I have taken in my field of expertise; any previous work history; the professional organizations I belong to and the rank held in each organization, especially any officer positions; and a listing of the awards that may have been given to me, such as being listed in Who's Who in America.*

*I then list the technical papers I have published and describe with short paragraphs the facts of the accident, the inspections of the vehicle and/or site, the injuries of the individuals or occupants that were involved in the accident, a short reconstruction of the accident, and a short opinion. This gives the attorney client a yardstick that will allow him/her to tackle your qualifications on a basis you are familiar with so that you both are tracking together during the deposition or the trial testimony (Figure 17.1, at the end of chapter).*

## How to Describe the Research

How many of you have had the experience of putting the jury to sleep or boring them with too much detail? You must be very careful about this and try to present direct answers. I think the best kinds of answers that come from experts are the ones that are presented in the narrative fashion. You can talk for a while and the attorney can then ask another question and then you can continue further. Now I said do not bore them, but sometimes you do have to talk about the technical nature of your investigation or your test and here are some of the things that we like to include with the expert witness to make sure that what you say is credible. In short, what I am saying is that you want to impress them with your methodology. You want them to think that it is very valid. You should tell them how long you have looked into this. Secondly, you should say what you did. Which test did you perform? Thirdly, what was the rationale for doing the test? Why did you do this test and not some other test.

## Videotape — Visual Aids

I think that in some instances the videotape can be a very valuable tool in the presentation of your testimony. If it shows something in a dramatic manner or shows it better than what you would say, then the saying "a picture is worth a 1000 words" is very true here. If you can show your test on videotape, do not hesitate to do that. Also, if you can videotape your testimony before trial, you can iron out a lot of the problems with your statements. I would advise you though, in terms of using videotape for your presentation, to always have a backup system. We always have a second system standing by. Machines break down and there is nothing that makes a jury more angry than to sit there and wait while you have to correct the problem.

## Briefly State Overall Conclusion — Then Explain

The next thing I try to do is sensitize the expert witness to the ultimate issue in a case. When an attorney asks, "Have you reached a conclusion or opinion about the issue?" it is very critical that you just answer yes or no initially and give a short statement of what your conclusion is. Do not launch into an extensive rationale immediately, giving your whole presentation. Sum up your position at the end. Tell the jury your conclusion. "Yes, I thought there were grounds to feel that this was a definite manufacturer's error or whatever it is you are testifying about and then give your rationale and then explain how you arrived at that conclusion. It is critical that you give that short answer first so that your jury knows what point you are leading to. Once again, it helps the communication process because you say it more often. I would suggest that you find out what the jury instructions will be, because if you tailor some of your testimony and presentation to the instructions the jury will hear later, you are going to be more effective and helpful.

## Transcending Your Ego

I think someone outside the legal and medical profession needs to level with witnesses. My biggest problem working with experts has been their egos. Egos are a problem for a couple of reasons. I would remind experts that they are respected. They are very learned men and women, but still must ultimately work with the trial attorney. As an expert witness, you have got to work with the lawyer for your side. If you act like a prima donna or want to do it your way or say it your way that may be satisfying to you but you may not communicate effectively to the jury. My second point is that I think your goal should be to communicate to the jury. Remember that they are the ones that ultimately will say yes or no to you. They will grant adherence to your testimony or reject it.

*Commentary: I would disagree with the author at this point. He is correct concerning egos. My objection is not being able to say what you believe you need to do to make your point. It is imperative that you make the attorney aware you are working for him/her but he/she must understand why you need to do it your way before you go to a deposition or a courtroom. I have had the misfortune to be told by an attorney exactly what to say concerning my opinion.*

What they want and what you can give and stay within the bounds of your expertise and ethics are not necessarily the same. Remember, your reputation is on the line when you testify, not his/hers. Your credability, honor, and reputation are the only attributes you have going for you. Without them you can be called a "prostitute," an expert who says whatever he/she is asked to do. Once that word gets around your call rate may decrease dramatically. It is up to you.

Juries usually have less education than you. What does that mean in terms of tailoring your message so you communicate to them? Eliminate the unnecessary jargon. Experts may have a polysyllabic vocabulary, but using big words may not always be effective. Big words do not work in the courtroom unless you are trying to establish your credibility or to baffle the jurors. If your goal is to communicate, then try to do that. I have also noticed that a lot of experts try to talk down to the jury or the attorney. This can work against you as well. Some terminology can add to your credibility, but overdone, the big words may become counterproductive.

*Commentary: Once again the author and I agree. I, too, have seen many experts try to describe to the jury their field of expertise using the technical language of that field.*

*One thing I have learned about juries is that they have a lot of common sense. They can feel or have a sense for when an expert is trying to "snow them." It is necessary for the expert to use common language when describing the particular area of his/her expertise. There are many times when there are no common terms for a particular chemical or mechanical product. In that case, that terminology indeed must be used, but there can be some analogy used to indicate how that product is used.*

## Hypothetical Questions

A word about hypothetical questions for expert witnesses. How many of you have faced hypothetical questions? Should the attorney ask you how long you have thought about the hypothetical question that has just been presented, your reply should be, "I have thought about it for a couple of weeks." You can enhance your credibility in this way. This way it will not appear as if you are just "winging it" on the spot, but that you have studied and then seriously thought of the question. One word of caution, I am sure some of you had this happen to you. The other side's attorney pulls one or two facts out of the hypothetical question and asks if that changes your opinion. You should be careful about that.

*Commentary: Hypothetical questions can be a minefield to an expert witness. In preparation for deposition or trial, the expert should always try to analyze the case from the opposing expert's point of view. You must determine how you would handle the case if you were the expert on that side of the case. This allows you to think of the possible methods the expert might use to prove his/her point and therefore you would arm yourself with potential answers that the opposing counsel would ask you in the form of a hypothetical question. Be sure to look at the jury directly when answering a hypothetical question. Make sure you enunciate several times that this is a hypothetical question and then launch into an explanation, if possible, to answer the question. Do not be afraid to state that you have not considered that possibility but give a reason for that answer. An example might be the opposing counsel asking, "How would it affect your opinion if I were to tell you the driver the vehicle had a 2.0 blood alcohol level?" If you have no expertise in the effects of alcohol on the perception and reaction time of the driver then clearly state, "I am not an expert in that area and cannot give you opinion. However, it may have some effect but I cannot tell you how much that would be." You have honestly answered the question and have given a forthright answer.*

## Cross-Examination

How many of you fear cross-examination? How many of you get a little nervous about it or would rather not have it happen? How many of you have had some unpleasant experiences being cross-examined? How many have found cross-examination pleasant? What I try to do is warn the experts as to what is coming in cross-examination so that it is not unpleasant. First, there are usually questions about whether you are qualified in the area of dispute. You want to be sure that when you take on a trial, in fact, you are qualified! Secondly, in my experience, a lawyer occasionally will ask you about the qualifications of an opposing expertise or someone else in the field. Usually the answer is, "He is nice," or "He is learned."

You can hurt yourself by engaging in personal attacks on someone who is opposing you in the trial. The third area of cross-examination preparation is making our expert witnesses very knowledgeable about all the information in the trial. This helps make the experts' testimony more effective.

Another thing that you can expect in cross-examination is to be attacked for your bias. "How much are you being paid?" "How often do you testify?" "Which side?" "If you are making expert testimony a career, you may want to consider spacing out your presentation for both plaintiff and defendant. I am reminded of the Patty Hearst trial in which F. Lee Bailey went after one of the expert witnesses for being a "paid mouth" who will say anything!

## Handling Attack

There are other indirect ways the opposition will attack you. I think you can expect to be investigated. If you find yourself being subjected to a very strong attack by the other side, you should be flattered. That means you probably harmed their case pretty badly and they are worried. If they ask you a few polite questions you should assume that perhaps you are fairly inconsequential or they do not want to draw too much attention to you. But if you find a lawyer being very hard on you, you should be flattered. Another thing that you will be asked in cross-examination is to explain the nature of the disagreement between you and another expert. You should anticipate this. You should know who the others are and have an explanation ready for the question: "How is it that this other learned doctor who looked at the same set of facts came up with exactly the opposite conclusion?" Another word of caution about answers in cross-examination: you should answer exactly what is asked of you and not try to pontificate on the subject or volunteer more information than you were asked about. My article on cross-examination will help you better understand the goal and your role in the process.

The last thing that I have noticed is that some experts are belligerent. They decide that they are not going to cooperate with the attorney. Some experts are not going to answer the attorney's questions. "They are not going to give him an inch." I would encourage you not to act in this manner. It hurts you in the mind of the jurors. It makes you a little less credible. It often appears as if you have something to hide and of course the smart attorney will ask the judge to admonish you to answer the question and of course if that happens, your credibility decreases in some degree.

*Commentary: I have always considered cross-examination as an attack, as a challenge not only to my opinion but also my reputation and my credentials as an expert. In that manner I am not astonished when those types of questions have been asked. I am ready to defend myself. The author previously mentioned body language. I have watched other experts in court have an open and congenial appearance in their body language to the attorney client they work for and to the jury. When the opposing counsel starts the cross-examination, the expert crosses arms over his/her chest, grits teeth, and sets the jaw, assuming a posture that portrays to all who can see that he/she is ready to fight. This is incorrect and does not gain you any credence with the jury or the judge or for that matter with your own attorney client. It is difficult to maintain an open and congenial attitude when another individual is attacking you personally as well as professionally, but just like the duck in a rainstorm, you have to let it roll off your back and not let it bother you. Unfortunately for the novice expert, this open and congenial attitude comes only with practice and experience.*

*If you have adequately prepared your reconstruction and opinion, you firmly believe this is the only feasible scenario that could have taken place at the accident scene, you stick to your opinions, and do not to go beyond the limits of your expertise, you should not have any problems with the opposing counsel.*

*I might add a word of acknowledgment with the author's statement that once the opposing counsel decides to come at you with, as they say, "all guns blazing," you know that you have prepared a good case and have all but destroyed his/her chances of winning. When that has occurred to me, I have had a difficult time not smiling from the witness stand.*

## Summary

I have tried to show you that nonverbal communication in the courtroom is a little noticed, yet powerfully important part of the communication process. My research suggests that nonverbal communication might, under certain circumstances and conditions, change the outcome of a trial. Second and probably most importantly, I have tried to share with you the techniques and insights that I use as a consultant for law firms preparing for trial. I have explained pretrial preparation; the importance of physical appearance and establishing your expert qualifications; and how to describe your research, use videotape, state your conclusion, transcend your ego, answer hypothetical questions, and handle cross-examination.

## Nature of Jury Response to the Expert Witness[3]

The following is excerpted from Reference 3*:

My participation in this symposium stems from a long-standing interest in the subject of persuasion. The communication process that is specifically designed to influence human behavior, belief, and action has always fascinated me. While it may seem a somewhat remote approach, I want to start with an example from a political context. Briefly I want to discuss a theory of persuasion I have evolved over a 20-year study, then apply it to a particular case that I observed, and finally, I would like to make one or two comments about modern mass media and the courts.

My first major study was of the 1960 Presidential campaign and I found that a large percentage of the American electorate did not really understand the issues in the campaign. They did not understand gross national product, free-floating exchange rates, and inverse ratios of economic deprivation. The diction and jargon used by the major Presidential candidates was often unintelligible and failed to communicate any real information to the mass electorate. The net effect of the 1960 campaign was that the winner of the Presidency, John Kennedy, persuaded about 8 to 10% more voters than did Richard Nixon during the campaign period and the content of the issues did not seem to make any difference in what was going on persuasively.

In a face-to-face communication there is a large quantity of information, some of which we traditionally designate as the message, the verbal component that is the subject of the communication. There is also a large, but extremely difficult to catalog, quantity of information that I call the paramessage. This is verbal and nonverbal information emanating from the source and the environment that is peripheral to the subject matter of the communication. When the content of the message is meaningful, the message can drive the persuasive process. But for one reason or another that content is not always meaningful, and when it is not, the focus of attention shifts away from the message to the paramessage. If you study the communication carefully, you usually can discern whether the focus has been on the paramessage, on these peripheral kinds of information, or on the central content of the communication — the message. If there has been a persuasive effect, it can often be traced to the latter or to the former.

In 1960 John Kennedy did not convince more people that his economic and foreign policies and social programs were better than those of Richard Nixon. What he did do was convince the majority of the persuadable voters that he was a more interesting, more attractive, and more knowledgeable individual than his opponent, and this made the difference in the outcome of the election.

As I began to examine other kinds of communications, I found this phenomenon to be broadly applicable. In 1966 I had occasion to become interested in a particular legal controversy because it seemed to be a very good case to further investigate this theory. The case was the Watts Voiceprint trial: the first attempt in California to introduce what is called "voicegram" or "voiceprint" evidence. If you are not familiar with the technique, it is a process whereby a sound spectrograph produces on electrosensitive paper a series of shadings that are sometimes intense, sometimes very light, and often vague in definition. These images represent specific sound features of a voice and the theory behind voice identification is that no two voices are absolutely alike. If you can identify graphically the peculiar sounds of an unknown voice and you can match them with a known voice, you can thereby identify the source.

In this trial, the entire case hinged on the identification of the voice of the defendant. There was an audio tape that contained admissions of arson committed during the Watts riots; however, CBS News made the tape and when the identity of the source was requested, CBS refused to provide it. The prosecution enlisted the aid of a voiceprint expert who made spectrograms from a known exemplar tape recording of the defendant's voice that could not be introduced into evidence for other reasons, and compared them with spectrograms of the unknown voice on the tape. He concluded they were the same, and the prosecution then sought to introduce the voiceprint expert and the voiceprint testimony as a means of identifying the voice on the CBS tape. The trial was originally expected to last two or three weeks; it went almost seven and the bulk of the time was spent hearing expert testimony on the validity of voiceprint identification.

The usual test for the introduction of evidence by a new technology is whether or not it has achieved general acceptance in the scientific community of which it is a part. One of the difficulties in the Voiceprint case was that nobody quite knew to what field the technique properly belonged, and a large number of experts from different disciplines, for example, physics, linguistics, phonetics, and so forth were called to testify three for the prosecution and seven for the defense. The judge made a critical error in the case. He should have ruled on the basis of all the testimony whether the technology had achieved acceptance in the scientific community, but he did not. Instead, he admitted the voiceprint evidence and let the jury make that decision. This was later found to be reversible error and the conviction was overturned on appeal.

The admission of the evidence, however, allowed me to question the jurors afterwards as to how they reacted to all of this highly technical testimony. I interviewed eight members of the jury and what I learned reinforced the conclusion I had reached in studying political communications. I asked each member of the jury which witness impressed him or her the most and one witness continually emerged as the most effective in the entire case. He was from Stanford University, was extremely articulate, his hair was short and trim, he wore glasses and a brown business suit, and presented himself in a very conservative and positive way. What struck me about the jury's reaction to this witness was the universal perception that he was "a real scientist.... Some of the others looked like hippies." "This guy was a real scientist ... I could tell," were typical comments.

I had talked with this witness and the defense attorney during the course of the trial and at one point the attorney expressed some concern that his testimony was overburdened with technical language and was going over the heads of the jurors. The witness commented that he thought that would probably help rather than hurt his effectiveness, and he was right. After the trial I asked the jurors a series of questions to see whether they had understood the basic technology of voiceprint identification. I asked if they knew what a format or a frequency response was and whether they had understood the argument about the theoretical dot (the size of the point of electrical contact on the electrosensitive paper).

As it turned out, the jury comprehended very little about the technical aspects of voiceprint identification. Much of the testimony was simply too complex or too confusing and the jury responded in the same way as the voters in the 1960 Presidential campaign. Not really understanding the "message," they shifted their focus to something they could understand — the obvious personal and professional attributes of the witnesses themselves. What happened in the Voiceprint trial was a microcosm of what had happened in the larger political context and it convinced me that merely analyzing the message is not a realistic way of assessing what is influencing people, particularly when the communication involves technical experts and technical knowledge that is not easily translatable into terms that a jury can be made to understand. Then it is the manner of presentation rather than the matter presented that seems to make the difference.

Obviously, this does not apply to all expert testimony. Doubtlessly many of you are familiar with the ballistics tests in which bullets are rotated and you can see the markings match up perfectly or fingerprint overlays where you can see the exact match, pore for pore, break for break. That kind of graphically precise evidence can be made very clear to a jury. The problem with voiceprint evidence was that it did not have that kind of precision or specificity, and that can also be a problem in other fields, for example, psychiatry. In those instances, it becomes the personal characteristics, the peripheral information, that makes the difference. When you begin to catalogue this kind of peripheral data you are discussing factors such as fluency, vocal inflection, appearance, and the like. Some jurors reacted negatively to what they perceived as a "hippy" orientation of some very distinguished university faculty members. They thought that was not the way scientists ought to appear. The attitude or manner or confidence a witness projects is also part of this message. Voiceprint jurors commented on what they saw as a "fussy" quality of one of the witnesses and they did not think it helped the case. They did not have much confidence in him.

There are other characteristics like this and they are situation specific. It is impossible to say what will be operative in every case but if you examine a particular configuration of persuasive communication, you can begin to unravel little factors that made it effective as well as those that operated adversely. Peripheral information can emanate from the source and also from the message itself, not what is being said but ancillary aspects such as the order of ideas, the clarity of organization, and the specificity of the information. Some witnesses chose to be deliberately general. The one who was seen as the most scientific was inordinately specific. The more detailed he became, the less the jury understood, but they were impressed that he was being so specific and they appreciated the comprehensiveness of his knowledge. So there are characteristics of what is being said, peripheral characteristics, that can either inure the jurors to the persuasive effect or divert them from it.

Finally, there is information in the environment. My fellow panelist Thomas Miller has alluded to a study in which the judge's nods or seeming nonverbal cues made a difference in the ways in which juries reacted to witnesses. In the Voiceprint trial there were similar occurrences. For instance, at one point the judge obviously was not being very attentive and the jurors could see that and take cues from him. There was one incident that was less passive. A defense witness was sitting in the audience section while the prosecution witnesses were testifying and in the course of the presentation was exhibiting facial expressions of disapproval. Finally, the judge stopped the proceedings and said "I'm going to admonish you to cease shaking your head or making any kind of bodily facial suggestion as to the testimony of the witness. You are giving evidence to the jury, and when you want to give evidence to the jury you do it from the stand, you don't do it from the audience."

But the fact is that it is not always that easy to control that sort of peripheral information in the environment and jurors do look around and pick up cues from the reactions of others. When the "superstar" witness was testifying, there was a rapt attention by the audience. Everybody in the courtroom listened intently and the jurors were aware of that, too.

A live face-to-face communication is the closest analogy to what goes on in courts most of the time. However, a new element is being introduced which my fellow panelist, Godfrey Isaac, has already referred to as "trial by cinematography," and it is something that needs to be attended to with great care and caution. Those of us interested in communications study the mass media because they are the means by which this society comes to understand much of the rest of the world. I have been in broadcasting studios when documentaries and theatrical shows were being edited and you cannot help but be impressed with the knowledge that these people have about the use of film and videotape. The angle of a camera, the choice of what it will show, and the editing can dramatically affect the character of the information that is transmitted and the way it is received. There is no greater potential for the credible distortion of reality than in the film technique and it is something that I am not sure the courts are totally sensitive to. The idea of putting a video camera on a witness and letting it run seems to be a reasonable procedure, but the fact is that the angle or proximity of that camera, whether it comes up very tight or pulls back, and whether it moves or does not move can make a difference in the impact of the testimony. The medium can alter significantly the character of the information. It is part of the message and must always be considered.

## Source Credibility[4]

Excerpts from Reference 4 follow[*]:

Source credibility has a long and noble history in the study of communication. It goes back to ancient Greece and it comes out of classical rhetorical theory that was concerned with persuasion. Aristotle, for example, talked about three major forms of proof that a communicator can use. In his book, *The Rhetoric*, he said the three forms of proof are ethos or ethical proof, logos or logical proof, and pathos or emotional proof. He considered ethos the most persuasive. Aristotle suggested that the qualities of ethos or credibility resided within the speaker. Thus, if you were knowledgeable, competent, and had high moral character, you would be a persuasive communicator. And this is behind some of the questions people ask. They ask, "What can I do to be credible?"

The assumption behind such a question is that credibility is within the speaker, and that if you do certain things you will punch the right buttons in the listeners and certain effects will occur. Unfortunately (or fortunately), such is not the case.

"The current term that people in communication are using is not ethos, but source credibility, and it reflects not only a change in terminology, but a change in orientation and conceptualization. Source credibility, as communication researchers look it at today, is a perceptual process, and resides in the audience. If it were inherent within the communicator, all jurors would respond similarly to all expert witnesses. There would be no deviation in response. But we know that is not true. People respond differently to the same communicator. Some people may perceive the communicator to be highly credible, others may conceive the communicator to be lacking in credibility. This is not to imply that qualities and characteristics of the communicator are unimportant. They are important. But what actually

[*] Reprinted with permission from Reference 4, copyright American Society for Testing and Materials, 100 Barr Harbor Drive, West Conshohocken, PA 19428.

happens when we deal with this issue of source credibility is that there is an interaction between qualities and characteristics that the jury brings to the situation and the qualities and characteristics of the communicator. Depending upon a juror's psychological state, this individual will focus on different things, organize the material that an expert discusses in different ways, and formulate different inferences about what was said. Jurors do this differently because they are coming from "different places." What are the implications?

I suggest that there are two implications. One, specific communication behaviors that you engage in will not necessarily produce one-to-one reactions. So do not look for a prescription. The second implication I have already alluded to. Unless you know the qualities and characteristics of the jurors, you cannot prescribe beforehand absolute qualities of the expert witness that will be effective. As was clearly pointed out by a previous speaker, what is considered to be effective or ineffective depends upon, for example, the part of the country that the individual is from, the cultural norms and expectations, and so forth. There is no magic formula or pill. Eric Weber made a pile of money on a little book called "*How to Pick Up Girls*." He gave prescriptions of all the things one can do. And they do not work! These books never work. People wish they would work, but they do not because people cannot be categorized in real life as they can be in a book. I will now discuss some of the research that actually has gone on in the area of source credibility.

This research really began in earnest on a scientific basis back in the 1940s. It started during WWII, actually, when people began doing research on propaganda effects. There were a few prior studies, but no systematic body of research. What was found from this research was that certain people were more persuasive than others, but they did not know why exactly. So the search went on to try to find out what the components of credibility were that led to the effectiveness of a particular communicator's presentation. This led to a flurry of research that bloomed between the mid-1960s and the mid-1970s that attempted to identify the major factors, components, and dimensions of source credibility. Researchers used a technique called factor analysis, which attempts to see how a multitude of characteristics can be broken down into a few fundamental elementary qualities or characteristics.

A whole spate of research was done attempting to find out what the fundamental dimensions of credibility were. This research focused on trying to identify what dimensions were and secondly on how to measure these reactions. There has been little research on verbal and nonverbal communication as it is directly related to specific dimensions of credibility. Most of the advice that is given in the area, particularly as it relates to the courtroom, is based upon a few isolated studies and courtroom experience. There is little solid scientific research on the effects of particular communication qualities to credibility of expert witnesses. Conclusions or inferences that people make have to be taken with a great deal of caution. Some of the major dimensions of credibility about which researchers seem to have reached a fair amount of unanimity across a wide variety of studies follow.

These factors or dimensions are called by different names but they refer to the same quality or dimension. One major component of credibility is what might be called competence, expertise, or authoritativeness. A second important dimension of credibility is what might be called trustworthiness or character. A third fairly consistent dimension that researchers have identified is called dynamism. These three dimensions seem to be consistently identified by people who are attempting to determine the major components of credibility. Other components have been identified but do not appear consistently, such as co-orientation and charisma. One of the interesting theoretical notions that is being toyed with and talked about and studied to a certain extent, but not established absolutely, is that of the three dimensions one might intuitively assume that expertise is the most important. But trustworthiness is often proposed by theorists as being more important, and I think that was demonstrated by the examples that some of the other speakers gave. Jurors may not have understood the testimony. But if there was a quality of trust and believability that seemed to come forth from the expert witness's testimony that was influential. Let me discuss some of the possible applications of this theoretic kind of orientation to expert witnesses.

The role of the attorney is significant. The attorney has a responsibility to help establish the credibility of a witness. He must be careful to ask questions ensuring that competence is established through expertise, knowledge, and experience. That certainly is important. But the other dimension of character or trustworthiness has to be brought forth also if you are going to be maximally effective. The kinds of questions that the attorney must ask that produce the idea of trustworthiness are ones that deal with the potential or the lack of bias that your witness has. If you do not establish that your witness is unbiased, you may hurt his or her credibility. The manner in which the attorney questions the witness can have a lot to do with the way the jury will perceive the credibility of that witness.

If the attorney in direct examination cuts the witness off or attempts to dominate the conversation, one of the perceptual consequences may be that the jury might feel that the attorney does not trust the competence or intelligence of the witness. Why is the attorney cutting the expert off? And, as was pointed out, you have to work closely with the witness so that there is some expectation about length of discussion, so that the expert witness is not led to believe that he will be explaining or expressing ideas in great detail and the attorney in his own mind is looking for short answers. In cross-examination the point has already been made that cutting off a witness or using snideness or sarcasm in delivery may make certain logical points, but could hurt in terms of the jury's reaction, because they may feel that the attorney is not being fair. Let me move now to a consideration of actual verbal behavior of the witness.

One major characteristic of a witness's presentation that seems to make a witness credible is that the delivery seems thoughtful. The person is "right here" and is thinking about the question and responding in an immediate way. This is in contrast to what might be a very thoroughly rehearsed presentation. People sense rehearsed presentations. They may not be able to tell you why, but they can tell. One of the problems that come about when there is a rehearsed presentation is that during cross-examination the expert witness's delivery will be totally different. This discrepancy could possibly hurt credibility.

What characteristics of delivery can influence your credibility? There is a whole list but I will discuss just a few. For example, the pronunciation of words is important. The dialect is important depending upon the locale of the trial. For example, most Americans do not have a positive attitude of people who speak a dialect other than the one they speak. Americans tend to have positive attitudes toward certain British dialects — not all — but some. We tend to have negative reactions to dialects that are not quite American sounding. I am speaking in very broad sweeping terms; if you have a very strong southern accent and you are giving expert testimony in Los Angeles, you may not be as credible as if you were giving expert testimony in Louisiana. Some of the research that has been done in this area suggests that people with different dialects are perceived not only as having differing intellectual capacities, but their moral character is also perceived as being different; people of certain differing dialects (for example, ethnic minorities) are perceived as not having the same high moral standards as people who speak in a general American dialect. So if you are an expert witness or are dealing with an expert witness who comes from a different region of the country this is something that you should consider. It may not necessarily hurt you, but there are people who do tend to respond this way.

In terms of language, it has already been noted that jargon has its good and bad points. A certain amount of jargon is necessary and important, and the good expert witness will give the parenthetical explanation of what the expression means so that the layperson on the jury will understand. This will enhance the witness's credibility because it shows the expert's sensitivity to the person who is attempting to understand the testimony. In some of the research that I have done, I have focused on the effects of presentational characteristics such as nonfluencies and disruptions in speech, such as "uh," "ers," stutters, repetitions, and tongue slips on perceptions of credibility. I have done a series of studies in which I have attempted to determine the effects of increasing numbers of nonfluencies inserted into a 15-min presentation upon perceptions of credibility and persuasive impact. One of the interesting findings is that as nonfluencies and disruptions increase, judgments of competence went down, which is what you would expect. But, fascinatingly enough, perceptions of trustworthiness did not go down; and, the speaker was still capable of producing strong persuasive impact. Perceptions of "competence" that might be related to fluency do not necessarily diminish persuasive impact.

Nonverbal characteristics include clothing. Depending upon the area of the country that you are in, cultural expectations of proper clothing differ. In a metropolitan area such as Los Angeles, the most appropriate colors to jurors who are middle class or higher are deep blues, blues, grays, whites, and tans, never green and never dark brown. The same colors apply with dresses. Dark brown does not come off well. If you are coming to the courtroom and it is a rainy day, your raincoat must always be beige or tan, never black. In terms of dress, if we continued it would come down to fine points such as the necktie you wear and how neckties represent differing status levels. So depending upon the status level of the jury, you would wear a different type of tie. For example, the highest status tie is a solid color tie that is either blue or wine colored basically and has a very small subtle pattern; a club pattern, for instance, would be very good with middle class and upper middle class jurors. But if you were not dealing with receivers who were of that status level, you would not want to come in with a deep navy blue pinstripe suit with a silver tie that had subtle gray dots on it. Even if this were very elegant, you would not do that. You would wear a medium blue suit and a burgundy tie, which is more typically middle class.

Now we could refer to many items like these. Remember that these are just generalizations, and do not necessarily fit all situations. So if you are looking for particular characteristics it is difficult to say that if you do this you will always be perceived as credible. If you do that you will not. People who have dogmatic personalities who are authoritarian in their own approach to life tend to respond very favorably to people who speak in absolute and categorical ways. On the other hand, people who are more "open-minded" and less dogmatic do not respond favorably to people who speak in absolute categorical terms. These people feel that nothing is absolute, that there is always some weakness or difficulty. Thus, when you speak too glibly and too broadly the latter group will respond negatively. Is the juror an authoritarian type who needs some kind of absolute structure, or is the individual no authoritarian or nondogmatic?

One other example: if you are dealing with jury members who are highly intelligent, research tends to suggest that when testimony seems to reflect only one side or point of view, this does not go over well because highly intelligent people tend to know that there is more than one side to an issue and that there are likely to be some loopholes and difficulties in your particular interpretation. If you are dealing with jurors who are not particularly intelligent and you strongly present an absolutely one-sided point of view, you are likely to be believed, because such individuals may not have the intellectual capacity to know that there are probably weaknesses in any perspective or point of view, that there are inferences and interpretations that have to be made, and that there are gaps.

One final note about dialects. European dialects are variously rated. People who have Germanic-type dialects, Austrian dialects, Viennese dialects, and so on, are sometimes perceived lower in credibility because Americans tend to perceive speakers of this dialect as having authoritarian personalities. And when one says "dis" and "dat" for this and that, many Americans have a negative attitude toward that particular dialect for it sometimes reflects a lower social class.

## Conclusion

So there are a variety of qualities and characteristics of the witness that can influence the juror, but there is no single variable that uniformly will produce a single effect. You first must consider qualities and characteristics of jurors that seem to be primarily important; then determine how these qualities affect what juries select as being important and unimportant in expert witnesses.

*Commentary: I have found that the attorney/client may require a script as assistance when I undergo direct examination either in a deposition or in a trial.*

*Therefore, I have developed what I refer to as direct examination questions that I give to the attorney a few days before the deposition or trial (see Figure 17.1, end of chapter). Remember that it might be several months between the time of your deposition and your appearance in court. Therefore, a document such as the direct examination questions is helpful for both the expert accident investigator/reconstructionist as well as the attorney.*

*Each of these indirect examination question scripts must be tailored to the particular case. For example, if the investigator/reconstructionist is working on a vehicle collision case, then the highlights of his/her background should be directed more toward past work experience and education in the automotive field. If the case involves a slip and fall, then the investigator/reconstructionist must include experience and education in the fields of biomechanics, human factors, construction, or any related type of experience or education.*

*The direct examination questions are rather simple from the standpoint of what needs to be included. It should, of course, have your full name, professional address, and your profession; and then a listing of your education starting with your earliest college degree and ending with your latest degree. These should include the institution and the dates of granting of these degrees. If the investigator or reconstructionist has had a special seminar or continuing education program in a particular area that might be applicable to this particular case, then that should be included also.*

*Next should come your work experience. Once again keep the direct examination questions as brief as possible. You would only include work experience relevant to the case at hand. In some areas you may want to expand the details such as working for a university involved in on-site accident investigation in conjunction with the local police department. If the investigator/reconstructionist* has had both hands-on experience as well as in-house design experience, both should be included. Both the plaintiff and defense parties are always interested in the expert's work schedule. I have found that a single statement such as the length of time you have been consulting either full-time or part-time, as well as the breakdown in percentages with respect to the amount of work being done for a plaintiff and/or a defense firm, works very well.

Many times the length of the depositions and/or trials can be shortened when an expert delineates an area of expertise in specific instead of general terms. As an example, the general term "accident reconstructionist" is not sufficient. You should include the types of accidents that you investigate and reconstruct, such as cars, trucks, buses, trains, motorcycles, vans, or any other vehicles in the transportation field. The statement is succinct and detailed enough to provide the attorney with basic information.

From this point onward the direct examination script should be aimed primarily at the case at hand. First, give the date of retention of your work on the case. This could include an introductory telephone conversation or the first date of receiving any information on the case. Next would come the short detailed information concerning your inspection of the accident vehicles, and the accident site. If no inspection was performed, then a statement should be made to that fact and the reason that the inspection was not conducted. As an example, the vehicles were repaired prior to your becoming involved in the case.

The next action involves the materials that you have reviewed that assisted you in developing your reconstruction and opinions. This again should be as short as possible and cover not only the information such as complaints, interrogatories, photographs of the scene and the vehicles, and depositions of participants and witnesses but also any standards that you have used to bolster your opinion.

The next section has a short paragraph on the reconstruction of the accident. This must be brief because it is only a reminder to the expert as to what he/she has done that will also lead the attorney through your reconstruction. It should include a short sentence or two stating the background of the case, a few sentences on the defects that may have been found, what you believe occurred during the accident based on the evidence you have reviewed, and the depositions and statements of the witnesses and participants.

The last portion of the direct examination is your opinion. This is crucial to the case. It must include how or why the problem occurred and what was the result of that problem occurring in terms of the injury to the parties involved. A short statement should be made concerning how the standards bolster your opinion, showing the particular defects as a violation of that standard.

A script such as I have described is very helpful to any case you may be involved with. It is memory aid for both you and your client. It saves the client a great deal of time in developing questions that he/she believes are relevant to *the case while making sure to cover the reconstruction opinion. The attorney client is not as conversant with the case from the expert's point of view and therefore may not review all the elements that the expert needs to cover in testimony.*

## Figure 17.1   Direct Testimony

Direct Examination Questions — A. Smith vs. Mr. and Mrs. Y.

*Full Name*: John J. Engineer

*Professional Address*: 1234 Tesla Boulevard – Suite 1 - Metropolis

*Profession*: Registered Professional and Consulting Engineer

*Education*: B. S. Mechanical Engineering, M.I.T., 1975; M.S. Engineering Mechanics, University of Michigan, 1977.

*Work Experience*: XYZ Motor Corporation. Junior engineer in charge of design standards and changes for the small car platform braking system including parking brakes and service brakes. Senior engineer in charge of steering systems and suspensions.

*Safety Office*: Worked with outside consultant on accident investigation studies for the latest safety installations on new product vehicle lines. Assisted in presentations to all departments and upper management. Set up investigation teams to collect data on accidents of XYZ Corporation vehicles in and around the city of Metropolis. Reviewed and studied films of high-speed barrier crash test vehicles as well as partial testing of interior components.

*Experimental Vehicle*: Worked as a member of a team to develop and build a vehicle that could be crashed into a concrete barrier at 50 mi/h and have the occupants survive the impact. Conducted computer analysis of the occupant's movements and many recommendations on location of various interior energy-absorbing devices. Study crash films of both the standard vehicle and the experimental vehicle for comparison purposes and data collection.

*Special Assignments*: Worked with outside vendors on various types of new vehicle concepts for low-production options on standard and luxury vehicles.

My function was to ensure that the proposed options met corporate and federal motor vehicle standards for crash worthiness, ease of operation, service ability, endurance, noise, vibration, and quality control. I was called on several times by the office of general counsel to assist and/or act as an expert witness for the corporation and litigation against the company. This included not only vehicle design but also reconstruction of the accident and the occupants' movements before, during, and after the vehicle had come to rest.

*Consulting Experience*: Full-time consulting engineer since 1985, 70% plaintiff and 30% defense work.

*Expertise*: Accident investigation and reconstruction — types of reconstruction include cars, motorcycles, buses, trucks, and various other products that produce injuries and require a reconstruction to determine the cause of injury.

*Data Retention on Case*: January 5, 1996

*Inspection of Accident Site*: An inspection was made of the accident site on September 21, 1996. The site appears to be in the same condition as it was on the day the accident. Measurements and photographs were taken showing some residual gouging of the concrete roadbed. No other evidence was present at this location during the inspection.

*Inspection of Vehicles*: No inspections of either vehicle could be conducted due to the fact that the defendant's vehicle was scrapped out by the insurance company and the plaintiff's vehicle had been repaired and was back in service.

*Materials Reviewed*: Complaint, interrogatories from both sides, photographs of the accident site taken by the police and by the investigator, and depositions of the participants and two witnesses.

*Reconstruction of Incident*: On July 10, 1995 at approximately 7:30 p.m. Mr. A. Smith was driving his vehicle on Highway 106 northbound looking for exit ten.
    As he approached the exit he slowed down to the proper speed to exit when he was rear ended by Mr. Y. and his vehicle at approximately 45 mi/h. Mr. Y. did not have the vehicle under control and was following too closely to be able to bring his vehicle to a stop. Mr. Smith had all lights working at the time of the impact.

*Opinion*: It is my opinion based on my experience, education, and the materials I have reviewed to date that Mr. Y. was following too closely at the nominal highway speed and did not have sufficient time or distance to stop his vehicle without an impact to Mr. Smith's vehicle. This impact caused severe injuries to Mr. Smith. Had Mr. Y. followed at a safe distance he would have had sufficient time to determine that Mr. Smith was slowing down and Mr. Y. would have been able to brake his vehicle in time to prevent a rear-end impact.

**John J. Engineer P.E.**

# References

1. Kessler, J. B., The expert witness and the use of videotape recordings, *J. Forensic Sci.*, 28(2), April 1983, 518.

2. Miller, T. H., Nonverbal communication in expert testimony, *J. Forensic Sci.*, 28(2), April 1983, 523.

3. Rosenthal, P., Nature of jury response to the expert witness, *J. Forensic Sci.*, 28(2), April 1983, 529.

4. Sereno, K. K., Source credibility, *J. Forensic Sci.*, 28(2), April 1983, 532.

# Educating the Client

"I never guess. It is a shocking habit destructive to the logical faculty"

**Sherlock Holmes**
*The Sign of the Four*

## Technology and Basic Language

The author has always felt it was part of his duty as a member of the investigation/reconstruction team to educate the client in the technology and basic language of accident investigation and reconstruction. Some attorneys were educated as engineers and even they need some assistance in understanding the precise information the investigator/reconstructionist is trying to impart.

## Terminology

Terminology is a very large part of the education process. This means that any time the accident investigator/reconstructionist is describing reconstruction and/or giving an opinion to the client, he/she must listen and look at the client to determine, by nonverbal communication, if the client does not understand what is being communicated. This may include a blank look, a furrowed brow, a slight shaking of the head, or even a distant, "Yeah ... I guess ... I understand." Any of these are indications that the explanation just given has not been understood.

Therefore, the reconstructionist must go back and think about what terminology may have been used that is confusing to the client. These terms might be related to the vehicle, such as "squirrel cage motor," the "banjo" of the rear axle, and many other pseudo-technical terms that are common expressions used by engineers and the automotive industry.

Accident reconstruction terminology and calculations many times are additional factors in the communications process. These could include specialized terminology, such as Newton's laws of motion and the conservation of linear momentum; or even the basic series of calculations that would allow the reconstructionist to develop a scenario of the accident by starting with the vehicle rest point and calculating the velocity lost by the vehicle at various points along the path it underwent from the moment the brakes were applied through the collision and final sliding to the point of rest. Interrogatories, the specialized questions for the opposing side to provide information that hopefully can be useful in preparing reconstructions, are discussed later in this chapter.

Again, the investigator/reconstructionist is educating the client in terms of the information that is needed to complete a reconstruction as well as how the questions should be worded to evoke the best responses from the first set of interrogatories without requiring a second, third, or even a fourth set to be propounded to opposing counsel.

## Preparation for Deposition

The attorney/client may request a meeting with the investigator/reconstructionist to "prep" for deposition or trial. This prep time is dependent on the relationship between the attorney and the investigator/reconstructionist from the standpoint of previous work done as well as trust and understanding between both parties. The investigator/reconstructionist can assist the attorney/client by providing what I have previously mentioned as a report titled "Direct Testimony." This is usually provided to the attorney client approximately 4 weeks before the known trial date, and allows the attorney to determine if he/she needs any further preparation time with the "expert" before trial. It also tells the attorney/client that the expert knows and understands the case and has become prepared for the trial. If the investigator/reconstructionist has been communicating to the attorney client throughout the course of the investigation, a rapport is being built that can prevent a lot of miscommunications between both parties.

Whenever there is a potential problem, inform the attorney/client immediately so that he/she may take whatever actions are necessary or may instruct the reconstructionist to continue. The primary reconstructionist may discover that in his/her opinion additional parties should be considered as part of the legal action. This information must be conveyed to the attorney/client as soon as possible to assist in deciding to proceed with this suggestion. Any adverse information the investigator/reconstructionist develops through the review of information provided by the attorney/client should also be conveyed as soon as possible. Suggestions such as these may provide the attorney client with sufficient information to determine that it would be better for the client to cease all action to prevent further expenditures.

Many times a client may describe a set of facts of an accident to the investigator/reconstructionist that appear to fit his/her area of expertise. The natural action would be for the investigator/reconstructionist to start a preliminary investigation with the vehicle and/or the scene to determine if there is a case for the client.

Once this determination is made — whether it is positive or negative — a call to the client is mandatory as soon as possible, to advise if there is a case or if the case should be dropped to prevent any further use of funds. Unbeknown to the expert, there may be several other experts working on the case, assuming that there is a case. To allow the case to continue is a needless expenditure of funds if there is no hope of the client recovering this loss. Never be afraid to tell the client that there is no case. Be sure of the facts before doing this, especially if it is a new client and does not understand the method of investigation/reconstruction. The client may take the case to another expert who might say that there is a case based on information that the first reconstructionist did not have or may not have considered previously — this can be embarrassing and detrimental to his/her career and reputation.

## Mutual Building of Trust and Understanding

There must be a mutual building of trust and understanding between the attorney/client and the investigator/reconstructionist during the initial investigation and subsequent work on the case. An open and honest attitude is the best policy. If the reconstructionist is not sure of a particular area of the case, then he/she should not be afraid to admit it. It is better to call in another expert than to try and solve all the problems alone. The attorney/client will understand that he/she is trying to stay within the bounds of one's own expertise. Going too far afield can result in embarrassing situations for both the reconstructionist and clients.

The same advice is appropriate when discussing testimony for a deposition or trial. The attorney may want the reconstructionist to couch his/her answers in a specific legal format. This is fine if it does not go beyond his/her area of expertise.

*Commentary: We all have a great deal of general knowledge about many things. We must be constantly on guard that we do not let that knowledge lead our egos into thinking we have sufficient knowledge about almost any subject.*

# Interrogatories

## Discovery

Every legal case that the author has ever been involved with has had a period of time after the case was filed that is called discovery. This is legal terminology for the period of time allowed by the court for each party involved in the lawsuit to discover what information is available from the other party and from all available witnesses and participants.

Of course, the plaintiff has done some preliminary discovery work to ensure that he/she has a viable case to bring before the judicial system, but in this context discovery means the period that occurs after the lawsuit has been filed and the judge sets the specific dates that must be met during the course of the lawsuit. One of those dates is the discovery period.

During this discovery period, interrogatories and requests for documents are sent between both parties involved in the lawsuit. These interrogatories and requests for documents must be very specific in their intent because the opposing party can answer them as being too vague or overly broad in their scope.

This is where the investigator/reconstructionist can become involved and assist the attorney client. The majority of attorneys are not engineers by training; therefore, they may not be able to ask the most significant questions that the investigator/reconstructionist needs to complete the reconstruction.

When first becoming involved in any case, the investigator/reconstructionist should ask the attorney/client if he/she would like assistance in forming interrogatories and requests for documents with respect to the accident itself, as well as the witnesses and on-scene investigators. Most attorneys welcome the assistance, because the interrogatories and requests for documentation must be framed in a specific language format that cannot be misunderstood by the opposing counsel or their experts.

Consider the example of a case against an automobile company. The accident investigator/reconstructionist would like information concerning the steering components of a particular four-passenger vehicle involved in the accident. The attorney might ask the question, "Please provide all information on the steering gear of the 1999 X Y vehicle." This question would most likely be answered by the following: "The interrogatory is too broad in its scope and cannot be answered in its present form." A more specific question must be framed as follows, "Please provide the assembly, subassembly, and all part drawings for the 1996 through 1999 X Y four-door sedan, including all design assumptions, Federal Motor Vehicle Safety Standards (FMVSS) certification tests, high-speed film and still photographs of the vehicle before and after testing, warranty reports for the same years, all technical bulletins, shop manuals, and customer complaints." These, of course, would be broken down into several questions concerning each particular item in the initial specific question, because opposing counsel would again decline to answer on the basis of it being too ambiguous.

## Questions about the Scene and Vehicle

We must assume at this point that the investigator/reconstructionist has completed an investigation of the scene as well as the vehicles involved in the accident. Therefore, he/she should submit a series of questions concerning the scene and the vehicles themselves. These would include the following:

- When was maintenance last performed on the vehicles?
- What maintenance was performed?
- What were the positions of all the occupants of the vehicle at the time of the accident?
- Where in the vehicle was the weight of all occupants of the vehicle located just prior to the accident?
- Were there any special equipment, luggage, or other items in the trunk or inside the vehicle at the time of the accident?
- Had either of the vehicles been in an accident prior to the date of the accident?
- What existing damage, if any, was present on the vehicle prior to the accident?
- Was the radio, tape deck, or compact disc (CD) player being used at the time of the accident?
- Was the driver or any of the passengers adjusting the radio, tape deck, or CD player just prior to the accident?
- Were any of the windows open prior to the accident; if so, which ones and how far were they rolled down?
- Were the vehicle lights on at the time of the accident, assuming it was dark enough to need these lights?
- Were there street lights on at the time of the accident?
- Were any streetlights not working at the scene of the accident?
- Were all traffic lights working prior to the accident; if not, where they blinking or completely inoperative?
- Were there any other traffic devices at or near the intersection of the accident that were hidden from view?
- Did the driver or any of the occupants in your vehicle see the other vehicle approaching just prior to the accident?
- Did the driver see the other vehicle at any time prior to the collision? If so, how long between the first sight of the other vehicle to the time of the collision?
- Did the driver apply his/her brakes prior to the collision?
- Did the driver hear the brakes or tires squealing prior to the collision?
- Did anyone observe any skid marks from either vehicle after the collision?

- Did any occupant feel the vehicle sliding in one direction or another prior to the impact?
- Where did your vehicle and the opposing vehicle end up after the collision, (the points of rest of both vehicles)?
- If injured, were you or any of the occupants treated at the scene?
- Who was the treating individual: emergency medical service (EMS), fire department, or private individual?
- Were any of the parties taken to an emergency room for treatment? If so, which hospital emergency room was used?
- Please describe all your injuries in as much detail as possible.
- Then please describe the events leading up to the collision from your seated position in the vehicle.
- Please provide any photographs taken by yourself, your family, or friends concerning the accident site or either vehicle that was involved in the collision.

These, of course, are only preliminary questions; a second set of interrogatories and possibly even a third or fourth set may be submitted, depending on the answers received from these preliminary questions. Some answers to these interrogatories may be very detailed depending on the memory of the participants involved in the collision.

If a lawsuit has been brought against an automobile company, then a specific set of interrogatories should be suggested to the attorney client based on information needed from that company. The following is a suggested list of specialized interrogatories and requests for documentation that might be used to obtain information from an automobile company whose vehicle had a failure in its structural system during a rollover accident:

- A full-size copy of all engineering drawings, including assembly, sub-assembly, details of the "A" post, front and rear headers, and side rails used in the 1998 X Y four-door sedan
- Copies of all engineering and manufacturing change requests for the "A" posts on the 1998 X Y vehicle
- Copies of all engineering, manufacturing, and management deviations that were in effect when the 1998 X Y vehicle was manufactured
- Full-size copy of the structural drawings of the 1998 X Y vehicle, including the "A" and "B" posts, front and rear headers, and all side rails
- A copy of all data collected by X Y Motors for the 1995 to 1998 X Y four-door sedan, from any insurance company or any other agency — institution or individual — that shows the type, rate, and number of accidents where the "A" post has collapsed into the passenger compartment and has compromised the occupant safety zone

- Copies of all certification tests conducted on the 1998 X Y four-door sedan vehicle, to meet the FMVSS standards in effect at that time, including all photographs of the testing
- A copy of all data collected by X Y Motors or any other agency that shows the type, rate, number, and methods of failure of the 1998 X Y four-door sedan "A" posts, roof headers, or side rails due to an automobile accident
- A copy of the failure mode and effects analysis or any other method used by X Y Motors to determine the number and type of component failure, with respect to the "A" post and headers, and corrective action performed prior to the release and sale of the 1998 X Y four-door sedan
- A copy of all the welding specifications and drawings showing the welds for the 1998 X Y four-door sedan "A" post, headers, and side rails
- Copies of all certification, development, and prototype rollover and roof crush tests, including all high-speed and still photographic material taken during any of the tests of the 1998 X Y four-door sedan, with and without a sunroof option installed; or prior model years that are carried over into the 1998 X Y four-door sedan, which may have been conducted to determine crashworthiness and energy absorption capabilities of the vehicle
- A copy of all complete or partial vehicle endurance testing done on the 1998 X Y four-door sedan, with and without sunroof option installed; or prior model years that are carried over into the 1998 X Y four-door sedan model, both long-term and short-term that was conducted to meet either the corporate, Japanese government, other foreign markets, and/or U.S. federal government standards
- Copies of the hardware, trim, chassis, and body manuals for the 1998 X Y four-door sedan with and without sunroof option installed
- Full-size copies of all body seating package drawings for the 1998 X Y four-door sedan
- Copies of all studies conducted by X Y Motors, an independent consultant, a university, or other agency by way of a contract or grant; or any other data used, referenced, reviewed, or relied on by X Y Motors to determine the strength capabilities of the "A" post, and body structural system of the 1998 X Y four-door sedan vehicle
- Copies of all tests, including laboratory static and dynamic tests of the individual components as well as the entire "A" post header complex; and all field, prototype, development, or production vehicle tests that show the interaction of the "A" post and headers of the 1998 X Y four-door sedan vehicle
- Copies of all service technical bulletins from X Y Motors service division to the X Y dealers, concerning any problems with the "A" post or header structure

- Copies of all roof crush tests used for certification of FMVSS 216 or 208, including all photographs and data sheets
- A copy of all complete or partial vehicle endurance testing done on the 1998 X Y vehicle; or prior model years that are carried over into the 1998 model, both long term and short term that was conducted to meet either the corporate, European Economic Community (EEC), Japanese markets, and/or U.S. federal government standards.

If the failure was in the steering gear, then a typical set of interrogatories might be developed as follows:

- Copies of all tests, including laboratory static and dynamic tests of the individual components as well as the entire steering gear assembly; and all field, prototype, development, or production vehicle tests that show the interaction of the steering gear and the possible loss of steering control in the 1998 X Y vehicle
- All warranty data for the steering gear and control valve unit for the 1998 X Y vehicle
- Copies of all drawings, graphics, installation sketches, or other product illustrations that show the installation of the steering gear assembly and control valve unit for the 1998 X Y vehicle
- A copy of the last two years of quality control inspection reports performed by X Y Motors on the steering gear assembly and control valve unit for the 1998 X Y vehicle
- A copy of all reports generated by the consumer affairs division of X Y Motors for the last 5 years with respect to injuries and/or incidents with the failure or partial failure of its steering gear assembly and control valve used in the fabrication of the 1998 X Y vehicle
- Copies of all presentations made of accident investigation and/or field studies of accidents of X Y Motors vehicles involving the steering gear assembly and control valve sponsored by X Y Motors through the Motor Vehicle Manufacturers Association, or any other Agency doing the same or comparable type work
- Copies of all manufacturing plant reports, which deal with any problems associated with the steering gear assembly and control valve used in the fabrication of the 1998 X Y vehicle
- Copies of all studies conducted by X Y Motors product planning, safety committee, office of general counsel, or any other agency contracted by X Y Motors to conduct such tests, with respect to the fail-safe devices for the steering gear assembly and control valve used in the fabrication of the 1998 X Y vehicle

Of course, there could be many other interrogatories sent to other parties in the lawsuit such as the county controlling the traffic signals, the ambulance or emergency response units, the fire department, the police department, the on-scene police investigator, and the police technician who may have photographed the scene and many of the pieces of evidence lying around the scene.

The investigator/reconstructionist must be prepared for specific questions during his/her deposition or trial testimony concerning his/her assistance in preparing the interrogatories for the client attorney. Be truthful, and answer the question in the following manner, "I submitted a set of questions and requests for documentation to the client, without reviewing each and every question I cannot tell you whether all my questions were used in the form I submitted or they were changed by the attorney."

*Commentary: I have never known an attorney client to turn down my suggestion of submitting a set of specific interrogatories and requests for documentation that I felt were necessary to complete my investigation and reconstruction of the accident scene so that I might have a more complete and optimum opinion to assist in the case.*

*Never be afraid to offer your services when you believe it can assist your client in some manner or form. The client may not be aware of your ability to assist, or of the specific questions that you may need answers to that can be framed by you and possibly reformatted for legal purposes. Remember the client is the head of the team and you are an assistant; any assistance you may be able to render can help the team.*

## Unusual Case Histories

One method of continuing education is reading journals related to the accident investigation and reconstruction field. These journals usually present unusual cases that are both interesting and informative.

### Case One — Injury to Cervical Airway

Mittleman[1] reported on a case of the injury to the cervical airway as a result of impact with a steering wheel rim. Excerpts* to follow:

> A head-on collision of a van and a multiton truck that allegedly had brake failure resulted in the inward crush of the left front of the van. The steering column was pushed upward and inward such that the upper edge of the

---

* Excerpts reprinted with permission from Reference 1, copyright American Society for Testing and Materials, 100 Barr Harbor Drive, West Conshohocken, PA 19428.

steering wheel rim was approximately 1 ft above the seatback. After the collision the driver exited the van through the right side door, walked a few steps and then collapsed. The rescue personnel on arrival found that he had a faint pulse. The trachea appeared elevated. Examination revealed a damaged airway. An endrotracheal tube was inserted and he was transported. All resuscitative efforts were unsuccessful.

The postmortem examination revealed a circumferential tear at the laryngotracheal junction. The dissection revealed a mild subluxation of the fourth and fifth cervical vertebra with an intact but swollen cervical cord. There were also lacerations and contusions of the lips. During the second collision the driver went forward as the steering column was coming rearward. His neck impacted the steering wheel rim resulting in the transection. The resulting blood in the tracheobronchial tree resulted in asphyxiation, which was the cause of death.[1]

## Case Two — Dragging Death

Dragging deaths are not unusual, but generally they are not reported in the literature. In 1988, Dix[2] reported on a dragging death case involving a 16-year-old boy who was riding his bicycle home from work. The following is excerpted*:

> While crossing the road, his bicycle was struck in the rear by a three-quarter ton truck. A witness to the accident saw and heard the collision, but saw or heard nothing from the victim. After the truck drove away, the witness called the police. The boy's body was found 15 min later 2.6 mi away from the scene of the accident alongside the road. Two hours later the truck was found in a nearby trailer park. The driver was intoxicated and said he remembers hitting the bicycle, but not the boy. Evidence was later found that the driver had tried to wash blood off some clothing he was wearing at the time of the accident.
>
> The passenger later confessed that they had both seen the boy at impact and realized about a mile or more from the accident site that they were dragging the boy. They pulled off the side of the road, backed the truck up, and manually dislodged the body from under the truck. The truck was found to have a dent in the hood that had to be done at impact by the boy as the bicycle was much lower to the ground. There was no blood, tissue, or hair found under the truck. Examination of the scene in the daylight hours revealed a continuous streak of blood 5 inches wide beginning approximately 250 yards from the initial impact and going all the way to the resting point of the body. The autopsy showed a young boy of 5 foot 8 1/2 inches in height and weighing about 120 pounds. There was a 24 1/2-inch by 6-inch deep abraded injury to the right flank that extended from

* Excerpts reprinted with permission from Reference 2, copyright American Society for Testing and Materials, 100 Barr Harbor Drive, West Conshohocken, PA 19428.

the midchest to the midthigh. The 10th and 11th ribs were ground down and the liver was exposed and abraded also. This indicted that the body was stuck in one place under the truck and was ground down as it was dragged along the highway. The question of time of death is important when determining the degree of driver negligence. Other than the dragging injuries there were no other significant injuries. The probability seems that the boy most likely died while being dragged or after he was left by the side of the road. The amount of blood that was deposited during the 2 1/2 mile dragging could not have done so without the heart still pumping.[2]

***Commentary:*** *I have seen two cases of dragging deaths in my practice. The first involved a woman who was thrown from a van during an accident, a passing vehicle caught her under the front of the vehicle and she was dragged 22 blocks down several city streets including several turns both in the left and right directions. The driver did not notice the body until a few hours later when he came out to go to the store and thought someone had placed the body there. The total injuries were all abrasions from constantly rolling and skidding along the road surface. The cause of death was listed as bled to death. The second case involved a woman who fell under the wheels of a bus; she was dragged approximately 20 ft, and the rear wheels of the bus then ran over her.*

## Case Three — Suicide by Self-Decapitation

A suicide by self-decapitation is unusual but not rare. Most cases are not reported in the literature for many reasons not germane to our analysis, which is to recognize that type of situation when an investigator sees it.

In 1993, Prichard[3] reported on a case that was unusual because it used a vehicle, as follows*:

The deceased was a 28-year-old male who was known to be depressed over pending criminal charges against him. He also was separated from his wife. The victim was found by two mushroom hunters on a logging road. The head, observed first, was found on the ground approximately 24 feet behind the rear of the deceased's vehicle. The head had been severed at the base of the skull. The torso of the victim was in the driver's seat of the car, which had crashed into a tree. Lying a few feet away was a 1/8-inch yellow nylon rope, approximately 25 feet long. One end of the rope was tied to a tree stump just off the roadway. The other end was lying loose and had been tied with a slipknot. A receipt from a building supply company dated earlier in the day was found in his trouser pocket. The receipt read *"25 feet of HB Poly Rope Yellow."* The price was 35 cents per foot for a total of $9.00

---

* Excerpts reprinted with permission from Reference 3, copyright American Society for Testing and Materials, 100 Barr Harbor Drive, West Conshohocken, PA 19428.

including tax. The bill had been paid with a $20 bill. Two $5 bills were found with the receipt.

Investigation disclosed that the decedent had purchased the rope at the store that was indicated on the receipt, earlier that same day. The clerk said he did recall the transaction, but noted there was nothing unusual about the sale. He stated that the person was very quiet. The victim then drove to the scene, tied the rope to a tree stump at the side of the road and fastened the other end around his neck. He then got into his truck, buckled the seat belt, accelerated, and was decapitated.

Observation of the remains at the mortuary disclosed a sharply defined wound. The appearance was similar to a decapitation wound that had been administered by a guillotine. The blood tested negative for alcohol. The urine drug screen also was negative. The death was officially certified as suicide by decapitation. After researching the coroner's files for as far back as records were kept in this county, the author was unable to locate any similar type of suicide. The Grays Harbor County Coroner, John Bebich, a long-time law enforcement officer, stated, "In 20 years as an Aberdeen police officer and 14 years as coroner, I've never run into this type of case before. It is very, very bizarre."

***Commentary***: *It seems that everyone has been involved with an unusual case at one time or another in his/her practice. I reconstructed a case in the northeast in which a woman apparently drove off the road onto an area between the road and the sidewalk that had a number of telephone poles set in a line. She continued driving in this manner and increased the speed of her car to approximately 50 mi/h. She drove in between the poles while sticking her head out of the window and was decapitated.*

## Summary

The investigator/reconstructionist (expert) must consider the relationship with the attorney as a team effort with the attorney as a player coach. He/she has the experience, knowledge, and abilities to work the entire playing field and knows how and when the other players (experts) are to be used. The players (experts) share their knowledge with the coach to help complete and enhance the plan for total team effort. It is a mutual respectful relationship, and both parties must accept that concept to be a winning team.

# References

1. Mittleman, R. E., Cervical airway injuries as a result of impact with steering wheel rim, *J. Forensic Sci.*, 33(5), September 1988, 1198.

2. Dix, J. D. and Bolesta, S., Dragging deaths: A case in point, *J. Forensic Sci.*, 33(3), May 1988, 826.

3. Prichard, P. D., A suicide by decapitation, *J. Forensic Sci.*, 38(4), July 1993, 981.

# Ethics

"It is a capital mistake to theorize before one has data."
**Sherlock Holmes**
*A Scandal in Bohemia*

As stated previously, I have read many texts on accident investigation and reconstruction. In each of these, I have never found a section or chapter discussing the ethics of the investigator/reconstructionist. In every professional organization, members of that group subscribe to a code or canon of ethics. It is a set of guidelines for them to go by in their professional lives.

## Derivations and Definitions

As I prepared this chapter I became interested in the derivation of the word ethics. It appears that it comes from the Greek "***ethikos***" meaning moral. Using several dictionaries, I came across the following definitions for ethics: a moral code, rules of conduct, moral philosophy, sense of right or wrong, sense of duty, conscience, decent, upstanding, fair, and aboveboard. A definition that makes most sense to me is the following: conforming to an accepted professional standard of conduct, a set of moral principles or values, the discipline dealing with what is good or bad, and with a moral duty and obligation.

Looking up the word ***moral***, I find it's defined as leading to a principle of right or wrong in behavior.

***Philosophy*** is defined as the pursuit of wisdom — a search for truth through logical reasoning instead of actual observations. Therefore, it would appear that a closed circle of definitions define morals, philosophy, and ethics.

Look at the word **reputation** for a moment. Reputation is defined as standing stature or reputed. Reputed is also defined as the character or stature commonly ascribed to a person. Reputation is also defined as the fact of being highly esteemed, the honor or credit belonging to one. It would appear to me that a person's ethics are tied to his/her reputation. For without them an ethical person can have no reputation. The loss of your reputation is the loss of everything. For without the respectability and esteem of your peers, family, co-workers or community, the individual has nothing.

Judging from the preceding definitions and information concerning both ethics and reputations, it would appear to me that the professional investigator/reconstructionist has to conduct his/her professional life on what he/she believes to be right and wrong. I then asked myself this simple question. Why do we need a code of ethics if we live moral lives and are concerned about our reputation with our peers, co-workers, and above all our families? It would appear that each of us, having been brought up in a society that respects law and order and that understands right from wrong, should have no problem dealing with the ethics of our professional life. Yet many professional organizations spend countless hours debating and evaluating the ethics of their members when the general public brings grievances to their attention.

In many of these cases the members are fined, suspended, or in the severest cases have their license to practice revoked. What causes these men and women to violate the ethics that they have sworn to uphold in their professional lives? Unfortunately, there are no simple answers.

Searching further among books on business ethics, I sought to find a reasonable answer to the question of the violation of ethical conduct. Are the codes of ethics too difficult for the membership to follow or are the members too weak to comply?

I could not find a satisfying answer, so I decided to check what other research may have been done to develop a comprehensive yet simple set of ethical standards that anyone could follow. The majority of the texts I reviewed contained many outlines, tasks, and other methods to develop an ethical workplace.

## Recommended Text on Ethics

Then I ran across a book by Dosick,[1] titled *The Business Bible — Ten Commandments for Creating an Ethical Workplace*. His method of presentation intrigued me and generated consciousness concerning ethical behavior in my daily life as well as in my profession. I present the following excerpts* to you without regard to their possible religious overtones:

* Excerpts from Reference 1, Reprinted with permission of HarperCollins Publishers, Inc.

In the American business community, there is a growing awareness that ancient wisdom has much to inform and influence the modern marketplace.

After decades of unparalleled growth and prosperity, in the aftermath of financial scandal, and in the midst of difficult financial times, the business world has been moved to an almost unprecedented soul-searching and self-examination.

Prominent — and highly successful — business leaders who, not too long ago, described the workplace only as a place for production and profit are now speaking about a business world defined by "*mission, vision, and values,*" a place where there are not only contracts but a "*covenant,*" a place where workers can find "*real meaning*" in their work, and where good management is a matter of "*love ... a calling ... a trust.*"

This newly evolving new business design — rooted, as it is, in age-old religious traditions — led *Fortune* magazine to proclaim that "*the language of the pulpit* has become the currency of the executive suite.*"

Ten Commandments were enough for Moses to bring down from the mountain, for he lived in much simpler times.

Our world is much more complex, much more complicated, much more challenging than his.

For us, the original ten as important and as enduring as they are — are not enough.

We need more.

We need commandments to guide us in the workaday world of our jobs, our businesses, our professions.

So here — steeped in antiquity and clothed in contemporary garb — are ten commandments for creating an ethical workplace — the ways to bring meaning and worth, values and ethics, into the modern marketplace.

## The First Commandment — *Your Ear Shall Hear; Your Eyes Shall See*

It is a well-known fact that we hear what we want to hear and we can tune out anything else.

The art of doing business depends on how well you hear, how well you listen. How many stories have you heard about silly — and the tragic — mistakes that have been made, the expectations that have been dashed, the deals that have been lost, the reputations that have been ruined, when someone doesn't listen well?

How well you listen depends on two people — the listener *and* the speaker. The first half of listening well is being spoken to — or speaking — clearly. When you want people to listen *to you,* you can begin by making sure that your words are simple, direct, and distinct.

People with different backgrounds, different education, different training, and different agendas may simply not hear and understand what is being said.

To make sure that you are understood, you can try to be sensitive to your listener's experience and perceptions, and speak words that your listener can comprehend.

The other half of listening is taking the time and the energy to listen to what is really said, to hear the words — spoken and, sometimes unspoken — that are being uttered.

When you listen well — and really, really hear — you can come a long way toward understanding and, ultimately, succeeding.

You can find a balance between speaking and listening by learning when to speak up and when to keep quiet.

There is one more art to listening that you can acquire. You listen not only to words but to the sound of the voice.

People can use words to try to fake or fool, but eventually the tone and the timbre of their voice lay open the truth.

In your voice — and the voices of the people to whom you listen — is your exhaustion or your exhilaration, your anger or your joy, your deception or your honesty. When you listen carefully, the sounds of the voice you hear will reveal what you need to know.

But even listening well is not enough. It is not your ears alone that need to be open. Your eyes need to see.

Vision is more than what you see. Vision is opening your eyes and your mind's eye, as well to that place where you see and foresee, where you dream and imagine and create. The success of your company, your business, your profession, your career, depends on your vision.

When you open your eyes, you open your possibilities, and you visualize not only what already is but what can be. No matter what you have already accomplished and become, you can always envision more. Yet vision alone is not enough. Vision can be no more than daydreams that disappear, no more than wisps of skywriting that drift away before the last word is finished. Vision realized is imagination coupled with the drive and determination, with courage and creativity, with sweat and hard work.

## The Second Commandment — *Do Not Utter a False Report*

Always tell the truth. Let your word be your bond, and let your honor be your word. It's good advice, while it's not always easy to follow.

Speaking words of truth may be more delicate and more difficult when the speaker must be direct and forthright, and when the listener's personal and professional ego and self-esteem are at stake. You could be brutally honest, telling it like it is, "telling" the truth, the whole truth, and nothing but the truth. But you have to be very cautious. Remember that at least some of your truth comes not from a dispassionate, objective standard, but through the prism of your background, your biases, and your subjective judgments. What is "true" for you may not be "true" for everyone around you.

And then you need to be very, very careful. For your words have a great power. Your words can doom dreams and destroy hope. Your words can humble and humiliate and crush the spirit. Your words can shatter worlds. So how shall you speak your words of truth — as frank and as painful as they may be?

Gently wrap your words of truth in the words of kindness. Temper your criticism with praise, your admonition with comfort, your reality with the reason.

Use your words of truth to build up instead of tear down, to instruct, to encourage, to uplift. Give your words of truth as a gift of caring and of sharing.

A lie may seem to save you at the moment, but eventually your lies will ruin you.

For no matter what their immediate benefit, lies follow you and hound you, mock you and torment you, haunt you and give you no rest. Ultimately, no matter what the monetary cost — the truth will set you free. Your pride in your integrity will be preserved, and you will be able to sleep at night.

There's another kind of false report that we all too often utter that brings pain and hurt and can cause irreparable damage — words that are a violation of confidence, of privacy, of trust, of decency.

It takes at least two people to sustain gossip and rumor, to prolong the life of the words that fly away and cannot be retrieved — the speaker and the listener.

By being neither a speaker nor a listener, you help sustain the honor of another human being, a touch more decency to your office, to your business, to your world.

## The Third Commandments — *Do No Unrighteousness in Weights and Measures*

Your measure as a human being — in your reputation, success, or failure in the world of business — is often determined by how accurately you measure, how meticulously you count, how honestly you deal.

Dishonesty is dishonesty, and cheating is cheating, whether it involves a little or lot. If you cheat, if you defraud, you diminish yourself as a human being, and you violate the trust that others have put in you. And eventually, you will pay.

If you cheat, if your weights and measures are inaccurate, if your financial dealings are shoddy, if you take things that do not belong to you, you won't be able to hide it forever. People will find out.

Then your reputation and your business will suffer, because people don't want to deal with someone who cannot be trusted.

The modern marketplace is full of opportunity to cheat and to steal, "to look the other way" at dishonesty and deceit, to profit from ill-gotten gain. But when you do what is right *because it is right*, when you measure accurately and count exactly, when you are scrupulous in your commerce and meticulous in your dealings, then your colleagues will respect you, your customers and competitors will believe you, and everyone will trust you. And ultimately you will succeed, for everyone likes to deal with an honest man, everyone wants to do business with an honest woman.

## The Fourth Commandment — *Love Your Neighbor As Yourself*

Treat every human being as you want to be treated — with understanding, with fairness, with kindness, and with compassion. Give everyone else the same decency, dignity, the same honesty and integrity, the same warmth and concern that *you* want.

When you begin with the big smile and a good word, when you are warm and friendly, when you are open and sincere, you can expect respect and regard; you build good will and trust; you create an atmosphere where anything … and everything … is possible.

## The Fifth Commandment — *Do Justly, Love Mercy, and Walk Humbly*

At one time or another, in one form or another, almost every person who works in the world of business will be called on to manage and to lead.

For to paraphrase, some are born to leadership, some achieve leadership, and some have leadership thrust upon them. It takes very special talent, very special skills, very special commitment, to be in management — to be responsible for directing and affecting other people's work and careers.

To be a real leader means to be a shepherd to a flock, to protect and defend, to nurture growth and tend to needs. To be a leader means to consider each life in your care as precious as your own.

Warren Bennis, Distinguished Professor of Business Administration at University of Southern California teaches, "Managers do things right. Leaders do the right thing."

As a manager striving to be a true leader, you can do the right thing when you *do justly*, when you set the right tone and create the right atmosphere in which to do business.

As a manager, striving to be true leader, you can increase your effectiveness, you can add to your success, when, as well as doing justly, you *love mercy*. When your people need guidance and direction, you can be patient and gracious. When your people need support and encouragement, you can be kind and generous. When your people are confused and uncertain, you can be compassionate and consoling. When your people make mistakes … and surely as they will … you can be understanding and forgiving. When your people achieve success, you can be complimentary and proud. You love mercy when you understand where your people are "coming from," and when you wisely and gently help them rise up to where you want them to be.

As a manager striving to be a true leader, you accomplish the most when you *walk humbly*, when you're modest and not pretentious, when you leave pride and arrogance and power trips at the front door.

You can never become a true leader foisting yourself on others, by flaunting power, by demanding loyalty. Rather, you rise to leadership through quiet determination, gentle persuasion, and humble presence. You can become a true leader when you earn the respect, the allegiance, and the admiration of those you seek to guide.

You can become a true leader when you truly understand that your power comes not from those who appoint you, not from your own sense of self-importance, but from the permission, acceptance, and grace of those you lead.

## The Sixth Commandment — *Bring Healing and Cure*

What is more important than the physical and mental health of those who work with and for you? Very few people can leave all feelings, all emotions, all concerns — sorrows or joys — at the office door. Every day there are those who come to work with personal issues swirling within: illness, physical pain, marital strife, a sick child, a dying parent, a new found love, a daughter's graduation, a son's wedding.

What role or responsibility does your company, your business, have in providing for the safety and protection, the health and dignity of your people?

This means that you can inspire confidence in your workplace by making sure that the work space and the working conditions are safe and secure. And if injury occurs, you can provide the time and the money to ensure complete healing.

It means that you can assure that all your people — and their families — are adequately protected, by providing comprehensive medical, dental, disability, and life insurances. Not only will your people benefit, but you and your business will gain, for an employee who feels appreciated and well cared for will be a better, a more effective, a more productive employee. A worker who knows that his or her family is protected in case of trauma or tragedy will be a more content, a more loyal worker.

Preventive health care can include providing for a comprehensive annual physical examination, for gyms and running tracks and workout equipment in the workplace, for stress reduction clinics, and for in-house psychologist or social workers to offer consul and advice; preventive health can even mean a roving massage therapist to give a ten minute "at your desk" neck and shoulder massage to relax and reinvigorate. With preventive health care, everybody wins.

You can help your people be healthy and well when you hear their concerns, and also their unspoken words, when you share their joy, feel their pain, celebrate their triumphs, and comfort them in their sorrow.

You can help your people do their best work when you see not just the worker — in the role he or she plays in your plans — but the person — a whole human being — who feels and responds, who laughs and cries, who hurts and can heal.

You do the most for your business when you have healthy, happy people. And you have healthy, happy people when you take care of them and meet their needs.

## The Seventh Commandment — *You Shall Surely Tithe*

Long before there were any reports, long before there were profit and loss statements, long before there were pretax earnings and tax deductions for charitable contributions, there was the basic human instinct to care for each other.

In the world of business, giving is usually more formalized, but it serves the same purpose. Giving provides for those who need. When you and your company give of your monetary resources, you respond to the public interest, the public good.

You are sharing, contributing members of the community and the society in which you live and work — and which supports your business by buying your product.

Equally important as giving your company funds, is giving the work of your company's hands.

When you open your heart to give of your time, your care, and your concern, when you give the gift of the work of your hands to those who need you, you give the greatest gift of all — the gift of yourself.

Even if you don't have a lot of money to give, even if your business is feeling the pinch of tough economic times, you can still respond to the very real needs of a very real people by giving the service of your corporate heart and hands.

You and your company will be active, participating, contributing members of the community where you live and work when you understand the wisdom of the saying that "service is the rent you pay for living on earth."

## The Eighth Commandment — *Remember the Sabbath*

Do you run your business, or does your business run you? Why do you work? Why do you earn money? Certainly you cherish the satisfaction of a job well done. Surely you need and want the things that money can buy.

But your job, your business, your profession, can become all-consuming. It can take up all your time, all your energy. It can seem to run your life.

After an entire career of working, contributing, and earning, when you retire, the company may give you — or you may treat yourself to — a gold watch. But no matter how hard you work, how many hours you put in, how much you earned, when you die, no one is going to give you a gold tombstone.

The harder the work, the more you need to rest — to reenergize your body and to rejuvenate your soul.

When you and the people who work for and with you take off at least one day a week — not an hour or two here and there, not a once in a while if you can find the time day, but a regularly scheduled day, which you can if you wish, call the Sabbath — you slow down and relax, you have time to think, to contemplate, to share with the ones you love.

Your Sabbath day can enrich you enormously, because at least once each week, you tell yourself — you show yourself — what is really important to you, what really, really counts in your life.

When you take time each week to rest and rejuvenate, you are able to stay in touch with your own needs, your own desires, your own priorities.

You can remember what is important to you, and what you and your family are really all about. You have the time to listen to your heart, to make choices, to set your direction, and to control your own destiny.

When you listen to both voices within you — the voice calling you to dedicated work and the voice calling you to your personal commitments — you can begin to find a balance between work and relaxation, it can be as simple as coupling your hard work with meeting your own needs, you can begin to truly understand why you work and for what you live.

## The Ninth Commandment — *Acquire Wisdom*

Every working day, for 40 years or more you wake up, get dressed, and go to your job, your business, or profession. You need to earn a living, to provide yourself and your family with the necessities — and hopefully a few of the luxuries — of life.

But is money enough?

When you spend the days of your entire lifetime at work, don't you want more than a paycheck?

Wouldn't you like your work to be exciting, meaningful enough to you that you are eager to get out of bed every morning?

How do you do it? How do you find and sustain the work that compensates you fairly, at the same time, worthwhile and meaningful to you?

The contemporary teacher Marcia Sinetar advises, "Do what you love, the money will follow."

You can choose work that you like and gives you pleasure. You can choose work that is important; that gives you deep personal fulfillment.

You can choose work that touches people's lives, that gives you a sense that you are making a real contribution to the world in which you live.

The good news is that the satisfaction that you see can be found in any work you choose.

In every single job, and every single business, and every single profession — in *whatever* you do — there can be the satisfaction and that comes from knowing that what you do is important, that what you do makes a difference in the lives of the people you serve.

Every working moment won't be fun. There will be problems and frustrations and stress.

But if, on balance, the good outweighs the bad, accomplishment outweighs the drudgery, and happiness outweighs the hassles, then your work can be worthy of your energy and your commitment, your work can be worthwhile.

If, at the end of most days, you can say to yourself, "what I did today made a difference, what I did today made a contribution, what I did today makes me feel good," then your work has meaning, your work life can bring you contentment and joy.

Everything depends on you being sure that you are doing your best.

For when you bring to your work your best effort, you can derive the most satisfaction.

When you give your people the freedom to use their own imagination, to tinker and to create, your company benefits not only from the resulting products but also from the presence of happy, satisfied workers who feel pride in their accomplishment and appreciation for their contribution.

Through your work, you can find meaning and value in your life, you can grow any policy human being, you can feel personal satisfaction and experience deep happiness from what you accomplish.

Through your work, you can achieve your noblest ambitions and sustain your greatest dreams.

Through your work, you can touch the finest within yourself.

Through your work, you can come to understand the good council of the modern writer Leo Rosten, who teaches, the purpose of life is … to matter, to be productive, to be useful, to have it make some difference that you lived at all.

And through your work, you can make this ancient entreaty your own: "Teach me to make good account of mine days, that I may acquire a heart of wisdom."

## The Tenth Commandment — *Know Before Whom You Stand*

Who is your boss? To whom do you answer? Who has the power? Who makes the final decisions? Who holds the ultimate authority?

No matter who may be, no matter what person seems to control your fate and your destiny, there's something else that is sure, something else that fashions your work and molds your conduct.

There is something beyond you, something greater than you, that defines and shapes you, that sets out for your standards of right and wrong, that demands your goodness and calls you to greatness.

Some people call it intuition. Some call it gut feeling. Some call it conscience. Some call it the inner force.

Some call it the higher spirit.

Some call it God.

No matter what you call it, it is always present, summoning you to heed its commands.

And you are always in its presence, compelling you to know before whom you stand.

When you know before whom you stand, you can know who you are.

When you know before whom you stand, you know your identity and your purposes, you know your value and your commitments.

When you know before whom you stand, you can be guided to do your best.

It can be difficult and confusing to do right, to do good — to accept a moral mandate and live up to an established standard of ethical behavior — when definitions, circumstances, and situations seemed constantly changing and subject to personal interpretation.

Get as the modern mystic Abraham Joshua Heschel taught, Man's understanding of *what* is right and wrong has often varied throughout the ages; yet the consciousness that *there is* a distinction between right and wrong is permanent and universal.

And modern technology has conveniently provided a measuring stick by which you can determine whether or not you are conducting your business in an acceptable, ethical way.

You can ask yourself: "How will I feel if my business dealings today become tomorrow morning's newspaper headlines?"

No matter how wise and talented you are, no matter how experienced you are, no matter how confident you are, your job, your business, will present you with situations that are hard to handle, problems that are hard to solve, decisions that are difficult to make, crises that demand immediate — and usually, very creative — solutions.

When you know before whom you stand, you can meet any challenge facing a leader, and overcome any obstacle, for the courage, the strength, and the help you need, not merely to endure but to prevail, is always with you.

These ten commandments for creating an ethical workplace offer you the foundation and the formula for bringing meaning and worth, values and ethics to your job, your business, or profession.

For all their wide-ranging concerns, their profile and depth and their practical relevance, these commandments can be summed up in *one* word."

So, remember

| The Business Bible's Word to Live by | |
|---|---|
| E | Everywhere |
| T | All the time |
| H | Be honest |
| I | Act with integrity |
| C | Have compassion |
| S | For what is at stake is |
| | Your reputation |
| | Your self-esteem |
| | Your inner peace |

## Suggested Conduct for Professional Investigators/Reconstructionists

The following is a list of examples concerning the way I believe a professional investigator or reconstructionist should conduct himself/herself:

- Do not continue working on a case if you know the results will not be favorable to your client.
- Call your client as soon as you are sure that the results of your investigation and reconstruction indicate that there is no theory of liability.
- Do not work for two parties on the same case, without getting approval from both parties to continue on that case.
- Do not work on cases involving friends, relatives, or co-workers because this can leave the impression with opposing counsel and the jury that you may be biased with respect to your work.
- Never discuss the particulars of any case with any attorney, insurance personnel, or other professional witnesses unless you know that they or the firms they represent are not connected with the case or your clients.
- Never prepare a report, give a deposition, or testify in court without being thoroughly prepared on the subject matter that you have been retained to analyze and reconstruct.
- Do not accept a contract that is not within the realm of your expertise and/or capabilities even if you have a peripheral knowledge of the work required.
- Be prepared to respond to your client's questions in a fair and equitable manner and if you are unable to accept his/her contract, then recommend another professional whom you know can give the client the necessary assistance to complete the contract.

In this business, word of mouth is the best if not the only method of promoting your business. Your reputation and ethical conduct are the only means by which clients can judge the way you conduct yourself and your business.

## Reference

1. Dosick, R. W. D., *The Business Bible* — Ten Commandments for Creating an Ethical Workplace, William Morrow, New York, 1993.

# Glossary

**AASHTO**   American Association of State Highway and Transportation Officials.

**ABS**   Antilock braking system. This is a braking system designed to brake the vehicle in the most effective manner, without locking up the tires and causing the tires to go into a skid. This system is used differently than standard brakes when braking in an emergency situation. The brake pedal is stepped on and held in place while the electronic system takes over and modulates or applies the brakes until the wheels want to lock up, and then releases and brakes again. The driver does not have to do anything else. The old system required the driver to pump his/her brakes, thus modulating the brakes and doing the same thing as the ABS system.

**Acceleration marks**   Marks that are just the opposite of skid marks. The tires are being rotated by the axle and when done fast enough, the outside of the tire, the tread, takes time to catch up to the rest of the tire, which is being held by the coefficient of friction between the tires and the road surface. Therefore, the acceleration marks are heavy at the beginning and lighten up as the tire tread catches up.

**Animation**   A computer program that allows the reconstructionist to develop a videotape of an accident sequence to be used as an exhibit to his/her opinion of the accident scenario.

**Apogee**   The maximum altitude a projectile will reach when shot in the air. Used here to define the maximum height the motorcycle driver or rider will reach when impacting an object, usually a vehicle.

**Base drawing**   The scale drawing made of the accident scene that shows all the landmarks and detail to set the scene. It generally does not contain any measurements or any points of impact (POI) or points of rest (POR).

**Body buck**   That portion of the vehicle that does not contain the suspension, transmission, engine, or any other equipment. It is only the exterior sheet metal with the windshield and side windows in place; if a sunroof is an option on that vehicle, then the body buck is also tested with that option in place.

**Body in white drawings**   Name given to full-size engineering drawings that show the structural layout of the vehicle without the overlaying external skin with anthropomorphic dummies in each of the seated positions.

**Break-over angles**   The angle between the point of contact of the front or rear tire of the vehicle and the lowest point of the vehicle. This angle is important for the vehicle to get up and down driveways, culverts, etc.

**Cab over tractors**   A type of truck where the cab sits directly over the engine of the vehicle.

**CDC — collision damage classification**   Discussed in detail in Chapter 11. It is a means by which the damage to the vehicle can be classified or indexed.

**Coefficient of friction**   A number that is dependent on the two materials that are acting on each other. These numbers can range from 0.1 to 1.0 $g$.

**Collision – primary**   The impact between a vehicle and another vehicle or a vehicle and a fixed object.

**Collision – secondary**   The impact between the occupant and some interior component of the vehicle.

**Collision–tertiary**   The impact between the occupant and the restraint system.

**Computer simulation**   A computer program that through a mathematical means and a series of data input into the computer program allows the solution to the equations of motion and renders a computer-generated drawing of the motion of the vehicle just prior to then through the collision, and then onto its point of rest.

**Data back**   A special electronic backing to a 35-mm camera that will imprint each photograph with the date, the time, or the number sequence of a film roll.

**Direct damage**   Damage or deformation of the vehicle that was directly caused by the collision itself.

**Diffuser**   A special filter that is attached to the flash unit of the camera to soften the light to prevent or at least minimize its reflection on the surface, to prevent hot or bright spots on the photograph, and to spread the light on the object.

**Drag factor**   Comes from the tool used to determine the value of the coefficient of friction of the road surface. A portion of a concrete-weighted tire is pulled or dragged along the roadbed by a "fish scale." The investigator reads the scale and divides by the weight of the tire to determine the coefficient of friction. It is called a drag factor because it is determined by dragging the tire.

**Driver's side**   (In the U.S.) The left side (from the inside looking out) of the vehicle.

**EDCRASH**   A sophisticated computer program used for accident reconstruction, which is used on personal computers (PCs).

**Edge ruts**   Are developed on a soft shoulder when a vehicle runs off the roadbed surface onto the shoulder and then presses the soil, forming a rut at least 2 to 4 in. deep.

**Exemplar vehicle**   A vehicle of the same make, model year, and accessories that the collision vehicle had at the time of the accident. It is meant to represent as closely as possible the actual collision vehicle.

**Far side**   The opposite side of the impact.

**Hot shoe**   A special device that allows the flash unit to be attached directly to the camera and synchronize the flash with the lens opening.

**Hysteresis**   A metallurgical phenomenon that allows the metal to lose a portion of its deformation.

**Impact**   Generally interchangeable with collision.

**Inboard**   Going toward the centerline of the vehicle.

**Induced damage**   Damage that was caused by components being squeezed together, causing the sheet to bend outward or inward from its normal position. The damage was not caused by an impact to the particular area of the vehicle.

**Interrogatories**   Set of specialized questions sent by one attorney to another concerning requested information of their clients and/or respective companies, such as maintenance and accident history of the vehicle, preexisting medical problems of the occupants, and other pertinent information with respect to the accident itself.

**Lateral axis**   The short axis of the vehicle, from the right side to the left side.

**Longitudinal axis**   The long axis of the vehicle, which runs from the front or hood to the rear, or trunk of the vehicle.

**Long-nose tractors**   A type of truck that has the engine in front of the cab.

**Motorized winder unit** An attachment to the bottom of a 35-mm camera that winds the film electrically after each photograph is taken.

**Near side** The side of the vehicle that is being impacted.

**Occupant** Can be one of the passengers or the driver of a vehicle.

**OEM** Original equipment manufacturer.

**Outboard** Going toward the outside of the vehicle from the inside.

**Overlay** A scale drawing with only specific data shown. It can contain the vehicles as the investigator determines the point of impact (POI) or just the measured data taken from the scene. Electronically in a computer-assisted design (CAD) program, these overlays are easily removed or laid over the base drawing as required. In court exhibits the base drawing is on opaque paper and all the overlays are on clear, partial see-through Mylar film.

**Parallelogram method** Graphic method by which vectors can be added. The two vectors are laid off graphically to scale in proper directions from a common starting point. They form two adjacent sides of a parallelogram. Drawing the two opposite sides meeting at the far end of the diagram then completes the parallelogram. The diagonal of the parallelogram is the resultant of the two original quantities both in length and in direction.

**Passenger** Includes everyone except the driver of a vehicle.

**Passenger's side** Position opposite the driver's side.

**Payout** The term given to a condition where the length of the webbing of the seat belt increases due to a malfunction of the retractor mechanism.

**PDOF** Principal direction of force. Many computer simulation programs today require an input telling it the principal direction from which the force was being applied to the vehicle. The clock directions usually do this, with the front of the vehicle being 12 o'clock.

**Perception time** The time it takes the human body to perceive that a situation is about to take place, or is taking place on the highway ahead, that requires some action.

**Photogrammetry** A scientific method used to determine from photographs the length of skid marks, width of roadways, or any other types of measurements needed.

**Preproduction defect reports** Report used by production engineers and technicians to list problems on preproduction vehicles that need to be repaired prior to, or after, the full production run begins.

**Polygon method**   Used for convenience to add three or more vectors (the parallelogram method being somewhat more difficult to use for this purpose). This method, starting from a common point of the vectors, is laid out in proper scale direction. From its terminal end another displacement is laid off similarly with the proper scale and direction until all the vectors have been placed head to tail or terminally. The last line drawn closes the figure forming a polygon; and this line is the resultant of the addition of all the vectors.

**Postimpact skid distance**   The distance a vehicle skids after an impact or collision.

**Postimpact velocity**   The speed of the vehicle after an impact or collision.

**Preimpact skid distance**   The distance a vehicle skids prior to an impact or collision.

**Preimpact velocity**   The speed of the vehicle prior to an impact or collision.

**Reaction Time**   How long it takes the human body to react to a perception that requires some action. It could be a brake application, or turning the steering wheel to move the vehicle out of the line of the action taking place ahead.

**REC-TEC**   A computer program used for basic accident reconstruction.

**Reference line**   An extension of the reference point (RP) from which the $X$ or $Y$ direction measurement is taken. Generally speaking, the RP is a pole or hydrant set back from the street or road. A straight line is drawn from the RP to the curb or edge of the road. The line from the pole to the curb is the vertical reference line. A second line is then drawn on the outside of the curb and is the horizontal reference line.

**Requests for documents**   Set of official requests sent out during the discovery process. They are requesting specific information from a singular party or business to the lawsuit, such as product specifications, and business or insurance contracts.

**Resolved**   To break up the original vector into two parts that are 90 degrees to one another at the origin of the original vector.

**Right front passenger**   The seat opposite the driver in the front seating area of the vehicle.

**Ring flash**   A special photographic flash unit that attaches to the lens of the camera for close-up pictures in dark areas or for concentrated light.

**RP   (Reference point)**   Chosen by the on-scene investigator, from which to take all measurements, in an $X$ and $Y$ or north and south direction.

**Skid marks**   Marks left on the road surface when the tire stops rotating, locks up, and skids.

**Stellar pattern**   A bull's-eye-type fracture of the windshield when struck by a human or anthropomorphic head during a collision. Damage occurs in the form of a circular pattern, with cracks radiating from the center.

**Striking vehicle**   The vehicle initiating the collision. This is sometimes referred to as the bullet vehicle.

**Struck vehicle**   The vehicle that was impacted by the other vehicle.

**Submarining**   Action of the occupant sliding forward underneath the lap belt portion of the restraint system, with the lap belt webbing resting above the pelvic girdle.

**Tire patch**   That portion of the tire that rests on the road surface. It is oval shaped and has its longest axis along the normal direction of travel of the vehicle. When a vehicle is sliding sideways, the tire marks left on the road get almost twice as wide as the tire turns sideways and the short axis is in the direction of travel that makes the tire marks.

**Truck**   A specialized vehicle that can be for commercial purposes, such as semitractor trailers, straight trucks, tankers, and stake trucks, or can be owned privately such as pickups, sport utility vehicles (SUVs), vans, and minivans.

**Tumblehome**   The curvature of the vehicle body inward toward the roof. This gives the vehicle a rounder look from the front and decreases aerodynamic drag.

**Unloaded tire**   Trailing tires that have less weight as a result of a weight transfer to the leading tires of a rotating vehicle. In this situation, some weight is shifted to those tires, but not enough to leave a gap between the tire surface and the ground, and not enough to allow downward force to produce a yaw mark.

**U-V filter**   A filter used on a camera to reduce the glare off an object being photographed.

**Vehicle**   Refers to all types of four- (or more) wheeled vehicles; everything except motorcycles, bicycles, and mopeds.

**Wear bars**   Marks on the tires where no tread appears. Manufacturers build these into the tires.

**Yaw marks**   Very distinctive marks left by a tire that is rotating and turning at the same time. Instead of the tire leaving dark marks parallel to the direction of vehicle movement, there are striations in the marks at various angles to the direction of travel. The direction of the marks is dependent on the amount of "rolling under" the tread does during the maneuver. In addition, the entire mark is curved. The width of the yaw mark as well as the number and angle of the striations are highly dependent on the speed of the vehicle.

# Index

## A

AASHTO, *see* American Association of State
    Highway and Transportation
    Officials
Abdominal injuries
  restraint systems, 182, 184, 256
  steering columns, 157
  steering wheel rims, 159
Abrasions, 120, 174, 177–178
ABS, *see* Antilock braking system
Acceleration
  calculations
    constant and linear motion, 341–342
    velocity, 366, 367, 378
  caudocephaled and occupant kinematics,
    248
  definition, 340–341
  linear, *see* Linear acceleration
  marks, 62, 75, 459
  occupant kinematics
    backward/forward, 254
    lateral, 258–259
  sudden, 17–18
Accident investigation forms
  damage measurements, 219–221
  exterior damage sketches, 218, 219
  injury mechanisms, 231–232, 234
  interior contacts, 223, 225
  interior seats, headrests, and steering wheel
    and column, 226–227
  internal damage sketches, 223, 224
  internal injuries, 229–230, 232
  notes and injury countermeasures, 233, 235
  occupant area intrusions, 221–223
  occupant information and injury data,
    229, 230
  seat belts and air bags, 227–229
  skeletal injuries, 230–231, 233
  soft tissue injuries, 229, 231
  tire data, 217, 219

vehicle data, 32, 215–217
Accident reconstruction
  checklist, 46
  detailed injury scale, 293–299
  drawing, 268, 269
  insufficient details, what happens, 27
  on-scene sketches, 67–72
  photographing the vehicle, 89
  real-world, 77–87
  rural setting
    debris pattern, 61
    lighting, 63
    point of impact, 64–65
    point of rest, 65–67
    poles, 63–64
    road surface and shoulders, 62–63
    roadbed damage, 61–62
    trees, 64
  sample case, 265–272
  tire marks, 74–77
  traffic light timing, 73–74
  urban setting
    configuration, 47, 48
    debris location, 51–54
    line of sight, 54–56, 57
    other details, 49
    point of impact, 49–50, 51, 52,
      53, 54
    reference points, 47, 48, 49
    witness marks, 51
  vehicular collisions, 45–47
  visualization, 72–73
  water on or over roadway, 87–88
Accident reconstructionist
  becoming one, 261–262
  defined, 263
  how to start the reconstruction, 263–265
  where to start
    basic knowledge, 15–19
    fresh scenes, 19–21
    requirements for, 11

sources of additional training, 11–15
stale or aged scenes, 21–22
Accident scene, interrogatories, 435–439
Accident victims, 18, 66, *see also* Occupant
Accidents, why investigate
causes, 4–5
criminal and civil litigation, 9–10
databases for road conditions and use of
restraint systems, 8–9
economic cost, 1–3
human costs, 3–4
investigative organizations, 8
methods to estimate costs, 5–6
prevention and elimination of on-the-job
injuries, 9
reasons for investigating, 7–8
reducing vehicular injuries, 6–7
Accuracy, measurement, 325
ACIR, *see* Automotive Crash Injury Research
survey
ACTAR, *see* American Council of Traffic
Reconstructionists
Active restraints, 181, *see also* Restraint
systems
Advanced Traffic Accident Reconstruction
Training Institute, 262
Adverse information, 432, *see also* Clients,
educating
Aerial photographs, *see* Photographs
Afferent fibers, 243
Age, 5
Agricultural stations, 384
Air bag restraint systems
accident investigation forms, 227–229
children, 8
components, use, and advantages/
disadvantages, 202–207
investigations of steering wheel rims, 159
reduction of vehicular injuries, 6
roof mounted, 208
side impact, 205
Air brake systems, 344, *see also* Braking systems
Air cushion, *see* Air bag restraint systems
Air force, 247
Alcohol, 4–5
Allen wrenches, 26
American Academy of Forensic Examiners, 14
American Association of State Highway and
Transportation Officials
(AASHTO), 389
American Council of Traffic Accident
Reconstructionists (ACTAR), 14,
262, 319
American Medical Association Abbreviated
Injury Scale, 287–293

American Medical Association Tissue Damage
Scale, 285
Angles, photography
automobile accidents, 93, 98, 100, 106
low angle, 115
motorcycle accidents, 304
Animals, 90, 257, 258
Animation
exhibit development, 331, 333–335
rendering and accident investigation, 38
usage of term, 459
Ankle, 241
Anthropomorphic dummies, 245–246,
249–250, 256, 258
Antilock braking system (ABS), 76, 77, 208,
459, *see also* Braking system
Aorta, 253
APGAR scale, 285
Apogee
calculation of velocity in motorcycle
accidents, 308–312
pedestrian accidents, 318
usage of term, 459
Appendicular skeleton, 240
Arteries, 244
Asphalt surfaces, 62, 76, 344–345
Attorney, 422
Automobile companies, 8, 436–439
Automotive Crash Injury Research (ACIR)
survey, 150–152
Autonomic nervous system, 244

# B

Baboons, 257, 258
Background noise, 92–93
Backup tape, 38
Backward acceleration, *see* Acceleration
Ballistics tests, 418
Barrel roll, 176, *see also* Rollovers
Barrier crash tests, 397
Base drawing, 459
Base metal, 122–125
Behavior, verbal, 423
Bending, steering column, 157
Bias, 422, 448–449
Billing, 38
Black ice, 385
Blade jackknife, 26
Blood and guts presentation, 406
Blood pooling, 180
Blowouts, 129, 130, 132, *see also* Tires
BOCA, *see* Building Owners and Construction
Association
Body duck, 460

Body in white drawing, 393–394, 460
Bones, 240–241
Bracket, bending, 196, 198–199, *see also*
    Restraint systems
Brain, 243
Brake fluid, 133
Brake light bulb, 135
Brake pads, 306
Braking system, *see also* Antilock braking
    system
    capacity and accident scene investigation, 76
    motorcycle accidents, 303
    velocity equations, problems, 365, 374, 375
Break-over angles, 460
Bridges, curve plotting, 71–72
Bronchus, 253
Bruising, 184, *see also* Restraint systems
Building Owners and Construction Association
    (BOCA), 400
Bulbs, 138
Bull's eye pattern, 145, *see also* Windshield
Bumpers
    front-of-vehicle pedestrian accidents, 314,
        316
    photographing the accident vehicle, 113,
        114, 119
    rear-end impact accidents, 173–174
Business bible, 456
Business cards, 37

**C**

Cab over tractors, 460
CAD, *see* Computer-aided design program
Cadavers, 249–252, 253, 256, *see also*
    Kinematics, occupant
Camera, *see also* Video camera
    panoramic lens, 34
    single-lens reflex 35-mm, 32–33
    still/35 mm, 93–109
Camera cases, 35
Cannonball method, 307–312
Capillaries, 244
Cardiovascular system, 244–245
Cartage, vehicle, 25
Cartilage, 241
Case, determination if there is one, 433
Case histories, unusual, 439–442
Caudocephaled acceleration, *see* Acceleration
CDC, *see* Collision damage classification
Cellulose nitrate, 143, *see also* Windshields
Central nervous system (CNS), 243
Chain of custody, evidence, 31–32
Chain reaction, 110
Chalk, 27–28

Charging device, video camera, 36
Charisma, witness, 422
Checklists, 46, 166–167
Chest injuries
    impact acceleration and occupant
        kinematics, 253–254
    instrument panels, 152, 153
    steering columns, 157
    steering wheel rims, 158
Child seats, 8, 210, 235
Children, restraint systems, 210–212
Circular pattern, 145, *see also* Glass;
    Windshields
Civil litigation, 9–10
Classes, injury criteria, 293–296
Clay, children's, 30
Clients, educating
    interrogatories, 433–439
    technology and basic language, 431–433
    unusual case histories, 439–442
Clock direction system, 277–278
Close-up views, 94, 95, 96, 97, 99–106,
    104–105, 115, 116, 119, 120, 121,
    *see also* Views
Clothing, witness, 424
CNS, *see* Central nervous system
Coefficient of fraction
    calculations
        distance equations, 364, 372
        momentum equations, 380
        rear-end impact, 347
        resting points of vehicle-to-vehicle colli-
          sion, 359
        velocity and motorcycle accidents, 308,
          310
    definition, 344–345
    impact velocity determination in pedestrian
        accidents, 319–320
    tire marks and accident scene investigation,
        76
    usage of term, 460
Cold fracture, 136
Collapse, steering column, 157
Collision damage classification (CDC), 221,
    460
Collisions
    secondary and air bag restraint systems,
        202–207
    usage of terms of primary/secondary/
        tertiary, 460
    vehicular and basic knowledge of
        investigator, 45–46
Commandments, *see* Ethics
Communication, nonverbal, 407–416
Compass, handheld, 30–31

Competence, witness, 422, 424
Comprehensive costs, estimating, 5–6
Comprehensive Research Injury Scale, 289, 290
Compression injuries, 203
Computer
    mainframe and Vehicle Deformation Index,
        277
    networking, 38
    programs, 40–41
    requirements, 38–41
    simulations
        accident investigation, 13, 102, 103
        bumpers and investigations of rear-end
            impacts, 173
        exhibit development, 335–338
        usage of term, 460
Computer-aided design (CAD) program
    accident reconstruction, 30, 52, 153,
        268–269
    exhibit development, 324
Conclusion, stating, 411–412
Concrete surfaces, 62, 76, 344
Concussions, 250–252
Cones, orange, 36–37
Constant angle method, 68–69
Constant distance method, 69–71
Construction zone, 388–390
Contacts, interior, 223, 225
Contusions, 184
Costs, accident investigation, 1–5
Crash sensors, 204, 205
Crash signature, 262
Credibility, witnesses, 407, 408, 419–420
Criminal litigation, 9–10
Criminal science, training, 11–12
Cross-examination, 414, 415
Culverts, 66–67
Curbs, 47, 65, 129
Curves, methods for plotting
    constant angle method, 68–69
    constant distance method, 69–71
    median system, 70, 71–72
Customer service bulletins, 394–395
Cuts, tires, 132

**D**

D ring system, 193, 196–202, *see also* Restraint
        systems
Damage
    environmental, 19
    induced, 100, 110, 117, 461
    marring, 131, 217
    measurements and accident investigation
        forms, 219–221

noncollision, 89–90
photographing the accident vehicle, 97,
    104–105
property costs and accidents, 1
rolled and noting/recording metal folds, 112
unexplained, 138
Data back, 33, 460
Data research companies, 399
Database analysis, 398
Day of week, 5
Deaths, 1–2
Debris
    marking with index cards, 29
    pattern
        accident investigation of fresh scenes, 20
        location and investigation, 18
        rural accident scenes, 61, 64–65, 66
        urban accident scenes, 50, 4
        visualization of scene, 73
Decapitation, 181–182, 441–442
Deceleration velocity, 364, 365, 372–373, *see*
        *also* Velocity
Deformable materials, 173
Deformation Index, *see* Vehicle Deformation
        Index
Deformations
    base metal separations, 122–123
    energy absorption and sheet metal thickness,
        124–125
    fresh scenes, 20
    motorcycle accidents, 305–306
    steering wheel rim, 159
    videotaping at accident scene, 91–92, 93,
        99–100
Delivery, testimony, 423
Dents, pedestrian accidents, 316, *see also*
        Vehicle exterior
Department of transportation, 344
Deposition/courtroom appearance
    direct testimony, 427–428
    expert witness and use of videotapes,
        403–407
    nature of jury response to expert witness,
        416–420
    nonverbal communication in expert
        testimony, 407–416
    preparation of client, 432–433
    review, 270
    source credibility, 420–427
Depth/counter gauge, 29
Dialects, witness, 423, 424–425
Diesel fluid, 133, 135
Diffuser, 460
Digestive system, 245
Direct damage, 460

Direct examination, 425–426
Direct testimony, 410–411, 427–428, 432
Dirt roads, 61, 178, 345, *see also* Roads
Disabilities, 318
Disassembly, vehicle, 26, 27
Discovery, 433–434
Distance traveled, calculations, 341, 363–365
    linear motion with constant acceleration,
        341–342
    problems, 371–373
DNA analysis, 146
Documentation, ownership, 41
Door panels, 171
Doors
    photographing the accident vehicle,
        101–102, 104, 106, 120
    side impacts and damage investigation, 169
Double lock system, 179
Drafting equipment, 39
Drag factor, 345–347, 461
Drag test, 346–347
Dragging death, 440–441
Driver education classes, 4
Driver's side, 461
Dynamism, witness, 422

**E**

EA, *see* Energy absorbing steering column
Economic costs, estimation, 5
EDCRASH, 461
Edge ruts, 62–63, 461
Efferent fibers, 243
Ego, witnesses, 412–413
Ejection, occupants
    caudocephaled acceleration, 248–249
    moon/sun/T roofs, 161–162
    rear-end impacts, 176
    rollovers, 178–179
    use of surrogates in exhibit development,
        331, 333
Elastic deformation, 120
Electromechanical sensors, 203, 204
Electronic measuring device, 267, 324, *see also*
        Measurements
Electronic sensors, 204
Emergency room, 3
Endocrine system, 245
Endoskeleton, 239
Endurance testing, 396
Energy absorbing (EA) steering column, 156,
        *see also* Steering column
Energy absorption, 124
Engine oil, 133
Environmental information, 419

Ethics
    derivations and definitions, 445–446
    recommended text, 446–456
    ways reconstructionists should conduct
        themselves, 456–457
Evasive action, 65
Evidence
    accident scene, 15
    chain of custody, 31–32
    examination and investigation of stale
        scenes, 22
    loss of and photographing the accident
        vehicle, 90–91
    management and vehicle interiors, 141
    ownership, 42
Evidence tags, 31–32
Exemplar vehicle, 461
Exhibits, preparation
    animations, 331, 333–335
    computer simulations, 335–338
    measurements, 324–327
    photographs, 323
    scale drawings, 324
    surrogates, 327–331, 332, 333
Exit velocity, 311
Exoskeleton, 239
Expenses, tracking, 38
Expert witness
    credibility, 419–420, 421–425
    nonverbal communication in testimony,
        407–416
    use of videotape, 405–406
Eye heights, 58
Eyebrow, instrument panels, 149
Eyewitnesses, 63

**F**

Face, 158, 250–252
Factor analysis, 421
Fading, 92
False report, 448–449
Far side, 461
Fatal squad, 7
Fatalities, motorcycle accidents, 301
Federal government, accident investigation, 8
Federal Motor Vehicle Safety Standards
        (FMVSS), 13, 147, 173, 396
Felt tip pens, 29
Femur, 250
Fender, damage, 100–105, 117, 118, 120
Filament, damage, 135–138
File server, 38
Film, 34
Flash unit, 34

Flasher, yellow, 37
Flat room drawing, 223
Fluid leaks, 133, 135
FMVSS, *see* Federal Motor Vehicle Safety
    Standards
Force absorber, 155–156
Force–deformation characteristic, 151–152
Forward acceleration, *see* Acceleration
Forward-force accidents, 297
Fractures, 249–250, *see also* Kinematics,
    occupant
Fracturing, instrument panels, 153–154
Free-running loop, 184, 188, 192–193, 194,
    199, 202
Fresh scenes, 19–21
Friction force, 314, 315
Fuel tank, 135

**G**

*g* force tests, 254
Garments, 316
Gas, injury-related problems with air
    bags, 203
Gasoline, 133, 135
General Medical Index, 276
Glass, 147, 172, *see also* Windshields
Glove boxes, 155
Gouge marks
    inspection of accident vehicle, 125–128
        undercarriage, 133
    motorcycle accidents, 303–304
    outlining and special equipment for
        accident investigation, 27
    rural accident scenes, 61–62, 67
Graph paper, 30
Grass surfaces, 178
Gravel surfaces, 345
Gravity calculations, 308, 309
Grease pencils, 28–29, 71
Grille, 115, 116, 117, 119
Grinding marks, 130
Guard door beam, 169

**H**

Hair strands, 174–175
Hand, 240–241
Hand controls, 212
Handicaps, 212–214
Handles, door, 172
Handling damage, 89
Head
    bones, 240
    impact

occupant kinematics, 250–252
    rearview mirrors, 163
    windshields, 143, 144, 145–146
    sun visor injury, 160
Headlights, 116, 135–138, 302
Head-on collision, 129
Headrests, 165–166, 226–227
Head stars, 223
Healing, 451–452, *see also* Ethics
Health organizations, 8
Hearing/listening, 447–448, *see also* Ethics
Heart, 244
Hedge, 57
Helix rollover, 176, 177, *see also* Rollovers
Helmet, 305
High-penetration resistant (HPR) glass, 144,
    *see also* Glass
Highway Department, 387–388
Hood
    pedestrian accidents, 315
    photographing the accident vehicle,
        116–117, 120, 124
    separation of welds and inspection of
        accident vehicle, 123, 128
Horse collar effect, 143
Hot fracture, 136
Hot shoe, 461
House, urban accident scenes, 55
HPR, *see* High-penetration resistant glass
Hubcaps, 130–131
Human body
    basic systems, 239–245
    kinematics, 238–239
Human factor data, 399–400
Human factor testing, 343
Humility, 450, *see also* Ethics
Hydraulic devices, 212
Hydroplaning, 87–88
Hypothetical case, 265–272
Hypothetical questions, 413–414
Hysteresis, 461

**I**

Impact
    angle and motorcycle accidents, 304
    calculation of resting points of vehicle-to-
        vehicle collision, 353, 355
    pedestrian accidents
        front of vehicle, 313–314
        velocity, 319–320
    rear-end
        accident investigations, 147
        momentum equations calculations,
            367–368

relations to interior components, 173–176

solving the problem mathematically, 347–353

rock-type impact and windshields, 145

side

occupant kinematics, 259

relations to interior components, 168–172

type and investigations involving windshields, 144–145

usage of term, 461

Impound yard, 89

Inaccuracy, measurements, 449

Inboard, 461

Independent agencies, 397–398

Independent study programs, 13

Index cards, 29

Induced damage, see Damage, induced

Inflator systems, 9

Information

background, 15

gathering and accident reconstruction, 267

overload and perception/reaction time, 343

sources

accident intersection data, 387

aerial photographs, 392–393

construction zone, 388–390

meteorology experts, 384–385

power and telephone poles, 390–392

professional associations, 401

state highway department photographs, 387–388

state maintenance records, roads, and trucks, 392

trade associations, 400–401

vehicle documentation, 393–400

vehicle statistics, 385–387

vision and lighting experts, 385

weather sources, 383–384

Injuries

correlation and Traffic Accident Data Index, 275

instrument panels and accident investigations, 150–152

mechanisms/countermeasures and accident investigation forms, 231–232, 234, 235

pedestrian accidents, 314

prevention and elimination of on-the-job, 9

unusual case histories, 439–440

vehicular accidents, 2

reducing, 6–7

Injury criteria, 293–296

Injury reports, 257–258

Injury scales

accident investigation, 293–299

American Medical Association Abbreviated Injury Scale, 287–293

medically acceptable, 285–287

Installation, restraint systems, 212

Instantaneous velocity, 340, see also Velocity

Institute of Police Technology and Management (IPTM), 12, 262

Instrument panels, accident investigations

lower surfaces, 150–155

side impacts, 171–172

upper surfaces, 148–150

Insufficient details, accident reconstruction, 272

Insurance companies, 8

Interior seats, 226–227

Internal damage, 223, 224

Internal injuries, 229–230, 232

Internet, 43–44, 395

Interrogatories, 433–439, 461

Intersections, 58–59, 73–74, 387

Invertube, 155–156

Investigative organizations, 8

IPTM, see Institute of Police Technology and Management

**J**

Jargon, 412, 423

Jewelry, conspicuous on expert witnesses, 410

Joints, 241–242

Journals/periodicals, 398–399

Judge, nonverbal communication, 408

Junkyard, 90, 94, 95, 96, 97

Jury

response to expert witness, 416–420

source credibility, 420–421

videotapes, 404–405, 406

**K**

Kinematics, occupant

anthropomorphic dummies, 245–246

backward acceleration, 254

basic systems in the human body

cardiovascular system, 244–245

muscular system, 242

nervous system, 242–244

skeletal system, 239–242

visceral system, 245

computer simulations for exhibit development, 337

general physiological effects, 255

impact acceleration, 246

injuries, 255–258
lap belt injuries in aircraft/automotive
    accidents, 255
lateral acceleration, 258–259
linear acceleration, 247–254
longitudinal acceleration, 254
terminology definitions, 238–239
Kinetic energy, 142
Knee/hip/thigh complex, 151, 152, 153

**L**

Laboratory testing, 396
Laminated safety glass, 142–143, *see also* Glass;
    Windshields
Lap belt, 148–149, 182, 183, 255
Lateral acceleration, *see* Acceleration
Lateral axis, 461
Launch velocity, 309–312, *see also* Velocity
Law enforcement personnel, 11
Law of conservation of momentum, 379, 381,
    *see also* Momentum
Lay the bike down, 303, *see also* Motorcycle
    accidents
Lenses, cracked, 171
Letter code, 280–283, *see also* Vehicle
    Deformation Index
Light, 91
Lighting, 63
Lighting experts, 385
Limbs, 249–250
Limitations, computer simulations,
    337–338
Line of sight, 54–56, 58
Linear acceleration
    actual incidences of vertebral injury,
        248
    caudocephaled acceleration, 248
    directional coordinates, 247–248
    experimental studies, 248–249
    impact
        chest, 253–254
        head and face, 250–252
        lower limbs, 249–250
        neck, 252–253
    occupant kinematics, 246
Linear motion, 339, 341–342
Load absorption, 164–165
Lockup, tire, 130, *see also* Tires
Longitudinal acceleration, *see*
    Acceleration
Longitudinal axis, 461
Long-nose tractors, 461
Low angle, *see* Angles, photography
Lug nuts, 126–128

**M**

Magazines, 43
Magnifying glasses, 31
Maintenance history, 21
Maintenance records, 392
Manhole covers, 47
Marring damage, *see* Damage, marring
Mass media, 419
Master cylinder, 374, *see also* Braking system
Matching procedures, 146
Mathematical analysis, 339–341
    appendix: equation workbook
        distance equations, 363–365
        momentum equations, 367–371
        velocity equations, 365–367
    definition of terms, 342–347
    detailed look at the appendix
        distance equations, 371–373
        momentum equations, 379–382
        velocity equations, 374–378
    detailed look at vehicle-to-vehicle collisions
        rear-end impact, 347–353
        resting points, 353–363
    linear motion with constant acceleration,
        341–342
MATIA, *see* Michigan Association of Traffic
    Investigation and Reconstruction
Measurements
    accident scenes
        motorcycle and impact angle, 304
        photographing and deformation zone,
            100–101
        rural, 59–60
        urban, 49, 50, 52, 54
    exhibit development, 324
    on-scene sketches, 67
Median system, 70, 71–72
Medical school libraries, 399
Memory storage, power seats, 163–164
Meninges, 243
Menu boards, 30, 92
Metal depressions, 313
Metal folds, 109–113, 118–120, 122, 124,
    125, 126
Meteorology experts, 384–385
Michigan Association of Traffic Investigation
    and Reconstruction (MATIA), 14
Michigan State University Civil and
    Environmental Engineering
    Department, 13
Microphones, omnidirectional, 92–93
Missing parts, 132–133
Models, exhibit development, 327
Moldings, 166

Momentum
    calculation of resting points of vehicle-to-
        vehicle collision, 361
    equations calculations, 367–371
    problems, 379–382
Monopods, 36, 91
Moon roofs, 160–162
Moral, definition, 445
Motion, geometry, *see* Kinematics
Motor functions, 243
Motorcycle accidents
    accident scene
        rural, 59, 60
        urban, 53–54
    details to investigate, 302–306
    determination of velocity at impact,
        306–312
    factors involved, 301–302
Motorized winder unit, 462
Movements, 242
Moving barrier, 169
Muscular system, 242

**N**

NAPRS, *see* National Association of
    Professional Reconstructionists
National Association of Professional
    Reconstructionists (NAPRS),
    14, 262
National Highway Traffic Safety
    Administration, 210
National Highway Transportation Safety
    Agency, 395
National Oceanic Atmospheric Administration
    (NOAA), 383–384
National Safety Council, 2, 398–399
Near side, 462
Neck, 252–253
Net-type restraint systems, 209, *see also*
    Restraint systems
Networking, 38
Newspapers, information source, 384
Newton's laws of motion, 142, 379
NOAA, *see* National Oceanic Atmospheric
    Administration
Noncollision damage, *see* Damage,
    noncollision
Noninfluencies, 423
North, identifying in sketches, 68
Northwestern University Traffic Institute
    (NUTI), 12–13, 262
Numerical rating system, 289
NUTI, *see* Northwestern University Traffic
    Institute

**O**

Occupant
    accident investigation forms, 221–223, 229,
        230
    ejection
        exhibit development, 331, 333
        from moon/sun/T roofs, 161–162
        rear-end impacts, 176
        rollovers, 178–179
    gathering information on injuries and
        accident reconstruction, 267
    restrained/unrestrained
        instrument panels, 149, 150
        sheet metal deformation, 124–125
        side impacts, 171
        steering column, 156
        windshields, 142–143
    second collision and vehicle interiors, 141
    usage of term, 462
Occupational Safety and Health
    Administration (OSHA), 9, 400
Office equipment, 37–38
Oil trail, 304–305
On-the-job injuries, 9
Open mind, 17
Original equipment manufacturer (OEM),
    160, 462
OSHA, *see* Occupational Safety and Health
    Administration
Outboard, 462
Overlay drawings, 268–269, 325–326, 462

**P**

P&R, *see* Perception and reaction times
Padding, instrument panel, 149
Paint transfers, 112, 120–122, 125, 127, 128
Panoramic views, 323, *see also* Views
Parallelogram method, 462
Paramessage, 416
Parked car, 56
Passenger, 462
Passenger's side, 462
Patella, 241
Payout, 462
PDOF, *see* Principal direction of force
Pedestrian accidents
    details to be examined, 313–317
    determination
        distance thrown, 318–319
        impact velocity, 319–320
        walking or running speed, 318
    witness statements, 320–321
Pelvic girdle, 241

Penetration resistance, 143, 144
Perception and reaction (P&R) times
  definition, 342–344
  distance equations
    calculations, 363–364
    problems, 371, 373
  usage of term, 462
Peripheral information, 418–419
Peripheral nervous system, 243–244
PGMs, see Poly Gel Mitigators
Philosophy, 445–446
Photogrammetry, 462
Photographic equipment, 32–35
Photographic recording, 27–30
Photographs
  accident reconstruction, 262–263, 266, 269
  aerial as information source, 392–393
  exhibit development, 323, 327, 328
  front of vehicle and pedestrian accidents, 313
  hair strands and accident investigations of rear-end impacts, 175
  highway department as information source, 387–388
  motorcycle accidents, 304
  real-world, 77–87
  stale accident scenes, 21
Physical appearance, expert witnesses, 409–410
PIs, see Private eyes
Pitch, 247
Placards, 29–30
Planes, occupant kinematics, 238
Plastic laminate, 143–144, see also Windshields
POI, see Point of impact
Point of impact (POI)
  accident scenes
    rural, 61, 64–65
    stale, 22
    urban, 48, 49–50, 51, 53
  determination and motorcycle accidents, 305
  side impacts, 170–171
  tire marks, 75, 77
Point of rest (POR)
  accident scenes
    rural, 65–67
    pedestrian, 318
    urban, 52, 53, 54
    visualization, 72
  calculations, 311, 353–363
  determination, 31
  tire marks, 75
Polaroid sunglasses, 149
Poles, power, 63–64, 67
  information source, 390–392

Police reports, 22
Poly Gel Mitigators (PGMs), 99, 113, 114, 173
Polygon method, 463
Polyvinyl butyral, 143, see also Glass; Windshields
POR, see Point of rest
Positive direction coordinates, 247
Post supports, 168, 169, 179, 221
Postimpact skid distance, 463, see also Skid
Postimpact velocity, 463, see also Velocity
Posttraumatic amnesia (PTA), 288
Potholes, 62, 63
Power seats, 163
Power source, videotaping, 91
Pregnant women, 209–210
Preimpact skid distance, 463, see also Skid
Preproduction defect reports, 394, 462
Presidential campaign, 416–417
Pretrial preparation, witnesses, 409
Preventive health care, 451–452, see also Ethics
Principal direction of force (PDOF), 221, 277–278, 462
Printers, 39, 41
Private eyes (PIs), 14
Product life tests, 396
Professional organizations, 399, 401
Propaganda effects, 421
PTA, see Posttraumatic amnesia
Public libraries, 384
Pulmonary system, 244
Puncture pattern, 126–128, see also Tires

Q

Qualifications, expert witnesses, 410–411
Quantitative Scale of Impact Injury, 285–286

R

Ramping, 174
Reaction time, see Perception and reaction (P&R) time
Rear-end impact, see Impact, rear-end
Rear windows, 147, 175–176, 329, 330
Rearview mirrors, 162–163, 317
Rearward-facing child seats, see Child seats
Recall campaigns, 395–396
REC-TEC, 463
Reference line, 463
Reference points (RP)
  accident scenes
    rural, 59, 60
    urban, 47, 48, 49, 50, 53, 56
  on-scene sketches, 67
  usage of term, 463

Refresher courses, 13
Rehearsed presentations, 423
Repair manuals, 43
Reputation, 446
Requests for documents, 463
Research, expert witnesses, 411
Resolution, video cameras, 91
Resolved, 463
Respiratory system, 245
Restraint systems
    accident investigation, 8–9
    air bags or supplemental systems, 202–207
    children, 210–212
    converted vehicles for handicapped,
        212–214
    impact acceleration and occupant
        kinematics, 255–259
    new developments, 207–209
    pregnant women, 209–210
    reduction of vehicular injuries, 6
    shoulder/lap belts, 182–202
    side impacts, 171
    standard, 181–182
    windshields, 142
Review, investigator, 93
Ribs, 240, 253
Right front passenger, 463
Rim beads, 219
Rim marks, 65–66
Rims, 129, 130, 306
Ring flash, 34, 463
Rise/fall of rider in space, 309–312
Roads
    coefficient of friction, 344, 345
    conditions and accidents, 8–9, 18, 19
    motorcycle accidents, 306
    rural accident scenes, 61–63
    skids relation to velocity equations
        problems, 376–377
    water on or over and accident scene, 87–88
    wet roads, 345
Roll, 247
Rollovers
    accident investigations, 125, 176–179
    noting/recording metal folds, 120
    static test, 177
    surrogates in exhibit development, 329, 330
    Vehicle Deformation Index, 278–279
Rotation of vehicle
    calculation of resting points in vehicle-to-
        vehicle collision, 357, 358, 360
    fluid leaks and inspection of accident
        vehicle, 135
    pedestrian accidents, 314–315
Rotational direction coordinates, 247–248

Rough roads, see Roads
RP, see Reference points
Runoff, vehicle fluids, 135
Rural settings
    debris pattern, 61
    lighting, 63
    point of impact, 64–65
    point of rest, 65–67
    poles, 63–64
    road surface and shoulders, 62–63
    roadbed damage, 61–62
    trees, 64
Rust, 123–124, 138–139

S

Sabbath, remembering, 452–453, see Ethics
SAE, see Society of Automobile Engineers
Safety gear, 36–37
Salvage yard, 89
Scale drawings
    exhibit development, 323
    pedestrian accidents, 320
    preparation for accident investigation,
        38–39
    urban accidents, 51–52
    line of sight problems, 55–56
Scale validation, 275
Scenario, development, 15–16
Scene investigation, see Accident
        reconstruction
Scrapes, 125–128
Scratches
    inspection of accident vehicle, 90–91,
        125–128
    undercarriage, 133
    motorcycle accidents, 303–304, 305
    vehicle exterior and pedestrian accidents,
        316
Screwdrivers, 26
Script, 335, 425–426
Seasons, 58
Seat belts, see also Restraint systems
    accident investigation forms, 227–229
    injury reduction, 6
    placement and occupant injury, 256
    retractors examination, 270–271
    use and accident reconstruction, 267
Seat cushions, 163–165
Seatback release latch, 176
Seatbacks, accident investigations, 163–165
    rear-end impacts, 174–176
    side impacts, 172
Secure the scene, 19
Self-decapitation, 441–442

Semiactive restraints, 181, *see also* Restraint systems
Senses, overload, 342–343
Sensory functions, 243
Severity indices
    American Medical Association Abbreviated Injury Scale, 287–293
    detailed injury scale for accident investigation, 293–299
    development of medically acceptable injury scale, 285–287
    Traffic Accident Data Index, 274–275
    vehicle deformation index, 275–285
Sewer grates, 47
Sheet metal, 124, 138–139
Shoe polish smears, 175
Shoulder/lap belt restraint, 182–202, 258, *see also* Restraint systems
Shoulders, 62–63
Side impact, *see* Impact, side
Side marker lights, 135–138
Side windows, 147
Sideswipe
    aluminum wheels damage, 129
    noting/recording paint transfers, 120, 121, 127
    pedestrian accidents, 316
Sidewalls, 130, 131, *see also* Tires
SIMBOL scale, 285
Simulations, computer, *see* Computer, simulations
Skeletal injuries, 230–231, 233, 314, 316
Skeletal system, 239–242
Sketches
    accident investigation forms
        exterior damage, 218, 219
        interior damage, 223, 224
    investigation of fresh scenes, 20
    on-scene, 67–68
        methods for plotting a curve, 68–72
Skid
    distance equations, 372
        vehicle-to-vehicle rear-end impact, 347, 348, 351, 352–353
    momentum equations, 380
    marks
        accident scene investigation, 75–77
        motorcycle accidents, 303
        rural accident scenes, 62, 65
        urban accident scenes, 51, 52, 53
        usage of term, 464
    velocity equations, 362, 366, 374, 375–377
Skull fractures, 250, 251
Slides, 125, 130
Smart bag system, 9

Smears
    blood, 175, 180
    instrument panels, 154
    windshields, 142, 147
Smudge patterns, 145
Snowy road, 345, *see also* Roads
Society of Automobile Engineers (SAE)
    accident investigation, 14
    courses on accident reconstruction, 262
    determination of velocity and motorcycle accidents, 306
    testing using anthropomorphic dummies, 245–246
    vehicle interiors, 146–147
Socket set, 26
Soft tissue injury, 182, 229, 231, 256
Sokkia Total Station, 67
Soundtracks, 406
Spares, 217, *see also* Tires
Specific Trauma Medical Index, 276
Speedometer assemblies, 154–155
Stale scenes, 21–22
Standing water, 87
Stapp Car Crash Conference, 182
State Troopers, 261
Static rollover test, 177, *see also* Rollovers
Static tests, 174
Steering column, 155–157, 226–227
Steering wheel, 226–227, 306
Steering wheel rims, 157–159
Stellar pattern, 145, 146, 464, *see also* Windshield
Stopped vehicle, 368–369
Stopwatch, 74
Storage, vehicle, 25–26
Stress cracks, 144–145
Stress fracture, 133, 134
Stress riser, 144
Stretching, webbing, 184–191, 193, 194, *see also* Restraint systems; Seat belts
Striking vehicle, 464
Struck vehicle, 464
Submarining, 164, 202, 464
Sudden acceleration, *see* Acceleration
Suicide, 441–442
Sun visors, 159–160
Sunroofs, 160–162
Supplemental restraint systems, 205–206, *see also* Restraint systems
Surrogates, 327–331, 332
Surveyor pins, 31, 69
Switch, headlight position, 137
Synthetic fibers, 207–208, *see also* Restraint systems
Systemic circulation, 244

# T

TAD, *see* Traffic Accident Data Index
Taillights, 135–138, 302
Tape, 30, 36
Tape measures, 29, 100–101
Tape recorder, 32
Tears
    shape of, 126
    webbing, 194–196
Technical library, 42–43
Teenage drivers, 4
Telephone poles, 390–392
Telephones, cellular, 37
Tempered glass, 147, *see also* Glass; Windshield
Terminology, client education, 431–432
Test devices, *see* Anthropomorphic dummies
Testing, evidence, 42
Textbooks, 43, 262
Thorax, 253
Thrown distance, 318–319, 320
Tibia, 249–250
Time, accounting for, 38
Time lag, 269–270
Time of day, 5, 74
Tire marks, accident scenes, 74–77
    point of rest in rural scenes, 66
Tires
    accident investigation forms, 217, 219
    coefficient of friction, 344–345
    damage and inspection of accident vehicle,
        129, 130–132, 217
    drag factor, 346
    patch, 464
Title block, 56, 57, 68
Tools/equipment
    basic kit, 25–27
    computer, 38–41
    internet, 43–44
    office, 37–38
    ownership of documentation, 41
    ownership of evidence, 42
    photographic, 32–35
    preparation, 25
    safety gear, 36–37
    special, 27–32
    technical library, 42–43
    video, 35–36
Totally passive restraints, 181, *see also* Restraint
        systems
Tow trucks, 90, 133, 266
Track width, 77, *see also* Tires
Trade associations, 400–401
Traffic Accident Data (TAD) Index,
        274–275

Traffic Accident Investigation Training
        Institute, 12
Traffic lights, 73–74, 391
Training, 11, 261
Trajectory, pedestrian accidents, 314
Transmission fluid, 133
Tread area, 131, *see also* Tires
Trees, 64
Trial by cinematography, 419
Triangle, 26, 68
Tripods, 34
Trucks, 373, 392, 464
Trunk, 113, 122, 174
Trustworthiness, witness, 422, 433
T-tops, 160–162, 178
Tumblehome, 147, 219, 464

# U

UD-10 report, 21
Undercarriage, 133, 219
Unintentional deaths, 1
Unloaded tire, 464, *see also* Tires
Unrighteousness in weights/measures,
        449–450, *see also* Ethics
Urban settings
    debris pattern, 50, 51–54
    line of sight problems, 54–56
    point of impact, 48, 49–50, 51, 53
    reference points, 47, 49
    witness marks, 51
Urogenital system, 245
Utility pole, 47, 48, 49
U-V filter, 464

# V

Vehicle Deformation Index, 275–285
Vehicle deformation location, 279–280, 283
Vehicle exterior
    damage sketches and accident investigation
        forms, 218, 219
    details to be noted/recorded
        aluminum vs. steel wheels, 129–131
        fluid leaks, 133, 135
        head-, tail-, and side marker lights,
            135–138
        metal folds, 109–113, 118–120
        missing or misplaced components,
            132–133, 134
        paint transfers, 120–122
        scrapes, gouges, and scratches, 125–128
        tires, 131–132
        underside of vehicle and tow truck use,
            133

unexplained damage, 138
vehicle deterioration and rusting,
138–139
weld or base metal separation and rust,
122–125
pedestrian accidents, 316
photographing accident vehicles, 89–91
using still or 35-mm camera, 93–109
videotaping at the scene, 91–93
Vehicle identification number (VIN), 385–386
Vehicle interior
checklists, 166–167
collisions and occupant, 141
headrests, 165–166
instrument panels, 148–155
moldings, 166
rear windows, 147–148
rearview mirrors, 162–163
seat cushions and seatbacks, 163–165
smears and blood pooling, 180
steering columns, 155–157
steering wheel rims, 157–159
sun visors, 159–160
T-tops, moon roofs, sunroofs, 160–162
types of impacts related to interior
components
side, 167–172
rear, 173–176
rollovers, 176–179
windshields, 142–147
Vehicle posts, 168
Vehicle-to-vehicle crash, 49, 51, *see also* Point
of impact
Vehicle-to-motorcycle crash, 53–54, *see also*
Motorcycle accidents
Vehicle-to-pedestrian impact, 52–53, *see also*
Pedestrian accidents
Vehicle trajectory rods, 31
Vehicles
checklist, 46
data and accident investigation forms,
215–217
deterioration and inspection of accident
vehicle, 138–139
examination and accident investigation, 15
individuality of and accident reconstruction,
262
questions about and interrogatories,
435–439
right-angle collision and momentum
equations calculations, 369–371
side impacts, 170–171
statistics as sources of information, 385–387
usage of term, 464
Veins, 245

Velocity
equations
calculations, 365–367
deceleration and distance, 372, 373
problems, 374–378
linear motion with constant acceleration,
341–342
motorcycle accidents, 302, 306–312
resting points of vehicle-to-vehicle
collisions, 353–363
uniform linear motion, 339, 340
vehicle and inspection of wheels, 130
vehicle-to-vehicle rear-end impact, 347–353
Verbal attack, handling, 414–415
Vertebral column, 240
Vertebral injury, 248–249
Vertical bounce, 92
Vests, orange, 37
Video camera, 35–36, *see also* Videotaping
Videographer, 407
Videotaping
accident scene and accident investigation,
15, 91–93
fresh scenes, 20
rural scenes, 61
courtroom appearance of expert witnesses,
403–407, 411
occupant intrusion areas, 222–223
seatbacks and investigations of rear impacts,
176
tire and gouge marks, 27–28
Views, photographing the accident vehicle
front, 95, 97, 109, 111, 115
left, 96, 98, 109, 110
rear, 96, 98, 108, 111, 112, 114
right, 97, 99, 108, 119
sectional, 104–106
side, 108, 109, 110, 111, 112
three-quarter, 107, 108, 109, 111, 112,
119, 123
VIN, *see* Vehicle identification number
Visceral system, 245
Visual aids, 411
Visualization, accident scene, 72–73
Voice recording, 92–93
Volunteer experiments, 258

**W**

Walking/running speed, 318, *see also*
Pedestrian accidents
Warranty reports, 394
Watts Voiceprint trial, 417–418
Wayne State University, 150–153
Wear bars, 464

Wear patterns, tires, 219, *see also* Tires
Weather, 76, 90, 345, 383–384
Webbing
    accident investigation forms, 227–228
    examination of restraint systems, 184–195
        converted vehicles for handicapped, 213
Weights, vehicles and momentum, 379–380
Welds, vehicle inspection, 122–125, 138–139
Wet roads, 345, *see also* Roads
Wheel covers, 130–131
Wheelchairs, 212, 213
Wheels, 129–131
Whiplash injury, 166
Wide-angle views, 93–94, 114, *see also*
    Views
Wind drag, 308–312
Winder unit, 33
Windows, up/down position, 148
Windshield
    accident investigations, 142–147
        stress cracks and rollovers, 178
        use of surrogates in rollover exhibit,
            329, 330
    fracture and inspection of accident vehicle,
        132, 133, 134
    pedestrian accidents, 315–316

Wisdom, acquisition, 453–454, *see also*
    Ethics
Witness marks
    accident reconstruction, 270
    bumpers and investigations of rear-end
        impacts, 173, 174
    measurement and investigation of fresh
        scenes, 20
    motorcycle accidents, 303–304
    noting and recording, 101, 113
    occupants claim to be belted, 194
    restraint systems, 188
    rollover investigations, 178
    undercarriage inspection, 133
    urban accident scenes, 51
    vehicle interiors, 141
Witnesses, 21, 22, 320–321
Work experience, expert witnesses, 425
Wrenches, 26

## XYZ

Yaw marks
    accident scene, 52, 62, 75
    usage of term, 465
Zoom lens, 33